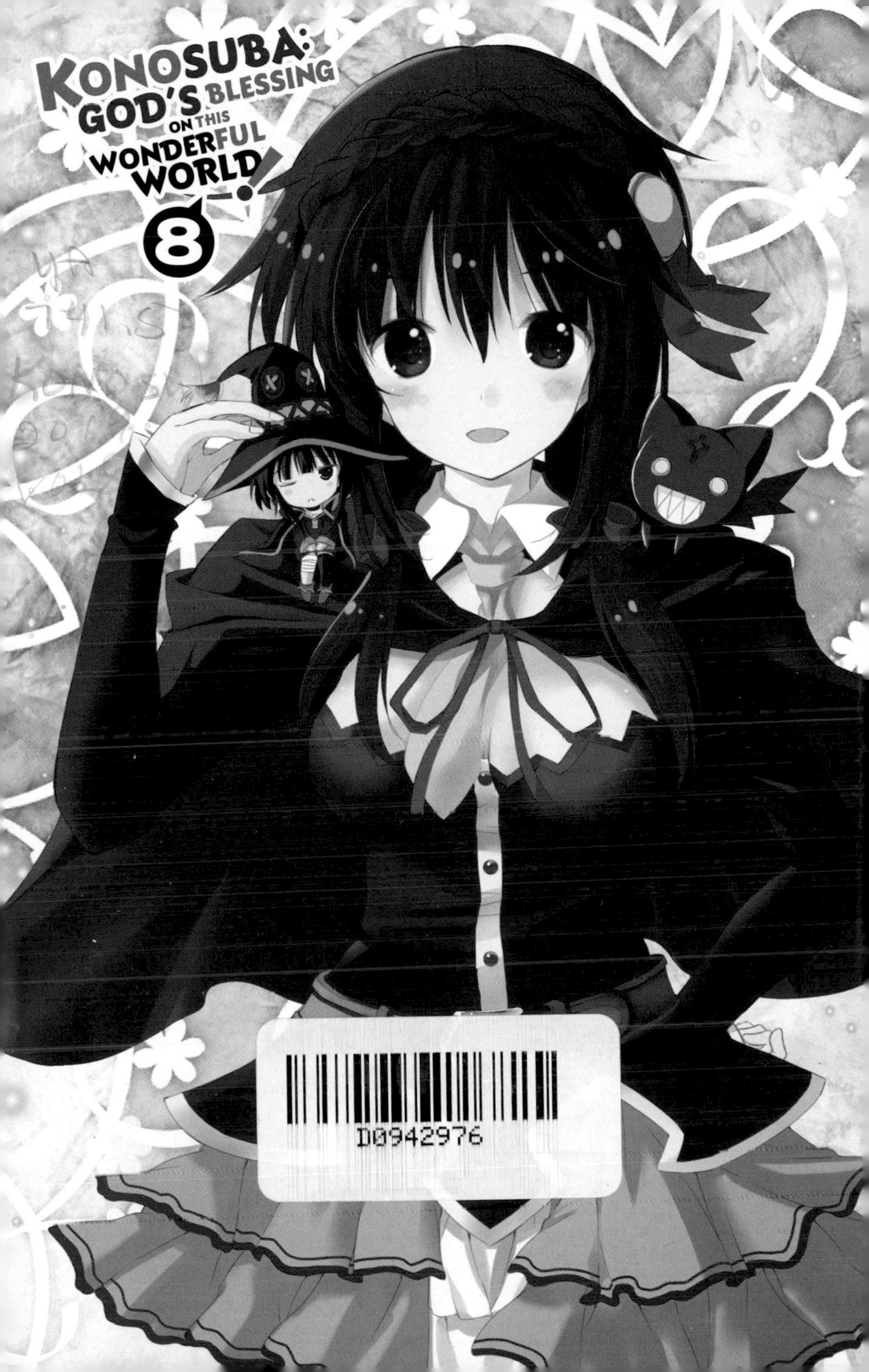
KONOSUBA: GOD'S BLESSING ON THIS WONDERFUL WORLD!
8

8
GOD'S BLESSING ON THIS WONDERFUL WORLD!
CONTENTS

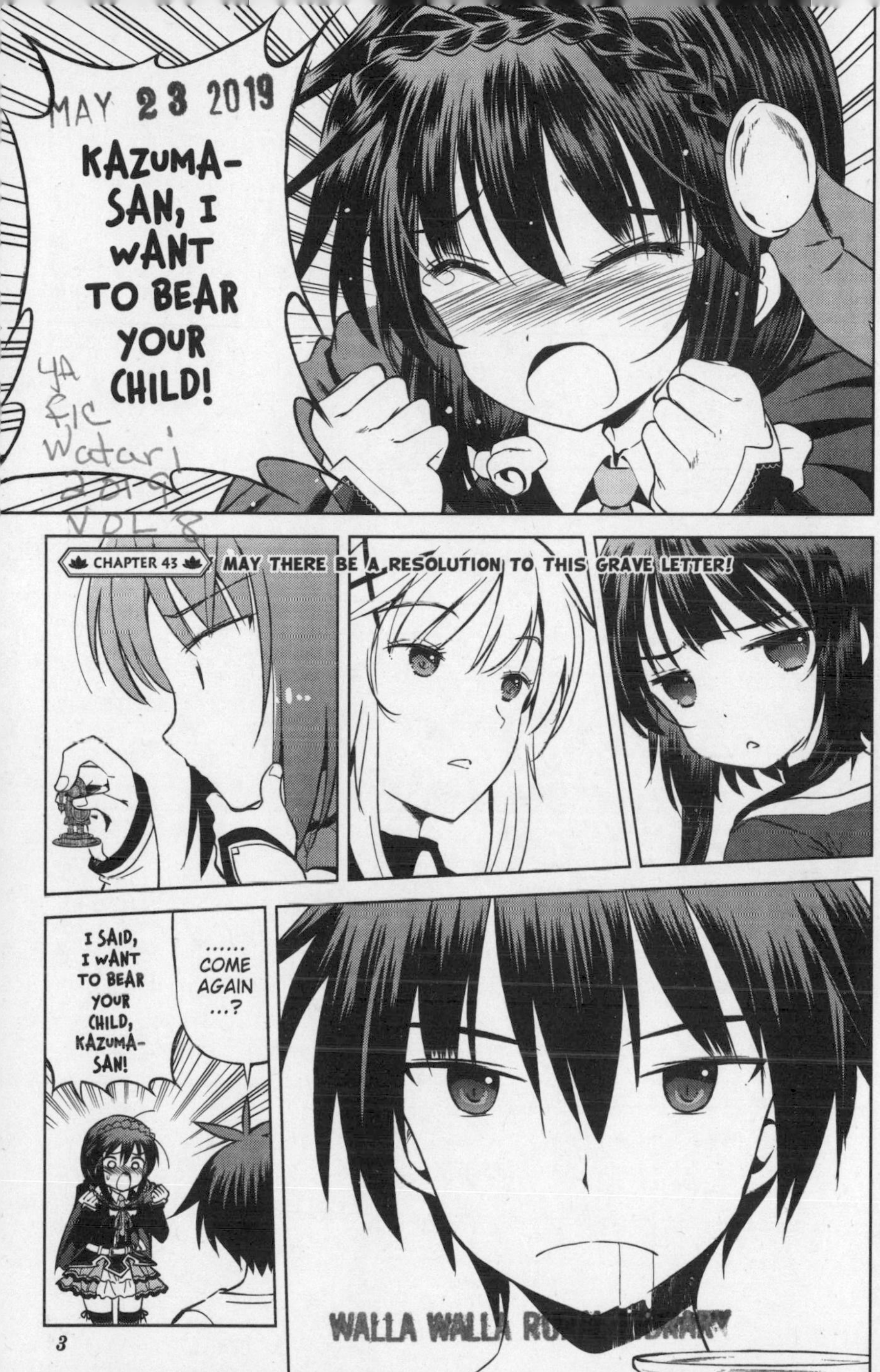
KAZUMA-SAN, I WANT TO BEAR YOUR CHILD!
CHAPTER 43
MAY THERE BE A RESOLUTION TO THIS GRAVE LETTER!
...
......COME AGAIN...?
I SAID, I WANT TO BEAR YOUR CHILD, KAZUMA-SAN!

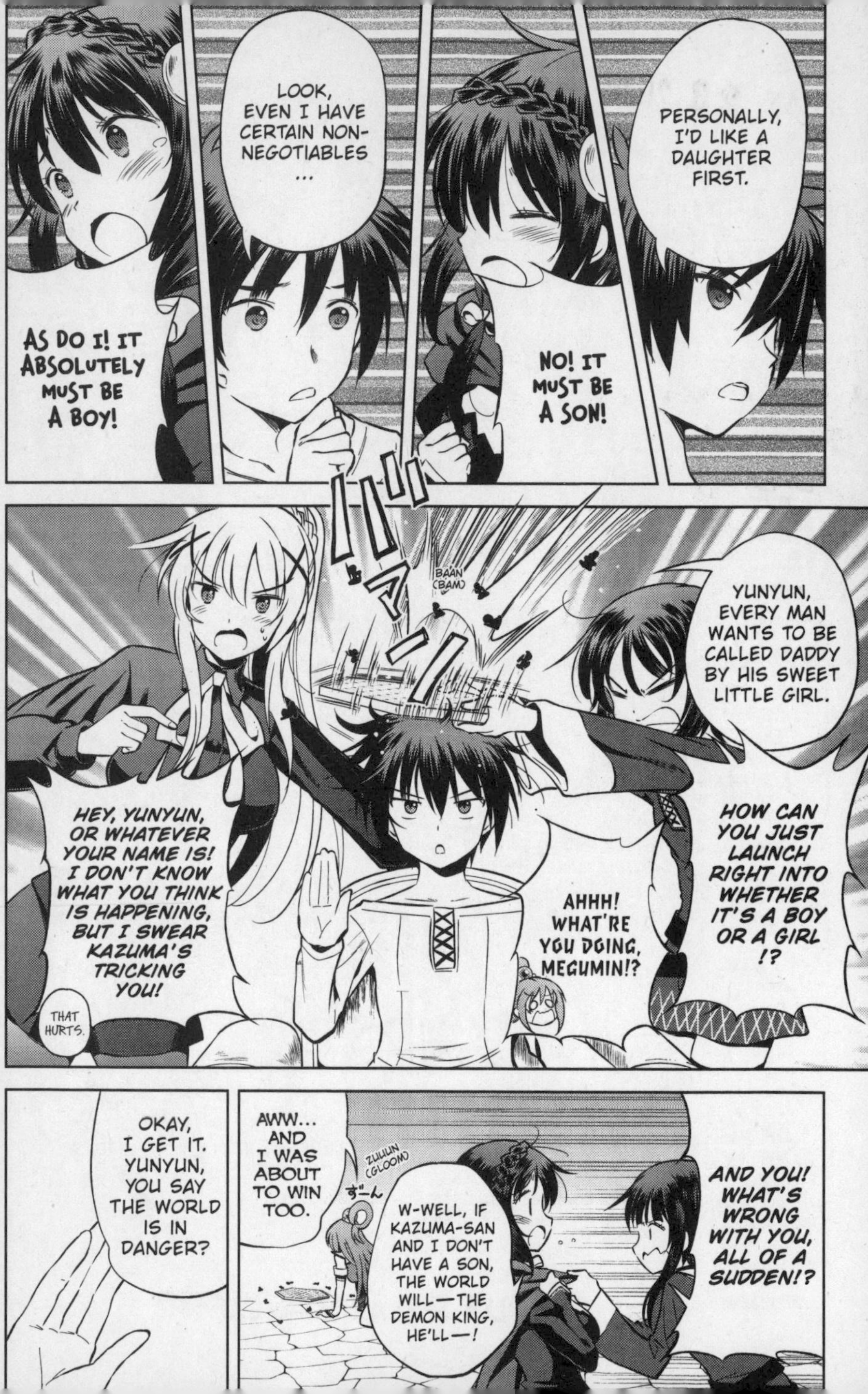
PERSONALLY, I'D LIKE A DAUGHTER FIRST.
NO! IT MUST BE A SON!
LOOK, EVEN I HAVE CERTAIN NON-NEGOTIABLES ...
AS DO I! IT ABSOLUTELY MUST BE A BOY!
BAAN (BAM)
YUNYUN, EVERY MAN WANTS TO BE CALLED DADDY BY HIS SWEET LITTLE GIRL.
HOW CAN YOU JUST LAUNCH RIGHT INTO WHETHER IT'S A BOY OR A GIRL !?
AHHH! WHAT'RE YOU DOING, MEGUMIN!?
HEY, YUNYUN, OR WHATEVER YOUR NAME IS! I DON'T KNOW WHAT YOU THINK IS HAPPENING, BUT I SWEAR KAZUMA'S TRICKING YOU!
THAT HURTS.
AND YOU! WHAT'S WRONG WITH YOU, ALL OF A SUDDEN!?
W-WELL, IF KAZUMA-SAN AND I DON'T HAVE A SON, THE WORLD WILL—THE DEMON KING, HE'LL—!
AWW... AND I WAS ABOUT TO WIN TOO.
ZUUUN (GLOOM)
ずーん
OKAY, I GET IT. YUNYUN, YOU SAY THE WORLD IS IN DANGER?

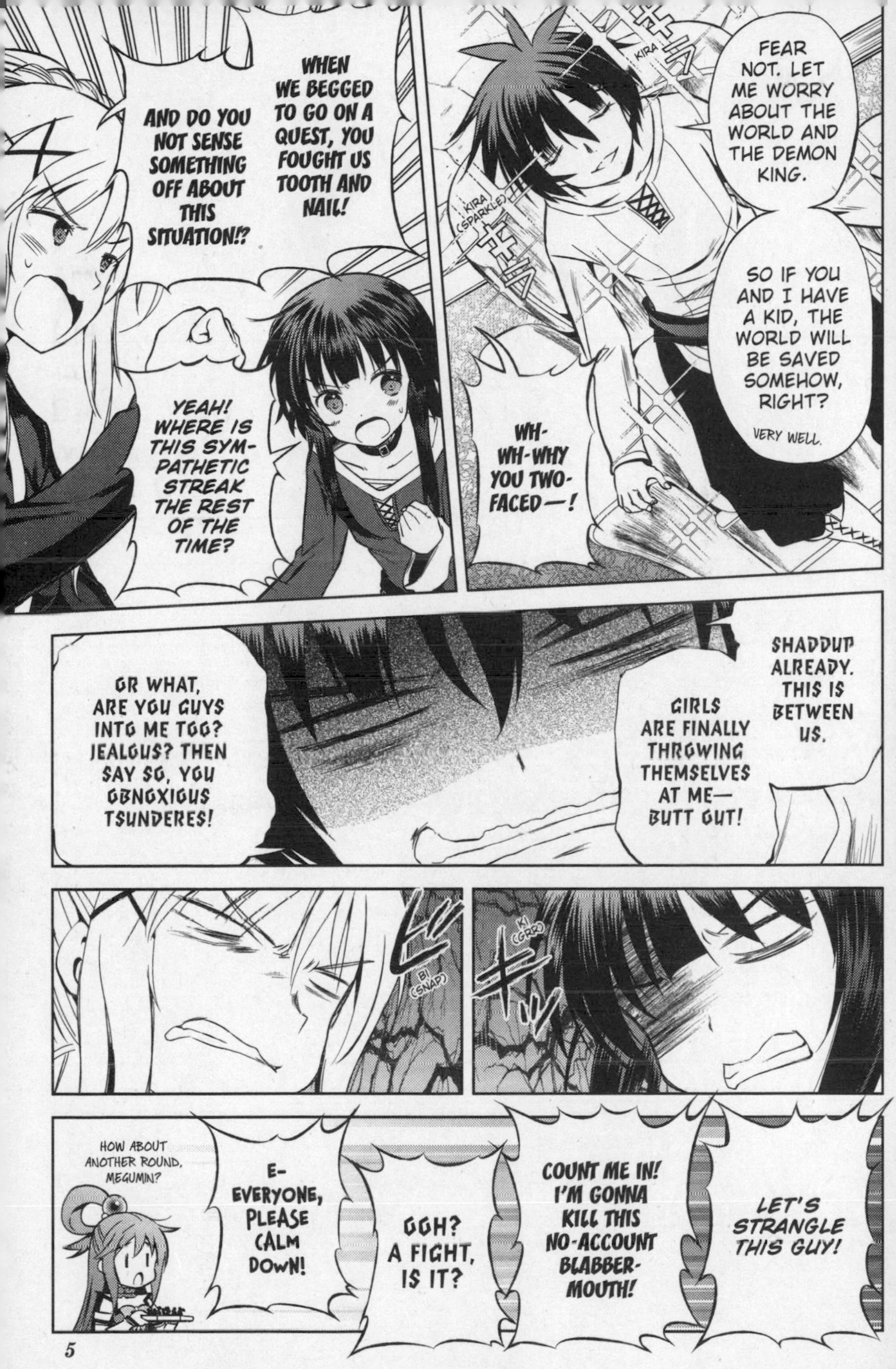
KIRA
FEAR NOT. LET ME WORRY ABOUT THE WORLD AND THE DEMON KING.
KIRA (SPARKLE)
SO IF YOU AND I HAVE A KID, THE WORLD WILL BE SAVED SOMEHOW, RIGHT?
VERY WELL.
WH-WH-WHY YOU TWO-FACED—!
WHEN WE BEGGED TO GO ON A QUEST, YOU FOUGHT US TOOTH AND NAIL!
AND DO YOU NOT SENSE SOMETHING OFF ABOUT THIS SITUATION!?
YEAH! WHERE IS THIS SYMPATHETIC STREAK THE REST OF THE TIME?
SHADDUP ALREADY. THIS IS BETWEEN US.
GIRLS ARE FINALLY THROWING THEMSELVES AT ME—BUTT OUT!
OR WHAT, ARE YOU GUYS INTO ME TOO? JEALOUS? THEN SAY SO, YOU OBNOXIOUS TSUNDERES!
KI (GRR)
BI (SNAP)
LET'S STRANGLE THIS GUY!
COUNT ME IN! I'M GONNA KILL THIS NO-ACCOUNT BLABBERMOUTH!
OOH? A FIGHT, IS IT?
E-EVERYONE, PLEASE CALM DOWN!
HOW ABOUT ANOTHER ROUND, MEGUMIN?

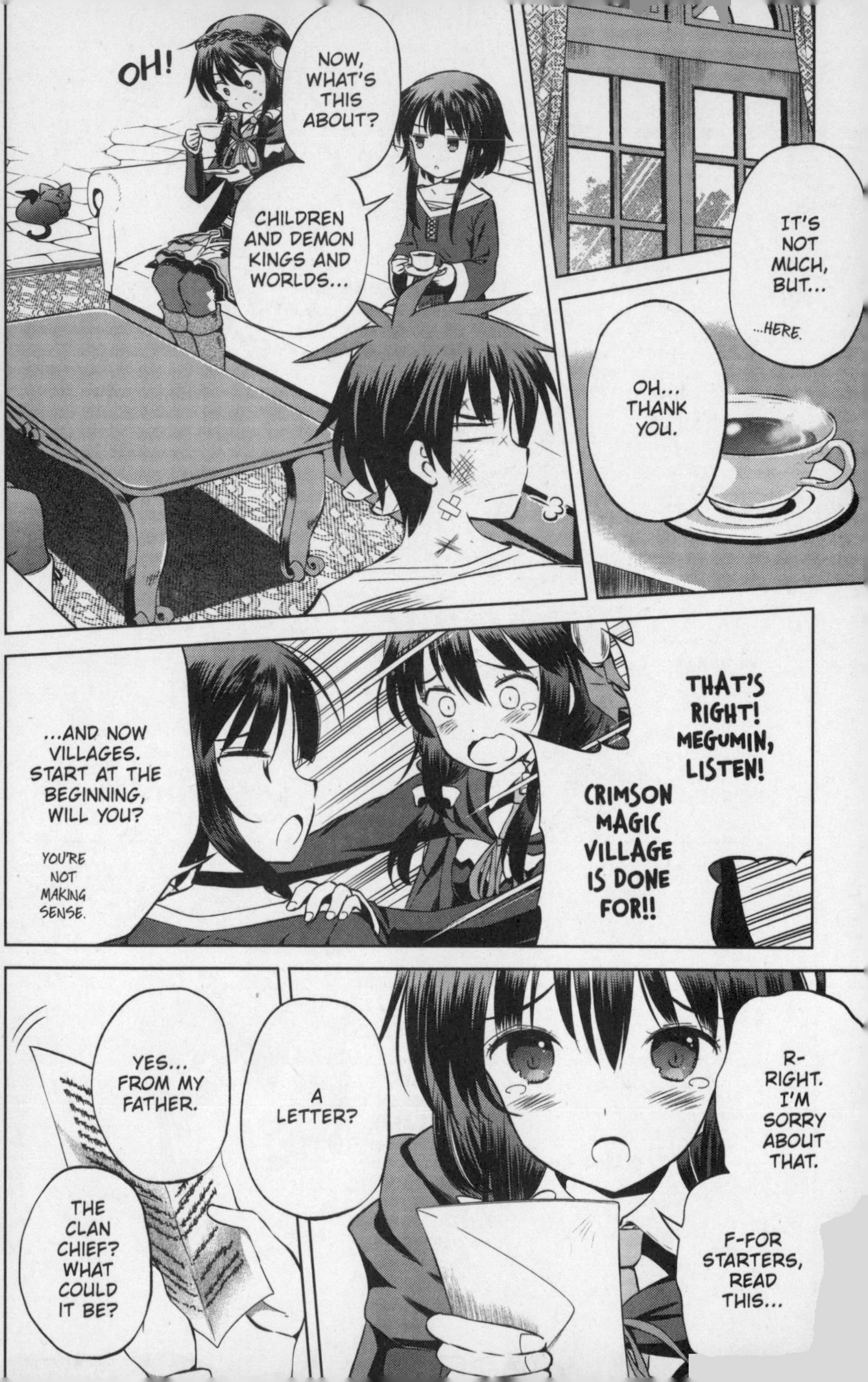
IT'S NOT MUCH, BUT...
...HERE.
OH... THANK YOU.
NOW, WHAT'S THIS ABOUT?
OH!
CHILDREN AND DEMON KINGS AND WORLDS...
THAT'S RIGHT! MEGUMIN, LISTEN!
CRIMSON MAGIC VILLAGE IS DONE FOR!!
...AND NOW VILLAGES. START AT THE BEGINNING, WILL YOU?
YOU'RE NOT MAKING SENSE.
R-RIGHT. I'M SORRY ABOUT THAT.
F-FOR STARTERS, READ THIS...
A LETTER?
YES... FROM MY FATHER.
THE CLAN CHIEF? WHAT COULD IT BE?

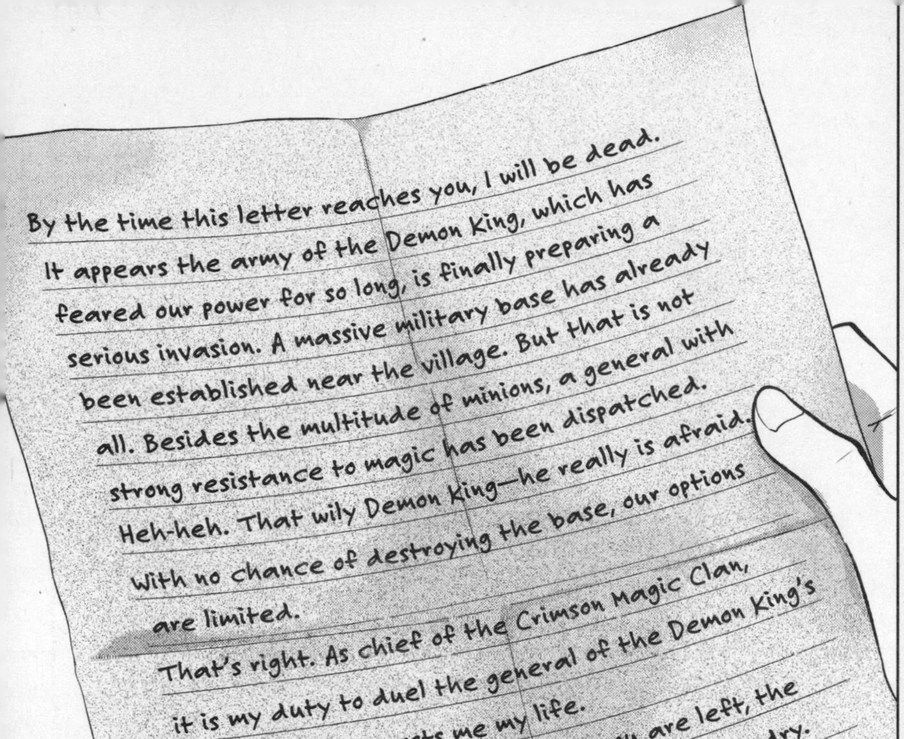
By the time this letter reaches you, I will be dead.
It appears the army of the Demon King, which has
feared our power for so long, is finally preparing a
serious invasion. A massive military base has already
been established near the village. But that is not
all. Besides the multitude of minions, a general with
strong resistance to magic has been dispatched.
Heh-heh. That wily Demon King—he really is afraid.
With no chance of destroying the base, our options
are limited.
That's right. As chief of the Crimson Magic Clan,
it is my duty to duel the general of the Demon King's
army, even if it costs me my life.
My beloved daughter, as long as you are left, the
blood of the Crimson Magic Clan shall not run dry.
I leave you my place as chief of our clan. You are
the last of the Crimson Magic Clan in this world.
Do not let it die out......

※ TRANSLATED FROM THE LOCAL WRITING SYSTEM

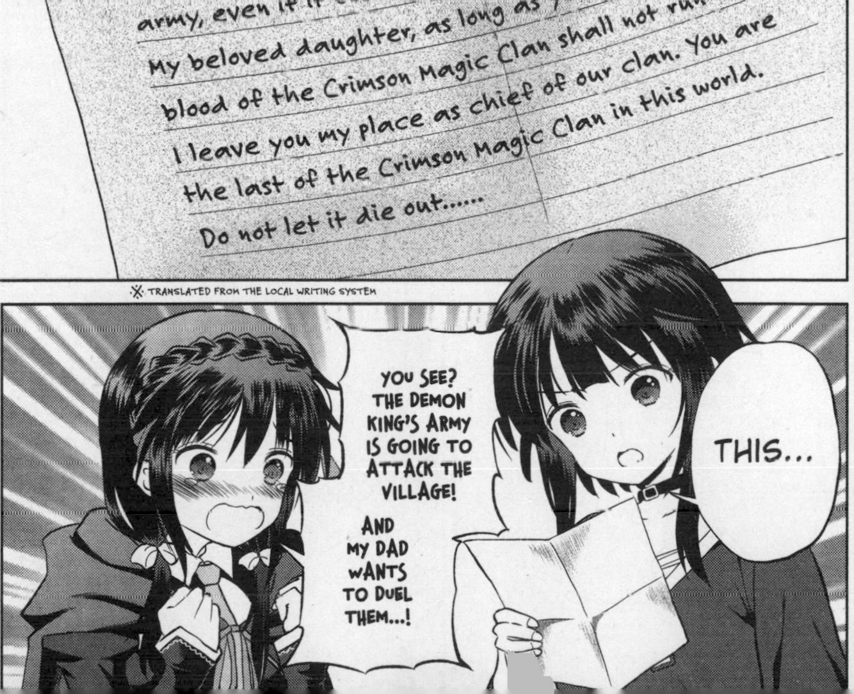
THIS...
YOU SEE? THE DEMON KING'S ARMY IS GOING TO ATTACK THE VILLAGE!
AND MY DAD WANTS TO DUEL THEM...!

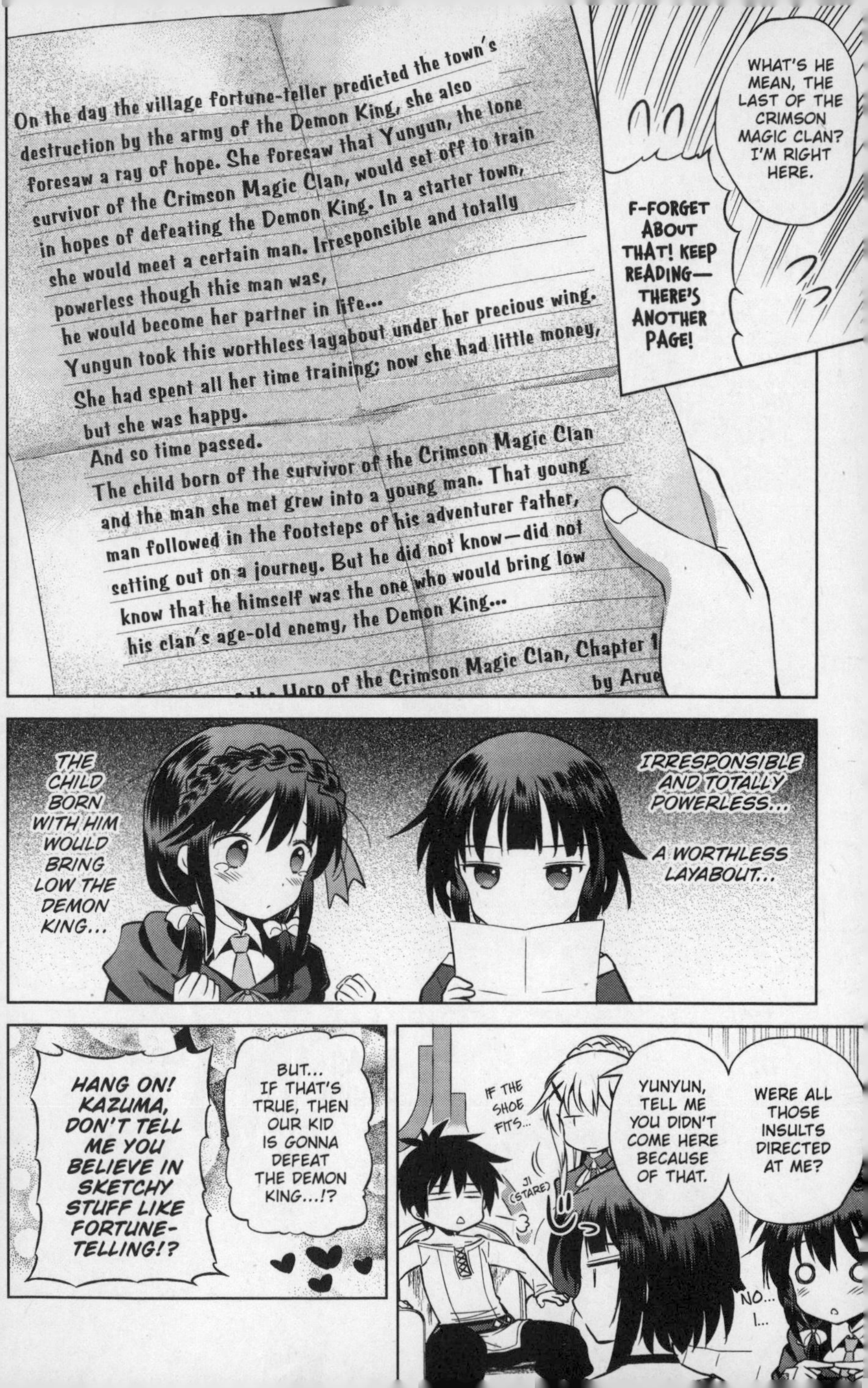
WHAT'S HE MEAN, THE LAST OF THE CRIMSON MAGIC CLAN? I'M RIGHT HERE.
F-FORGET ABOUT THAT! KEEP READING—THERE'S ANOTHER PAGE!
On the day the village fortune-teller predicted the town's destruction by the army of the Demon King, she also foresaw a ray of hope. She foresaw that Yunyun, the lone survivor of the Crimson Magic Clan, would set off to train in hopes of defeating the Demon King. In a starter town, she would meet a certain man. Irresponsible and totally powerless though this man was, he would become her partner in life...
Yunyun took this worthless layabout under her precious wing.
She had spent all her time training; now she had little money, but she was happy.
And so time passed.
The child born of the survivor of the Crimson Magic Clan and the man she met grew into a young man. That young man followed in the footsteps of his adventurer father, setting out on a journey. But he did not know—did not know that he himself was the one who would bring low his clan's age-old enemy, the Demon King...
the Crimson Magic Clan, Chapter 1
by Arue
IRRESPONSIBLE AND TOTALLY POWERLESS...
A WORTHLESS LAYABOUT...
THE CHILD BORN WITH HIM WOULD BRING LOW THE DEMON KING...
WERE ALL THOSE INSULTS DIRECTED AT ME?
YUNYUN, TELL ME YOU DIDN'T COME HERE BECAUSE OF THAT.
IF THE SHOE FITS...
JI (STARE)
NO... I...
BUT... IF THAT'S TRUE, THEN OUR KID IS GONNA DEFEAT THE DEMON KING...!?
HANG ON! KAZUMA, DON'T TELL ME YOU BELIEVE IN SKETCHY STUFF LIKE FORTUNE-TELLING!?

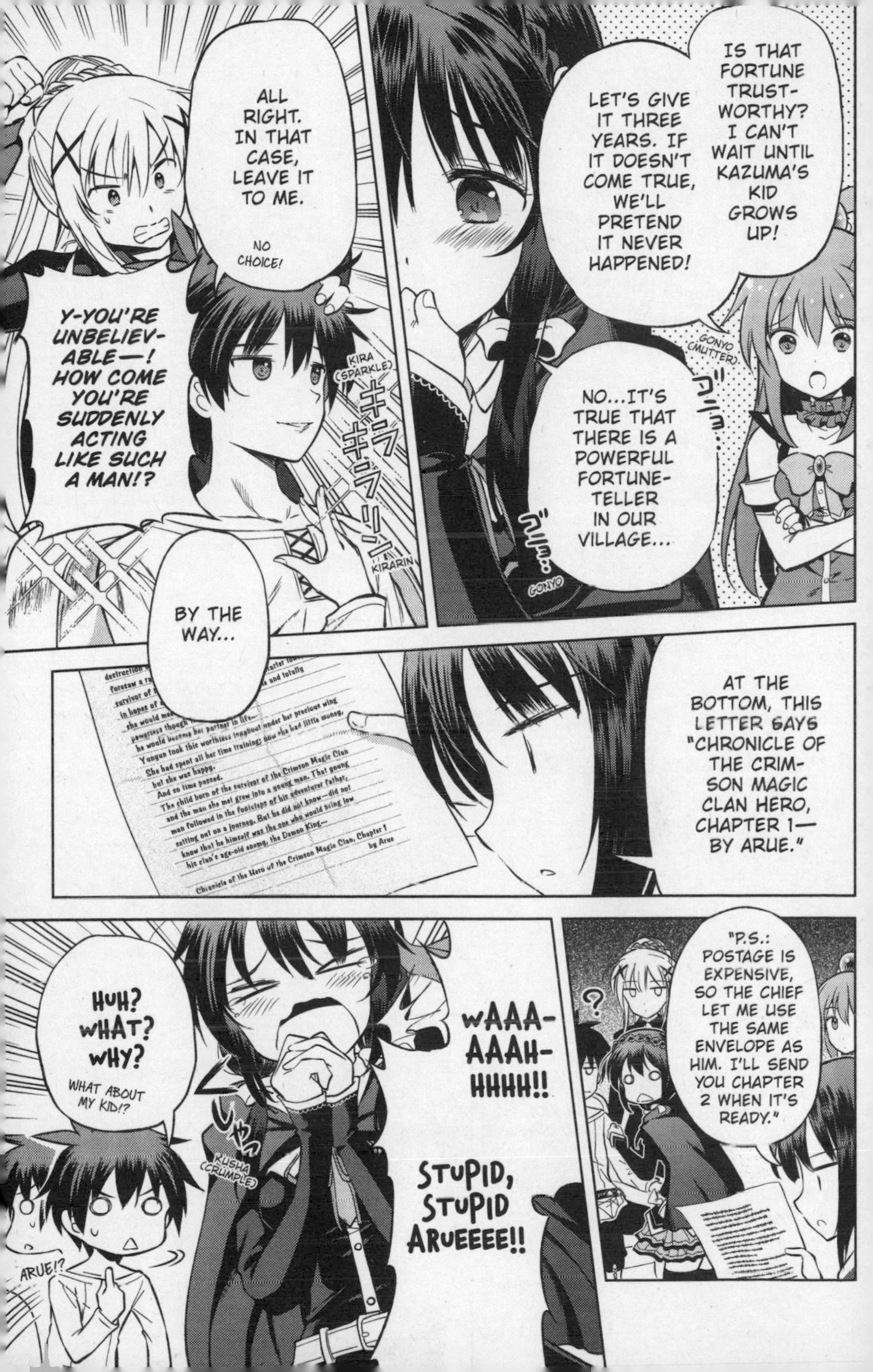
IS THAT FORTUNE TRUST-WORTHY? I CAN'T WAIT UNTIL KAZUMA'S KID GROWS UP!
LET'S GIVE IT THREE YEARS. IF IT DOESN'T COME TRUE, WE'LL PRETEND IT NEVER HAPPENED!
GONYO (MUTTER)
NO...IT'S TRUE THAT THERE IS A POWERFUL FORTUNE-TELLER IN OUR VILLAGE...
GONYO
ALL RIGHT. IN THAT CASE, LEAVE IT TO ME.
NO CHOICE!
KIRA (SPARKLE)
Y-YOU'RE UNBELIEV-ABLE—! HOW COME YOU'RE SUDDENLY ACTING LIKE SUCH A MAN!?
KIRARIN
BY THE WAY...
AT THE BOTTOM, THIS LETTER SAYS "CHRONICLE OF THE CRIM-SON MAGIC CLAN HERO, CHAPTER 1— BY ARUE."
but she was happy.
And so time passed.
The child born of the survivor of the Crimson Magic Clan
and the man she met grew into a young man. That young
man followed in the footsteps of his adventurer father,
setting out on a journey. But he did not know—did not
know that he himself was the one who would bring low
his clan's age-old enemy, the Demon King...
Chronicle of the Hero of the Crimson Magic Clan, Chapter 1
by Arue
"P.S.: POSTAGE IS EXPENSIVE, SO THE CHIEF LET ME USE THE SAME ENVELOPE AS HIM. I'LL SEND YOU CHAPTER 2 WHEN IT'S READY."
?
WAAA-AAAH-HHHH!!
HUH? WHAT? WHY?
WHAT ABOUT MY KID!?
KUSHA (CRUMPLE)
STUPID, STUPID ARUEEEE!!
ARUE!?

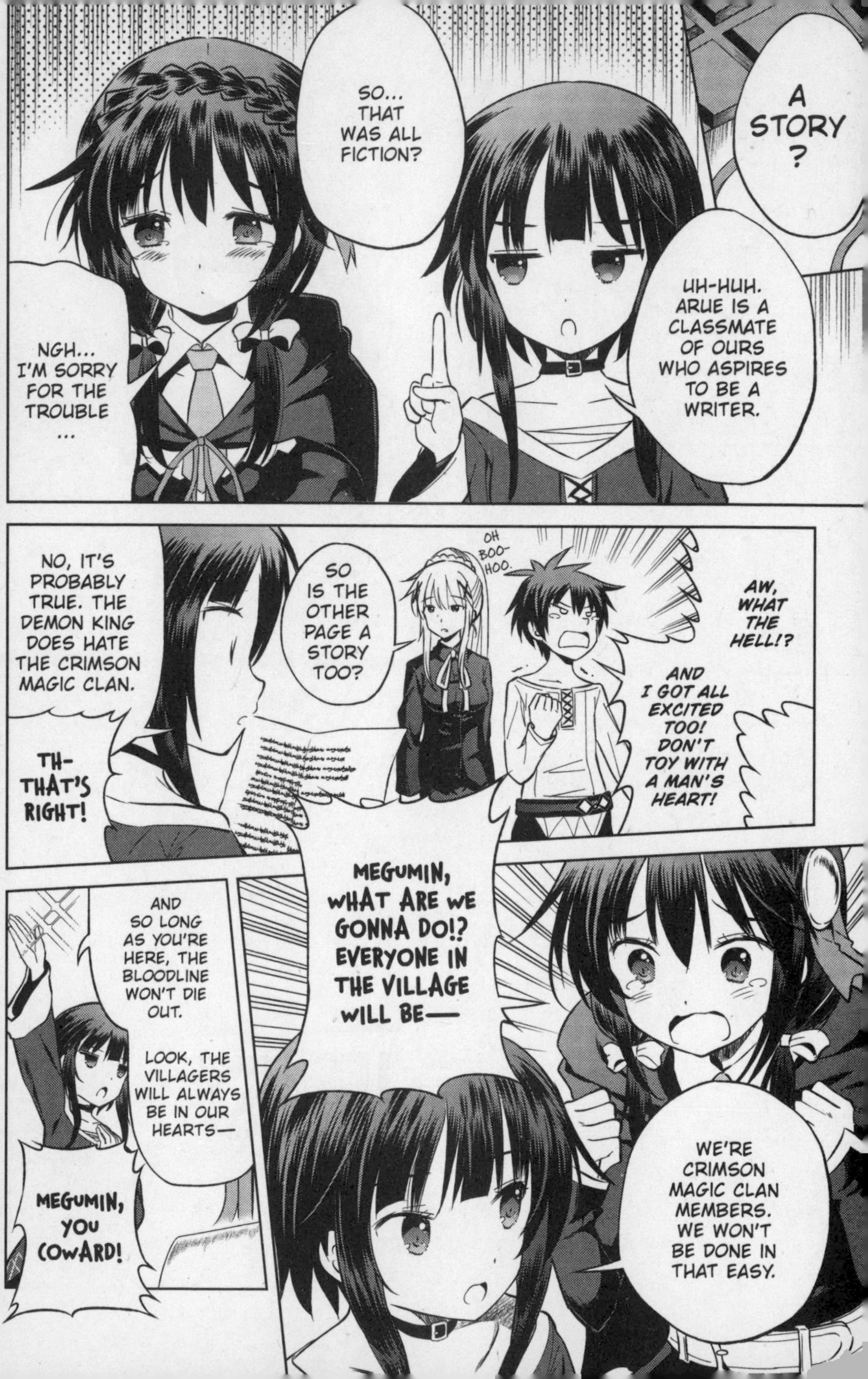
A STORY?
SO... THAT WAS ALL FICTION?
UH-HUH. ARUE IS A CLASSMATE OF OURS WHO ASPIRES TO BE A WRITER.
NGH... I'M SORRY FOR THE TROUBLE...
AW, WHAT THE HELL!?
AND I GOT ALL EXCITED TOO! DON'T TOY WITH A MAN'S HEART!
OH BOO-HOO.
SO IS THE OTHER PAGE A STORY TOO?
NO, IT'S PROBABLY TRUE. THE DEMON KING DOES HATE THE CRIMSON MAGIC CLAN.
TH-THAT'S RIGHT!
MEGUMIN, WHAT ARE WE GONNA DO!? EVERYONE IN THE VILLAGE WILL BE—
WE'RE CRIMSON MAGIC CLAN MEMBERS. WE WON'T BE DONE IN THAT EASY.
AND SO LONG AS YOU'RE HERE, THE BLOODLINE WON'T DIE OUT.
LOOK, THE VILLAGERS WILL ALWAYS BE IN OUR HEARTS—
MEGUMIN, YOU COWARD!

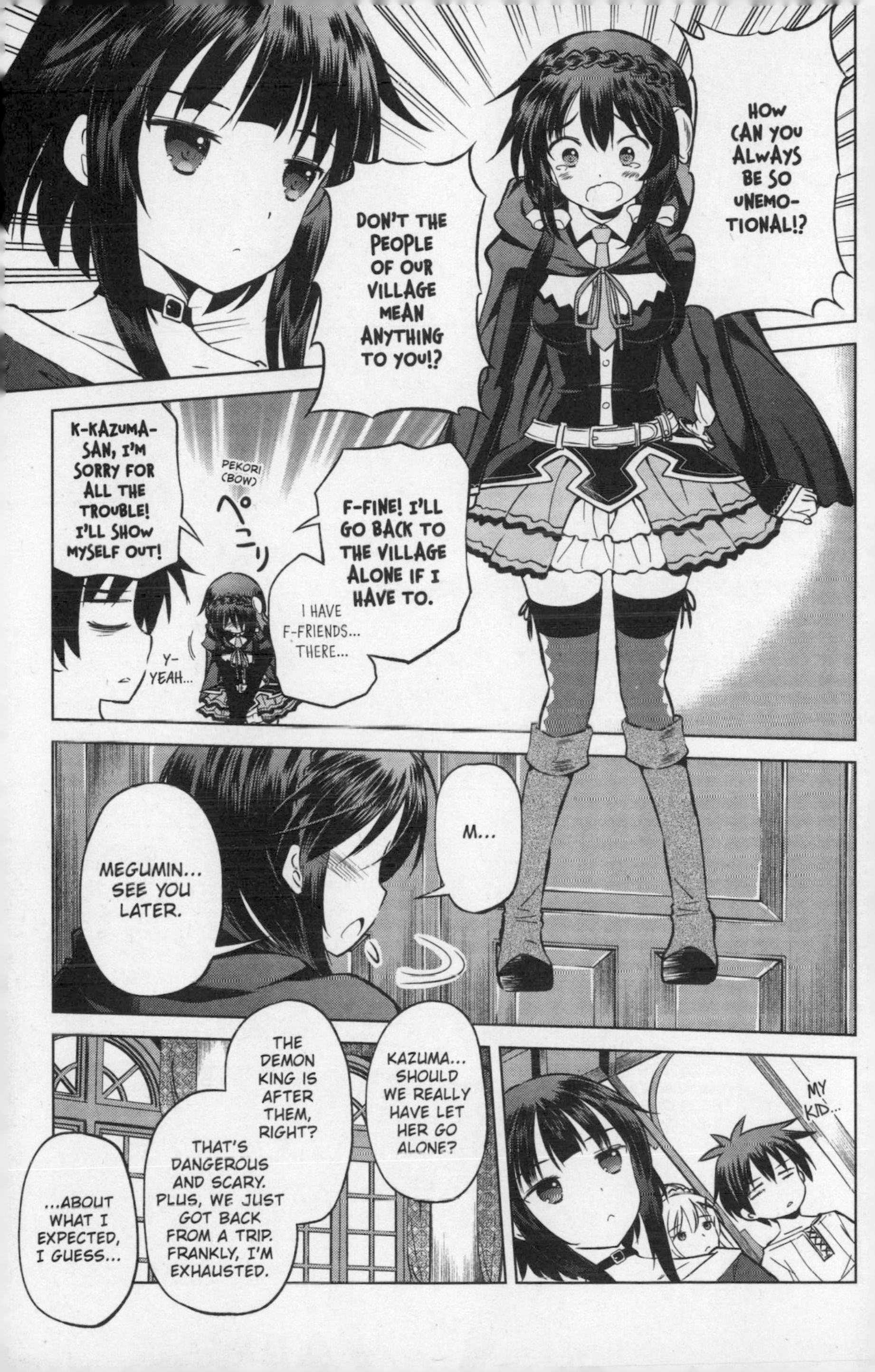

HOW CAN YOU ALWAYS BE SO UNEMOTIONAL!?
DON'T THE PEOPLE OF OUR VILLAGE MEAN ANYTHING TO YOU!?
F-FINE! I'LL GO BACK TO THE VILLAGE ALONE IF I HAVE TO.
I HAVE F-FRIENDS... THERE...
K-KAZUMA-SAN, I'M SORRY FOR ALL THE TROUBLE! I'LL SHOW MYSELF OUT!
PEKORI (BOW)
ぺこり
Y-YEAH...
M...
MEGUMIN... SEE YOU LATER.
MY KID...
KAZUMA... SHOULD WE REALLY HAVE LET HER GO ALONE?
THE DEMON KING IS AFTER THEM, RIGHT?
THAT'S DANGEROUS AND SCARY. PLUS, WE JUST GOT BACK FROM A TRIP. FRANKLY, I'M EXHAUSTED.
...ABOUT WHAT I EXPECTED, I GUESS...

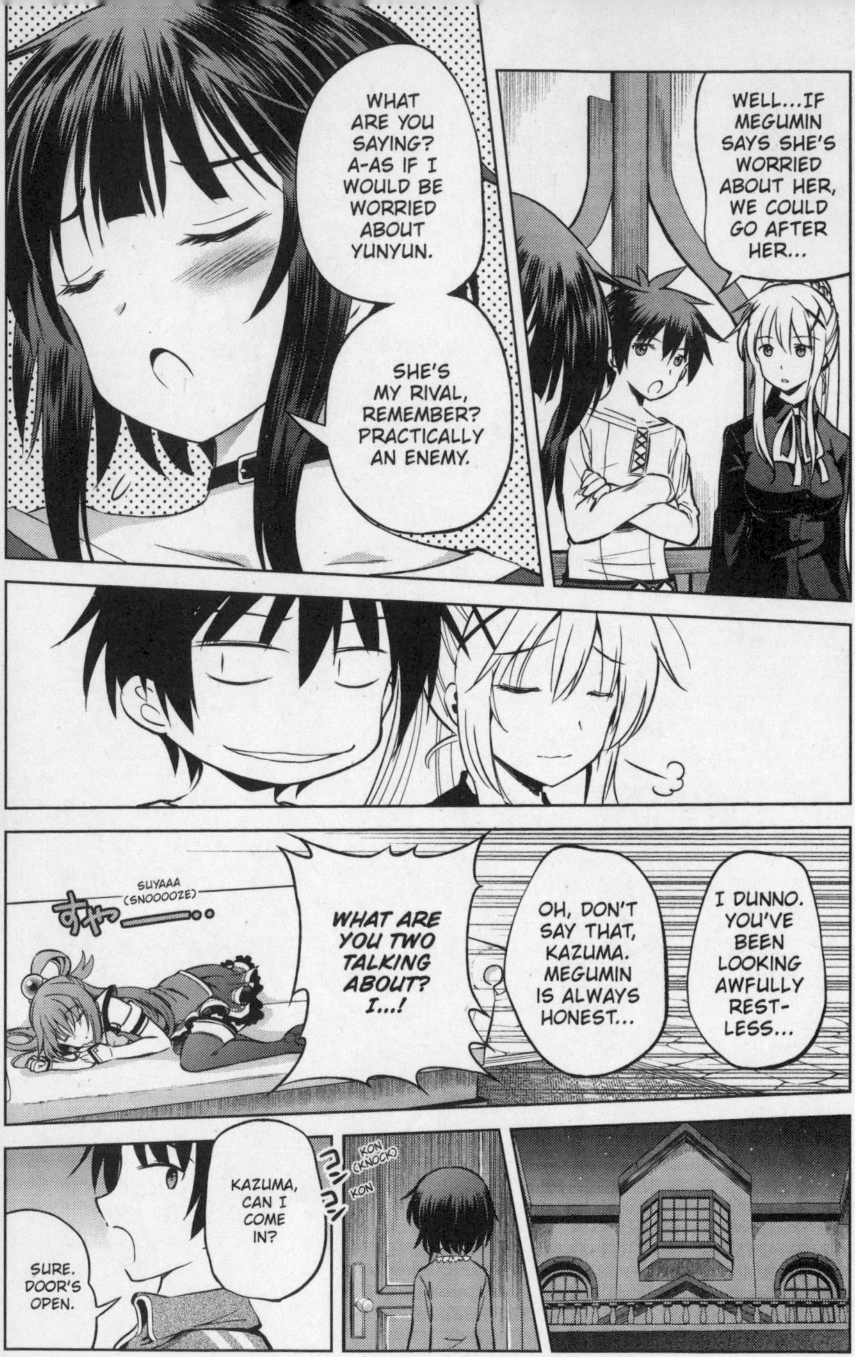
WELL...IF MEGUMIN SAYS SHE'S WORRIED ABOUT HER, WE COULD GO AFTER HER...
WHAT ARE YOU SAYING? A-AS IF I WOULD BE WORRIED ABOUT YUNYUN.
SHE'S MY RIVAL, REMEMBER? PRACTICALLY AN ENEMY.
I DUNNO. YOU'VE BEEN LOOKING AWFULLY REST-LESS...
OH, DON'T SAY THAT, KAZUMA. MEGUMIN IS ALWAYS HONEST...
WHAT ARE YOU TWO TALKING ABOUT? I...!
SUYAAA (SNOOOOZE)
KON (KNOCK)
KON
KAZUMA, CAN I COME IN?
SURE. DOOR'S OPEN.

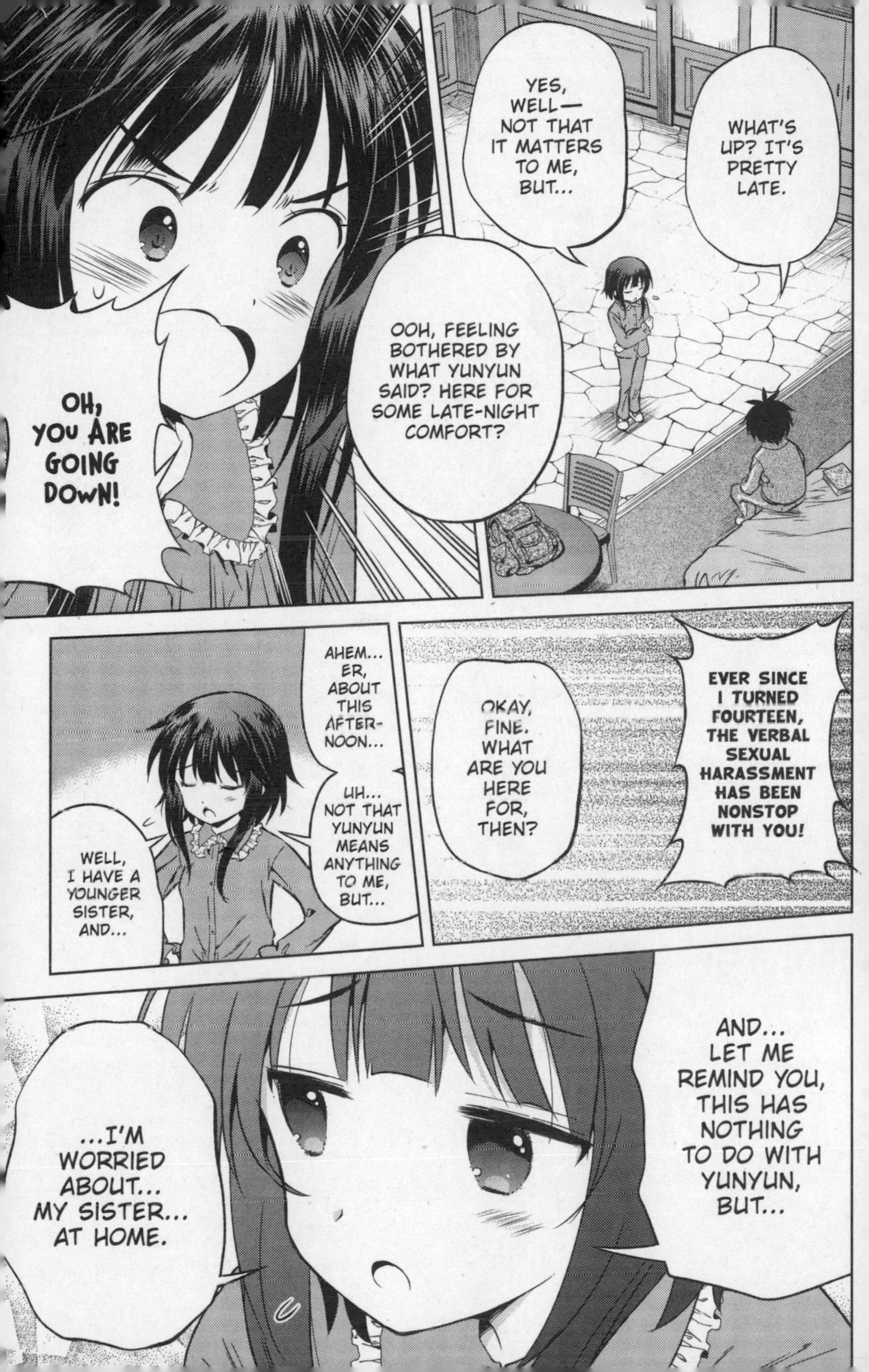
WHAT'S UP? IT'S PRETTY LATE.
YES, WELL— NOT THAT IT MATTERS TO ME, BUT...
OOH, FEELING BOTHERED BY WHAT YUNYUN SAID? HERE FOR SOME LATE-NIGHT COMFORT?
OH, YOU ARE GOING DOWN!
EVER SINCE I TURNED FOURTEEN, THE VERBAL SEXUAL HARASSMENT HAS BEEN NONSTOP WITH YOU!
OKAY, FINE. WHAT ARE YOU HERE FOR, THEN?
AHEM... ER, ABOUT THIS AFTER-NOON...
UH... NOT THAT YUNYUN MEANS ANYTHING TO ME, BUT...
WELL, I HAVE A YOUNGER SISTER, AND...
AND... LET ME REMIND YOU, THIS HAS NOTHING TO DO WITH YUNYUN, BUT...
...I'M WORRIED ABOUT... MY SISTER... AT HOME.

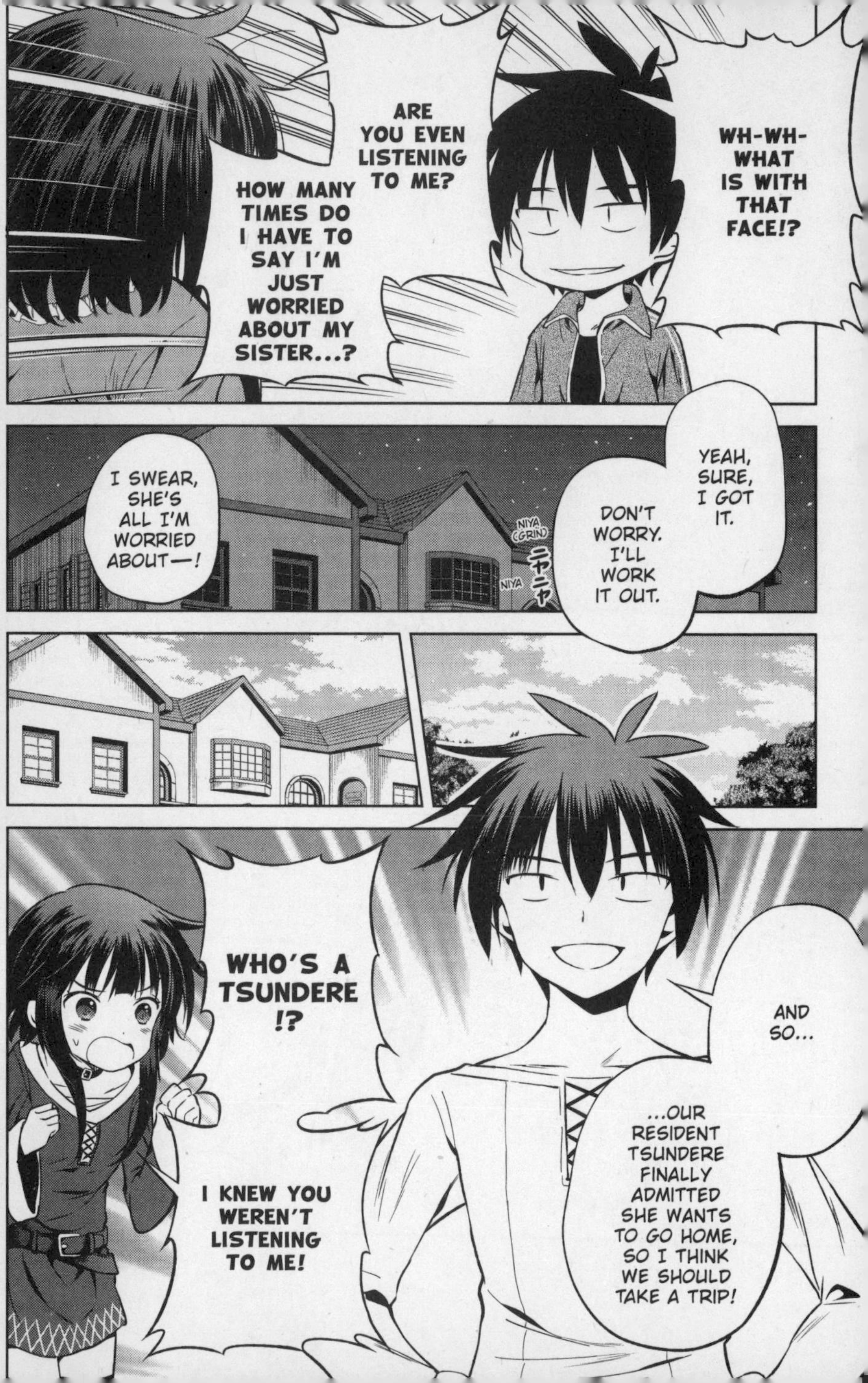
WH-WH-WHAT IS WITH THAT FACE!?
ARE YOU EVEN LISTENING TO ME?
HOW MANY TIMES DO I HAVE TO SAY I'M JUST WORRIED ABOUT MY SISTER...?
YEAH, SURE, I GOT IT.
DON'T WORRY. I'LL WORK IT OUT.
NIYA (GRIN)
ニヤニヤ
NIYA
I SWEAR, SHE'S ALL I'M WORRIED ABOUT—!
AND SO...
...OUR RESIDENT TSUNDERE FINALLY ADMITTED SHE WANTS TO GO HOME, SO I THINK WE SHOULD TAKE A TRIP!
WHO'S A TSUNDERE!?
I KNEW YOU WEREN'T LISTENING TO ME!

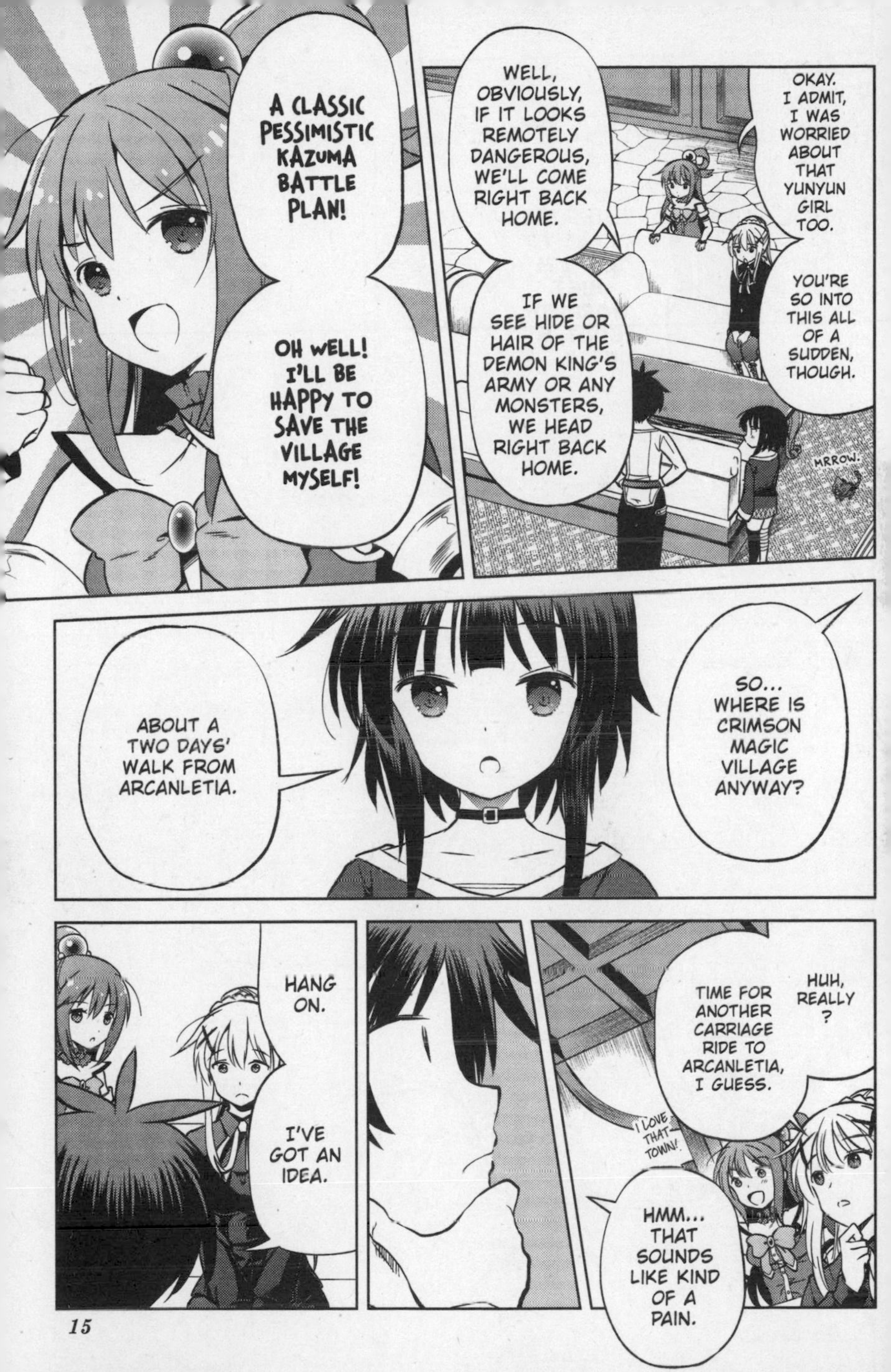
OKAY. I ADMIT, I WAS WORRIED ABOUT THAT YUNYUN GIRL TOO.
YOU'RE SO INTO THIS ALL OF A SUDDEN, THOUGH.
WELL, OBVIOUSLY, IF IT LOOKS REMOTELY DANGEROUS, WE'LL COME RIGHT BACK HOME.
IF WE SEE HIDE OR HAIR OF THE DEMON KING'S ARMY OR ANY MONSTERS, WE HEAD RIGHT BACK HOME.
MRROW.
A CLASSIC PESSIMISTIC KAZUMA BATTLE PLAN!
OH WELL! I'LL BE HAPPY TO SAVE THE VILLAGE MYSELF!
SO... WHERE IS CRIMSON MAGIC VILLAGE ANYWAY?
ABOUT A TWO DAYS' WALK FROM ARCANLETIA.
HUH, REALLY?
TIME FOR ANOTHER CARRIAGE RIDE TO ARCANLETIA, I GUESS.
I LOVE THAT TOWN!
HMM... THAT SOUNDS LIKE KIND OF A PAIN.
HANG ON.
I'VE GOT AN IDEA.

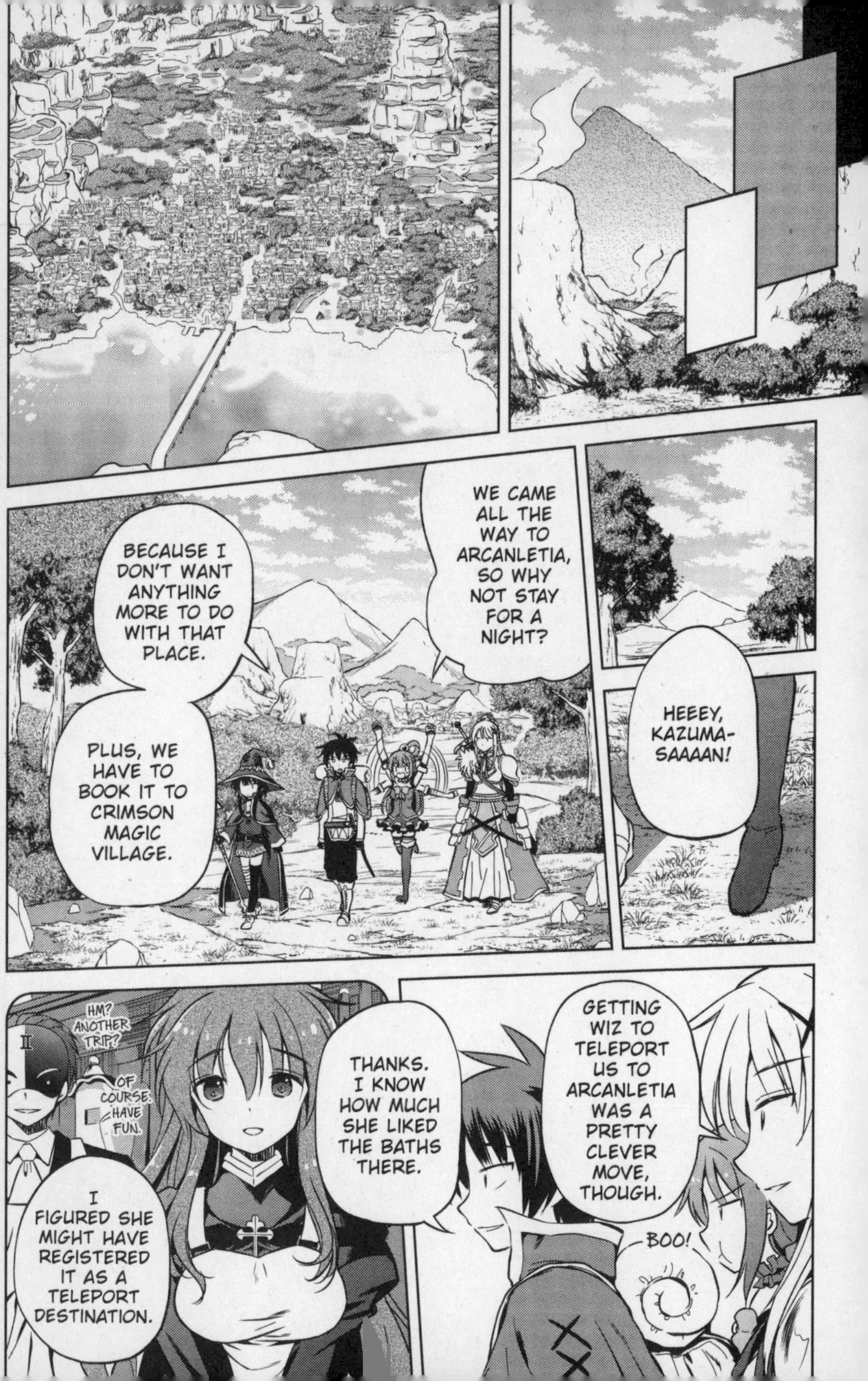
HEEEY, KAZUMA-SAAAAN!
WE CAME ALL THE WAY TO ARCANLETIA, SO WHY NOT STAY FOR A NIGHT?
BECAUSE I DON'T WANT ANYTHING MORE TO DO WITH THAT PLACE.
PLUS, WE HAVE TO BOOK IT TO CRIMSON MAGIC VILLAGE.
GETTING WIZ TO TELEPORT US TO ARCANLETIA WAS A PRETTY CLEVER MOVE, THOUGH.
BOO!
THANKS. I KNOW HOW MUCH SHE LIKED THE BATHS THERE.
HM? ANOTHER TRIP?
OF COURSE. HAVE FUN.
I FIGURED SHE MIGHT HAVE REGISTERED IT AS A TELEPORT DESTINATION.

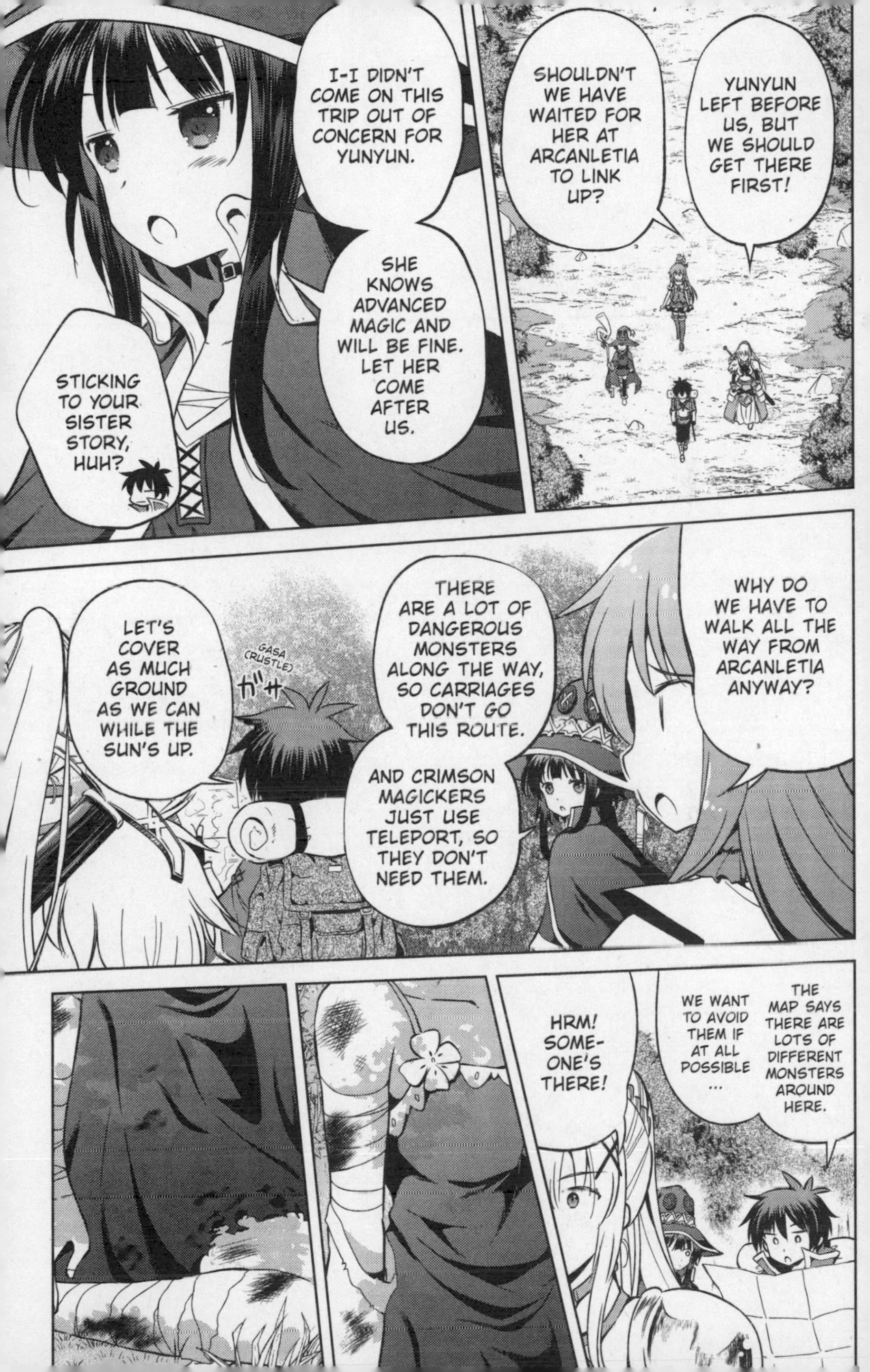
YUNYUN LEFT BEFORE US, BUT WE SHOULD GET THERE FIRST!
SHOULDN'T WE HAVE WAITED FOR HER AT ARCANLETIA TO LINK UP?
I-I DIDN'T COME ON THIS TRIP OUT OF CONCERN FOR YUNYUN.
SHE KNOWS ADVANCED MAGIC AND WILL BE FINE. LET HER COME AFTER US.
STICKING TO YOUR SISTER STORY, HUH?
WHY DO WE HAVE TO WALK ALL THE WAY FROM ARCANLETIA ANYWAY?
THERE ARE A LOT OF DANGEROUS MONSTERS ALONG THE WAY, SO CARRIAGES DON'T GO THIS ROUTE.
AND CRIMSON MAGICKERS JUST USE TELEPORT, SO THEY DON'T NEED THEM.
GASA (RUSTLE)
ガサ
LET'S COVER AS MUCH GROUND AS WE CAN WHILE THE SUN'S UP.
THE MAP SAYS THERE ARE LOTS OF DIFFERENT MONSTERS AROUND HERE.
WE WANT TO AVOID THEM IF AT ALL POSSIBLE...
HRM! SOME-ONE'S THERE!

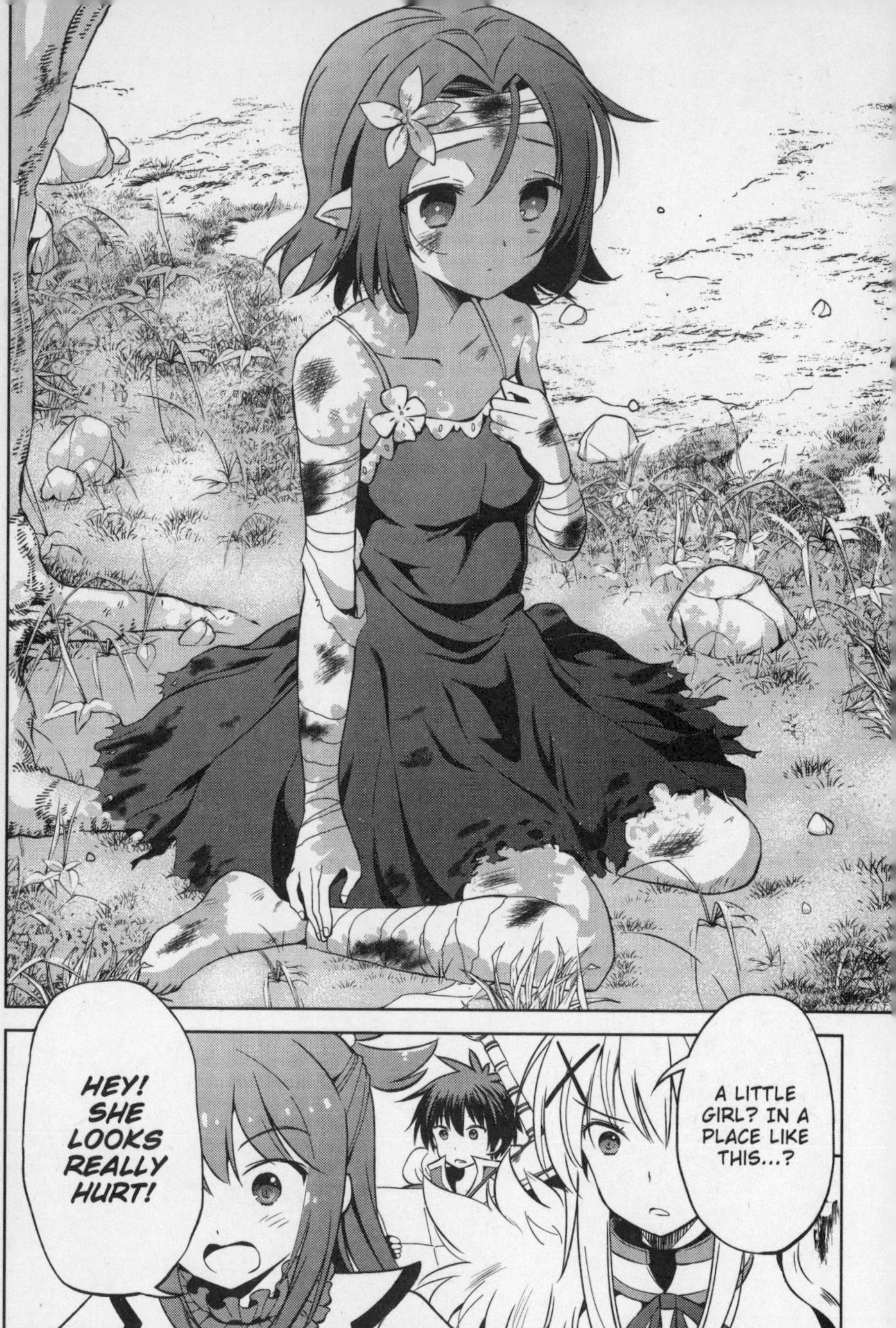
A LITTLE GIRL? IN A PLACE LIKE THIS...?
HEY! SHE LOOKS REALLY HURT!

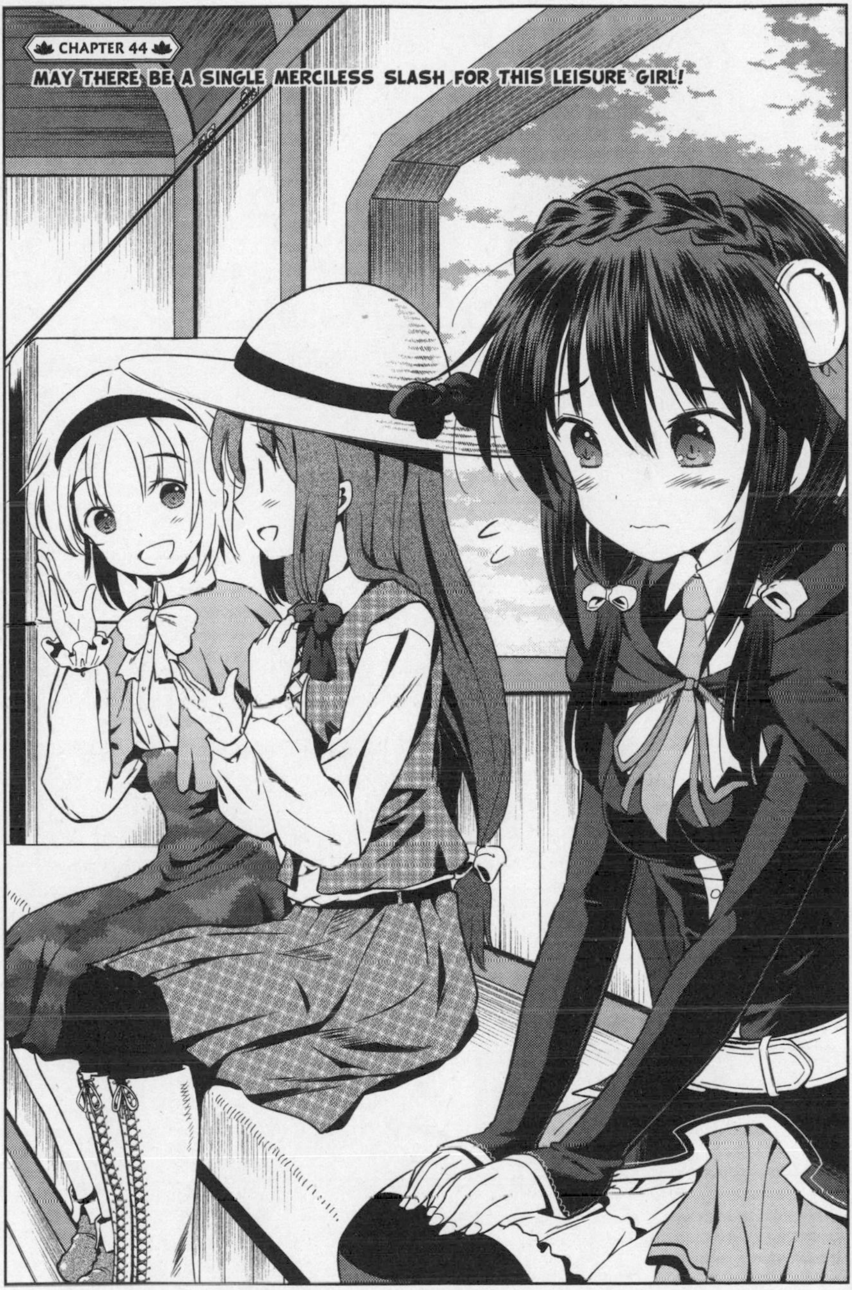
CHAPTER 44
MAY THERE BE A SINGLE MERCILESS SLASH FOR THIS LEISURE GIRL!

A PICTURE OF YUNYUN IN THE CARRIAGE, UNABLE TO TALK TO THE OTHER GIRLS HER AGE.

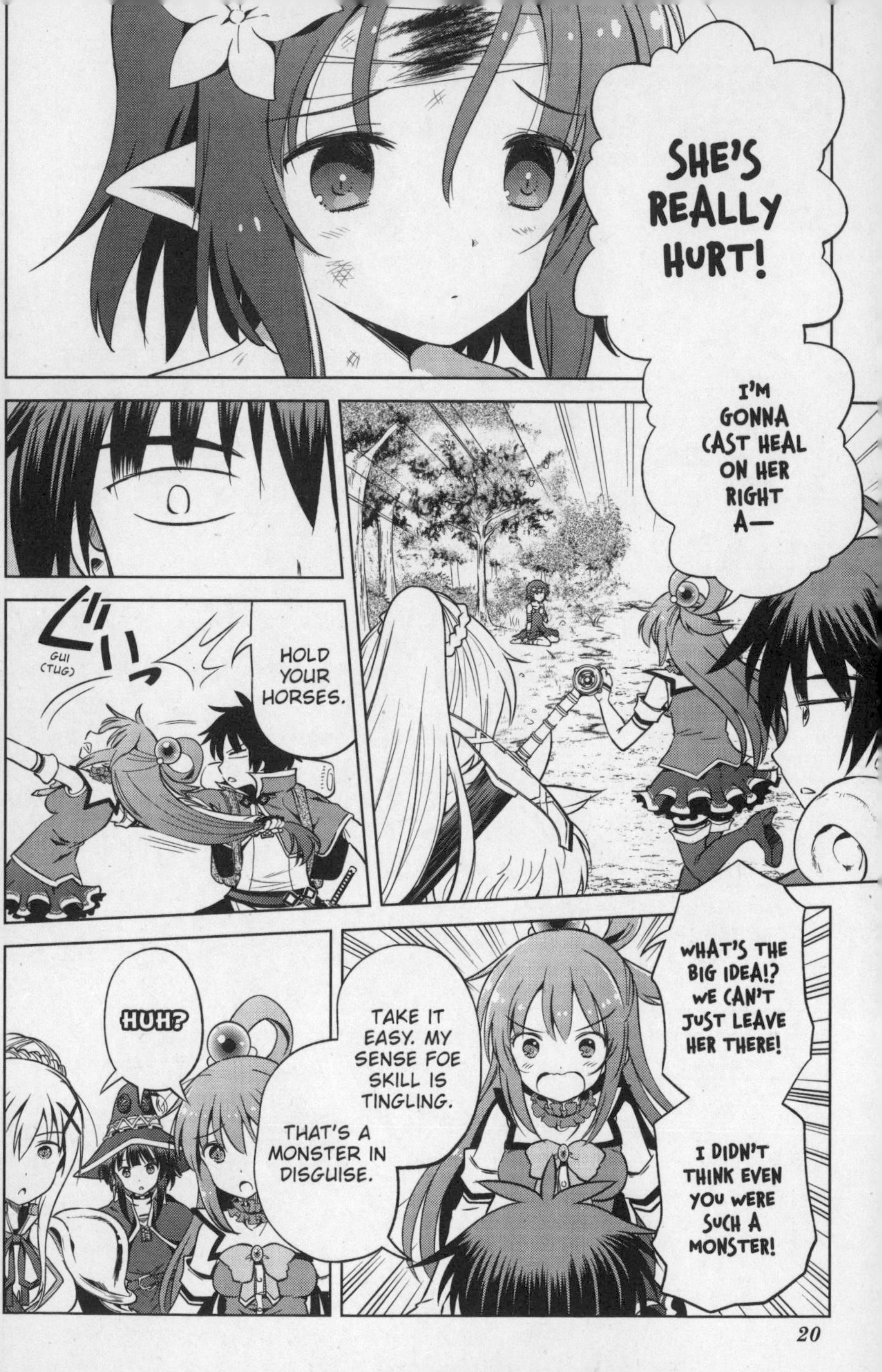
SHE'S REALLY HURT!
I'M GONNA CAST HEAL ON HER RIGHT A—
ぐいっ
GUI (TUG)
HOLD YOUR HORSES.
WHAT'S THE BIG IDEA!? WE CAN'T JUST LEAVE HER THERE!
I DIDN'T THINK EVEN YOU WERE SUCH A MONSTER!
TAKE IT EASY. MY SENSE FOE SKILL IS TINGLING.
THAT'S A MONSTER IN DISGUISE.
HUH?

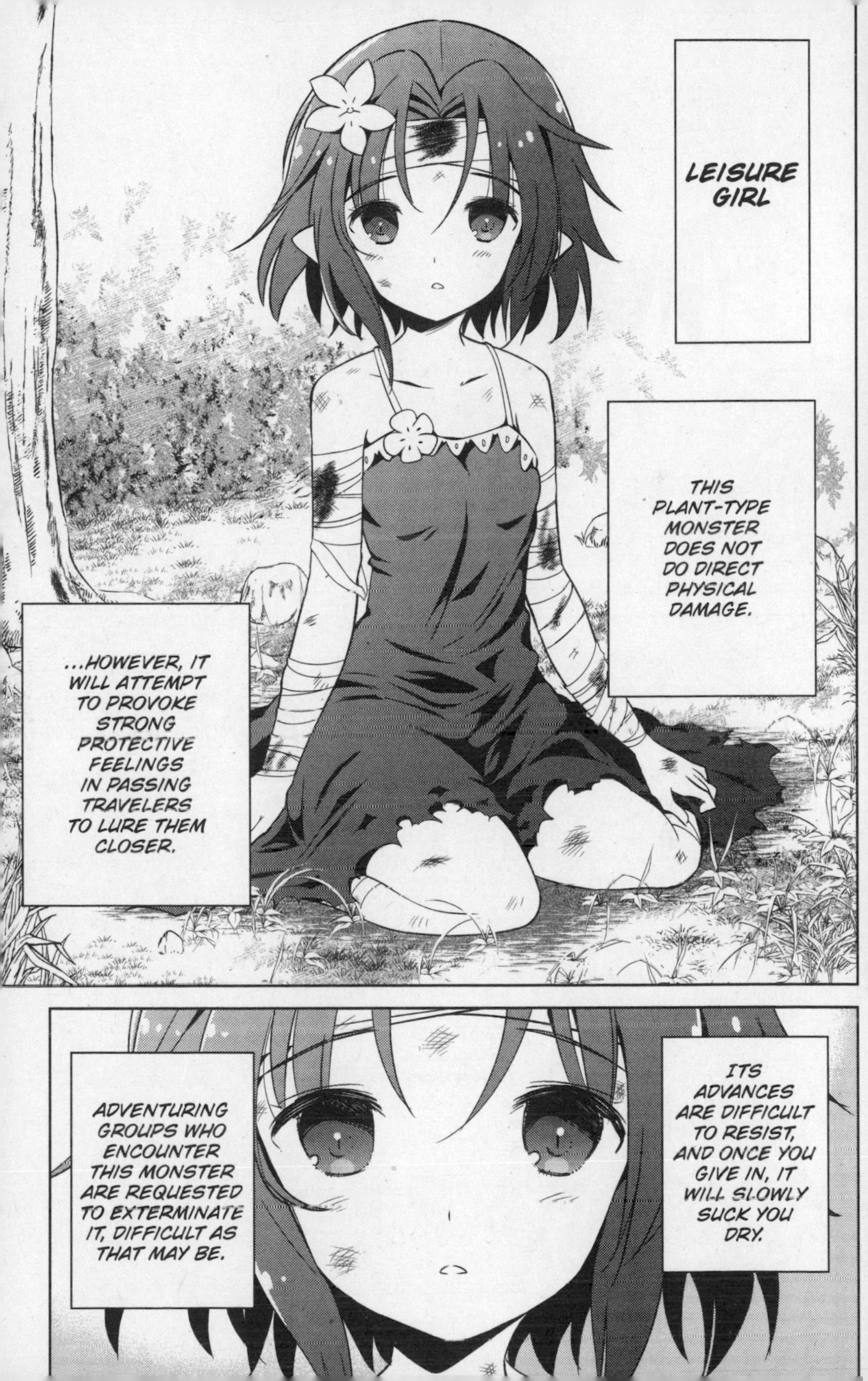
LEISURE GIRL
THIS PLANT-TYPE MONSTER DOES NOT DO DIRECT PHYSICAL DAMAGE.
...HOWEVER, IT WILL ATTEMPT TO PROVOKE STRONG PROTECTIVE FEELINGS IN PASSING TRAVELERS TO LURE THEM CLOSER.
ITS ADVANCES ARE DIFFICULT TO RESIST, AND ONCE YOU GIVE IN, IT WILL SLOWLY SUCK YOU DRY.
ADVENTURING GROUPS WHO ENCOUNTER THIS MONSTER ARE REQUESTED TO EXTERMINATE IT, DIFFICULT AS THAT MAY BE.

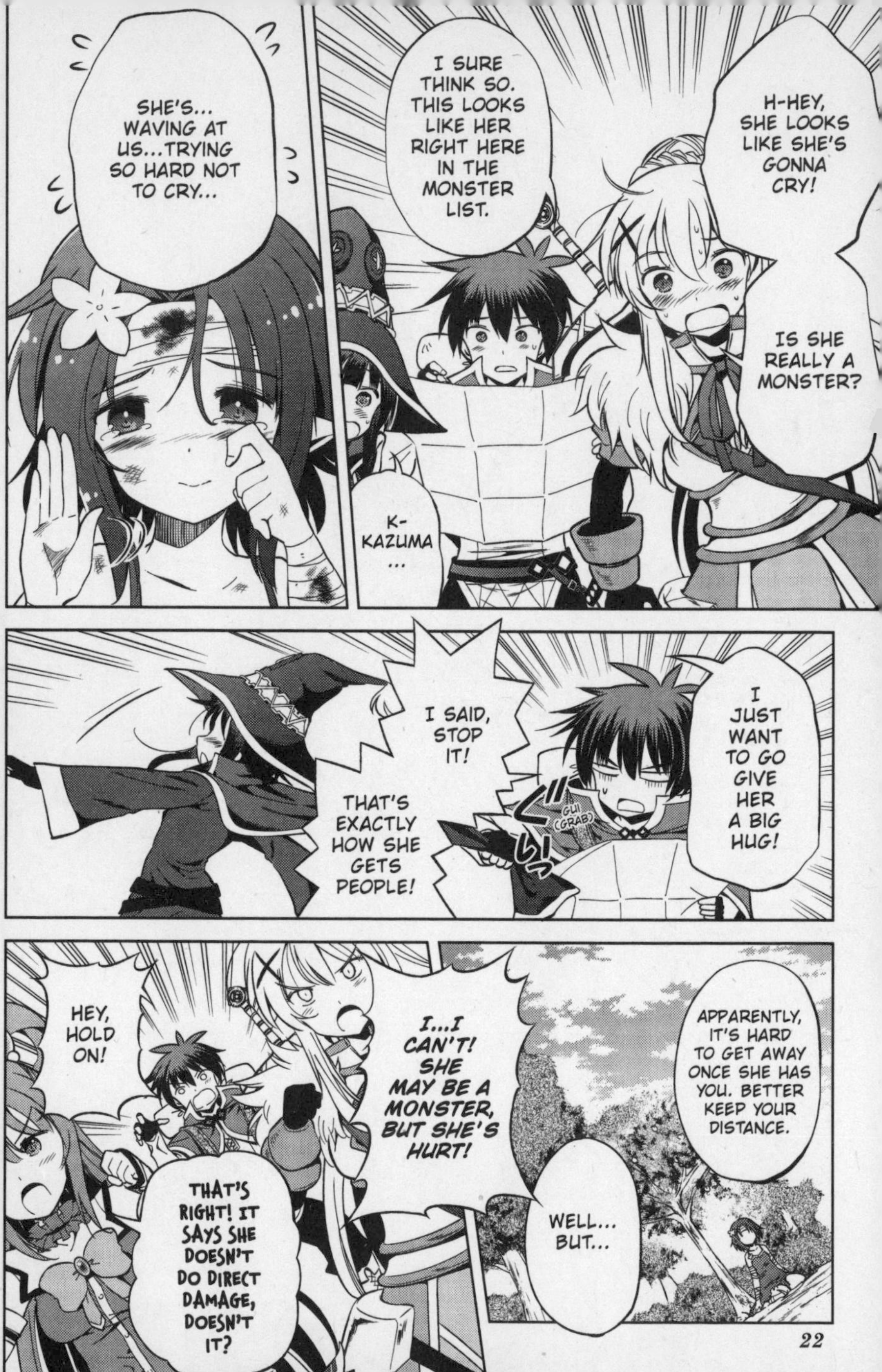
H-HEY, SHE LOOKS LIKE SHE'S GONNA CRY!
I SURE THINK SO. THIS LOOKS LIKE HER RIGHT HERE IN THE MONSTER LIST.
IS SHE REALLY A MONSTER?
K-KAZUMA...
SHE'S... WAVING AT US...TRYING SO HARD NOT TO CRY...
I JUST WANT TO GO GIVE HER A BIG HUG!
GUI (GRAB)
I SAID, STOP IT!
THAT'S EXACTLY HOW SHE GETS PEOPLE!
APPARENTLY, IT'S HARD TO GET AWAY ONCE SHE HAS YOU. BETTER KEEP YOUR DISTANCE.
WELL... BUT...
I...I CAN'T! SHE MAY BE A MONSTER, BUT SHE'S HURT!
HEY, HOLD ON!
THAT'S RIGHT! IT SAYS SHE DOESN'T DO DIRECT DAMAGE, DOESN'T IT?

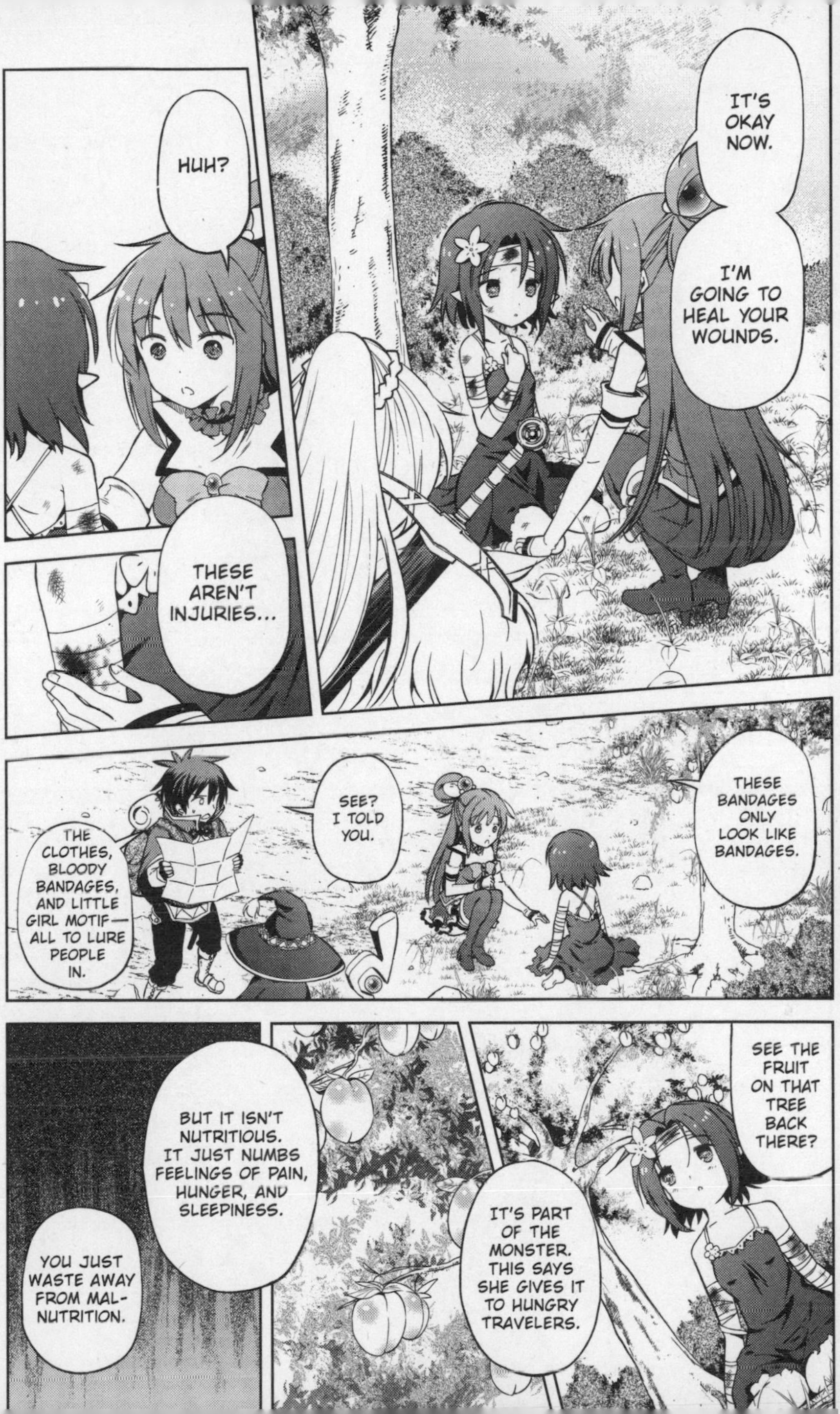
IT'S OKAY NOW.
I'M GOING TO HEAL YOUR WOUNDS.
HUH?
THESE AREN'T INJURIES...
THESE BANDAGES ONLY LOOK LIKE BANDAGES.
SEE? I TOLD YOU.
THE CLOTHES, BLOODY BANDAGES, AND LITTLE GIRL MOTIF—ALL TO LURE PEOPLE IN.
SEE THE FRUIT ON THAT TREE BACK THERE?
IT'S PART OF THE MONSTER. THIS SAYS SHE GIVES IT TO HUNGRY TRAVELERS.
BUT IT ISN'T NUTRITIOUS. IT JUST NUMBS FEELINGS OF PAIN, HUNGER, AND SLEEPINESS.
YOU JUST WASTE AWAY FROM MAL-NUTRITION.

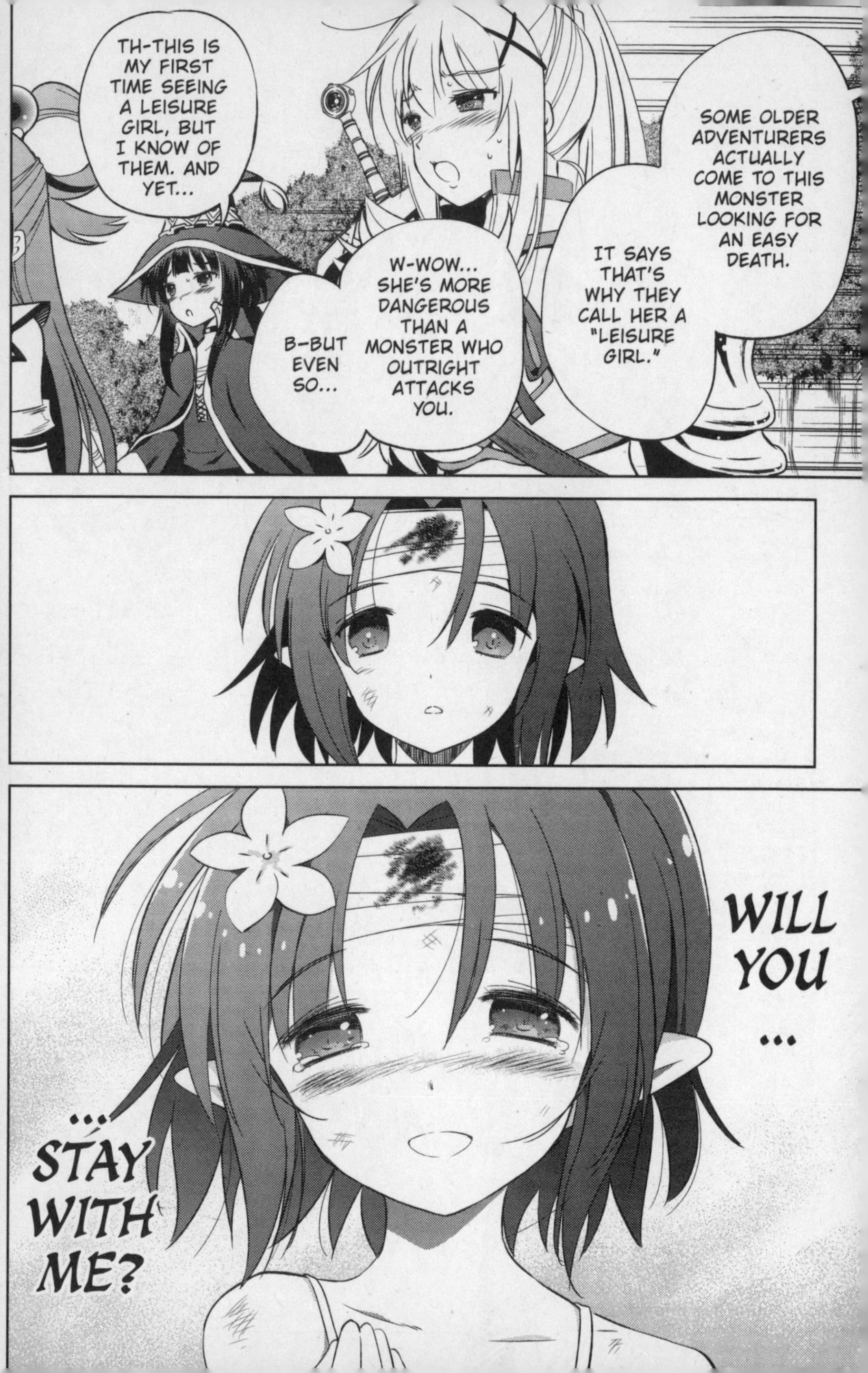
SOME OLDER ADVENTURERS ACTUALLY COME TO THIS MONSTER LOOKING FOR AN EASY DEATH.
IT SAYS THAT'S WHY THEY CALL HER A "LEISURE GIRL."
W-WOW... SHE'S MORE DANGEROUS THAN A MONSTER WHO OUTRIGHT ATTACKS YOU.
B-BUT EVEN SO...
TH-THIS IS MY FIRST TIME SEEING A LEISURE GIRL, BUT I KNOW OF THEM. AND YET...
WILL YOU ...
...STAY WITH ME?

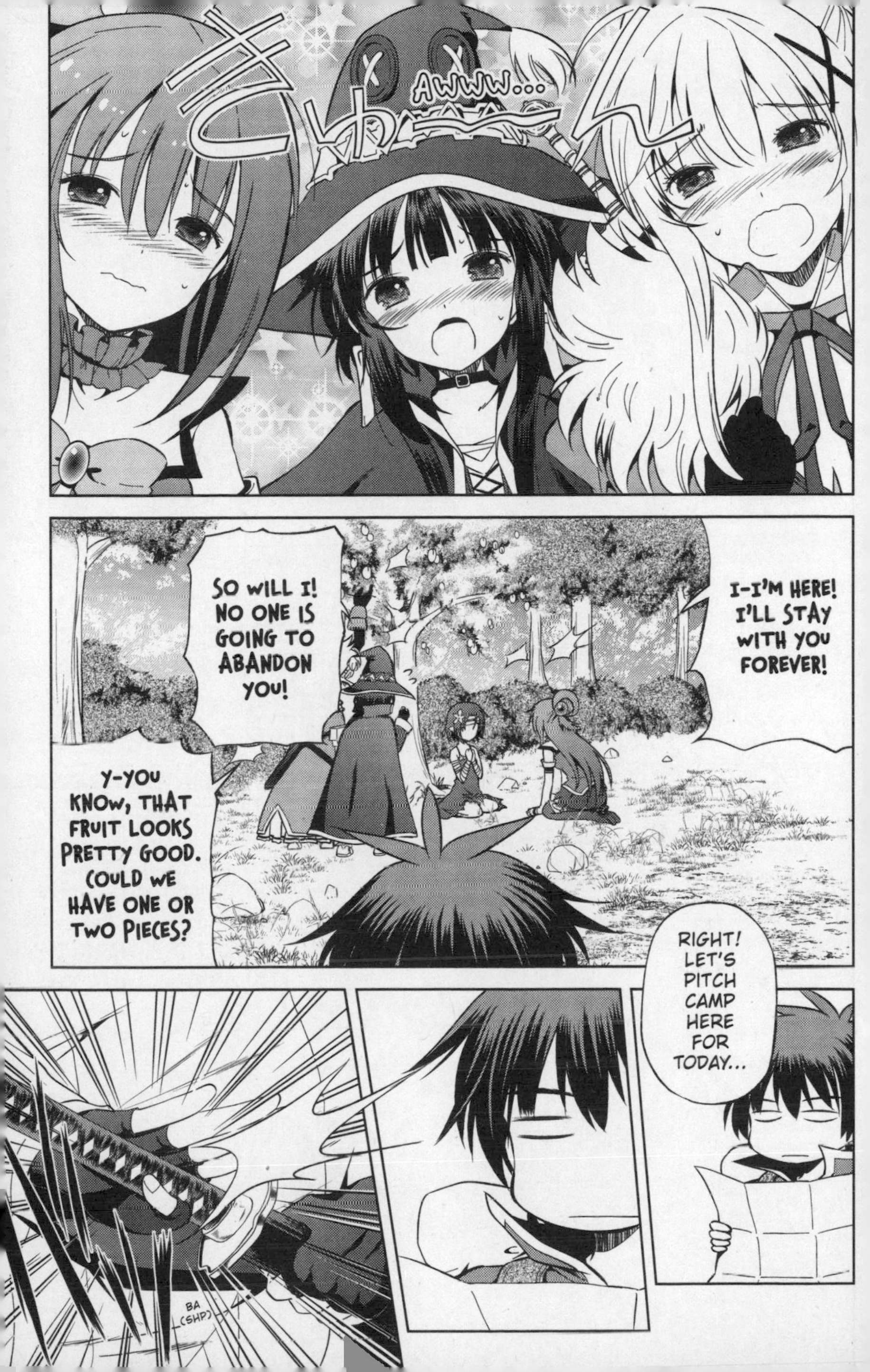
AWWW...
I-I'M HERE! I'LL STAY WITH YOU FOREVER!
SO WILL I! NO ONE IS GOING TO ABANDON YOU!
Y-YOU KNOW, THAT FRUIT LOOKS PRETTY GOOD. COULD WE HAVE ONE OR TWO PIECES?
RIGHT! LET'S PITCH CAMP HERE FOR TODAY...
BA (SHP)

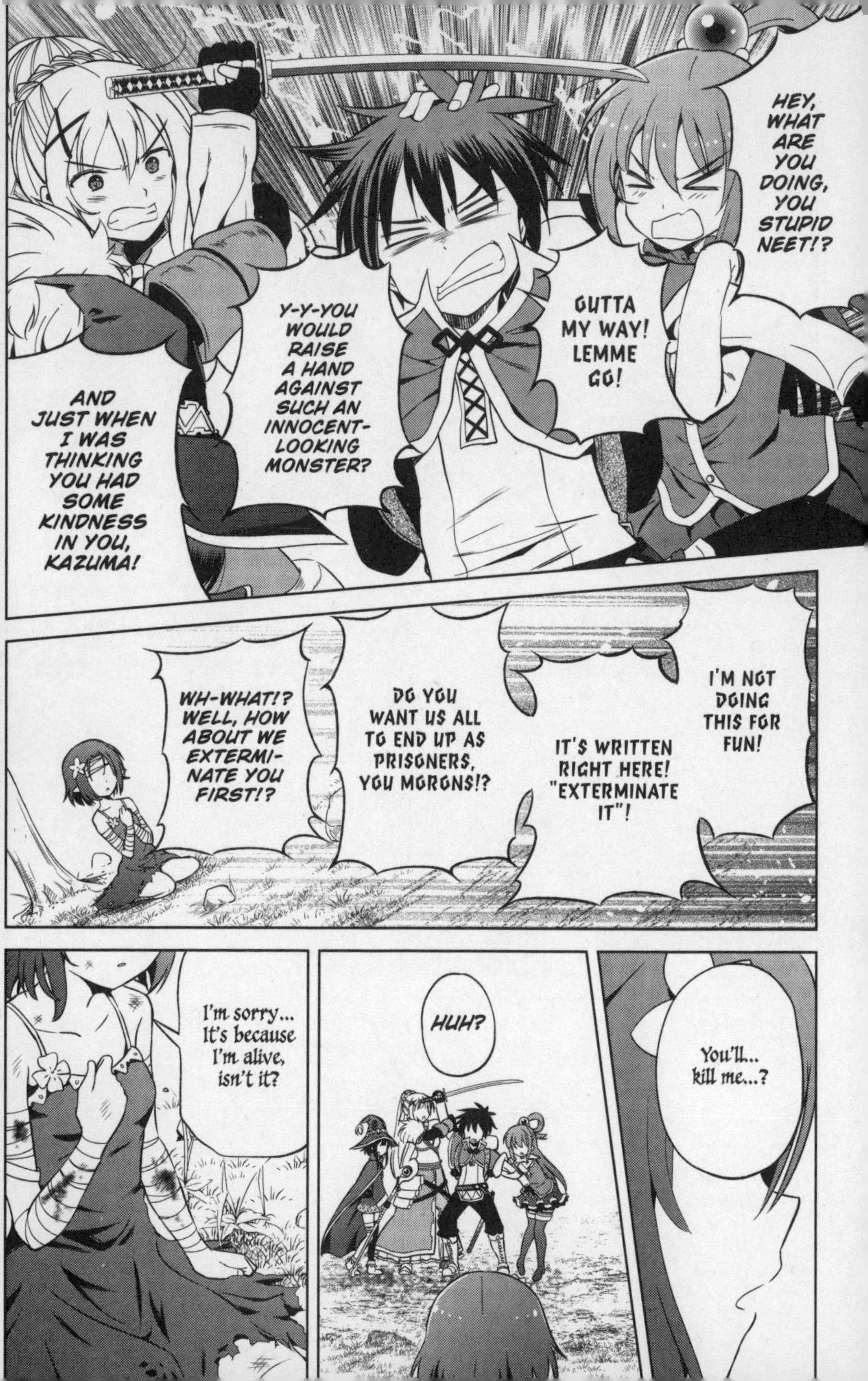
HEY, WHAT ARE YOU DOING, YOU STUPID NEET!?
OUTTA MY WAY! LEMME GO!
Y-Y-YOU WOULD RAISE A HAND AGAINST SUCH AN INNOCENT-LOOKING MONSTER?
AND JUST WHEN I WAS THINKING YOU HAD SOME KINDNESS IN YOU, KAZUMA!
I'M NOT DOING THIS FOR FUN!
IT'S WRITTEN RIGHT HERE! "EXTERMINATE IT"!
DO YOU WANT US ALL TO END UP AS PRISONERS, YOU MORONS!?
WH-WHAT!? WELL, HOW ABOUT WE EXTERMI-NATE YOU FIRST!?
You'll... kill me...?
HUH?
I'm sorry... It's because I'm alive, isn't it?

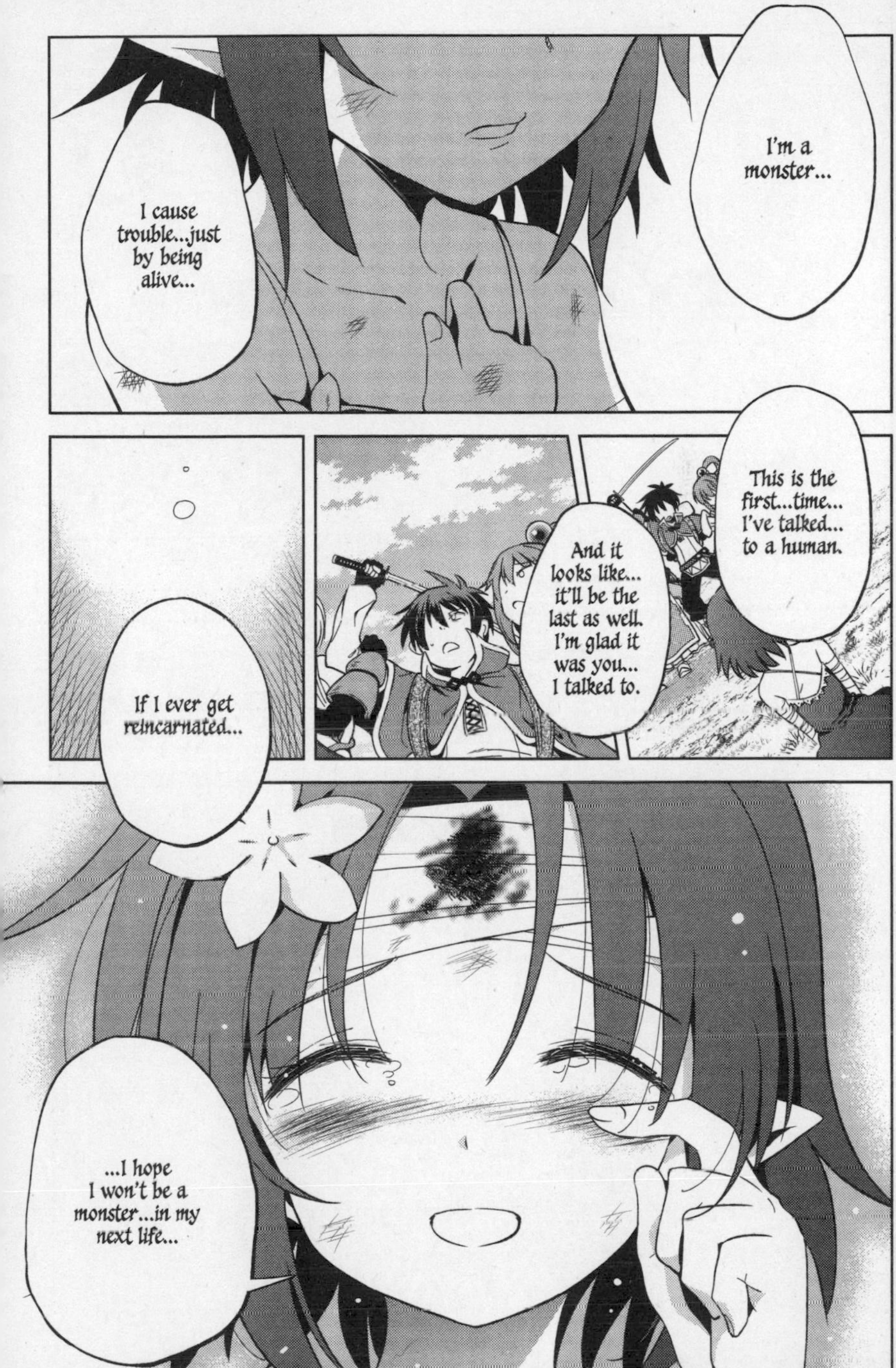
I'm a monster...
I cause trouble...just by being alive...
This is the first...time... I've talked... to a human.
And it looks like... it'll be the last as well. I'm glad it was you... I talked to.
If I ever get reincarnated...
...I hope I won't be a monster...in my next life...

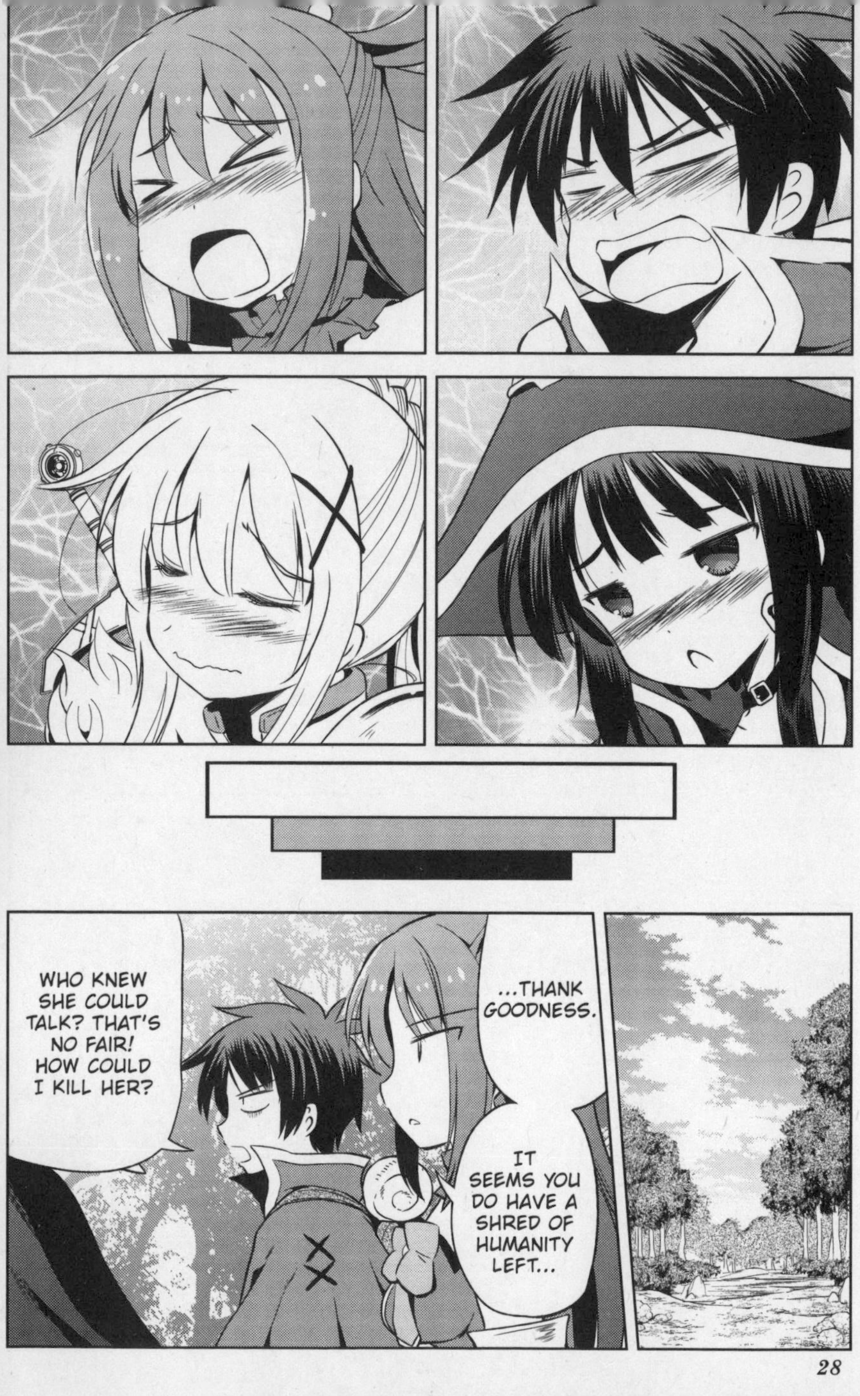
...THANK GOODNESS.
IT SEEMS YOU DO HAVE A SHRED OF HUMANITY LEFT...
WHO KNEW SHE COULD TALK? THAT'S NO FAIR! HOW COULD I KILL HER?

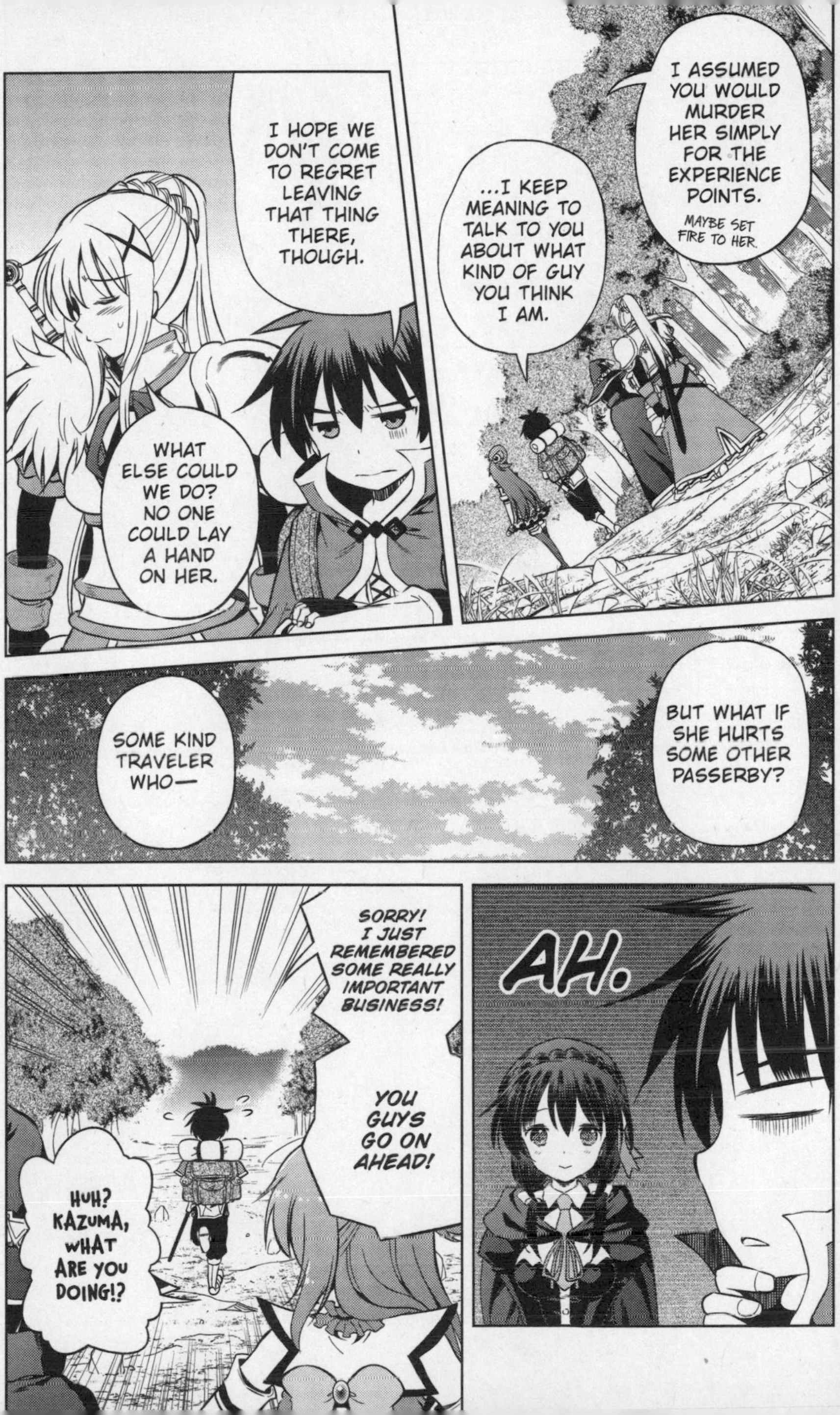
I ASSUMED YOU WOULD MURDER HER SIMPLY FOR THE EXPERIENCE POINTS.
MAYBE SET FIRE TO HER.
...I KEEP MEANING TO TALK TO YOU ABOUT WHAT KIND OF GUY YOU THINK I AM.
I HOPE WE DON'T COME TO REGRET LEAVING THAT THING THERE, THOUGH.
WHAT ELSE COULD WE DO? NO ONE COULD LAY A HAND ON HER.
BUT WHAT IF SHE HURTS SOME OTHER PASSERBY?
SOME KIND TRAVELER WHO—
AH.
SORRY! I JUST REMEMBERED SOME REALLY IMPORTANT BUSINESS!
YOU GUYS GO ON AHEAD!
HUH? KAZUMA, WHAT ARE YOU DOING!?

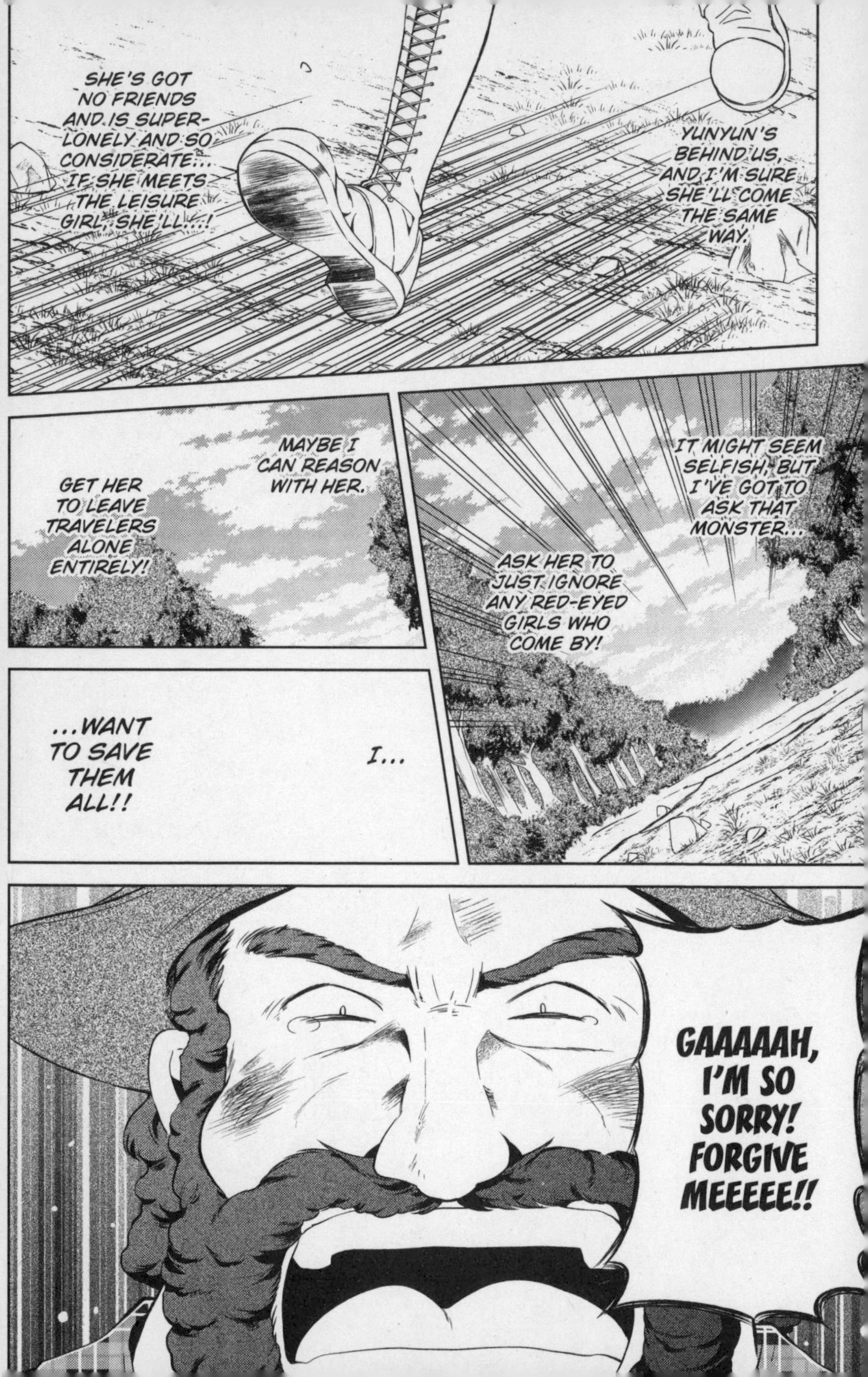
YUNYUN'S BEHIND US, AND I'M SURE SHE'LL COME THE SAME WAY.
SHE'S GOT NO FRIENDS AND IS SUPER-LONELY AND SO CONSIDERATE... IF SHE MEETS THE LEISURE GIRL, SHE'LL...!
IT MIGHT SEEM SELFISH, BUT I'VE GOT TO ASK THAT MONSTER...
ASK HER TO JUST IGNORE ANY RED-EYED GIRLS WHO COME BY!
MAYBE I CAN REASON WITH HER.
GET HER TO LEAVE TRAVELERS ALONE ENTIRELY!
I...
...WANT TO SAVE THEM ALL!!
GAAAAAH, I'M SO SORRY! FORGIVE MEEEEE!!

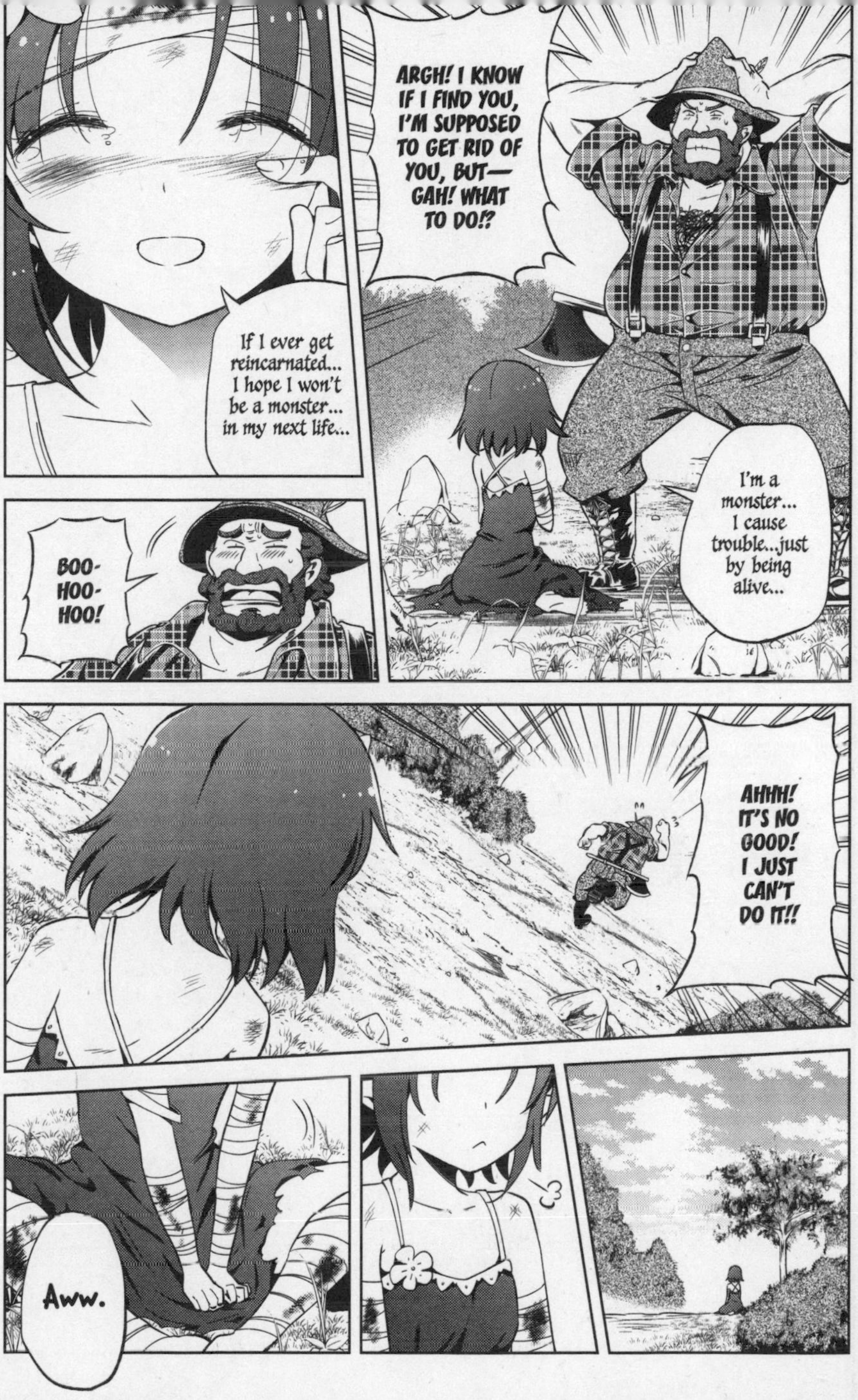
ARGH! I KNOW IF I FIND YOU, I'M SUPPOSED TO GET RID OF YOU, BUT— GAH! WHAT TO DO!?
I'm a monster... I cause trouble...just by being alive...
If I ever get reincarnated... I hope I won't be a monster... in my next life...
BOO-HOO-HOO!
AHHH! IT'S NO GOOD! I JUST CAN'T DO IT!!
Aww.

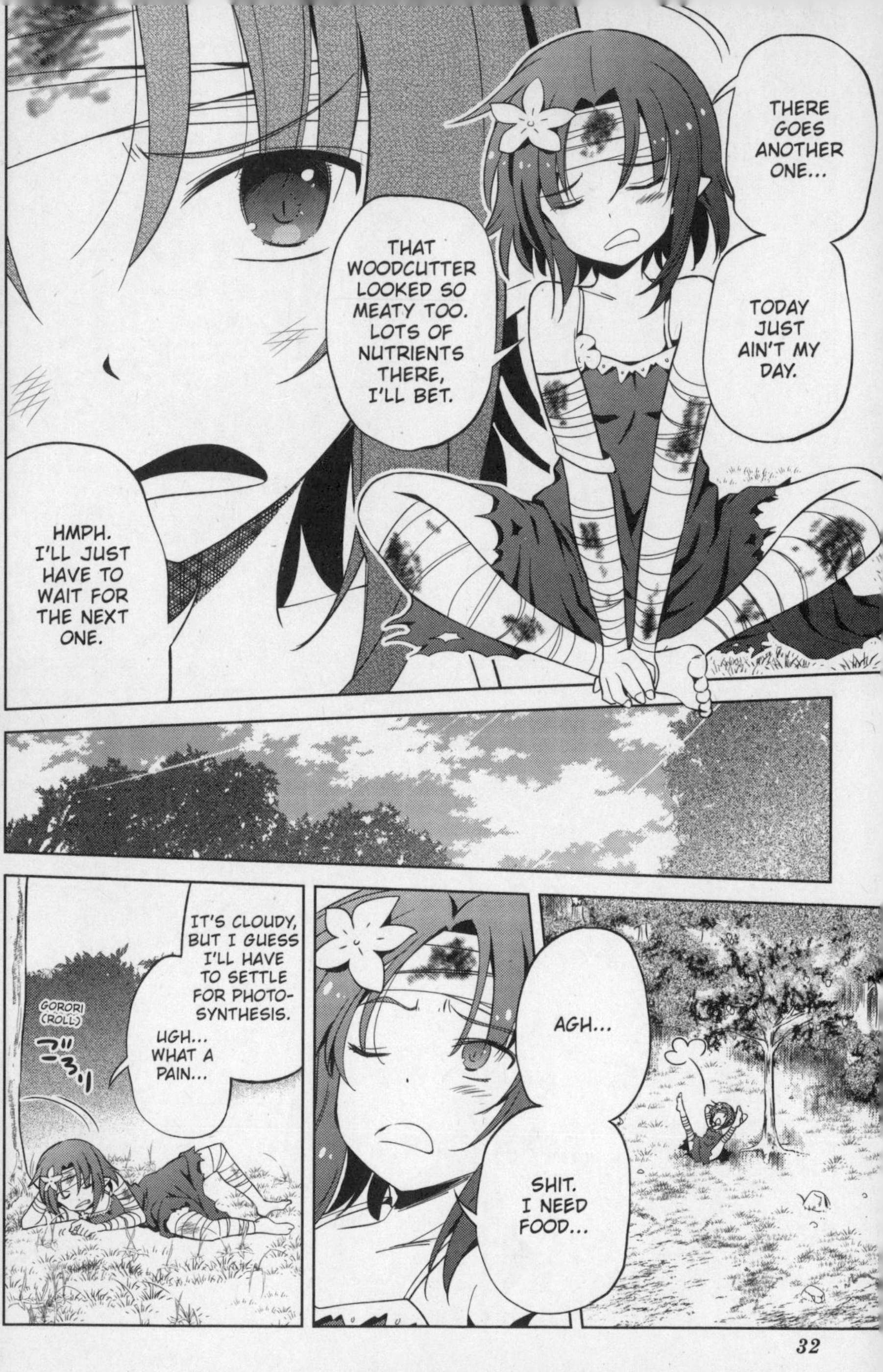
THERE GOES ANOTHER ONE...
TODAY JUST AIN'T MY DAY.
THAT WOODCUTTER LOOKED SO MEATY TOO. LOTS OF NUTRIENTS THERE, I'LL BET.
HMPH. I'LL JUST HAVE TO WAIT FOR THE NEXT ONE.
AGH...
SHIT. I NEED FOOD...
IT'S CLOUDY, BUT I GUESS I'LL HAVE TO SETTLE FOR PHOTO-SYNTHESIS.
UGH... WHAT A PAIN...
GORORI (ROLL)
ごろり

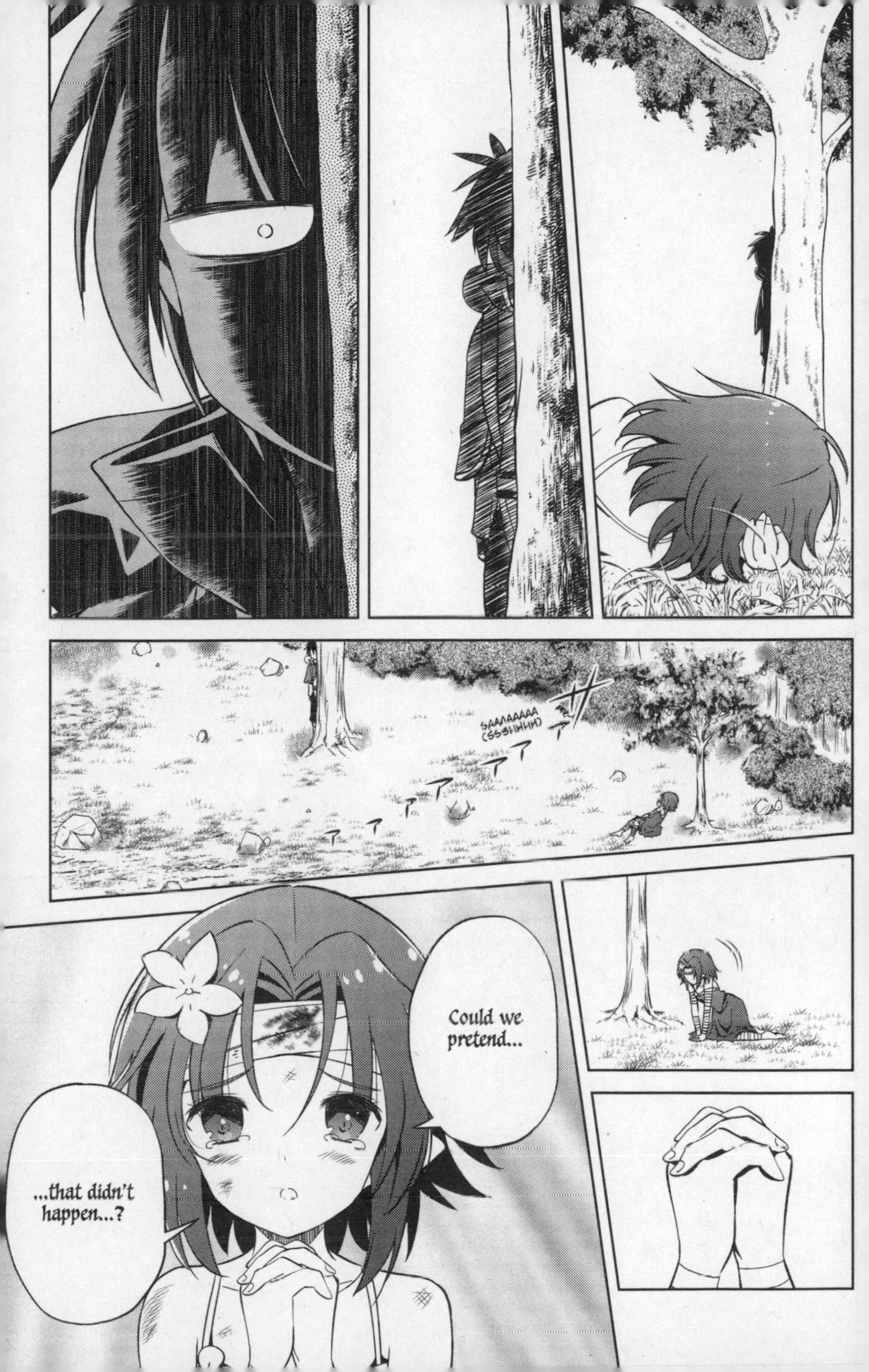
SAAAAAAAA
(SSSHHHHH)
Could we pretend...
...that didn't happen...?

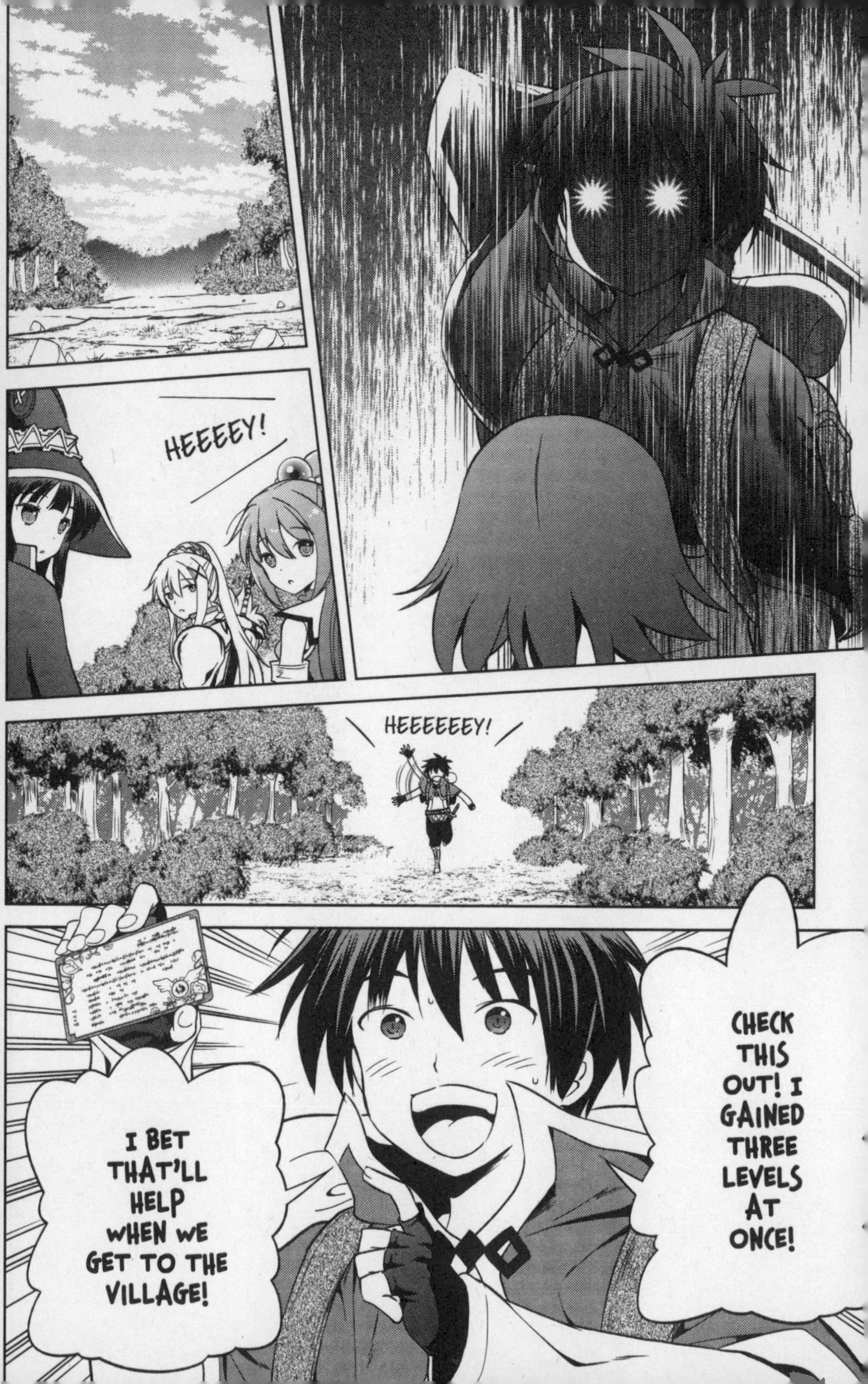
HEEEEY!
HEEEEEEY!
CHECK THIS OUT! I GAINED THREE LEVELS AT ONCE!
I BET THAT'LL HELP WHEN WE GET TO THE VILLAGE!

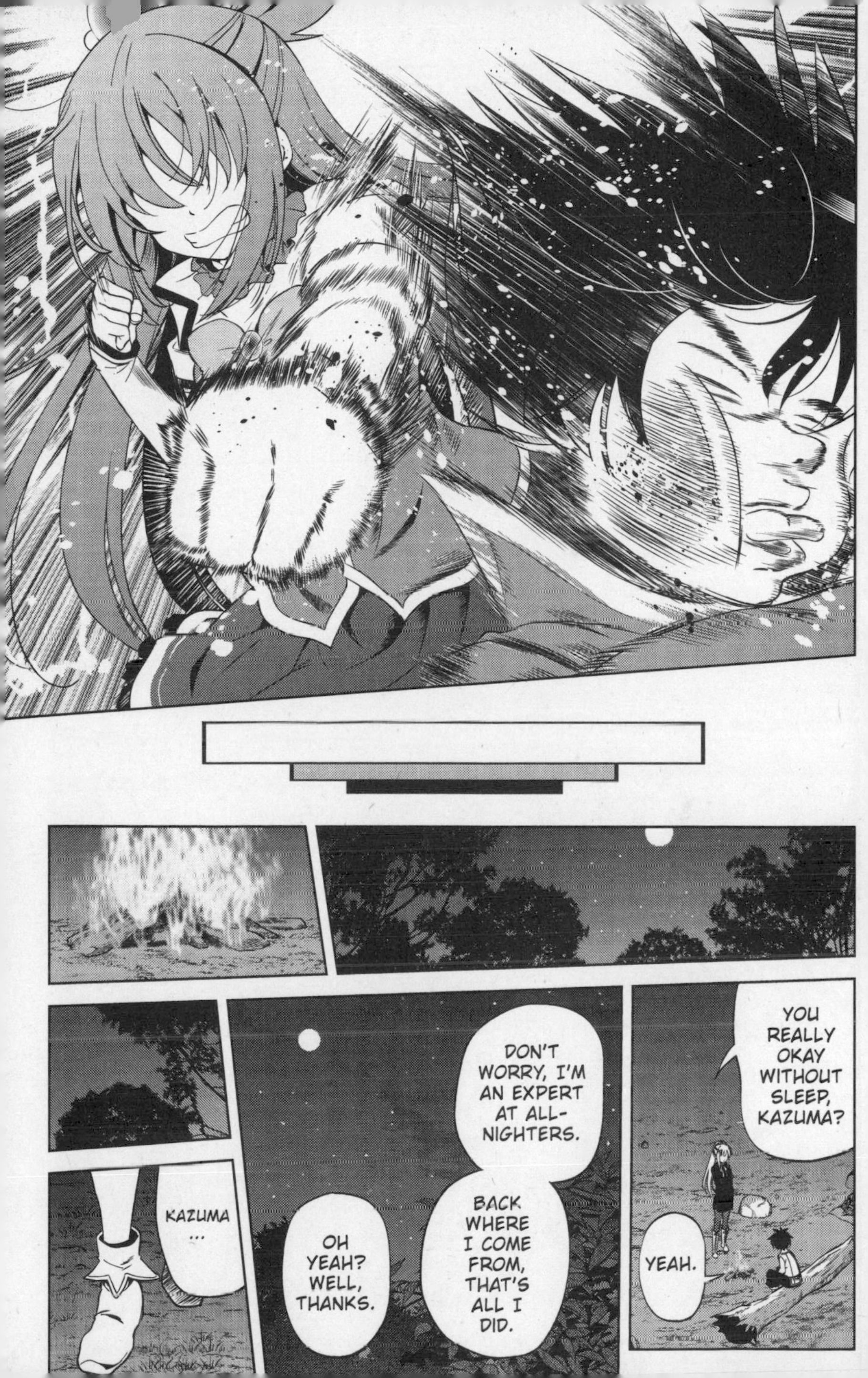
YOU REALLY OKAY WITHOUT SLEEP, KAZUMA?
YEAH.
DON'T WORRY, I'M AN EXPERT AT ALL-NIGHTERS.
BACK WHERE I COME FROM, THAT'S ALL I DID.
OH YEAH? WELL, THANKS.
KAZUMA ...

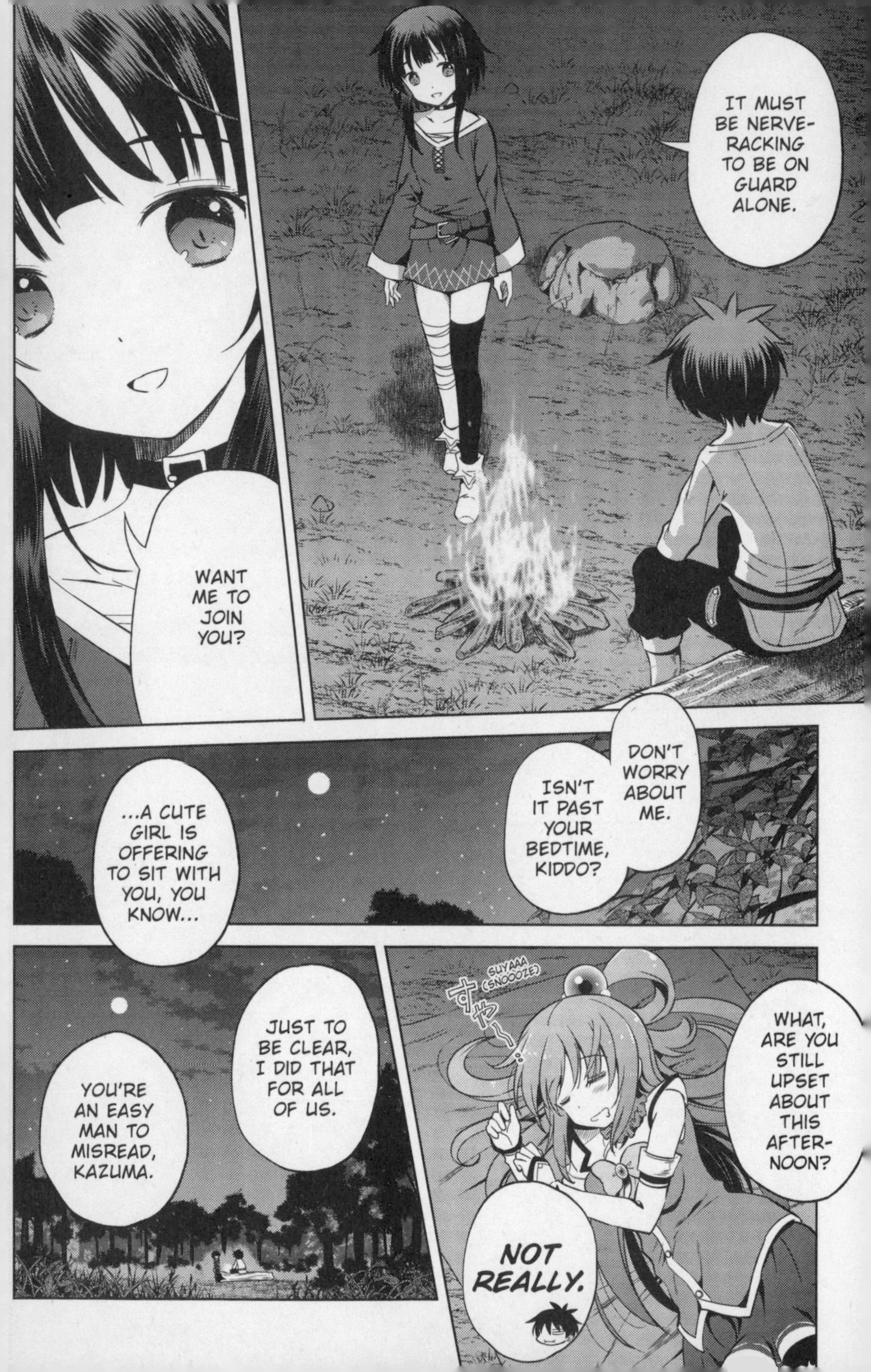
IT MUST BE NERVE-RACKING TO BE ON GUARD ALONE.
WANT ME TO JOIN YOU?
DON'T WORRY ABOUT ME.
ISN'T IT PAST YOUR BEDTIME, KIDDO?
...A CUTE GIRL IS OFFERING TO SIT WITH YOU, YOU KNOW...
すや～
SUYAAA (SNOOOZE)
WHAT, ARE YOU STILL UPSET ABOUT THIS AFTER-NOON?
NOT REALLY.
JUST TO BE CLEAR, I DID THAT FOR ALL OF US.
YOU'RE AN EASY MAN TO MISREAD, KAZUMA.

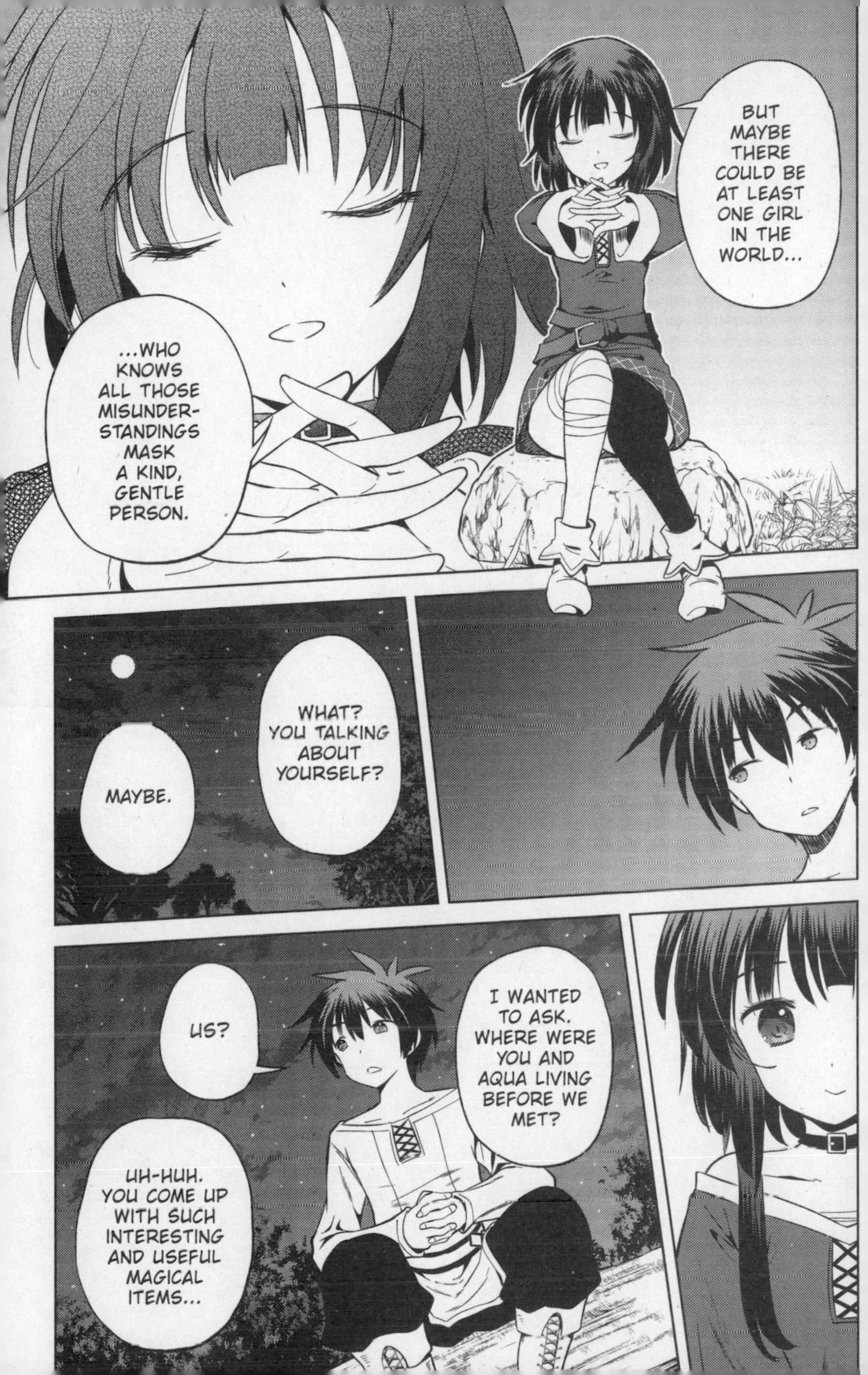
BUT MAYBE THERE COULD BE AT LEAST ONE GIRL IN THE WORLD...
...WHO KNOWS ALL THOSE MISUNDER-STANDINGS MASK A KIND, GENTLE PERSON.
WHAT? YOU TALKING ABOUT YOURSELF?
MAYBE.
I WANTED TO ASK. WHERE WERE YOU AND AQUA LIVING BEFORE WE MET?
US?
UH-HUH. YOU COME UP WITH SUCH INTERESTING AND USEFUL MAGICAL ITEMS...

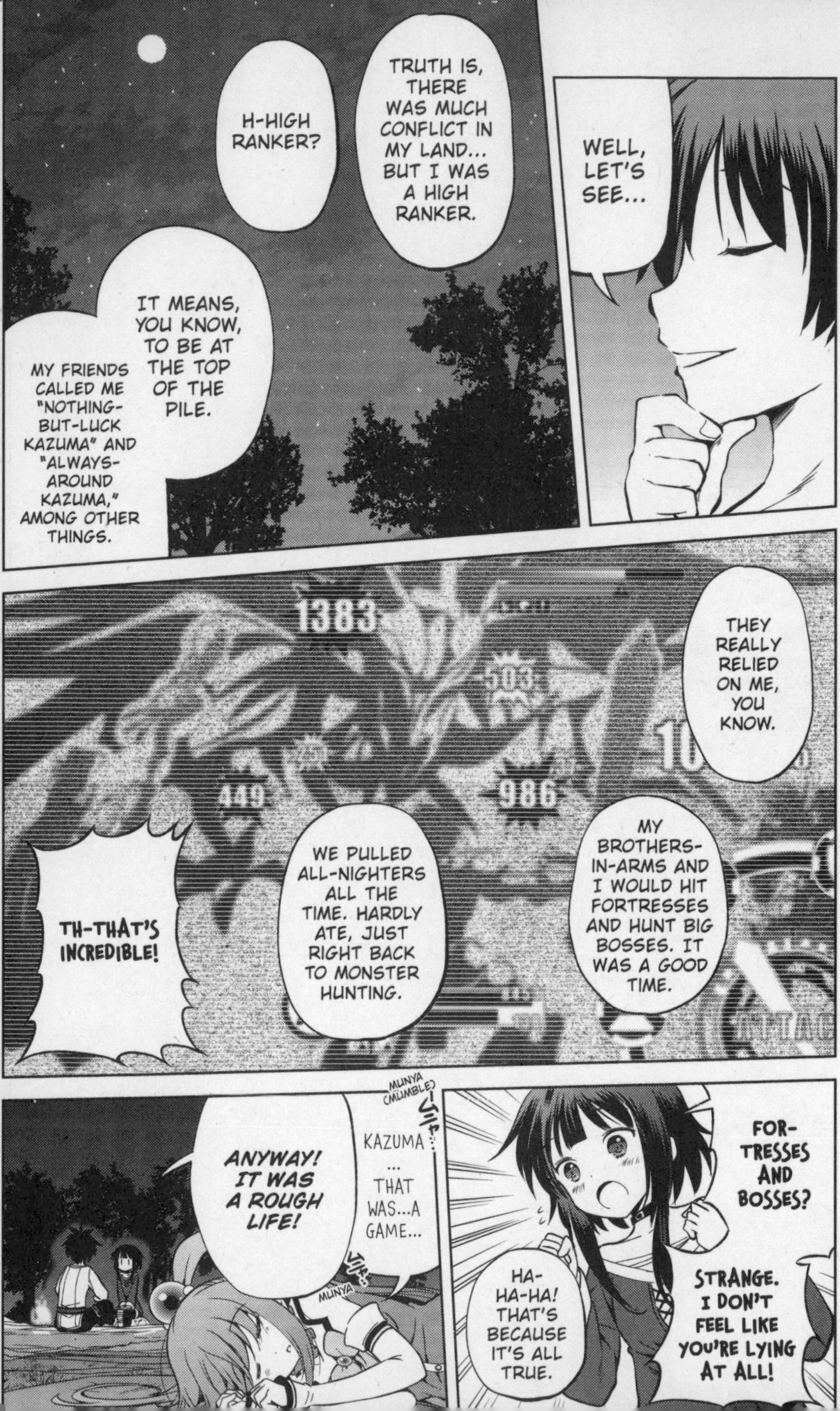
WELL, LET'S SEE...
TRUTH IS, THERE WAS MUCH CONFLICT IN MY LAND... BUT I WAS A HIGH RANKER.
H-HIGH RANKER?
IT MEANS, YOU KNOW, TO BE AT THE TOP OF THE PILE.
MY FRIENDS CALLED ME "NOTHING-BUT-LUCK KAZUMA" AND "ALWAYS-AROUND KAZUMA," AMONG OTHER THINGS.
THEY REALLY RELIED ON ME, YOU KNOW.
1383
503
986
449
MY BROTHERS-IN-ARMS AND I WOULD HIT FORTRESSES AND HUNT BIG BOSSES. IT WAS A GOOD TIME.
WE PULLED ALL-NIGHTERS ALL THE TIME. HARDLY ATE, JUST RIGHT BACK TO MONSTER HUNTING.
TH-THAT'S INCREDIBLE!
FOR-TRESSES AND BOSSES?
STRANGE. I DON'T FEEL LIKE YOU'RE LYING AT ALL!
HA-HA-HA! THAT'S BECAUSE IT'S ALL TRUE.
MUNYA (MUMBLE)
KAZUMA ... THAT WAS...A GAME...
ANYWAY! IT WAS A ROUGH LIFE!
MUNYA

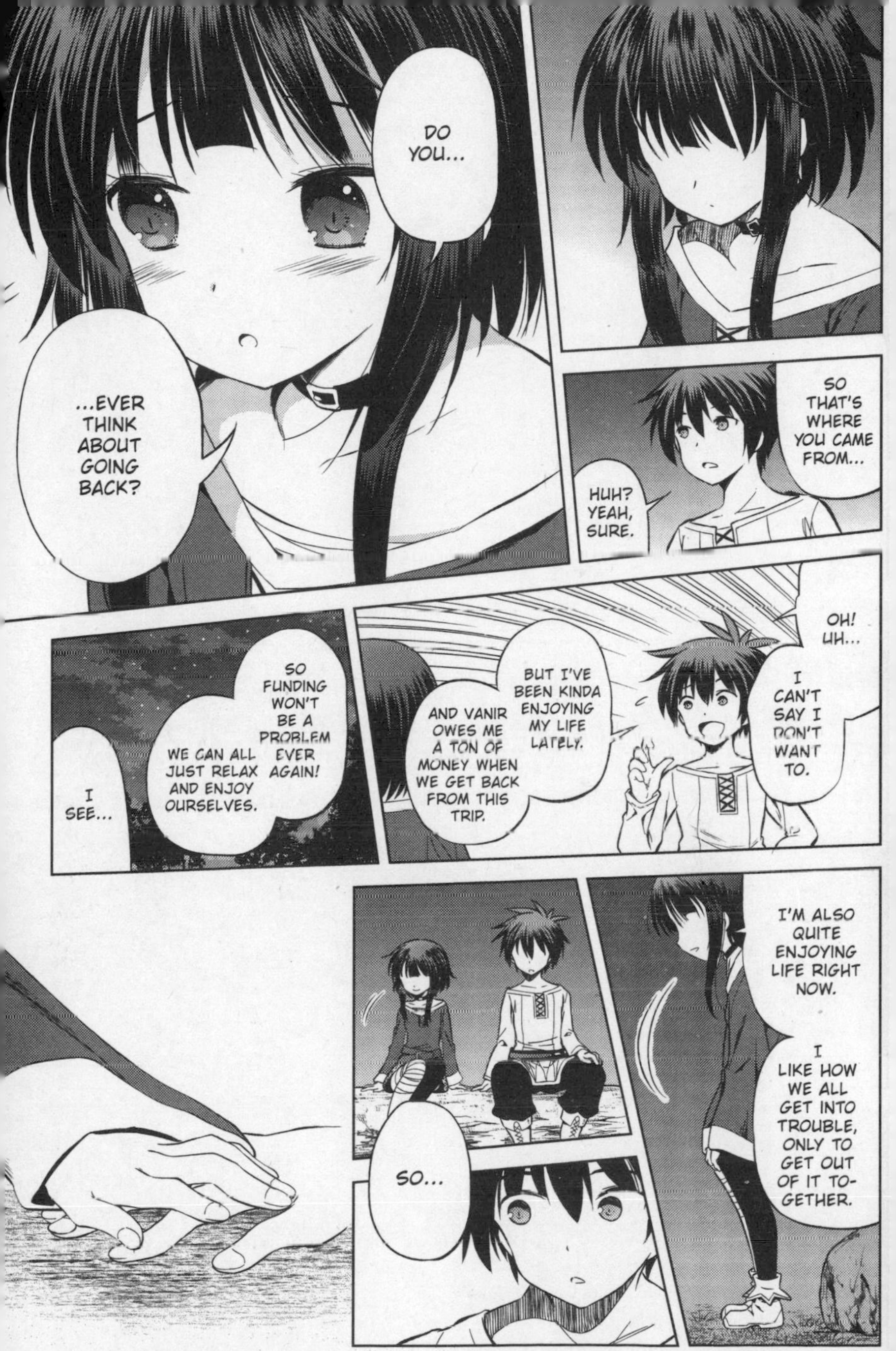
SO THAT'S WHERE YOU CAME FROM...
HUH? YEAH, SURE.
DO YOU...
...EVER THINK ABOUT GOING BACK?
OH! UH...
I CAN'T SAY I DON'T WANT TO.
BUT I'VE BEEN KINDA ENJOYING MY LIFE LATELY.
AND VANIR OWES ME A TON OF MONEY WHEN WE GET BACK FROM THIS TRIP.
SO FUNDING WON'T BE A PROBLEM EVER AGAIN!
WE CAN ALL JUST RELAX AND ENJOY OURSELVES.
I SEE...
I'M ALSO QUITE ENJOYING LIFE RIGHT NOW.
I LIKE HOW WE ALL GET INTO TROUBLE, ONLY TO GET OUT OF IT TO-GETHER.
SO...

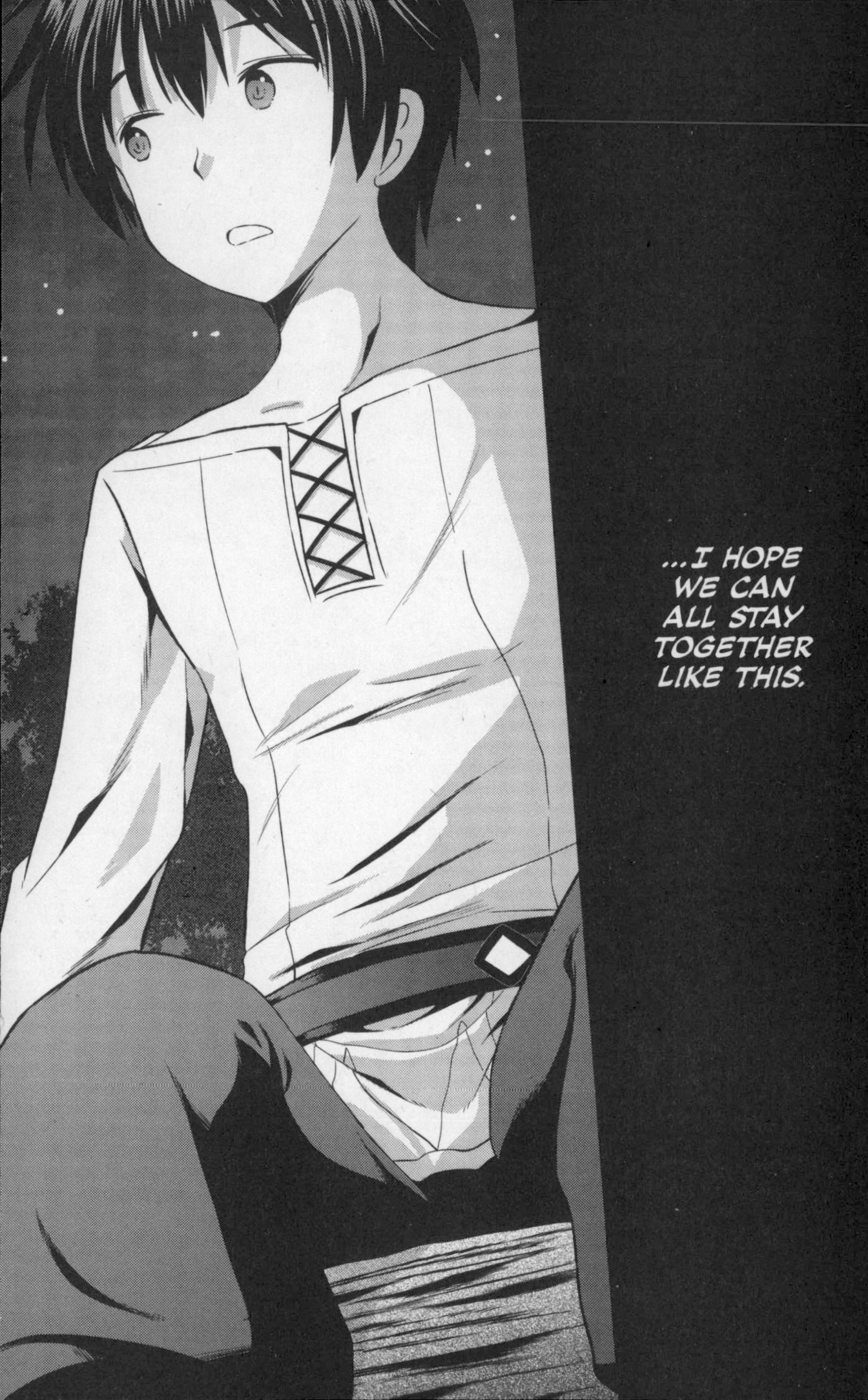
...I HOPE WE CAN ALL STAY TOGETHER LIKE THIS.

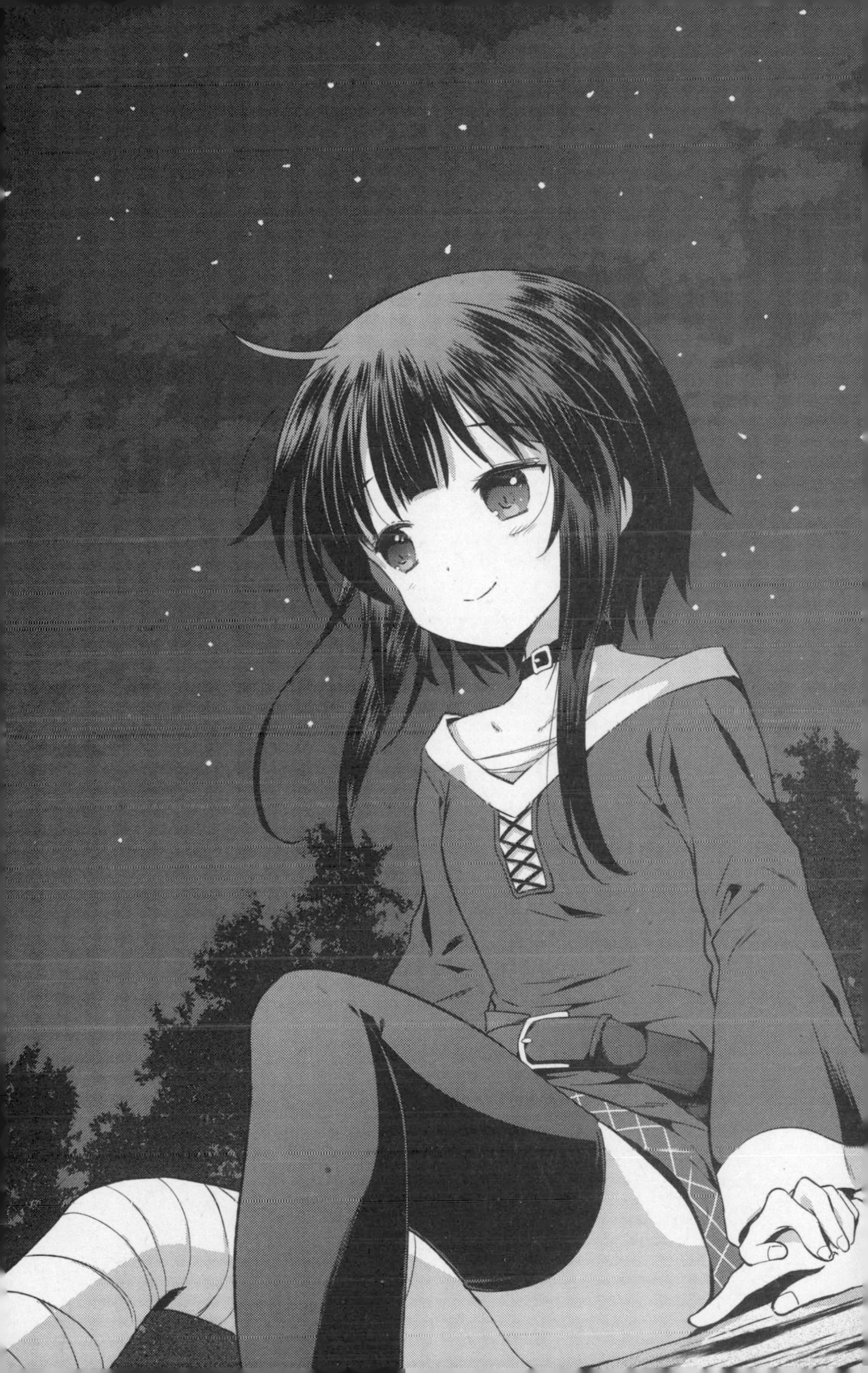

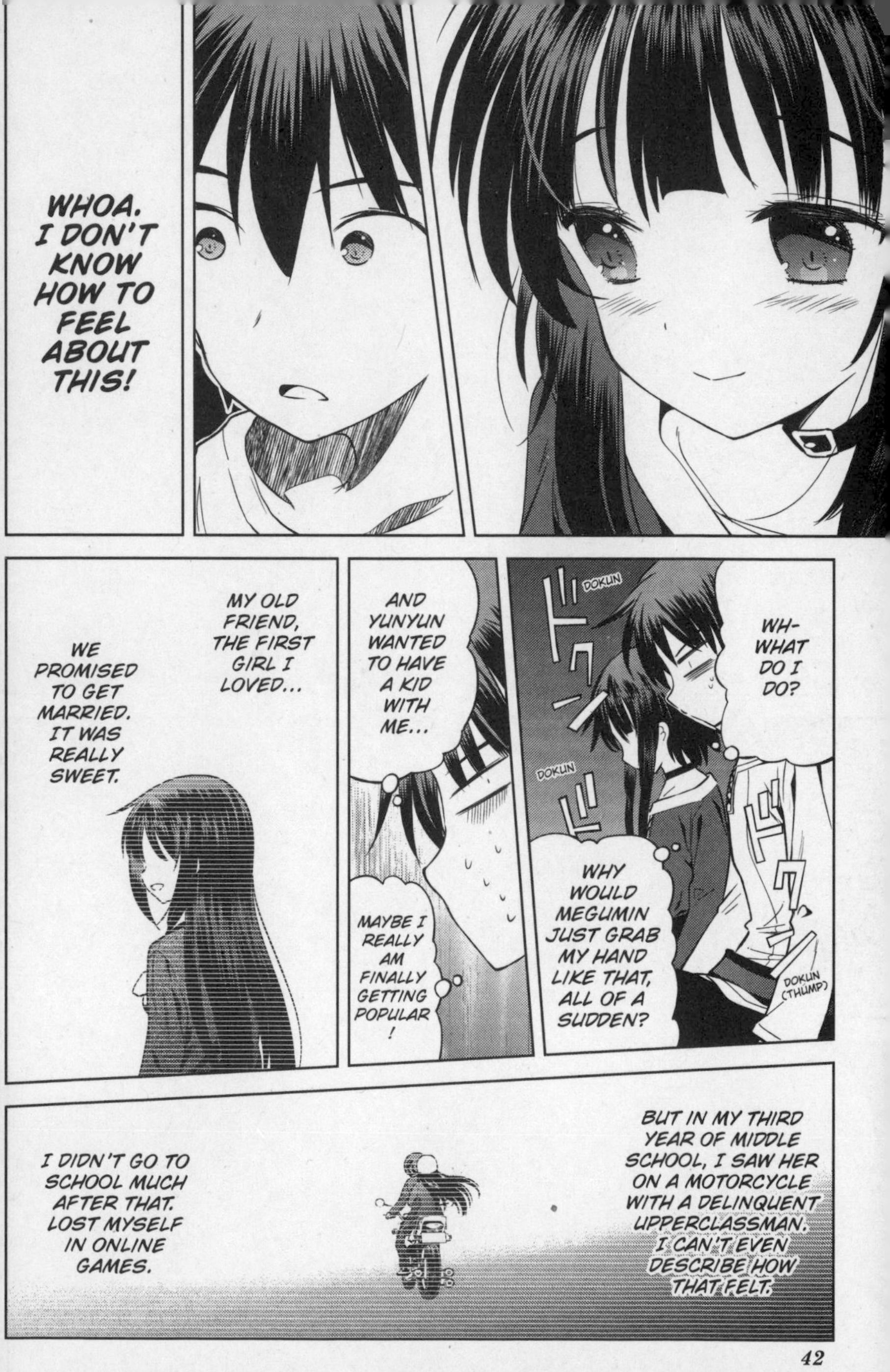
WHOA. I DON'T KNOW HOW TO FEEL ABOUT THIS!
DOKUN
WH-WHAT DO I DO?
DOKUN
WHY WOULD MEGUMIN JUST GRAB MY HAND LIKE THAT, ALL OF A SUDDEN?
DOKUN (THUMP)
AND YUNYUN WANTED TO HAVE A KID WITH ME...
MAYBE I REALLY AM FINALLY GETTING POPULAR!
MY OLD FRIEND, THE FIRST GIRL I LOVED...
WE PROMISED TO GET MARRIED. IT WAS REALLY SWEET.
BUT IN MY THIRD YEAR OF MIDDLE SCHOOL, I SAW HER ON A MOTORCYCLE WITH A DELINQUENT UPPERCLASSMAN. I CAN'T EVEN DESCRIBE HOW THAT FELT.
I DIDN'T GO TO SCHOOL MUCH AFTER THAT. LOST MYSELF IN ONLINE GAMES.

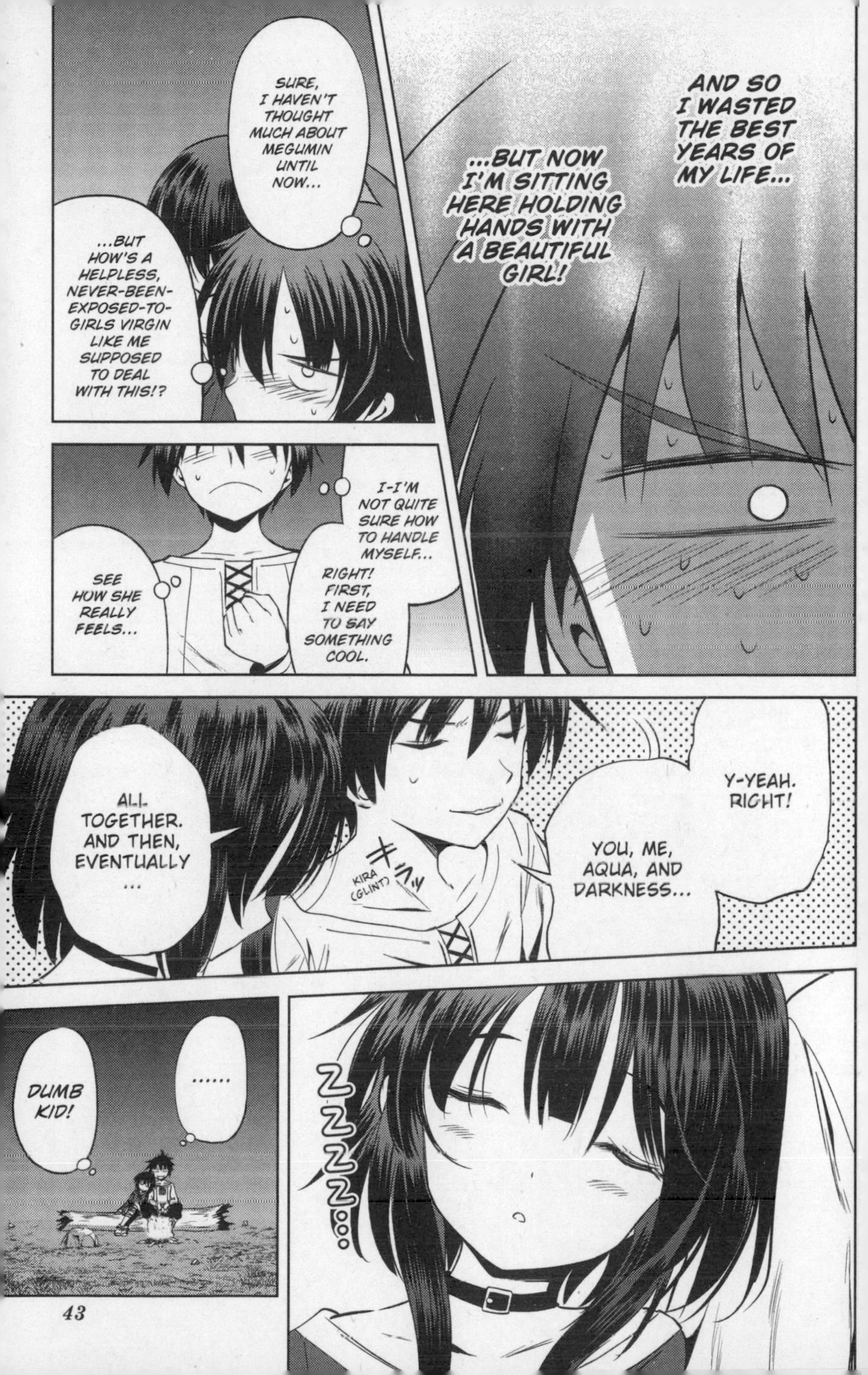
AND SO I WASTED THE BEST YEARS OF MY LIFE...
...BUT NOW I'M SITTING HERE HOLDING HANDS WITH A BEAUTIFUL GIRL!
SURE, I HAVEN'T THOUGHT MUCH ABOUT MEGUMIN UNTIL NOW...
...BUT HOW'S A HELPLESS, NEVER-BEEN-EXPOSED-TO-GIRLS VIRGIN LIKE ME SUPPOSED TO DEAL WITH THIS!?
I-I'M NOT QUITE SURE HOW TO HANDLE MYSELF...
RIGHT! FIRST, I NEED TO SAY SOMETHING COOL.
SEE HOW SHE REALLY FEELS...
Y-YEAH. RIGHT!
YOU, ME, AQUA, AND DARKNESS...
ALL TOGETHER. AND THEN, EVENTUALLY ...
KIRA (GLINT)
ZZZZ...
......
DUMB KID!

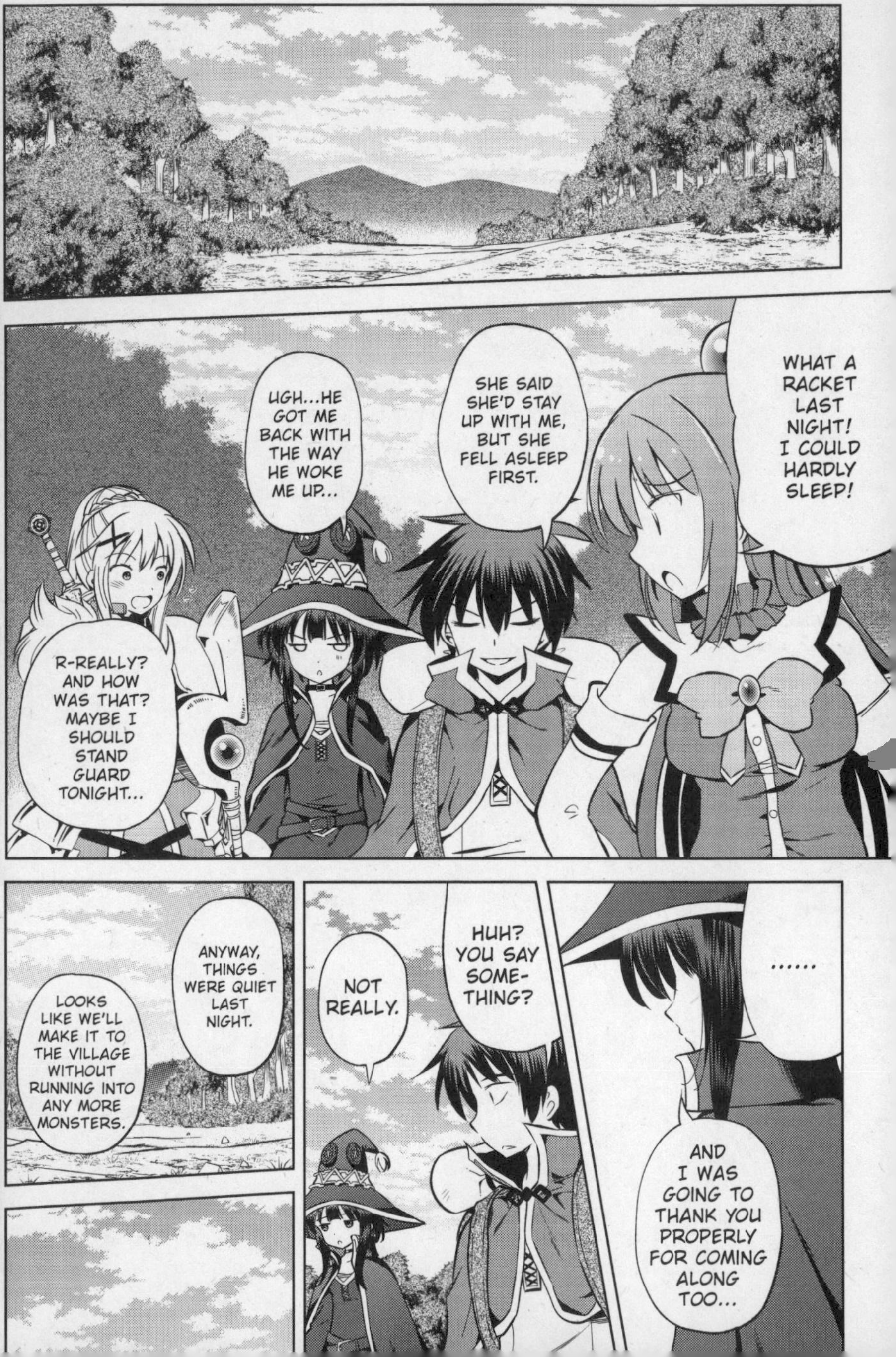
WHAT A RACKET LAST NIGHT! I COULD HARDLY SLEEP!
SHE SAID SHE'D STAY UP WITH ME, BUT SHE FELL ASLEEP FIRST.
UGH...HE GOT ME BACK WITH THE WAY HE WOKE ME UP...
R-REALLY? AND HOW WAS THAT? MAYBE I SHOULD STAND GUARD TONIGHT...
......
AND I WAS GOING TO THANK YOU PROPERLY FOR COMING ALONG TOO...
HUH? YOU SAY SOME-THING?
NOT REALLY.
ANYWAY, THINGS WERE QUIET LAST NIGHT.
LOOKS LIKE WE'LL MAKE IT TO THE VILLAGE WITHOUT RUNNING INTO ANY MORE MONSTERS.

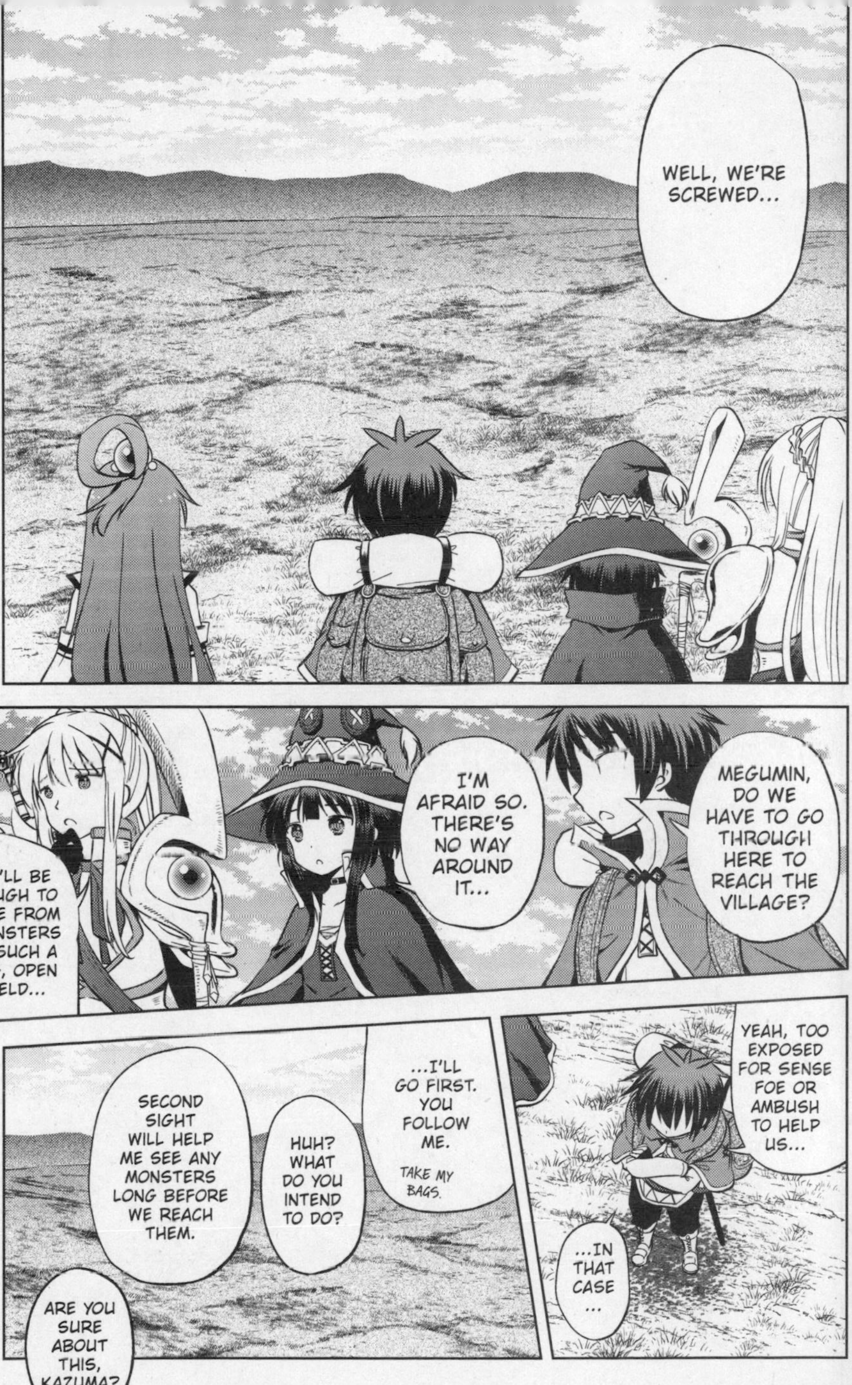
WELL, WE'RE SCREWED...
MEGUMIN, DO WE HAVE TO GO THROUGH HERE TO REACH THE VILLAGE?
I'M AFRAID SO. THERE'S NO WAY AROUND IT...
IT'LL BE TOUGH TO HIDE FROM MONSTERS IN SUCH A BIG, OPEN FIELD...
YEAH, TOO EXPOSED FOR SENSE FOE OR AMBUSH TO HELP US...
...IN THAT CASE...
...I'LL GO FIRST. YOU FOLLOW ME.
TAKE MY BAGS.
HUH? WHAT DO YOU INTEND TO DO?
SECOND SIGHT WILL HELP ME SEE ANY MONSTERS LONG BEFORE WE REACH THEM.
ARE YOU SURE ABOUT THIS, KAZUMA?

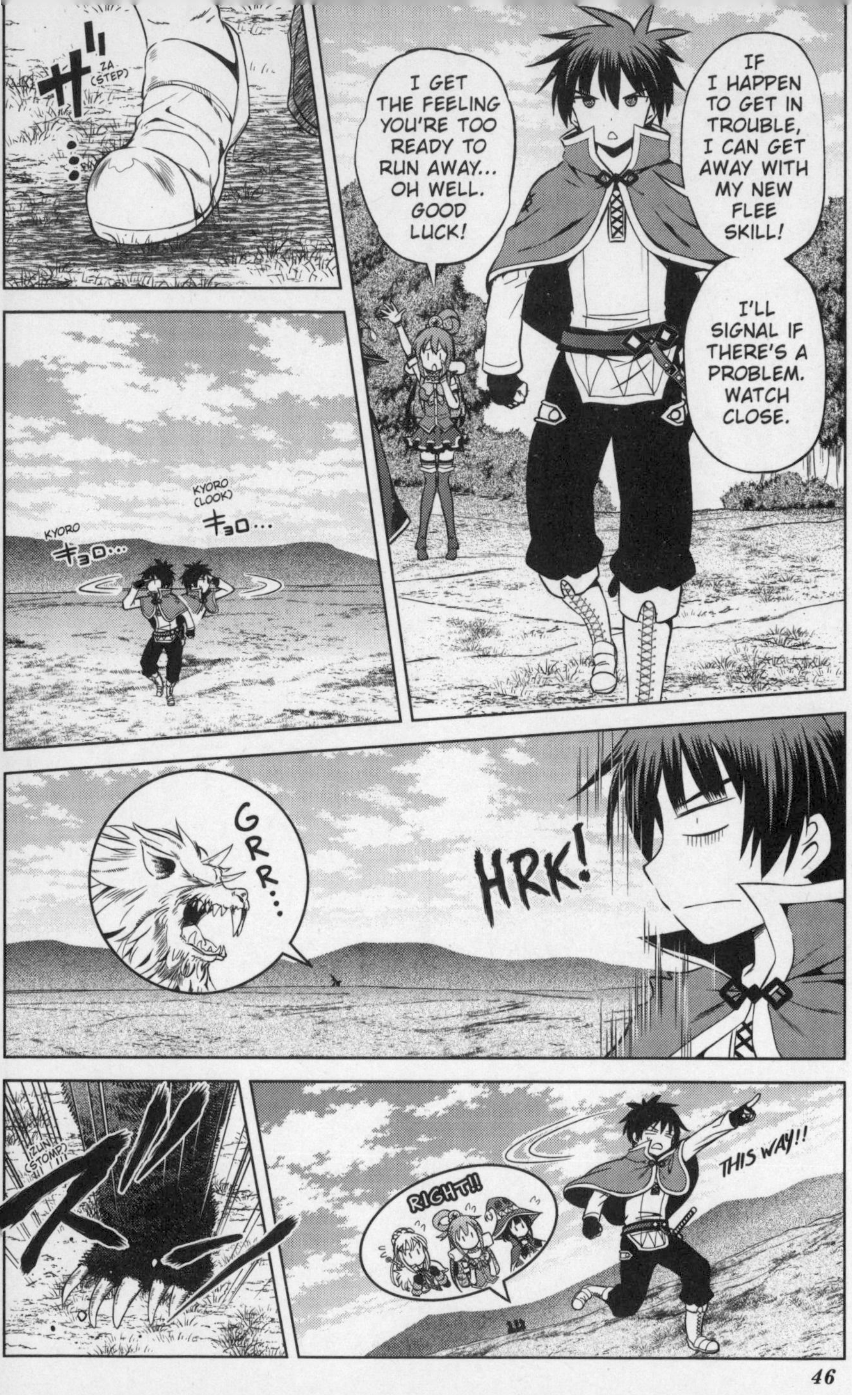
IF I HAPPEN TO GET IN TROUBLE, I CAN GET AWAY WITH MY NEW FLEE SKILL!
I'LL SIGNAL IF THERE'S A PROBLEM. WATCH CLOSE.
I GET THE FEELING YOU'RE TOO READY TO RUN AWAY... OH WELL. GOOD LUCK!
ZA (STEP)
KYORO (LOOK) キョロ...
KYORO キョロ...
HRK!
GRR...
THIS WAY!!
RIGHT!!
ZUN (STOMP)!!!

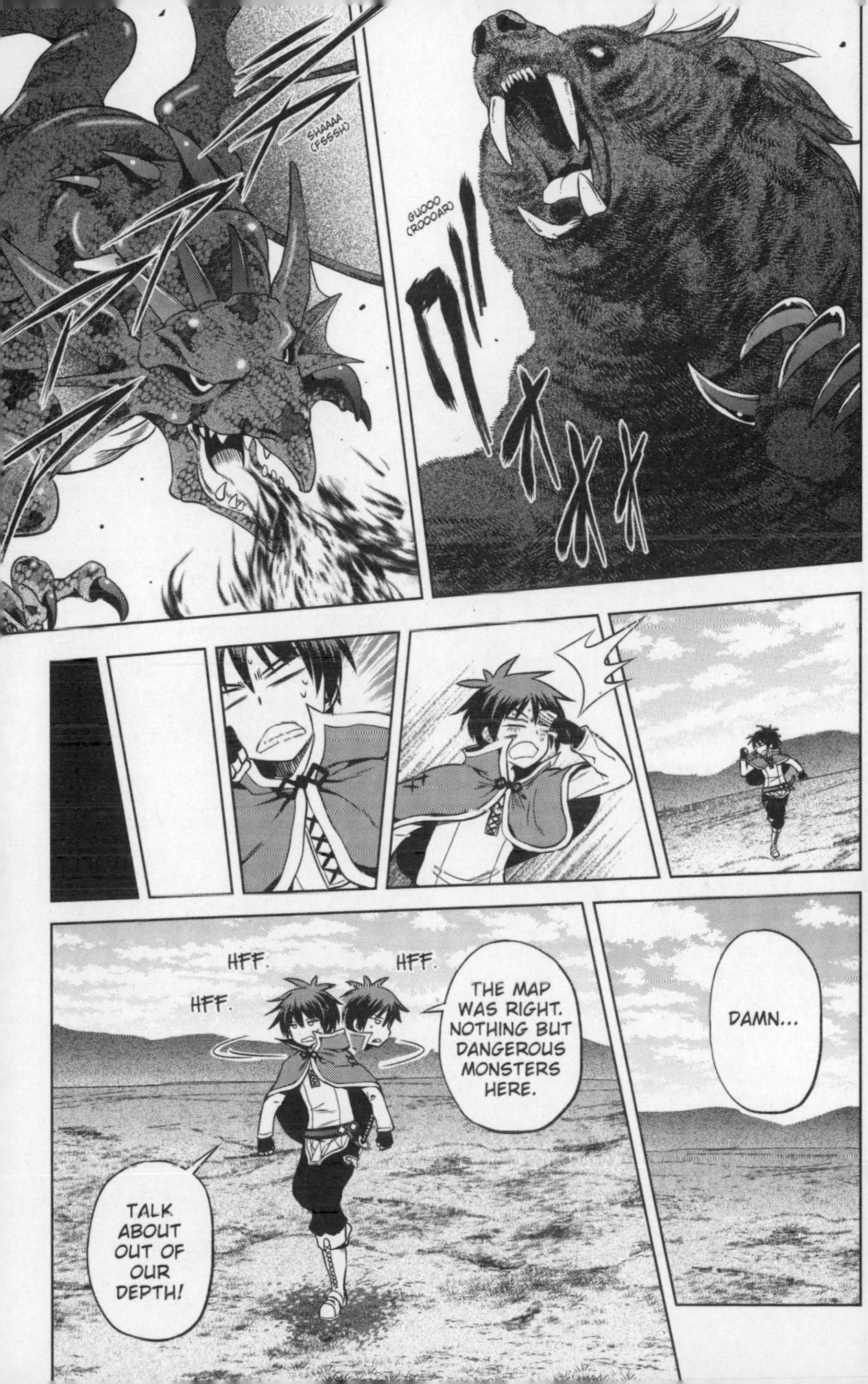
GUOOO (ROOOAR)
SHAAAA (FSSSH)
DAMN...
HFF.
HFF.
HFF.
THE MAP WAS RIGHT. NOTHING BUT DANGEROUS MONSTERS HERE.
TALK ABOUT OUT OF OUR DEPTH!

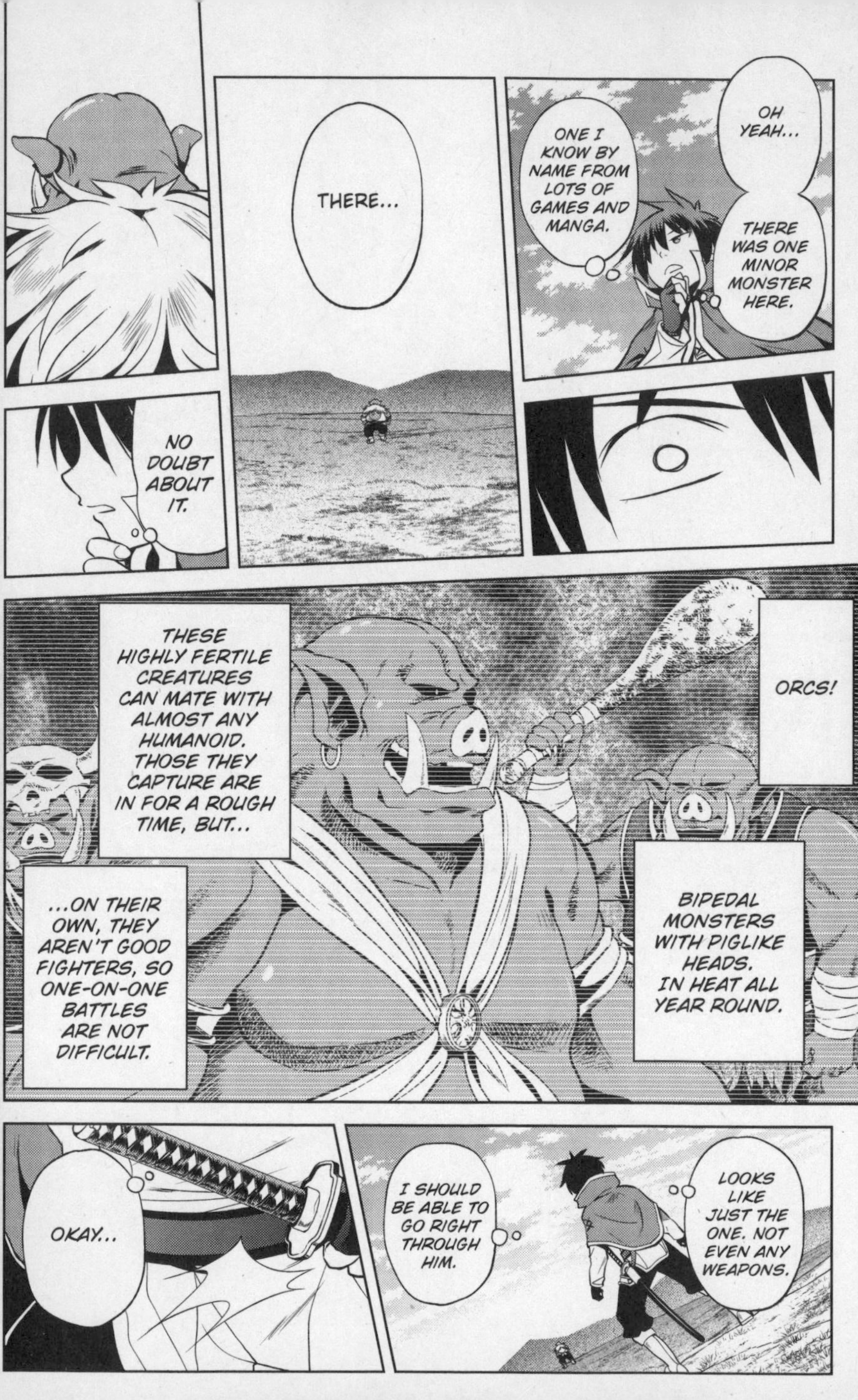
OH YEAH...
THERE WAS ONE MINOR MONSTER HERE.
ONE I KNOW BY NAME FROM LOTS OF GAMES AND MANGA.
THERE...
NO DOUBT ABOUT IT.
ORCS!
BIPEDAL MONSTERS WITH PIGLIKE HEADS. IN HEAT ALL YEAR ROUND.
THESE HIGHLY FERTILE CREATURES CAN MATE WITH ALMOST ANY HUMANOID. THOSE THEY CAPTURE ARE IN FOR A ROUGH TIME, BUT...
...ON THEIR OWN, THEY AREN'T GOOD FIGHTERS, SO ONE-ON-ONE BATTLES ARE NOT DIFFICULT.
LOOKS LIKE JUST THE ONE. NOT EVEN ANY WEAPONS.
I SHOULD BE ABLE TO GO RIGHT THROUGH HIM.
OKAY...

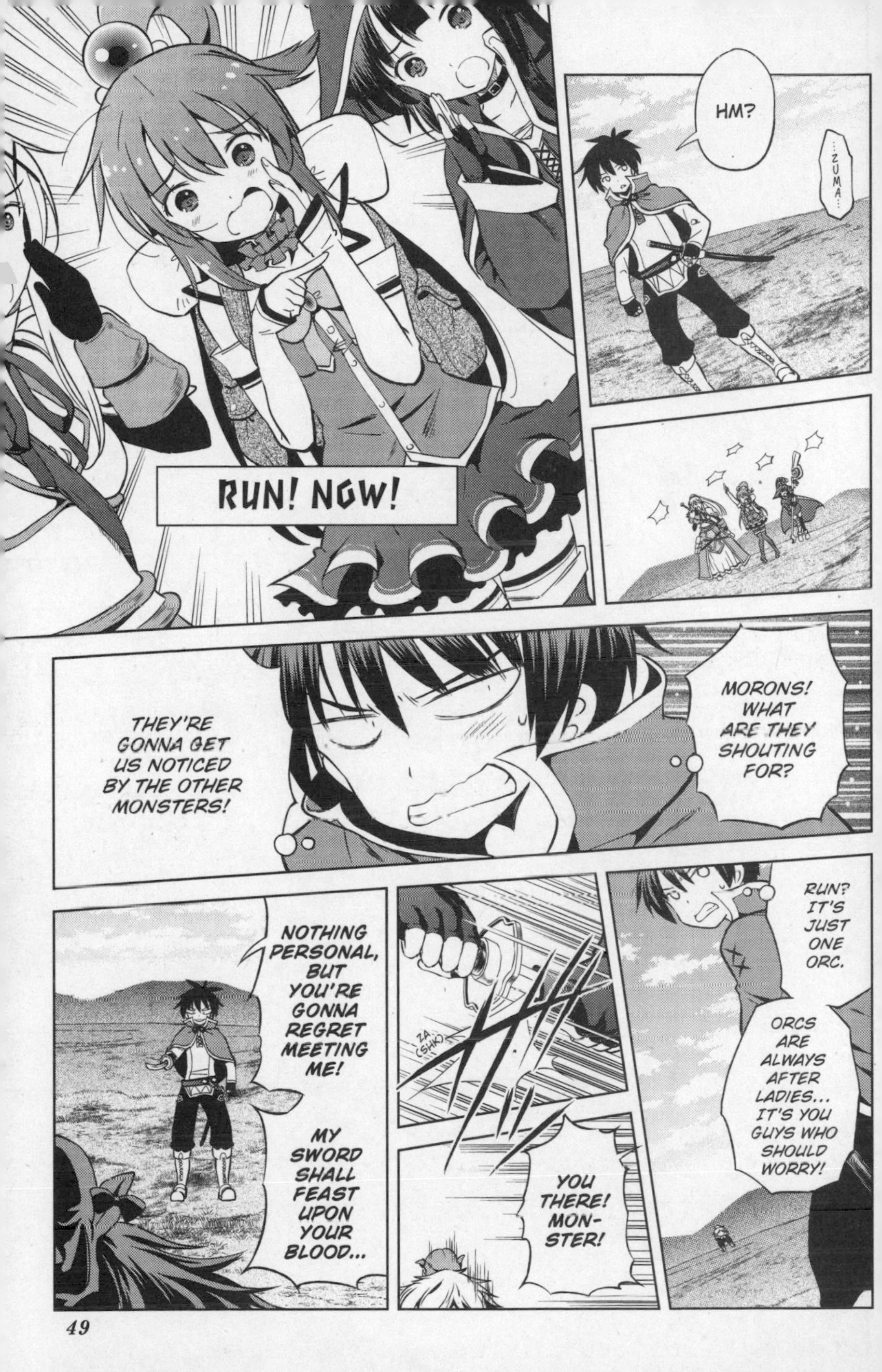

...ZUMA...
HM?
RUN! NOW!
MORONS! WHAT ARE THEY SHOUTING FOR?
THEY'RE GONNA GET US NOTICED BY THE OTHER MONSTERS!
RUN? IT'S JUST ONE ORC.
ORCS ARE ALWAYS AFTER LADIES... IT'S YOU GUYS WHO SHOULD WORRY!
ZA (SHK)
YOU THERE! MON-STER!
NOTHING PERSONAL, BUT YOU'RE GONNA REGRET MEETING ME!
MY SWORD SHALL FEAST UPON YOUR BLOOD...

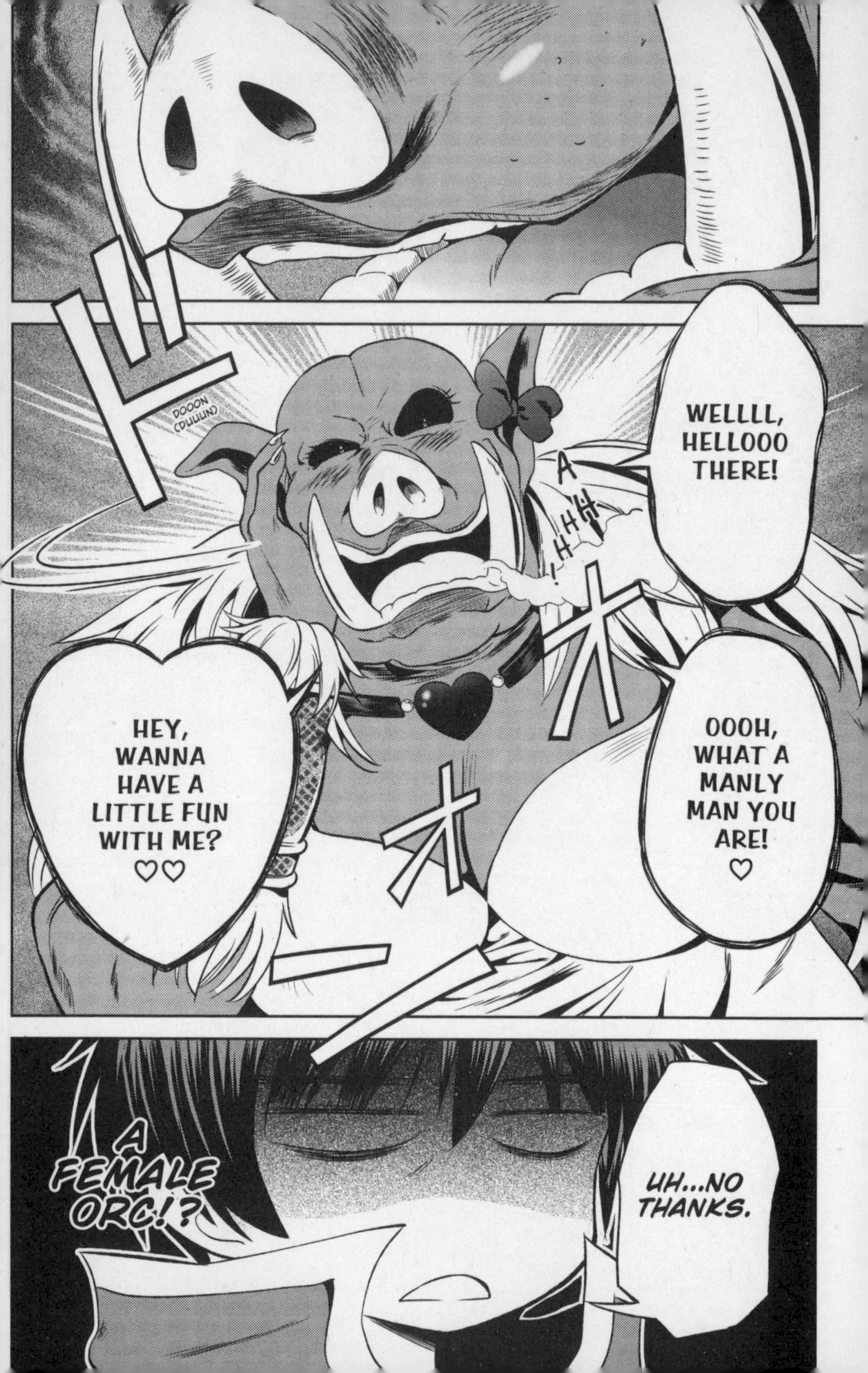
WELLLL, HELLOOO THERE!
AHHHH!
OOOH, WHAT A MANLY MAN YOU ARE! ♡
HEY, WANNA HAVE A LITTLE FUN WITH ME? ♡♡
DOOON (DUUUN)
UH...NO THANKS.
A FEMALE ORC!?

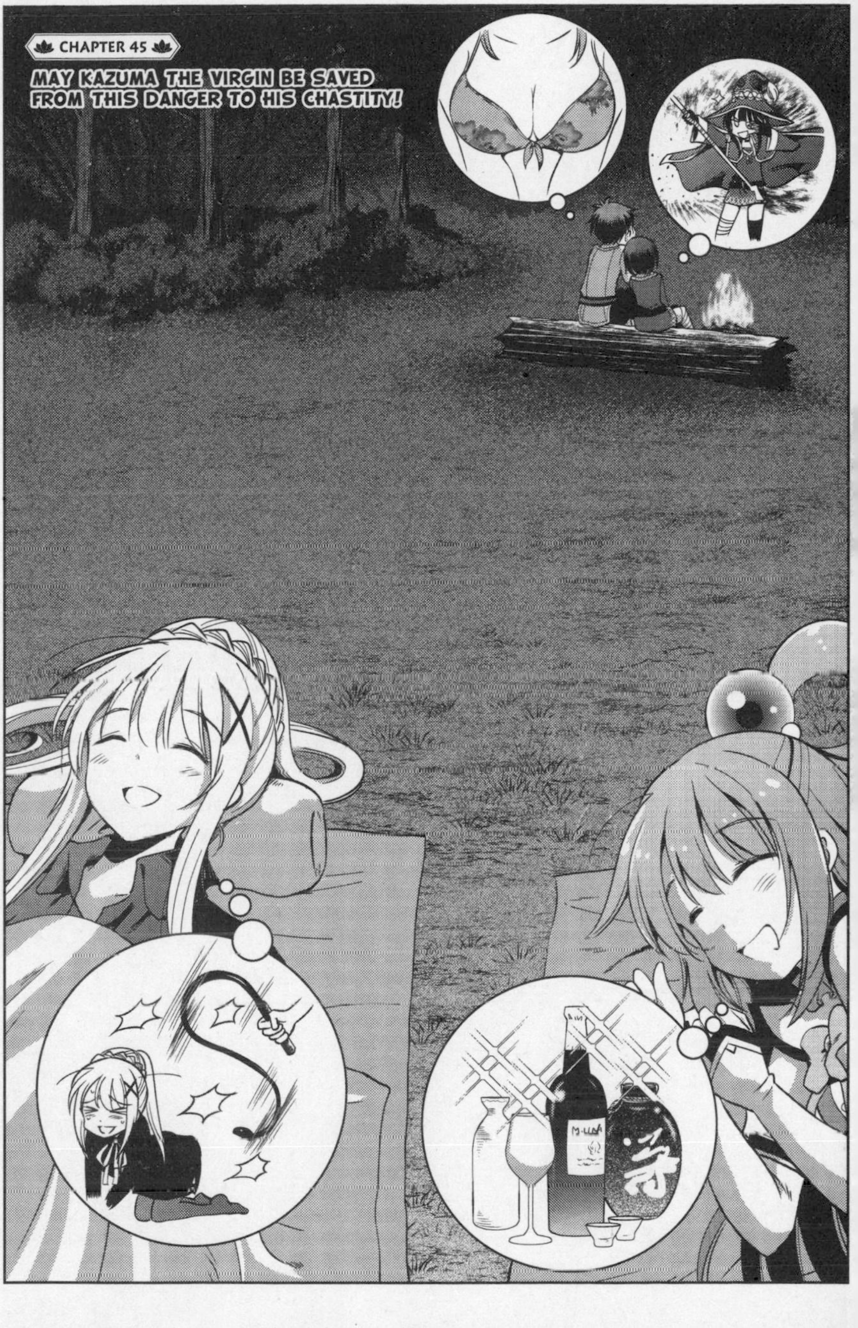
CHAPTER 45
MAY KAZUMA THE VIRGIN BE SAVED FROM THIS DANGER TO HIS CHASTITY!

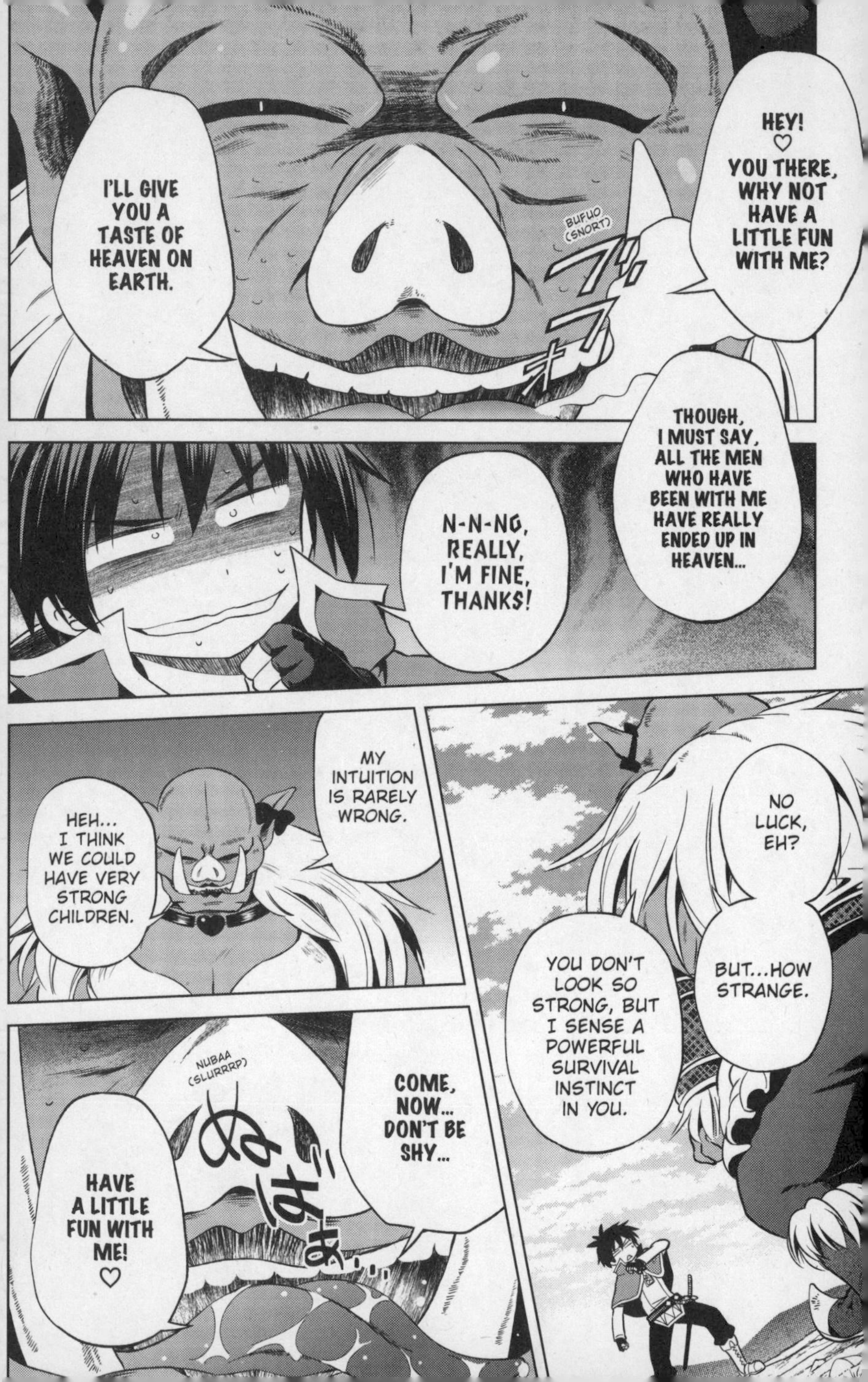
HEY! ♡ YOU THERE, WHY NOT HAVE A LITTLE FUN WITH ME?
BUFUO (SNORT)
I'LL GIVE YOU A TASTE OF HEAVEN ON EARTH.
THOUGH, I MUST SAY, ALL THE MEN WHO HAVE BEEN WITH ME HAVE REALLY ENDED UP IN HEAVEN...
N-N-NG, REALLY, I'M FINE, THANKS!
NO LUCK, EH?
BUT...HOW STRANGE.
YOU DON'T LOOK SO STRONG, BUT I SENSE A POWERFUL SURVIVAL INSTINCT IN YOU.
MY INTUITION IS RARELY WRONG.
HEH... I THINK WE COULD HAVE VERY STRONG CHILDREN.
COME, NOW... DON'T BE SHY...
NUBAA (SLURRRP)
HAVE A LITTLE FUN WITH ME! ♡

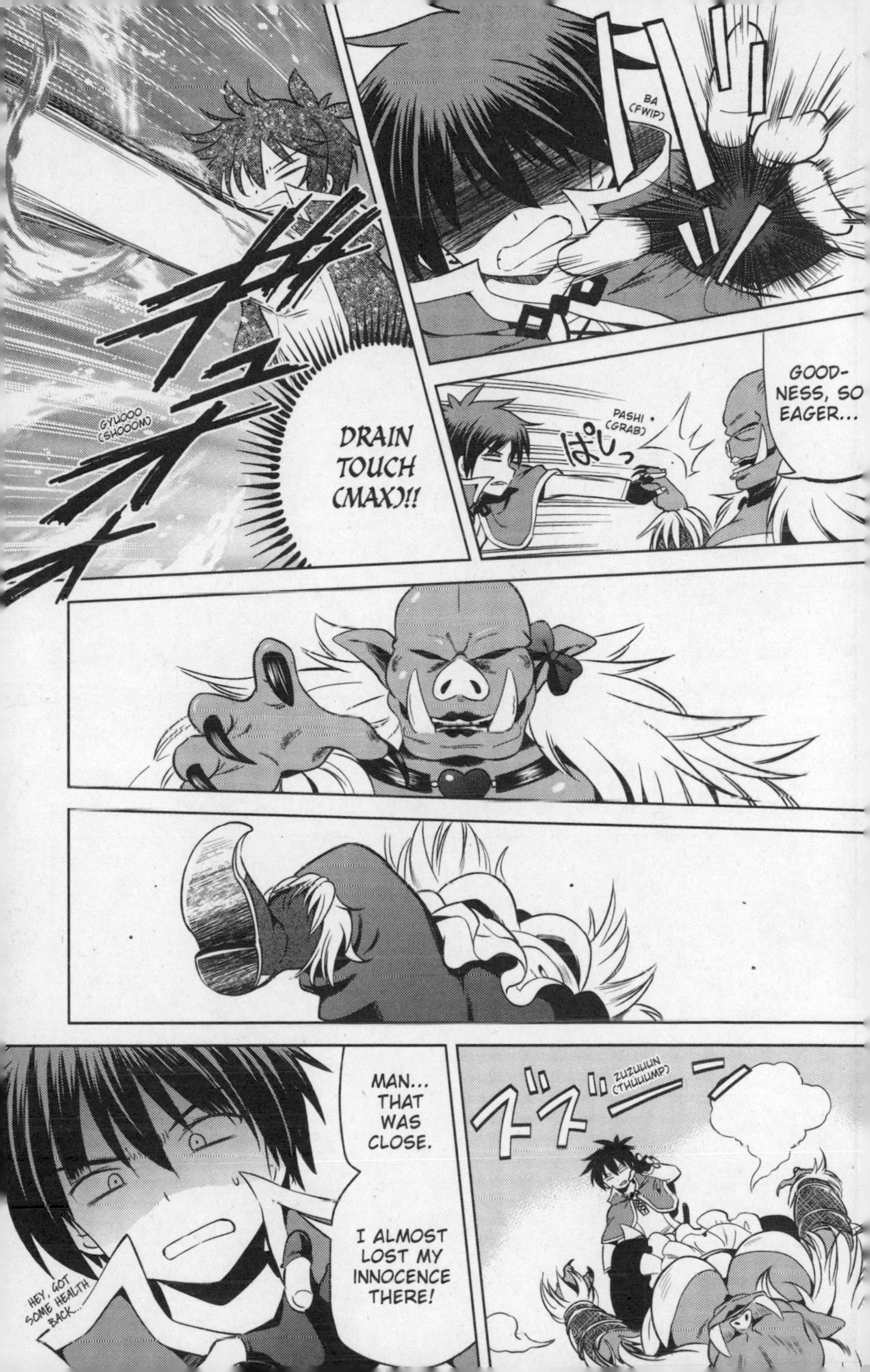
BA (FWIP)
GOOD-NESS, SO EAGER...
PASHI (GRAB)
ぱしっ
DRAIN TOUCH (MAX)!!
GYUOOO (SHOOOM)
ズズーー
ZUZUUUN (THUUUMP)
MAN... THAT WAS CLOSE.
I ALMOST LOST MY INNOCENCE THERE!
HEY, GOT SOME HEALTH BACK...

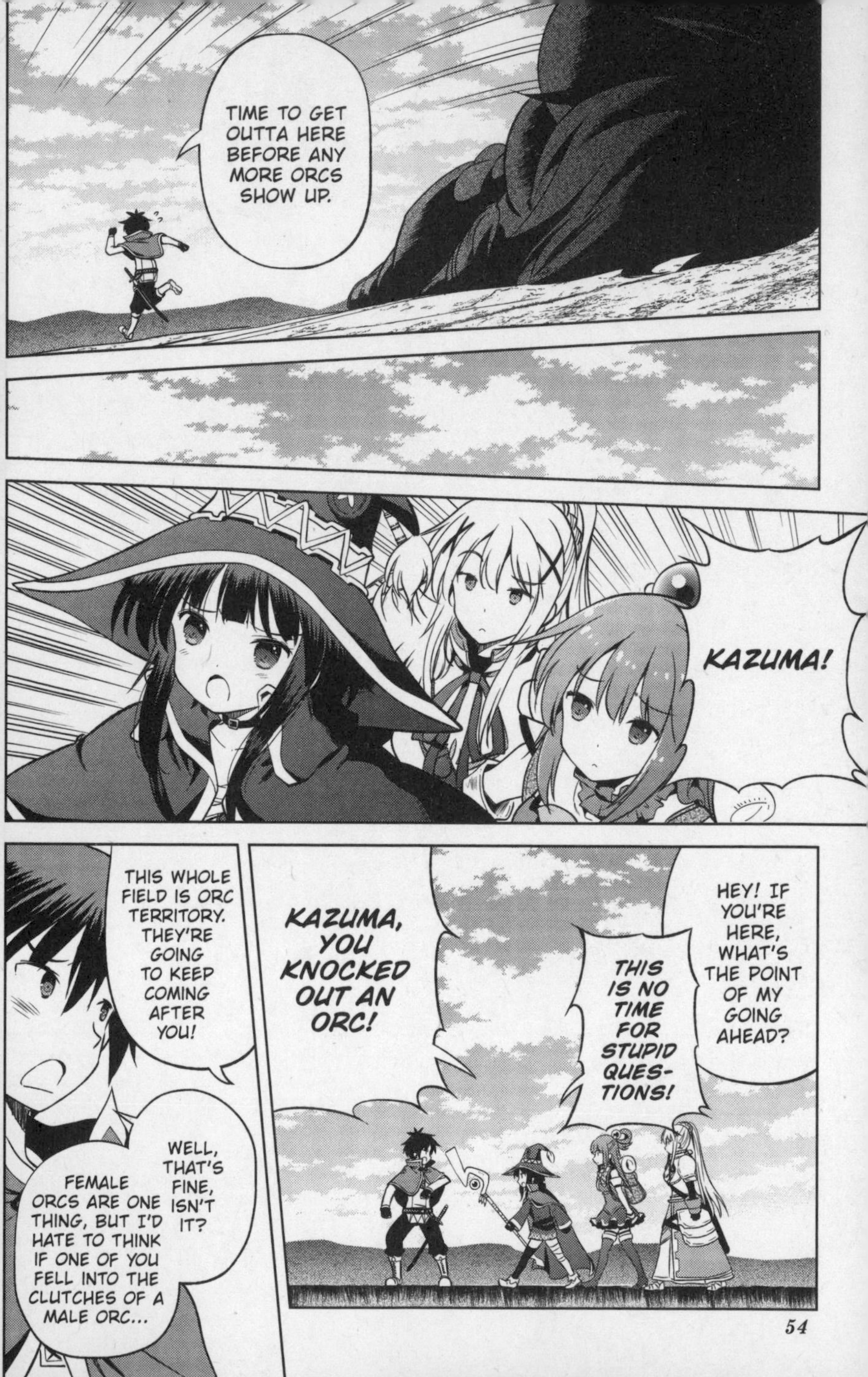
TIME TO GET OUTTA HERE BEFORE ANY MORE ORCS SHOW UP.
KAZUMA!
HEY! IF YOU'RE HERE, WHAT'S THE POINT OF MY GOING AHEAD?
THIS IS NO TIME FOR STUPID QUES-TIONS!
KAZUMA, YOU KNOCKED OUT AN ORC!
THIS WHOLE FIELD IS ORC TERRITORY. THEY'RE GOING TO KEEP COMING AFTER YOU!
WELL, THAT'S FINE, ISN'T IT?
FEMALE ORCS ARE ONE THING, BUT I'D HATE TO THINK IF ONE OF YOU FELL INTO THE CLUTCHES OF A MALE ORC...

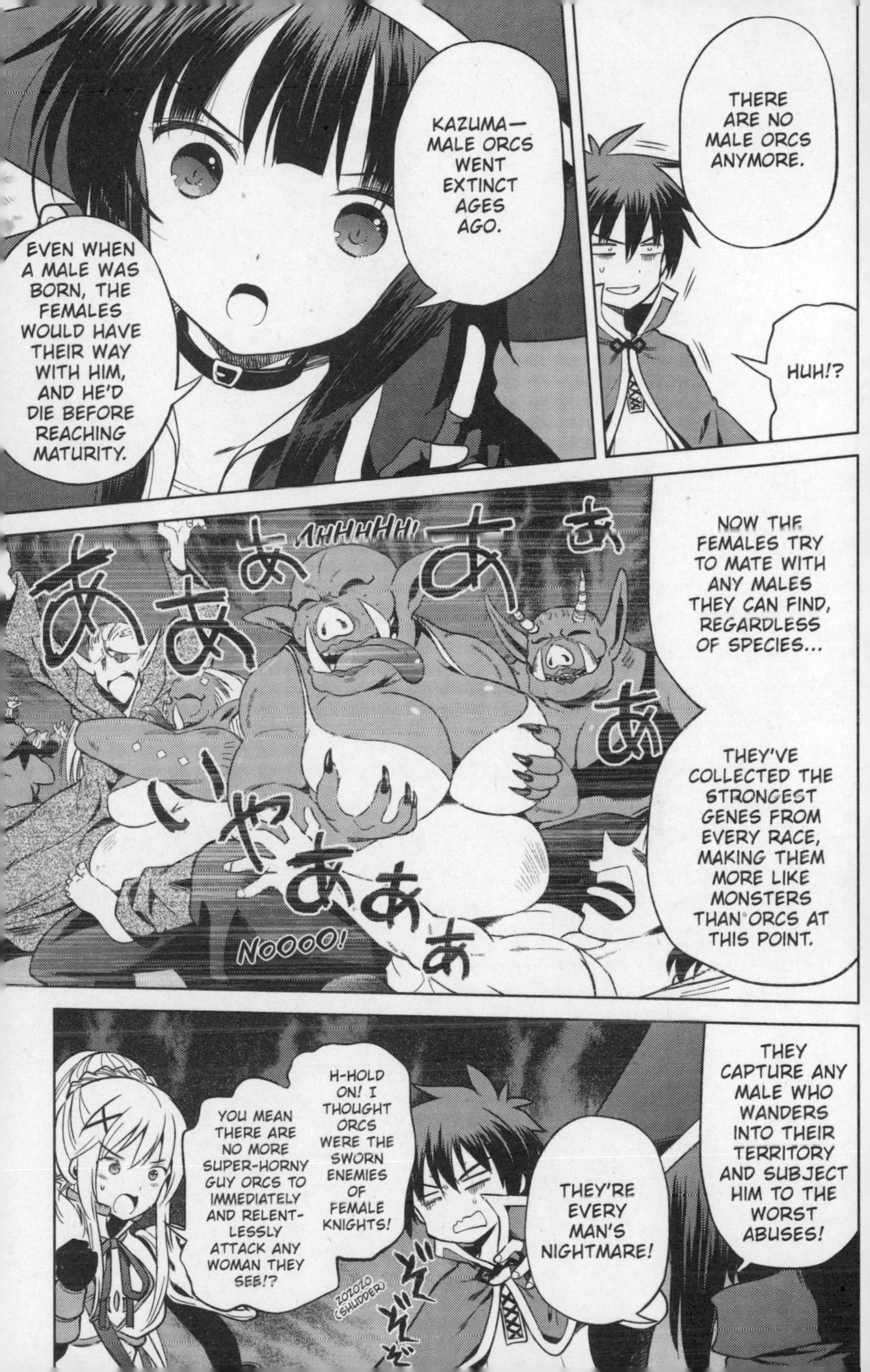
THERE ARE NO MALE ORCS ANYMORE.
HUH!?
KAZUMA—MALE ORCS WENT EXTINCT AGES AGO.
EVEN WHEN A MALE WAS BORN, THE FEMALES WOULD HAVE THEIR WAY WITH HIM, AND HE'D DIE BEFORE REACHING MATURITY.
NOW THE FEMALES TRY TO MATE WITH ANY MALES THEY CAN FIND, REGARDLESS OF SPECIES...
THEY'VE COLLECTED THE STRONGEST GENES FROM EVERY RACE, MAKING THEM MORE LIKE MONSTERS THAN ORCS AT THIS POINT.
AHHHHHH!
NOOOO!
THEY CAPTURE ANY MALE WHO WANDERS INTO THEIR TERRITORY AND SUBJECT HIM TO THE WORST ABUSES!
THEY'RE EVERY MAN'S NIGHTMARE!
H-HOLD ON! I THOUGHT ORCS WERE THE SWORN ENEMIES OF FEMALE KNIGHTS!
YOU MEAN THERE ARE NO MORE SUPER-HORNY GUY ORCS TO IMMEDIATELY AND RELENT-LESSLY ATTACK ANY WOMAN THEY SEE!?
ZOZOZO (SHUDDER)

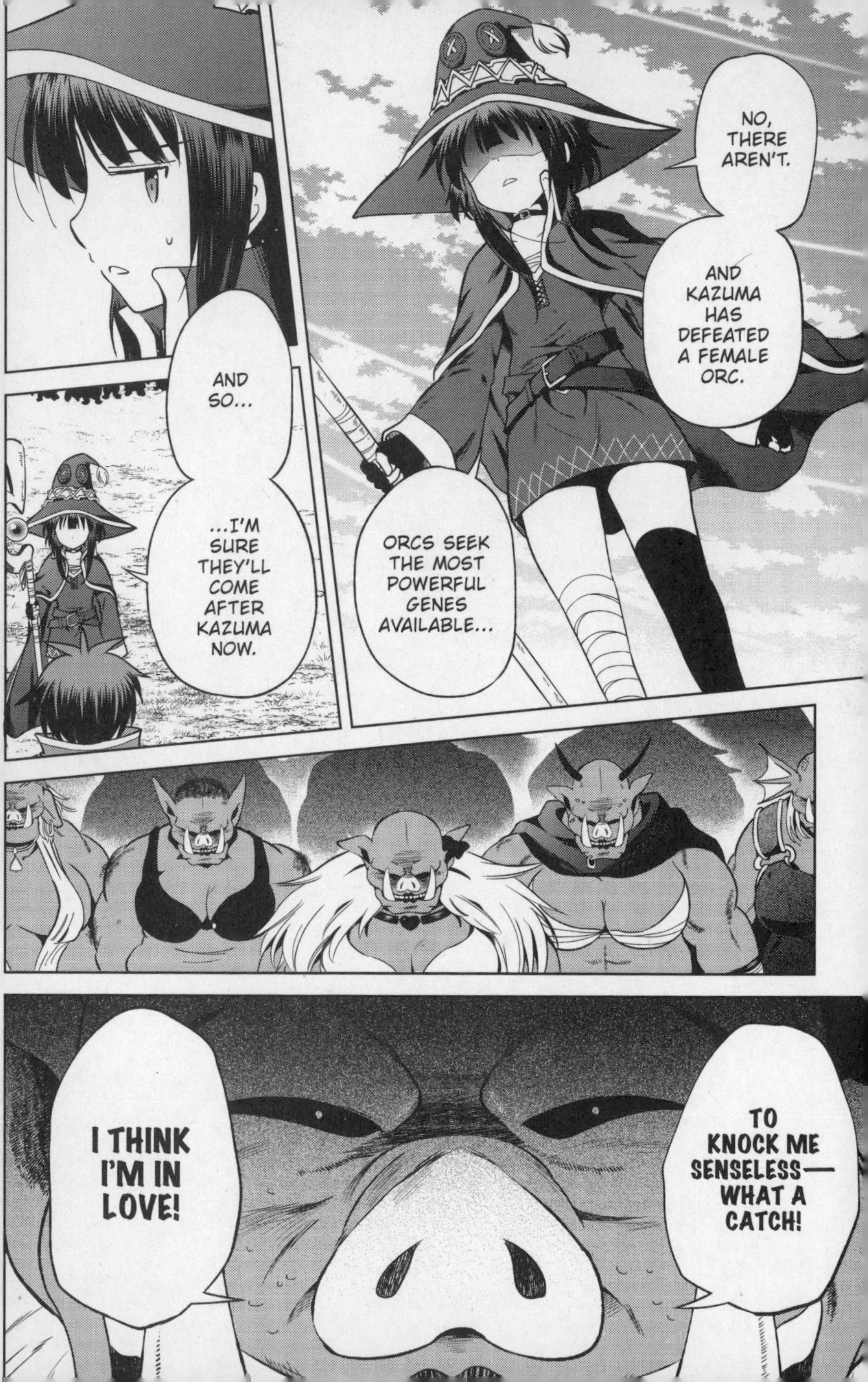
NO, THERE AREN'T.
AND KAZUMA HAS DEFEATED A FEMALE ORC.
ORCS SEEK THE MOST POWERFUL GENES AVAILABLE...
AND SO...
...I'M SURE THEY'LL COME AFTER KAZUMA NOW.
TO KNOCK ME SENSELESS—WHAT A CATCH!
I THINK I'M IN LOVE!

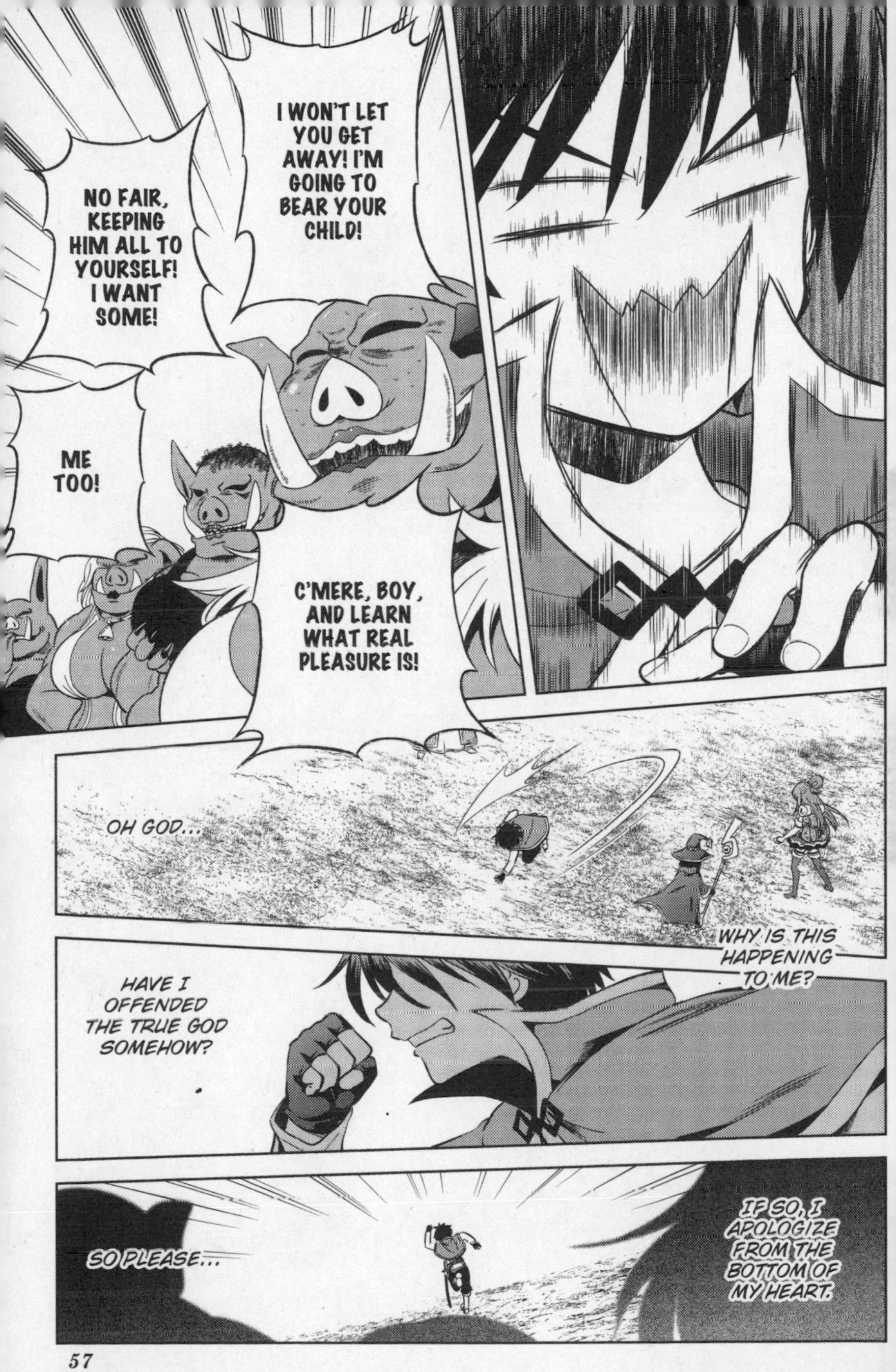
I WON'T LET YOU GET AWAY! I'M GOING TO BEAR YOUR CHILD!
NO FAIR, KEEPING HIM ALL TO YOURSELF! I WANT SOME!
C'MERE, BOY, AND LEARN WHAT REAL PLEASURE IS!
ME TOO!
OH GOD...
WHY IS THIS HAPPENING TO ME?
HAVE I OFFENDED THE TRUE GOD SOMEHOW?
IF SO, I APOLOGIZE FROM THE BOTTOM OF MY HEART.
SO PLEASE...

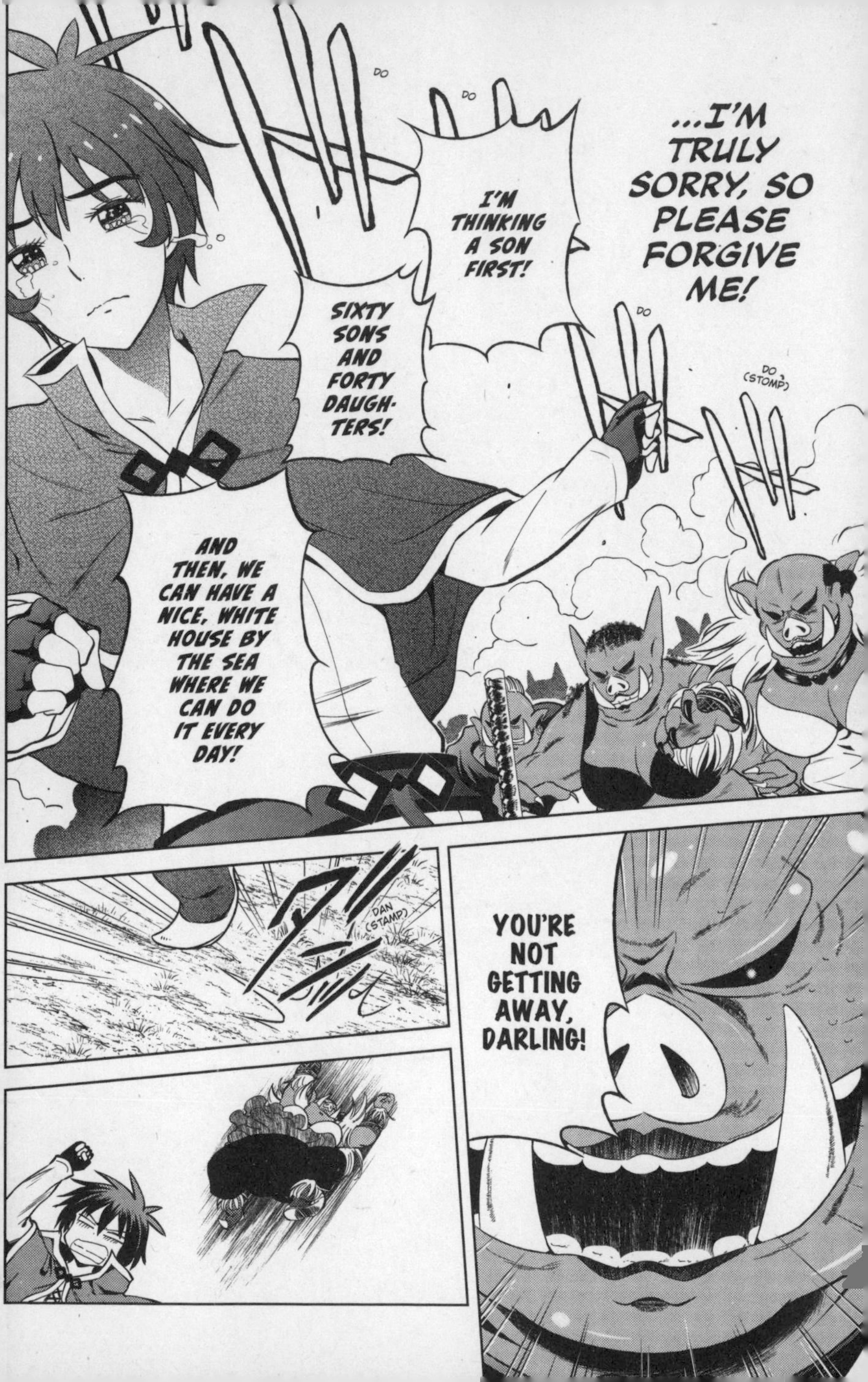
DO
DO
...I'M TRULY SORRY, SO PLEASE FORGIVE ME!
I'M THINKING A SON FIRST!
SIXTY SONS AND FORTY DAUGHTERS!
DO
DO (STOMP)
AND THEN, WE CAN HAVE A NICE, WHITE HOUSE BY THE SEA WHERE WE CAN DO IT EVERY DAY!
YOU'RE NOT GETTING AWAY, DARLING!
DAN (STAMP)

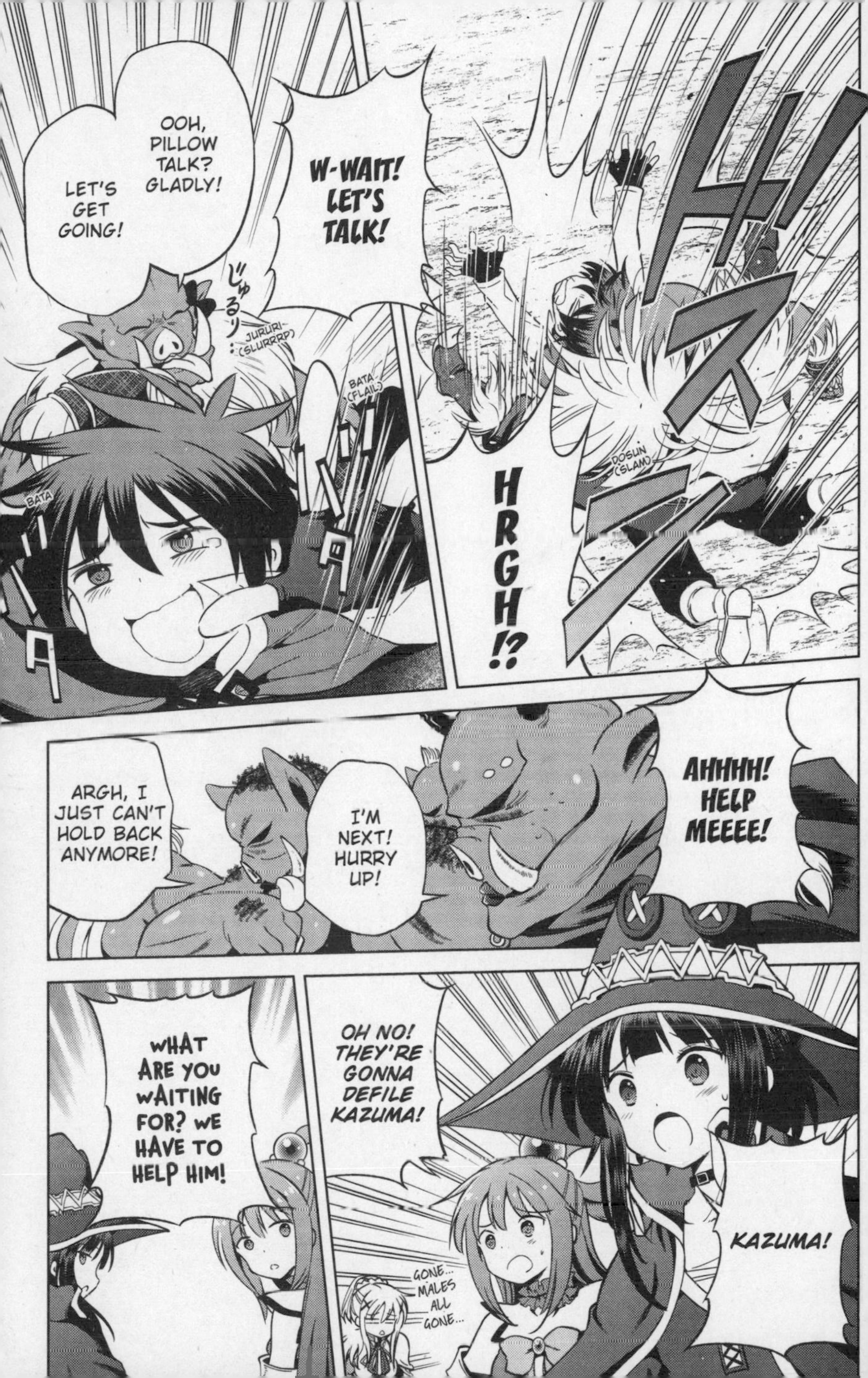
DOSUN (SLAM)
HRGH!?
W-WAIT! LET'S TALK!
OOH, PILLOW TALK? GLADLY!
LET'S GET GOING!
じゅるり
JURURI (SLURRRP)
BATA (FLAIL)
BATA
AHHHH! HELP MEEEE!
I'M NEXT! HURRY UP!
ARGH, I JUST CAN'T HOLD BACK ANYMORE!
KAZUMA!
OH NO! THEY'RE GONNA DEFILE KAZUMA!
GONE... MALES ALL GONE...
WHAT ARE YOU WAITING FOR? WE HAVE TO HELP HIM!

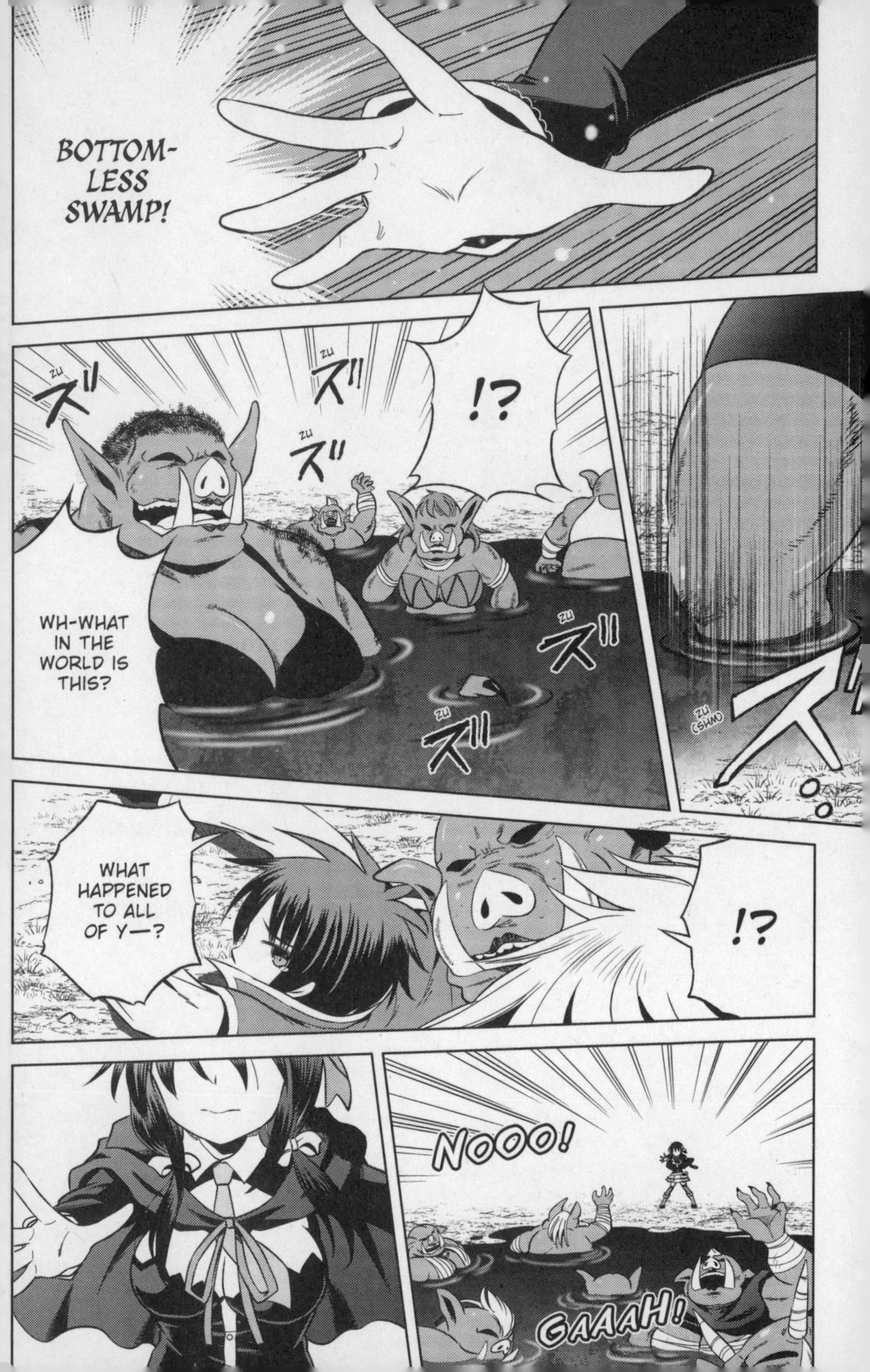

BOTTOM-LESS SWAMP!
ZU (SHM)
ズ
!?
ZU ズ
ZU ズ
ZU ズ
WH-WHAT IN THE WORLD IS THIS?
ZU ズ
ZU ズ
!?
WHAT HAPPENED TO ALL OF Y—?
NOOO!
GAAAH!

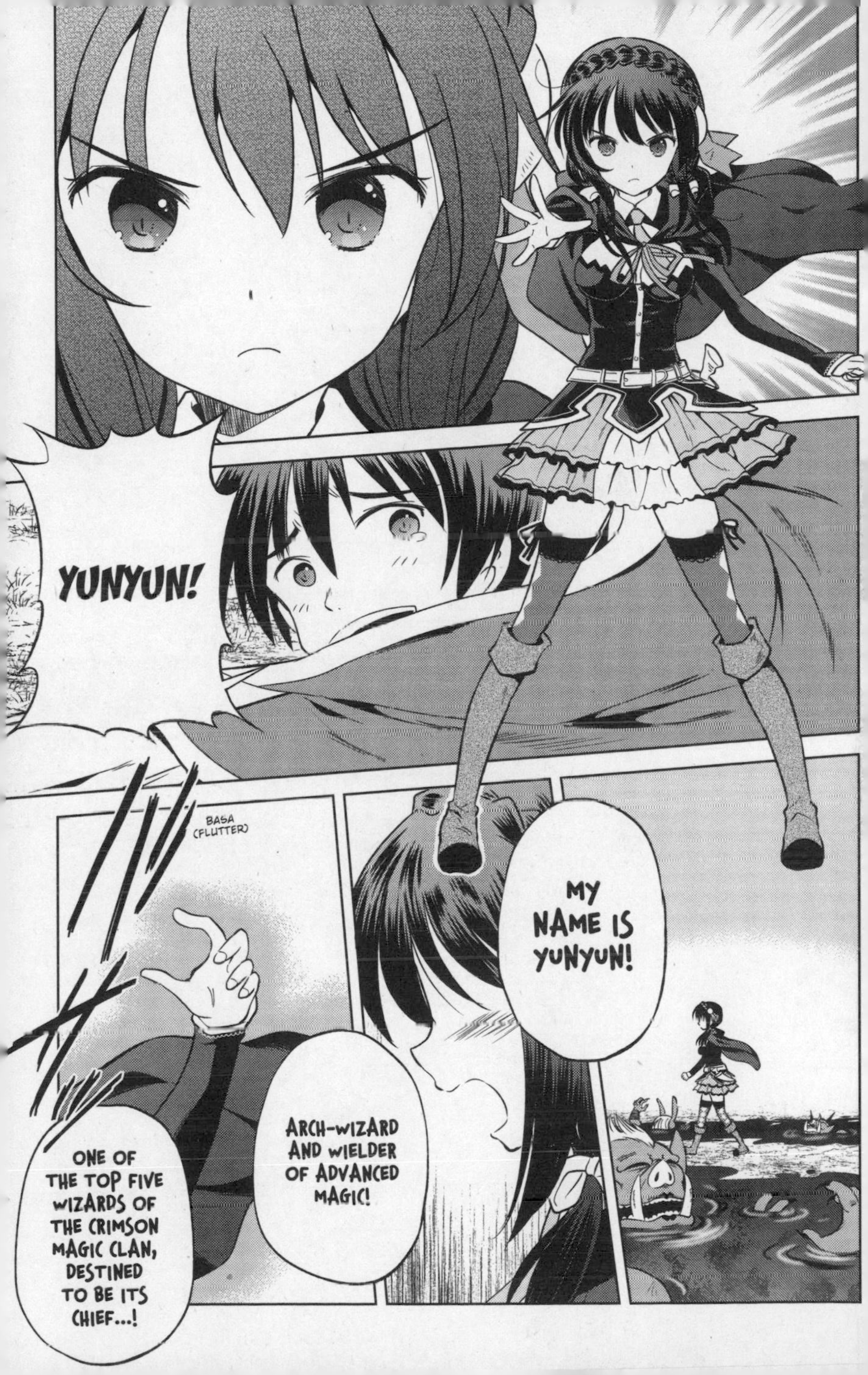
YUNYUN!
MY NAME IS YUNYUN!
ARCH-WIZARD AND WIELDER OF ADVANCED MAGIC!
BASA (FLUTTER)
ONE OF THE TOP FIVE WIZARDS OF THE CRIMSON MAGIC CLAN, DESTINED TO BE ITS CHIEF...!

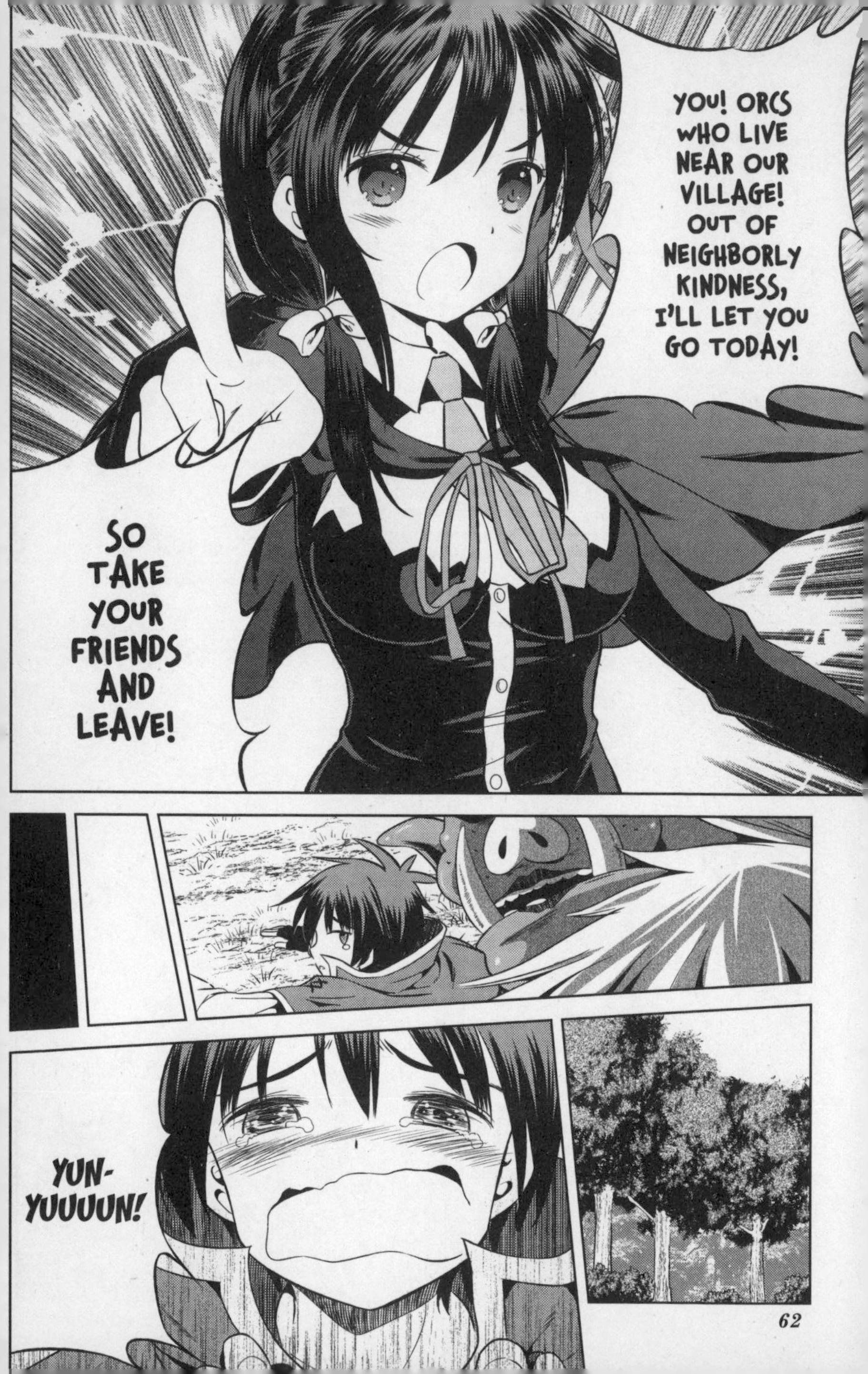
YOU! ORCS WHO LIVE NEAR OUR VILLAGE! OUT OF NEIGHBORLY KINDNESS, I'LL LET YOU GO TODAY!
SO TAKE YOUR FRIENDS AND LEAVE!
YUN-YUUUUN!

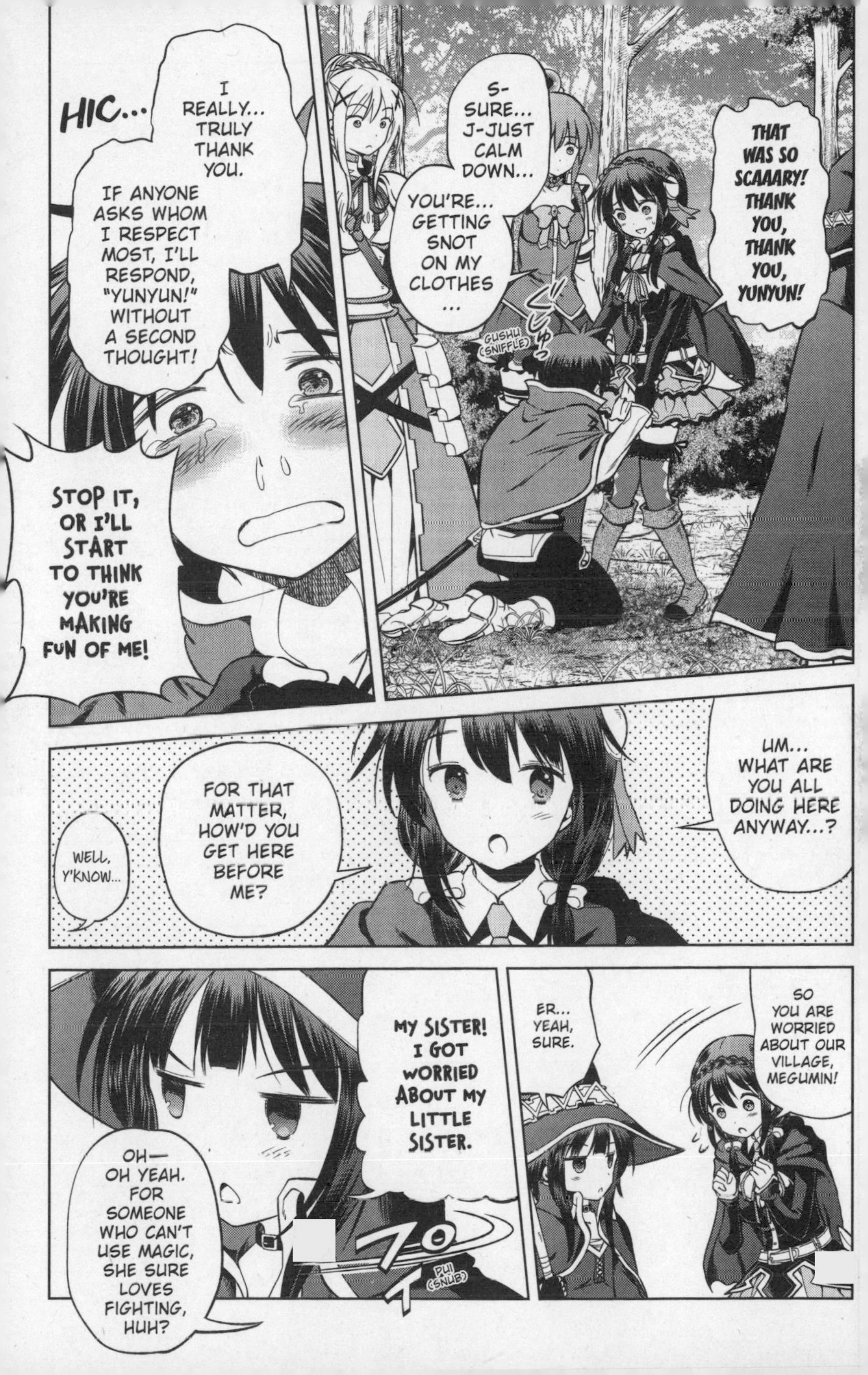
THAT WAS SO SCAAARY! THANK YOU, THANK YOU, YUNYUN!
S-SURE... J-JUST CALM DOWN...
YOU'RE... GETTING SNOT ON MY CLOTHES...
GUSHU (SNIFFLE)
HIC...
I REALLY... TRULY THANK YOU.
IF ANYONE ASKS WHOM I RESPECT MOST, I'LL RESPOND, "YUNYUN!" WITHOUT A SECOND THOUGHT!
STOP IT, OR I'LL START TO THINK YOU'RE MAKING FUN OF ME!
UM... WHAT ARE YOU ALL DOING HERE ANYWAY...?
FOR THAT MATTER, HOW'D YOU GET HERE BEFORE ME?
WELL, Y'KNOW...
SO YOU ARE WORRIED ABOUT OUR VILLAGE, MEGUMIN!
ER... YEAH, SURE.
MY SISTER! I GOT WORRIED ABOUT MY LITTLE SISTER.
PUI (SNUB)
OH— OH YEAH. FOR SOMEONE WHO CAN'T USE MAGIC, SHE SURE LOVES FIGHTING, HUH?

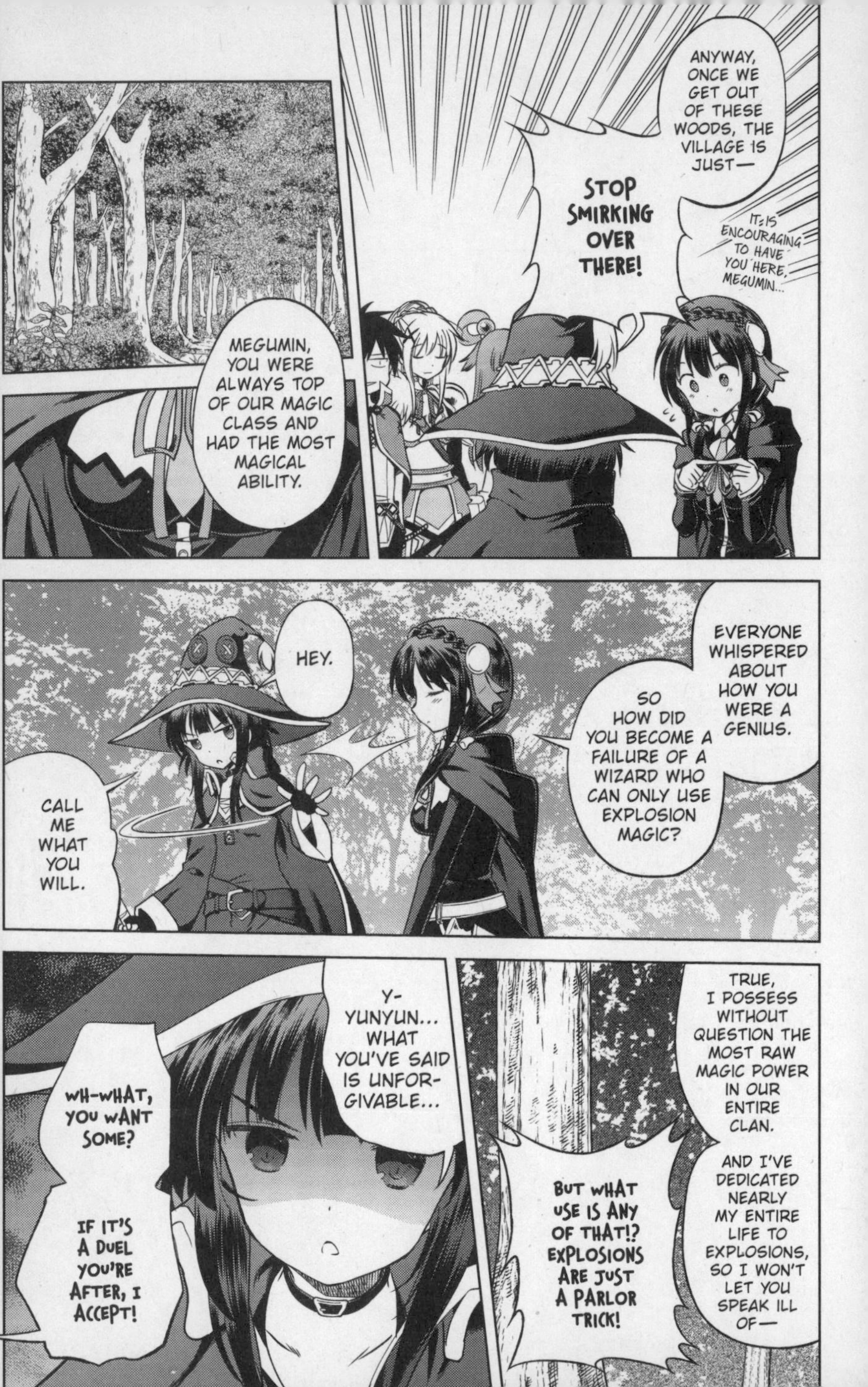
ANYWAY, ONCE WE GET OUT OF THESE WOODS, THE VILLAGE IS JUST—
STOP SMIRKING OVER THERE!
IT IS ENCOURAGING TO HAVE YOU HERE, MEGUMIN...
MEGUMIN, YOU WERE ALWAYS TOP OF OUR MAGIC CLASS AND HAD THE MOST MAGICAL ABILITY.
EVERYONE WHISPERED ABOUT HOW YOU WERE A GENIUS.
SO HOW DID YOU BECOME A FAILURE OF A WIZARD WHO CAN ONLY USE EXPLOSION MAGIC?
HEY.
CALL ME WHAT YOU WILL.
TRUE, I POSSESS WITHOUT QUESTION THE MOST RAW MAGIC POWER IN OUR ENTIRE CLAN.
AND I'VE DEDICATED NEARLY MY ENTIRE LIFE TO EXPLOSIONS, SO I WON'T LET YOU SPEAK ILL OF—
BUT WHAT USE IS ANY OF THAT!? EXPLOSIONS ARE JUST A PARLOR TRICK!
Y-YUNYUN... WHAT YOU'VE SAID IS UNFORGIVABLE...
WH-WHAT, YOU WANT SOME?
IF IT'S A DUEL YOU'RE AFTER, I ACCEPT!

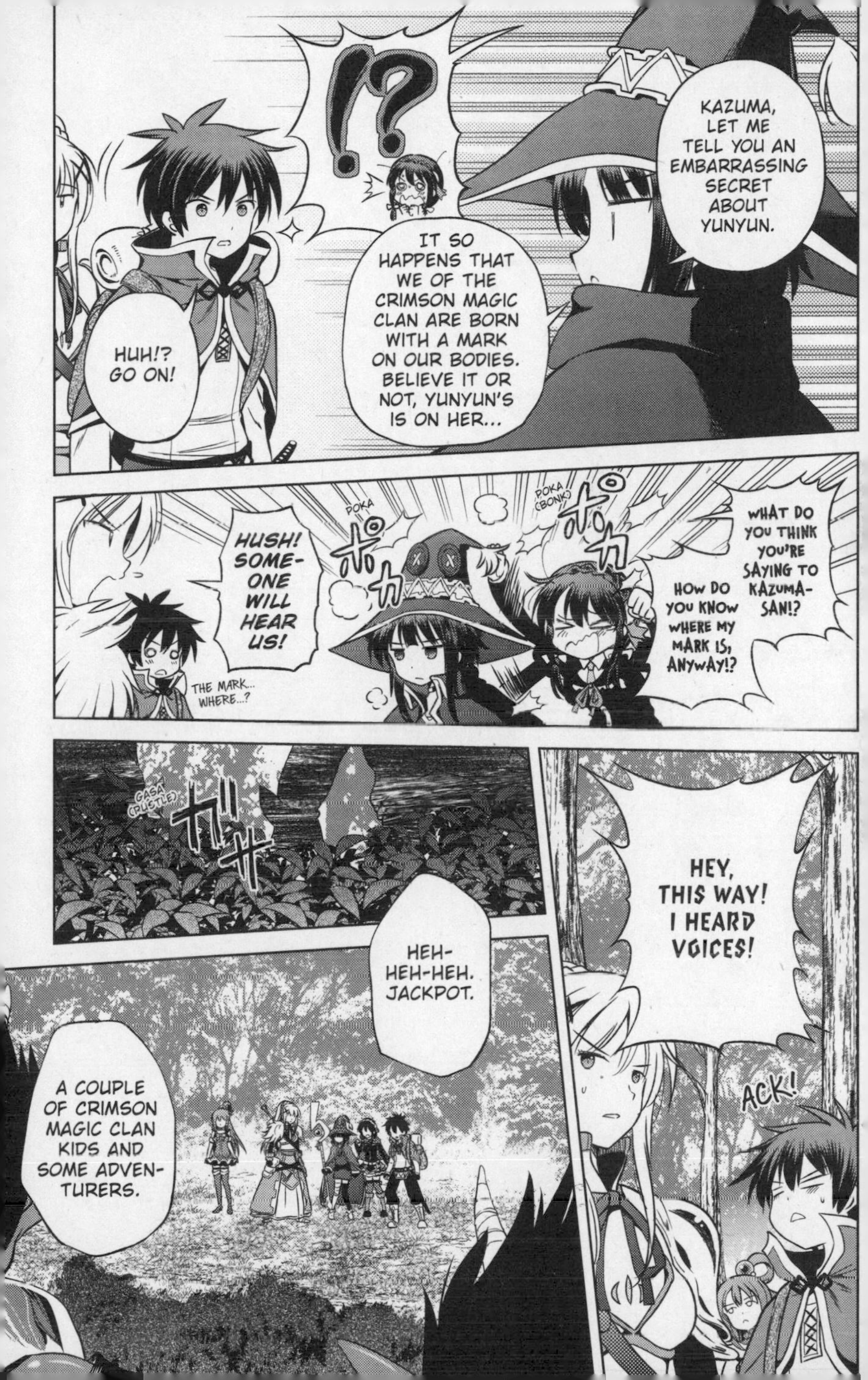
KAZUMA, LET ME TELL YOU AN EMBARRASSING SECRET ABOUT YUNYUN.
IT SO HAPPENS THAT WE OF THE CRIMSON MAGIC CLAN ARE BORN WITH A MARK ON OUR BODIES. BELIEVE IT OR NOT, YUNYUN'S IS ON HER...
!?
HUH!? GO ON!
WHAT DO YOU THINK YOU'RE SAYING TO KAZUMA-SAN!?
HOW DO YOU KNOW WHERE MY MARK IS, ANYWAY!?
POKA (BONK)
POKA
HUSH! SOMEONE WILL HEAR US!
THE MARK... WHERE...?
HEY, THIS WAY! I HEARD VOICES!
ACK!
GASA (RUSTLE)
HEH-HEH-HEH. JACKPOT.
A COUPLE OF CRIMSON MAGIC CLAN KIDS AND SOME ADVENTURERS.

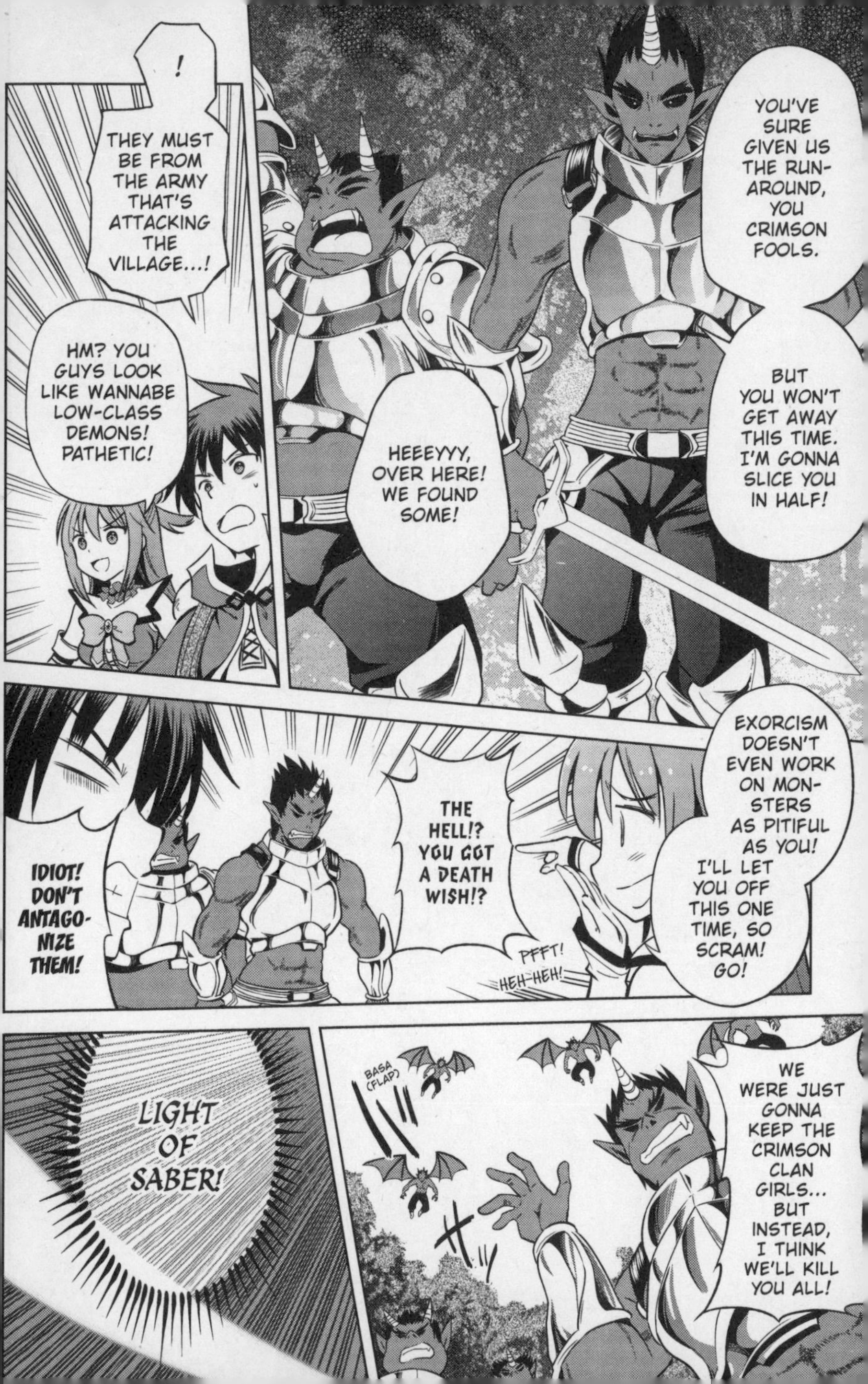
YOU'VE SURE GIVEN US THE RUN-AROUND, YOU CRIMSON FOOLS.
BUT YOU WON'T GET AWAY THIS TIME. I'M GONNA SLICE YOU IN HALF!
HEEEYYY, OVER HERE! WE FOUND SOME!
!
THEY MUST BE FROM THE ARMY THAT'S ATTACKING THE VILLAGE...!
HM? YOU GUYS LOOK LIKE WANNABE LOW-CLASS DEMONS! PATHETIC!
EXORCISM DOESN'T EVEN WORK ON MON-STERS AS PITIFUL AS YOU!
I'LL LET YOU OFF THIS ONE TIME, SO SCRAM! GO!
PFFT!
HEH-HEH!
THE HELL!? YOU GOT A DEATH WISH!?
IDIOT! DON'T ANTAGO-NIZE THEM!
WE WERE JUST GONNA KEEP THE CRIMSON CLAN GIRLS... BUT INSTEAD, I THINK WE'LL KILL YOU ALL!
BASA (FLAP)
LIGHT OF SABER!

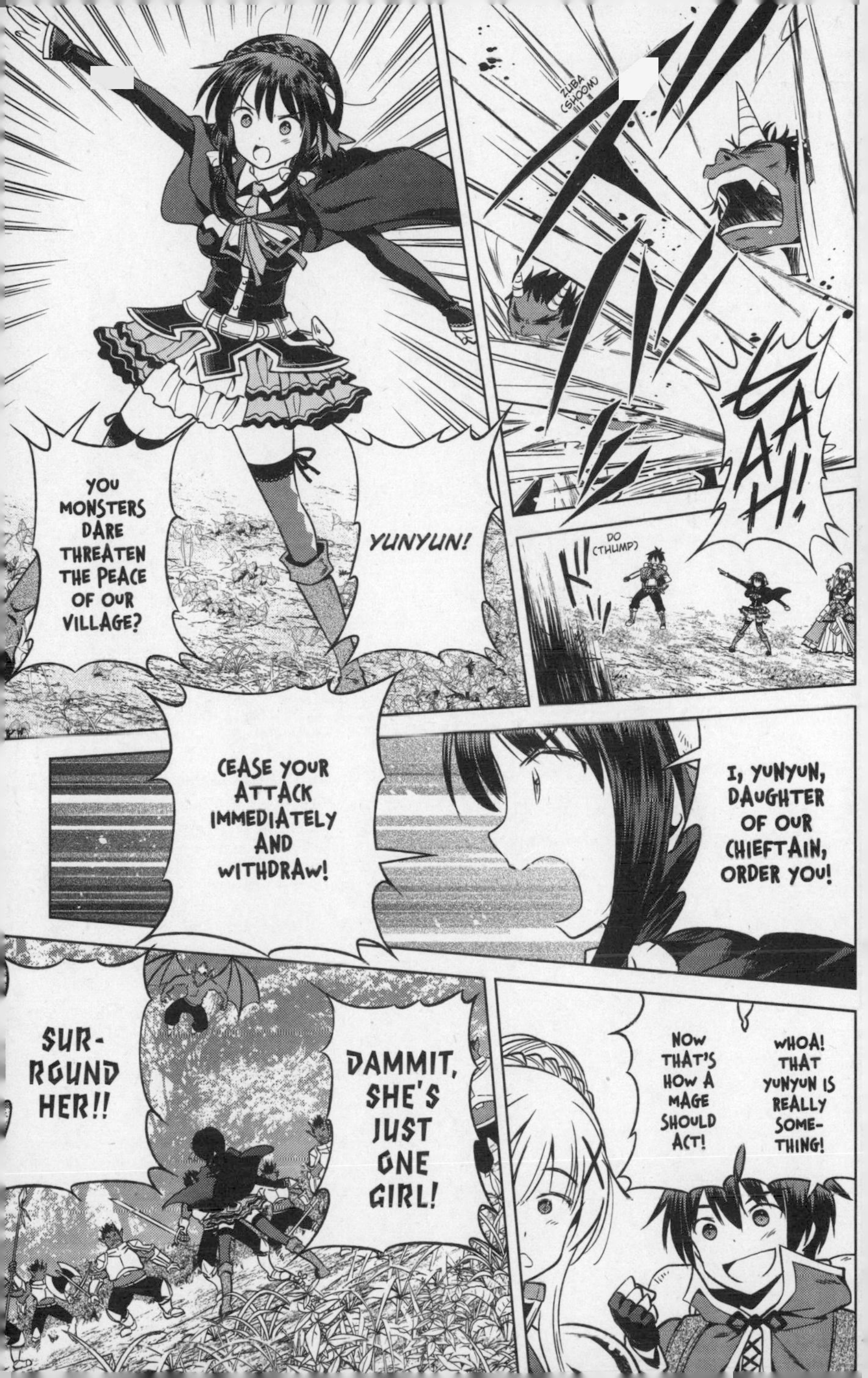
ZUBA (SHOOM)
UAAH!
DO (THUMP)
YUNYUN!
YOU MONSTERS DARE THREATEN THE PEACE OF OUR VILLAGE?
I, YUNYUN, DAUGHTER OF OUR CHIEFTAIN, ORDER YOU!
CEASE YOUR ATTACK IMMEDIATELY AND WITHDRAW!
WHOA! THAT YUNYUN IS REALLY SOME-THING!
NOW THAT'S HOW A MAGE SHOULD ACT!
DAMMIT, SHE'S JUST ONE GIRL!
SUR-ROUND HER!!

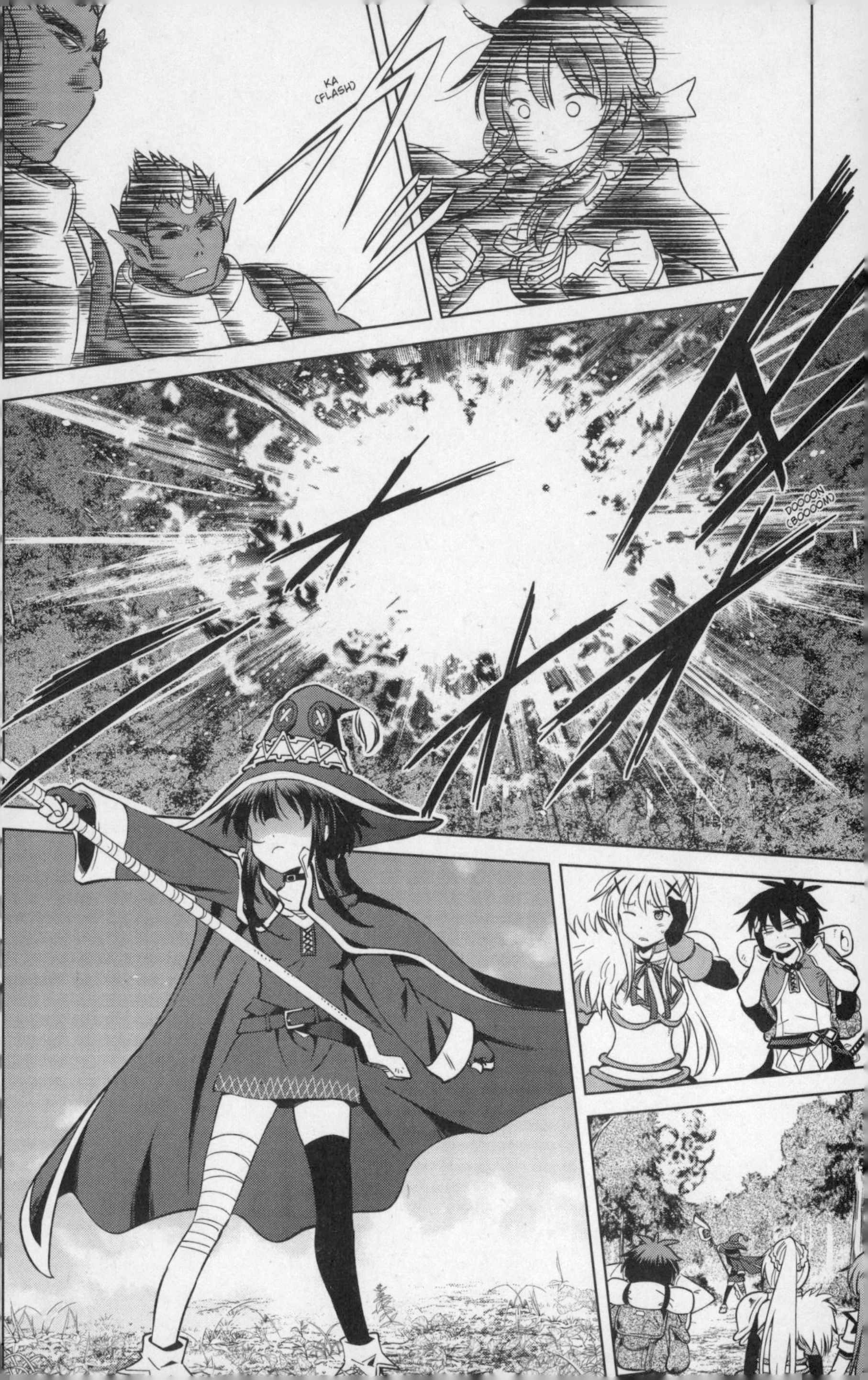
KA
(FLASH)
DOOOON
(BOOOOM)

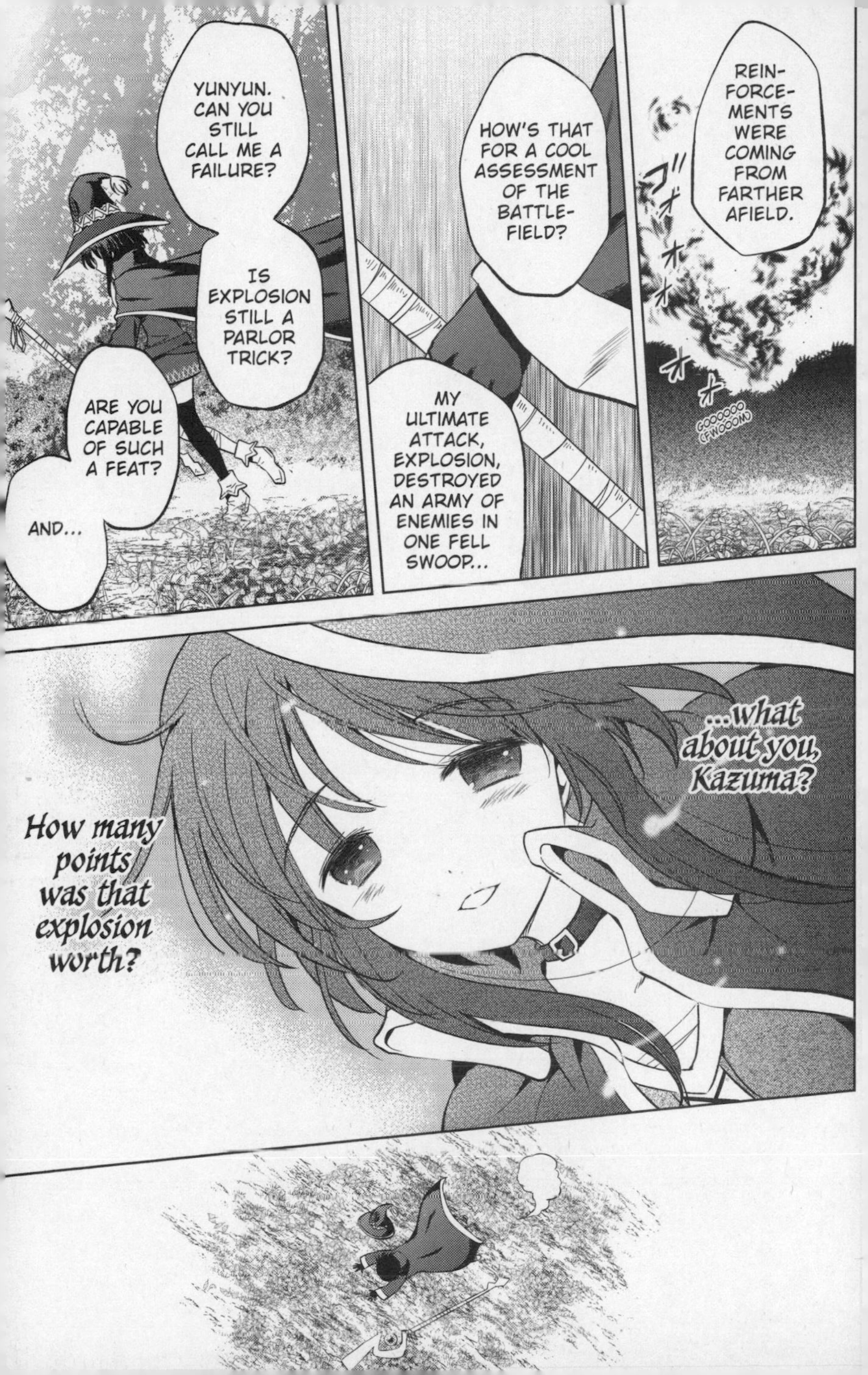
REIN-FORCEMENTS WERE COMING FROM FARTHER AFIELD.
GOOOOOO (FWOOOM)
HOW'S THAT FOR A COOL ASSESSMENT OF THE BATTLE-FIELD?
MY ULTIMATE ATTACK, EXPLOSION, DESTROYED AN ARMY OF ENEMIES IN ONE FELL SWOOP...
YUNYUN. CAN YOU STILL CALL ME A FAILURE?
IS EXPLOSION STILL A PARLOR TRICK?
ARE YOU CAPABLE OF SUCH A FEAT?
AND...
...what about you, Kazuma?
How many points was that explosion worth?

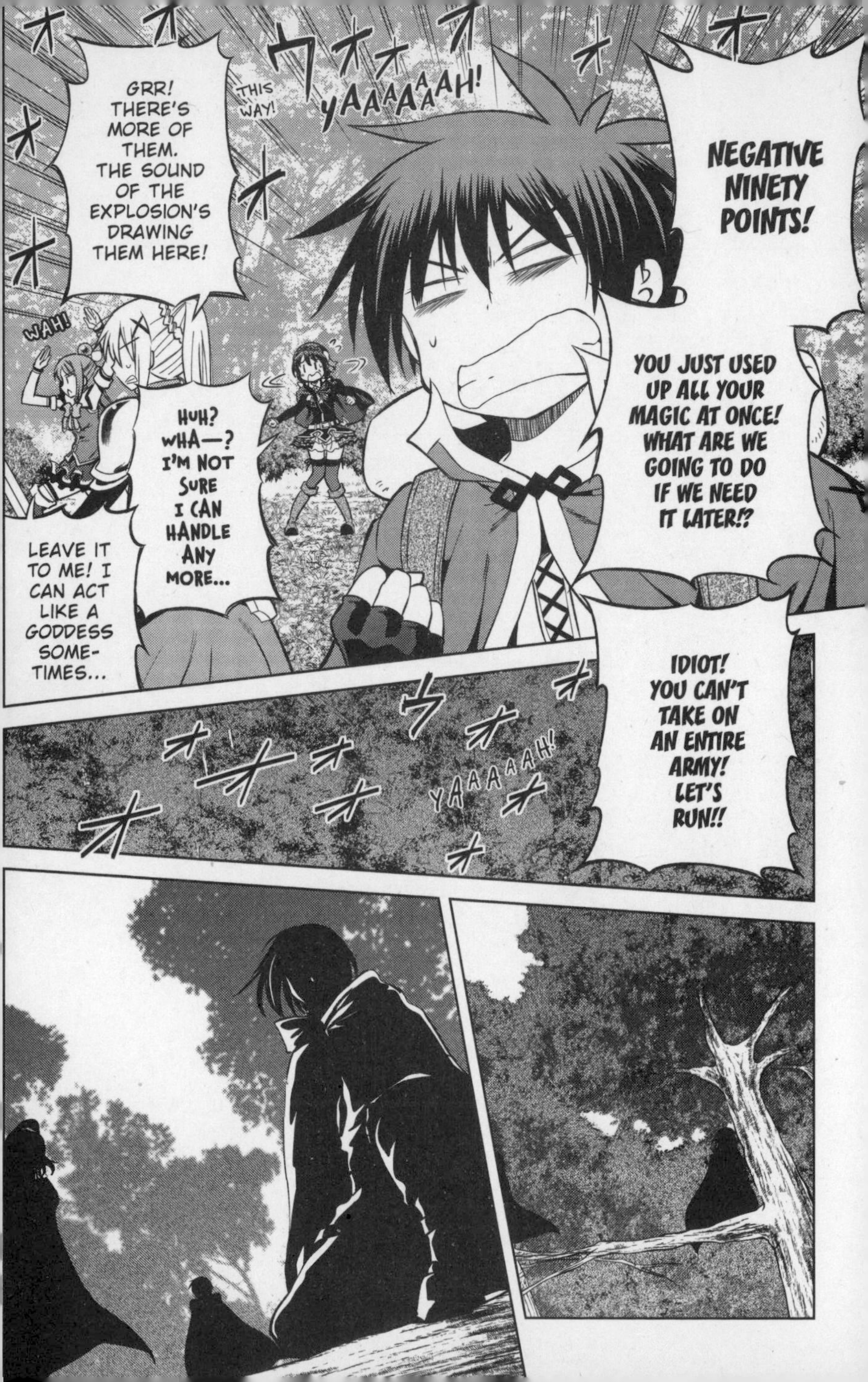

NEGATIVE NINETY POINTS!
YOU JUST USED UP ALL YOUR MAGIC AT ONCE! WHAT ARE WE GOING TO DO IF WE NEED IT LATER!?
YAAAAAAH!
THIS WAY!
GRR! THERE'S MORE OF THEM. THE SOUND OF THE EXPLOSION'S DRAWING THEM HERE!
WAH!
HUH? WHA—? I'M NOT SURE I CAN HANDLE ANY MORE...
LEAVE IT TO ME! I CAN ACT LIKE A GODDESS SOME-TIMES...
IDIOT! YOU CAN'T TAKE ON AN ENTIRE ARMY! LET'S RUN!!
YAAAAAH!

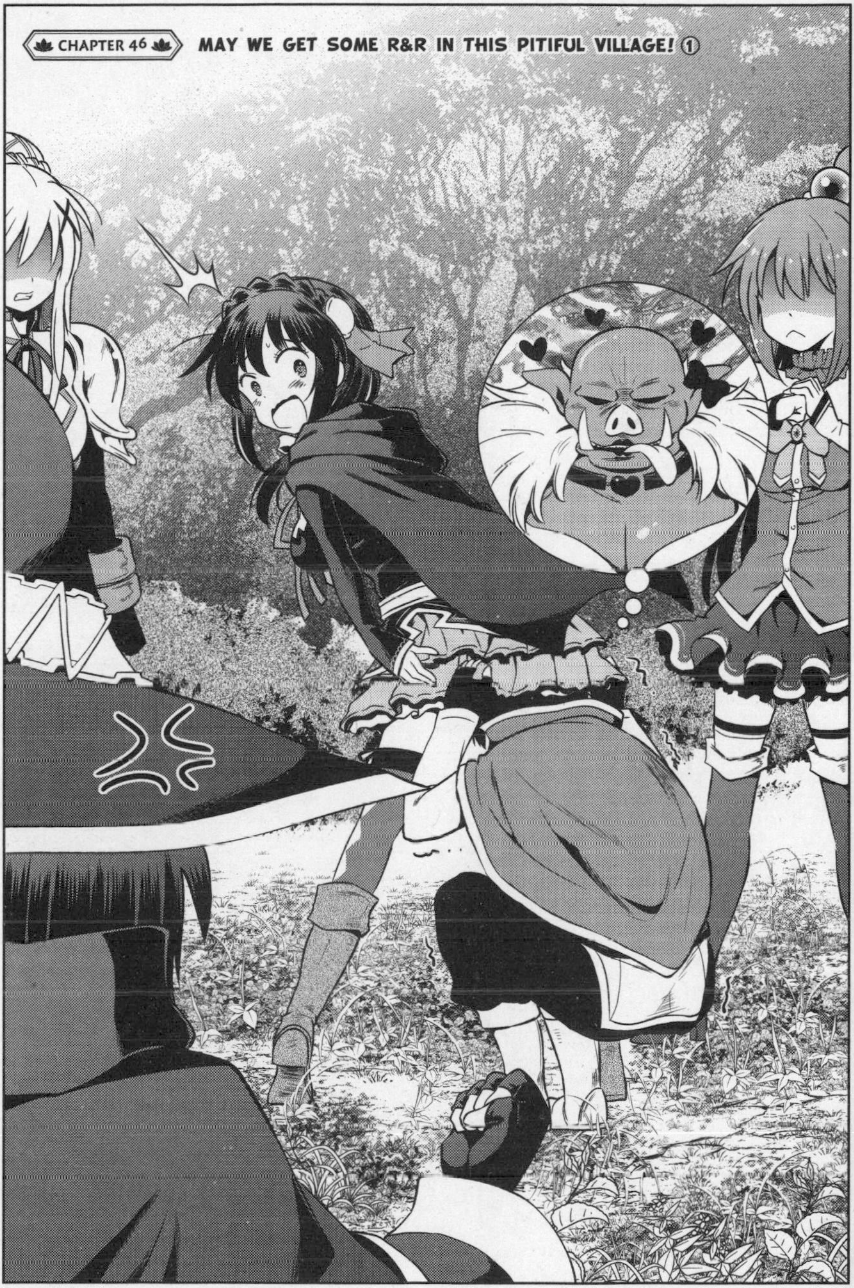

CHAPTER 46
MAY WE GET SOME R&R IN THIS PITIFUL VILLAGE! ①

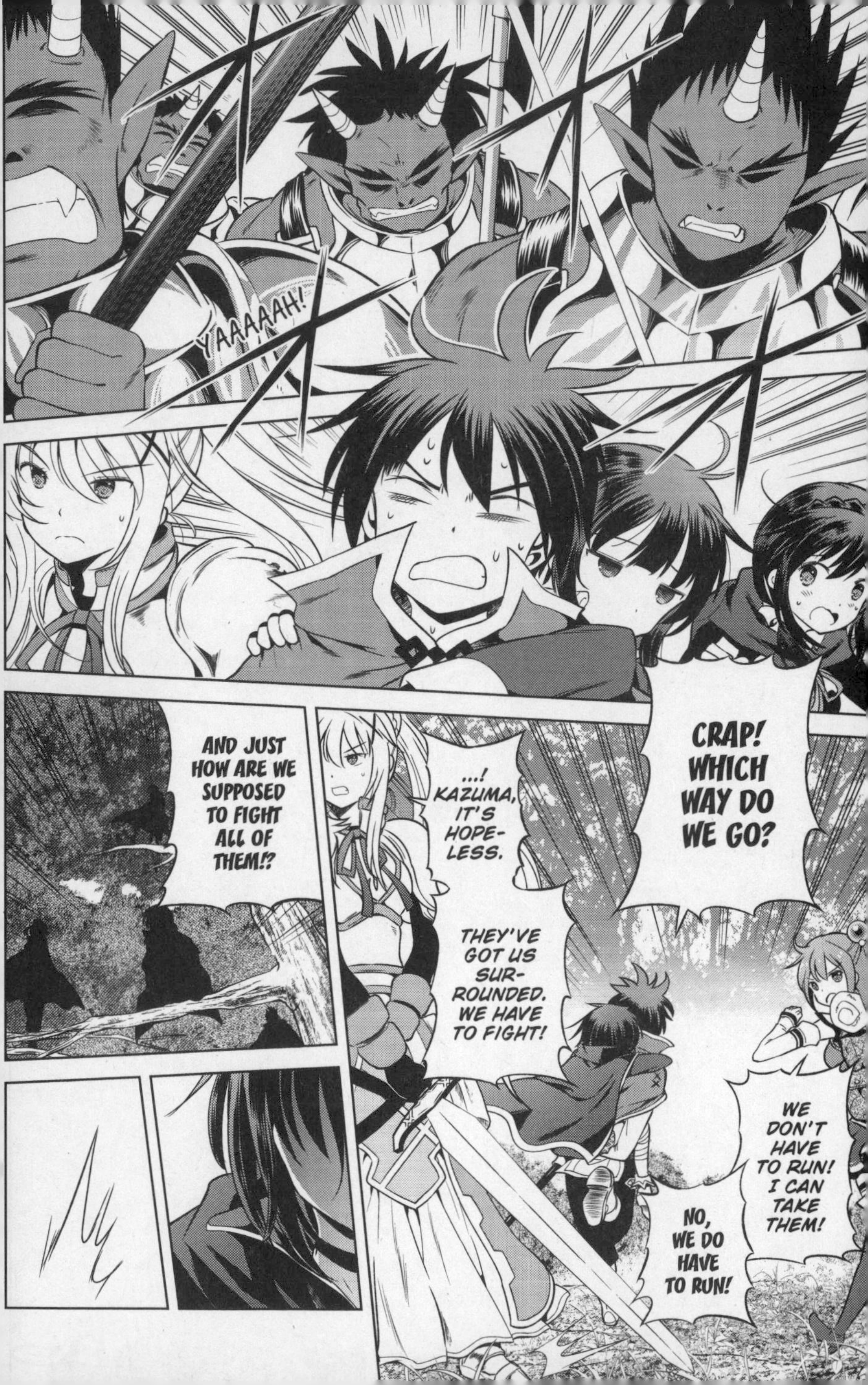
YAAAAAH!
CRAP! WHICH WAY DO WE GO?
...! KAZUMA, IT'S HOPELESS.
THEY'VE GOT US SURROUNDED. WE HAVE TO FIGHT!
WE DON'T HAVE TO RUN! I CAN TAKE THEM!
NO, WE DO HAVE TO RUN!
AND JUST HOW ARE WE SUPPOSED TO FIGHT ALL OF THEM!?

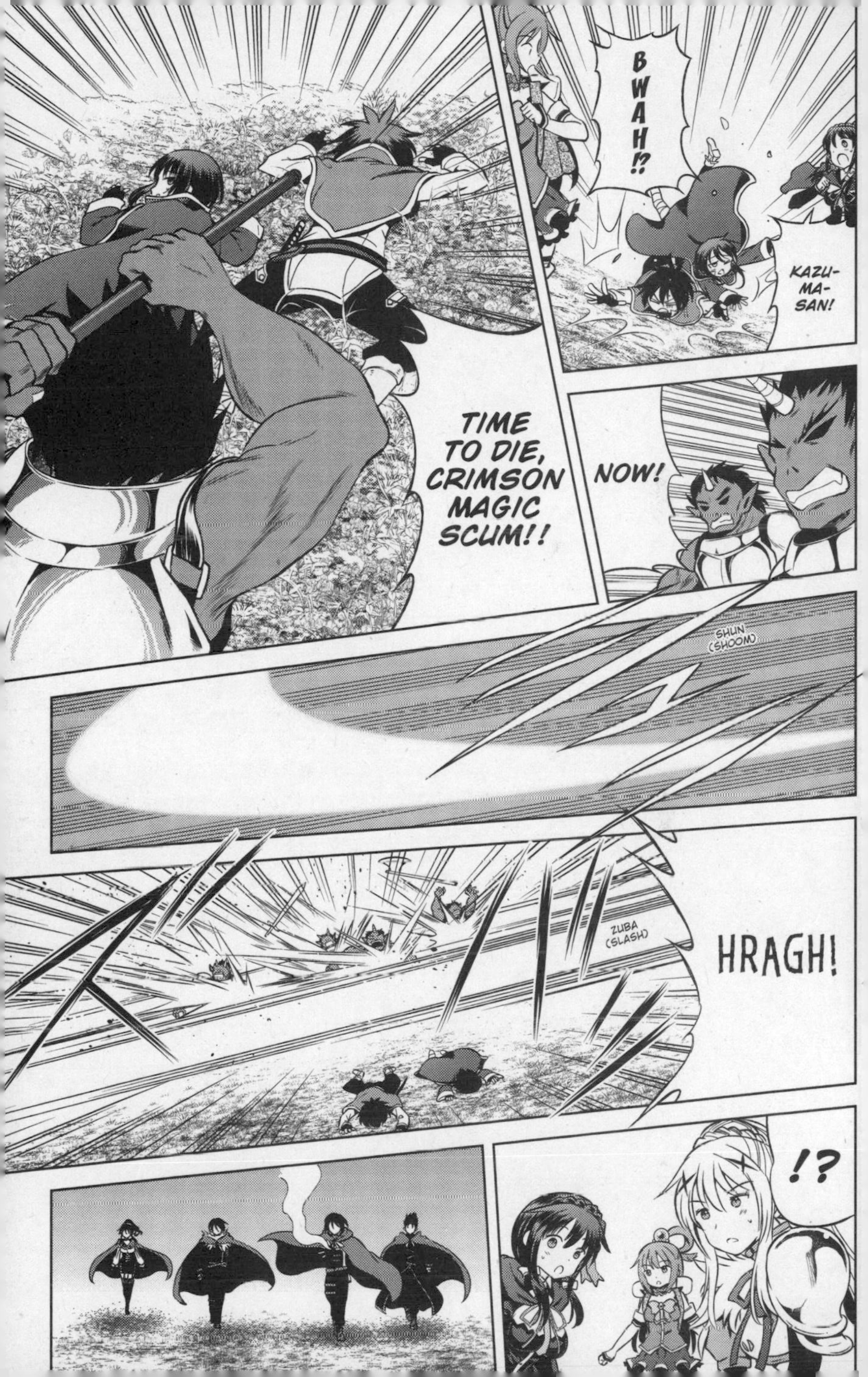
BWAH!?
KAZUMA-SAN!
NOW!
TIME TO DIE, CRIMSON MAGIC SCUM!!
SHUN (SHOOM)
HRAGH!
ZUBA (SLASH)
!?

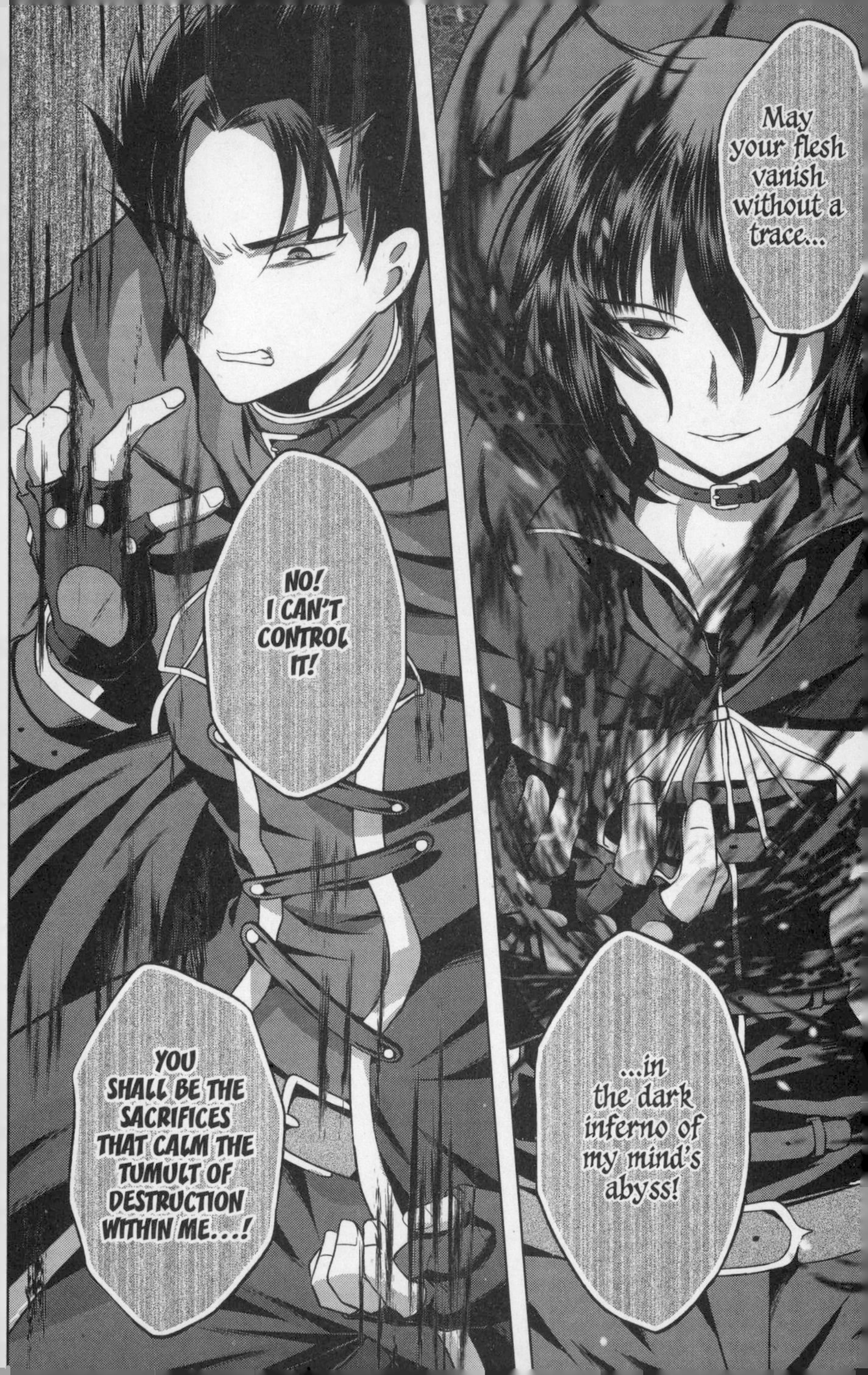
May your flesh vanish without a trace...
...in the dark inferno of my mind's abyss!
NO! I CAN'T CONTROL IT!
YOU SHALL BE THE SACRIFICES THAT CALM THE TUMULT OF DESTRUCTION WITHIN ME...!

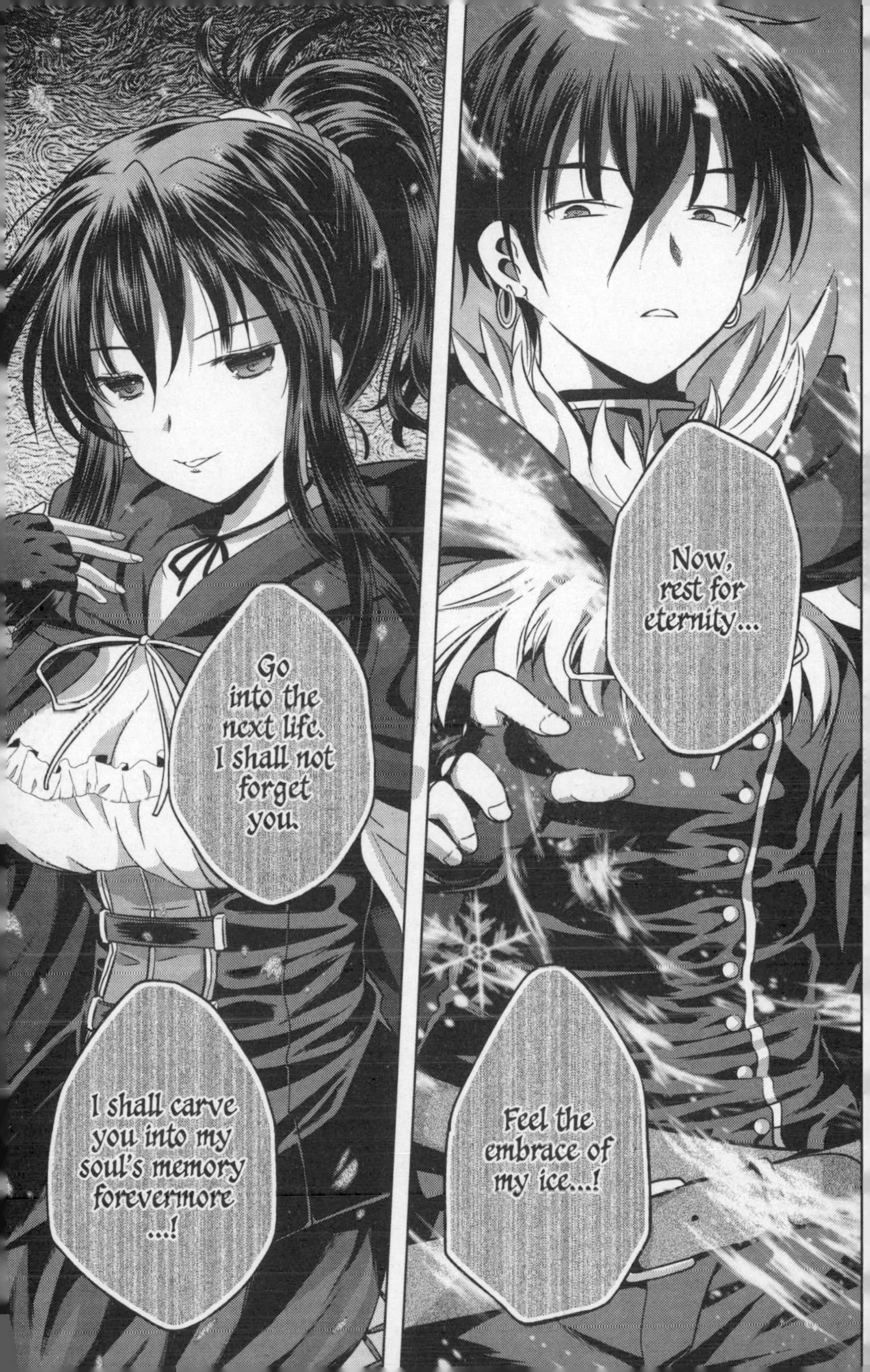
Now, rest for eternity...
Feel the embrace of my ice...!
Go into the next life. I shall not forget you.
I shall carve you into my soul's memory forevermore ...!

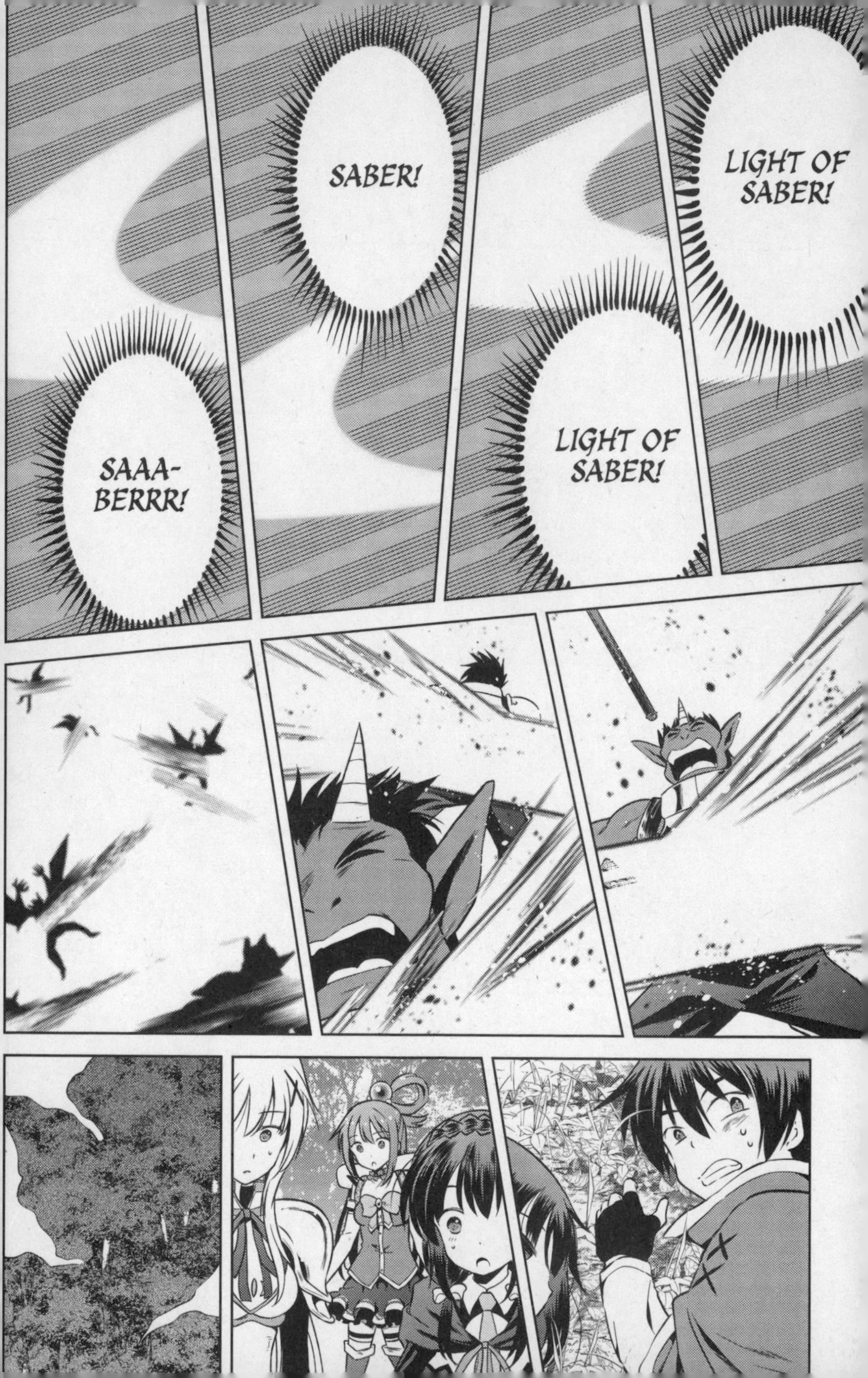
LIGHT OF SABER!
LIGHT OF SABER!
SABER!
SAAA-BERRR!

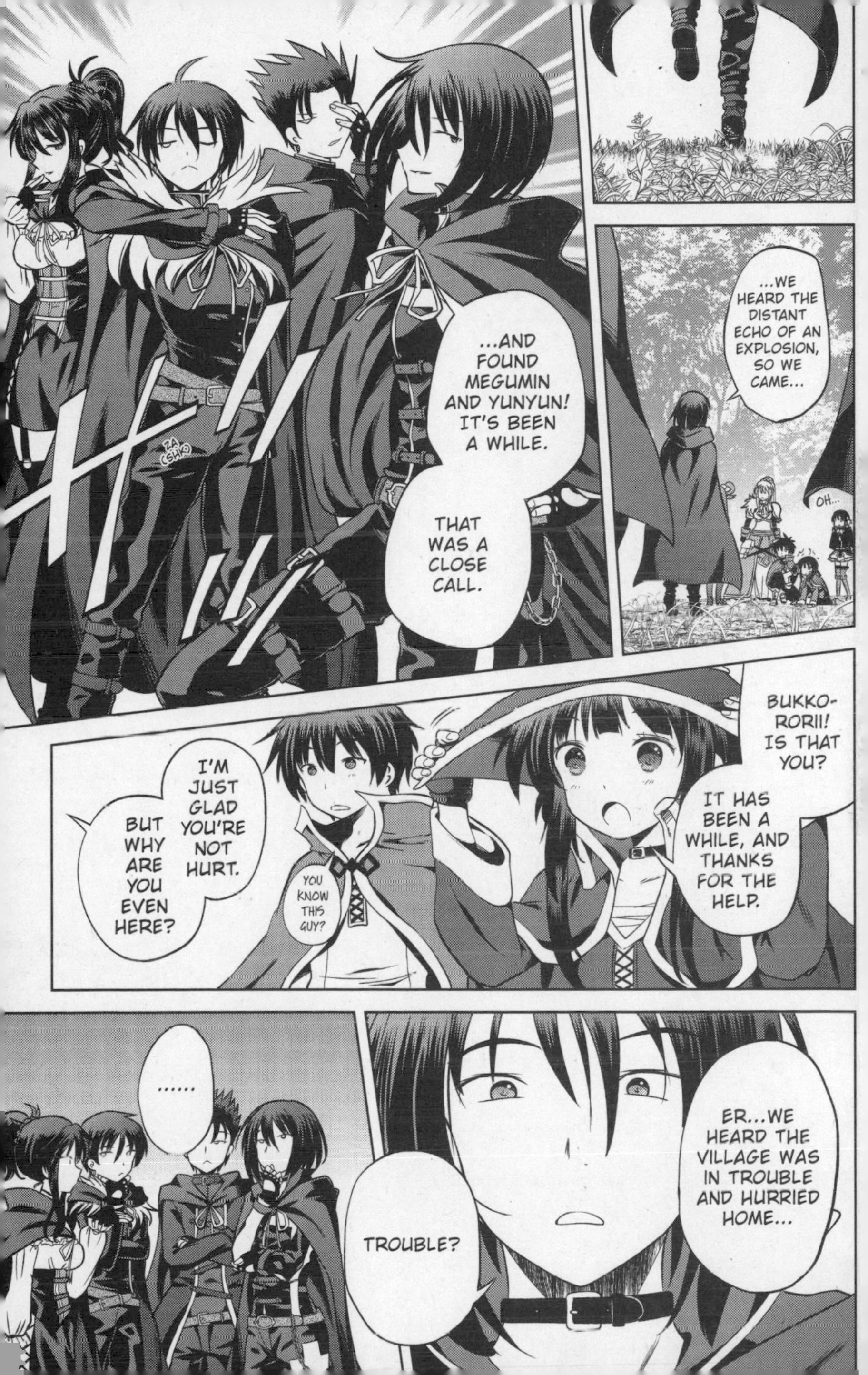
...WE HEARD THE DISTANT ECHO OF AN EXPLOSION, SO WE CAME...
OH...
...AND FOUND MEGUMIN AND YUNYUN! IT'S BEEN A WHILE.
THAT WAS A CLOSE CALL.
ZA (SHK)
BUKKORORII! IS THAT YOU?
IT HAS BEEN A WHILE, AND THANKS FOR THE HELP.
YOU KNOW THIS GUY?
I'M JUST GLAD YOU'RE NOT HURT.
BUT WHY ARE YOU EVEN HERE?
ER...WE HEARD THE VILLAGE WAS IN TROUBLE AND HURRIED HOME...
TROUBLE?
......

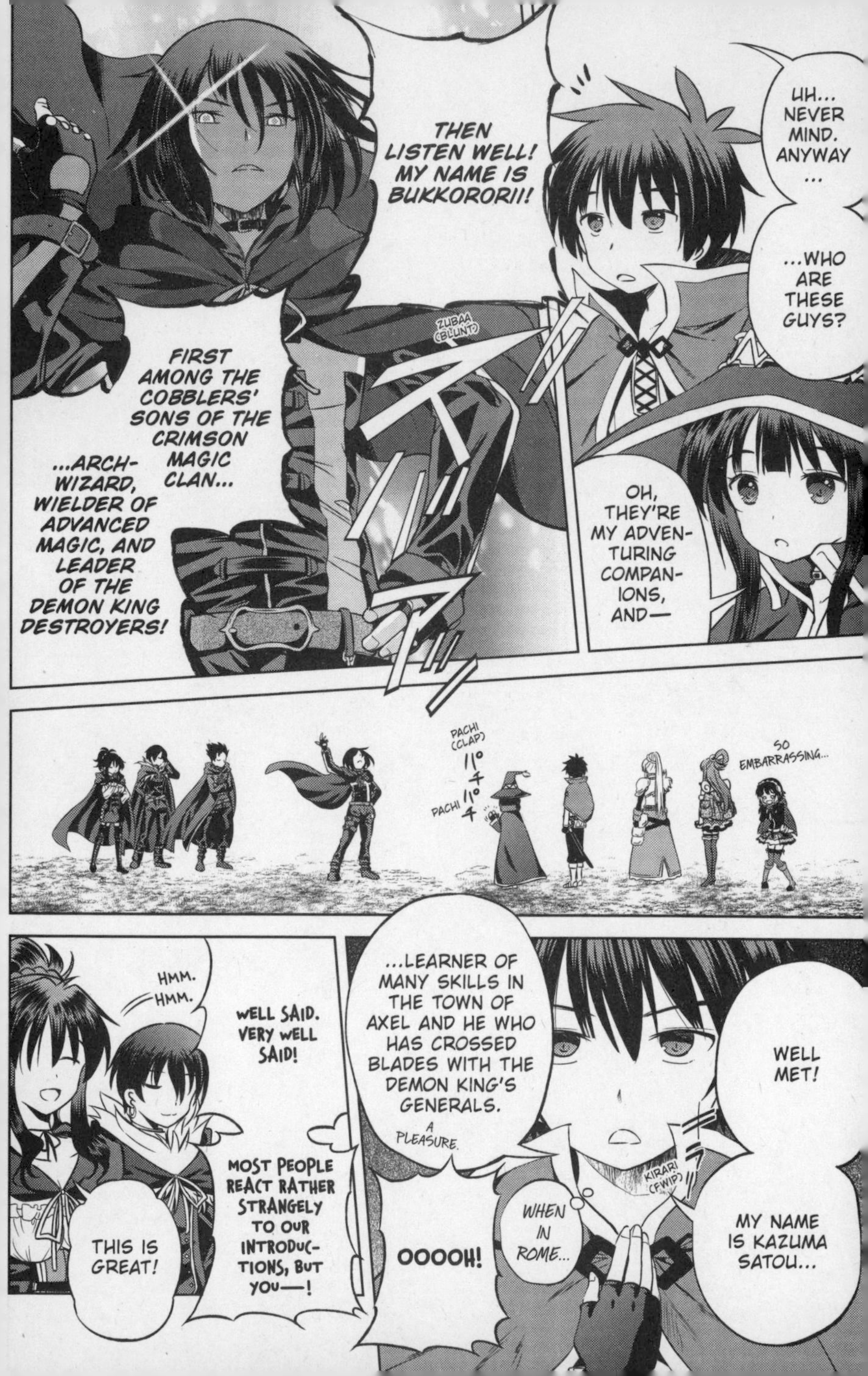
UH... NEVER MIND. ANYWAY ...
...WHO ARE THESE GUYS?
OH, THEY'RE MY ADVENTURING COMPANIONS, AND—
THEN LISTEN WELL! MY NAME IS BUKKORORI!!
ZUBAA (BLUNT)
FIRST AMONG THE COBBLERS' SONS OF THE CRIMSON MAGIC CLAN...
...ARCH-WIZARD, WIELDER OF ADVANCED MAGIC, AND LEADER OF THE DEMON KING DESTROYERS!
SO EMBARRASSING...
PACHI (CLAP)
PACHI
WELL MET!
MY NAME IS KAZUMA SATOU...
KIRARI (FWIP)
...LEARNER OF MANY SKILLS IN THE TOWN OF AXEL AND HE WHO HAS CROSSED BLADES WITH THE DEMON KING'S GENERALS.
A PLEASURE.
WHEN IN ROME...
OOOOH!
HMM. HMM.
WELL SAID. VERY WELL SAID!
MOST PEOPLE REACT RATHER STRANGELY TO OUR INTRODUCTIONS, BUT YOU—!
THIS IS GREAT!

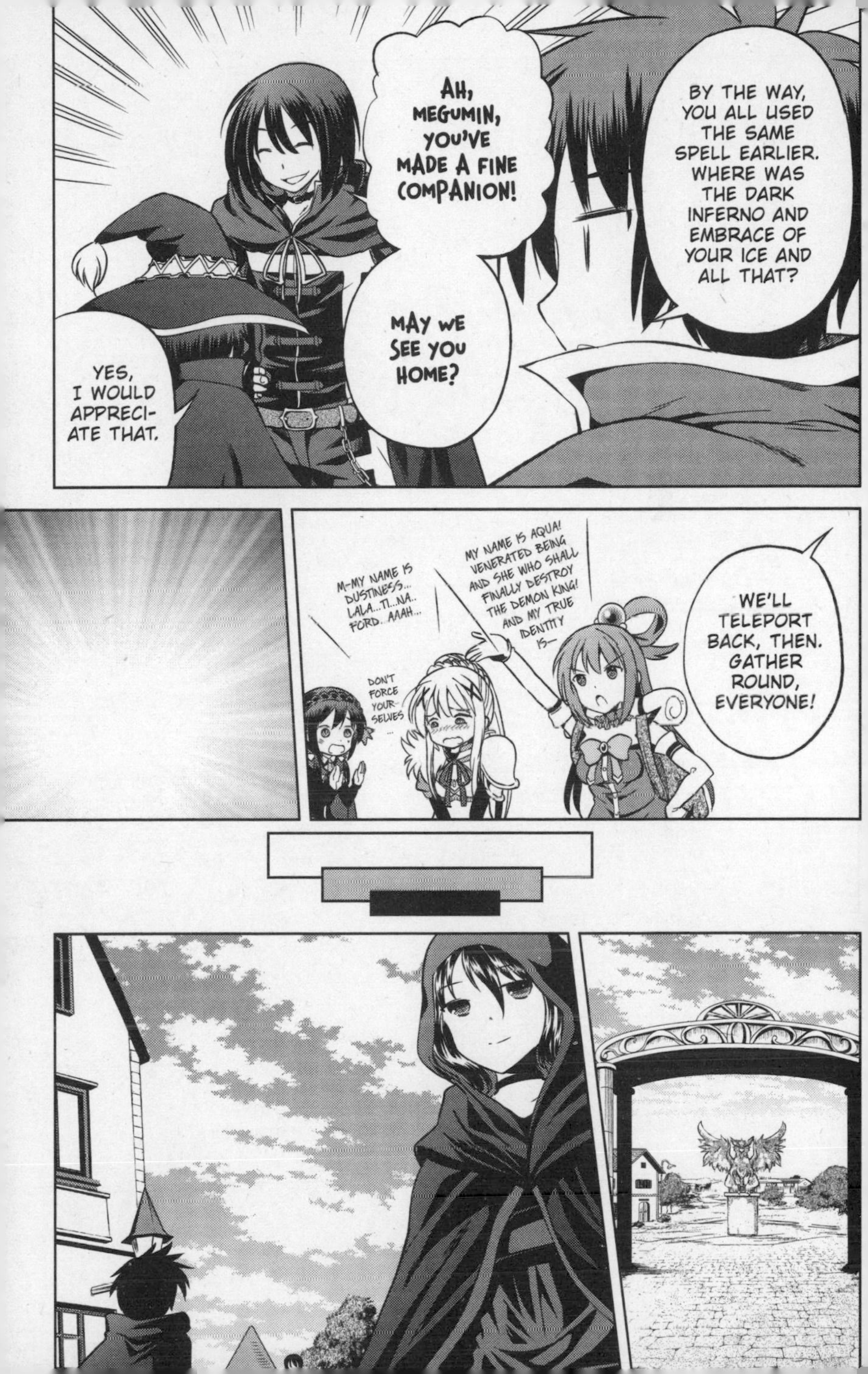
BY THE WAY, YOU ALL USED THE SAME SPELL EARLIER. WHERE WAS THE DARK INFERNO AND EMBRACE OF YOUR ICE AND ALL THAT?
AH, MEGUMIN, YOU'VE MADE A FINE COMPANION!
MAY WE SEE YOU HOME?
YES, I WOULD APPRECIATE THAT.
WE'LL TELEPORT BACK, THEN. GATHER ROUND, EVERYONE!
MY NAME IS AQUA! VENERATED BEING AND SHE WHO SHALL FINALLY DESTROY THE DEMON KING! AND MY TRUE IDENTITY IS—
M-MY NAME IS DUSTINESS... LALA...TI...NA... FORD...AAAH...
DON'T FORCE YOURSELVES...

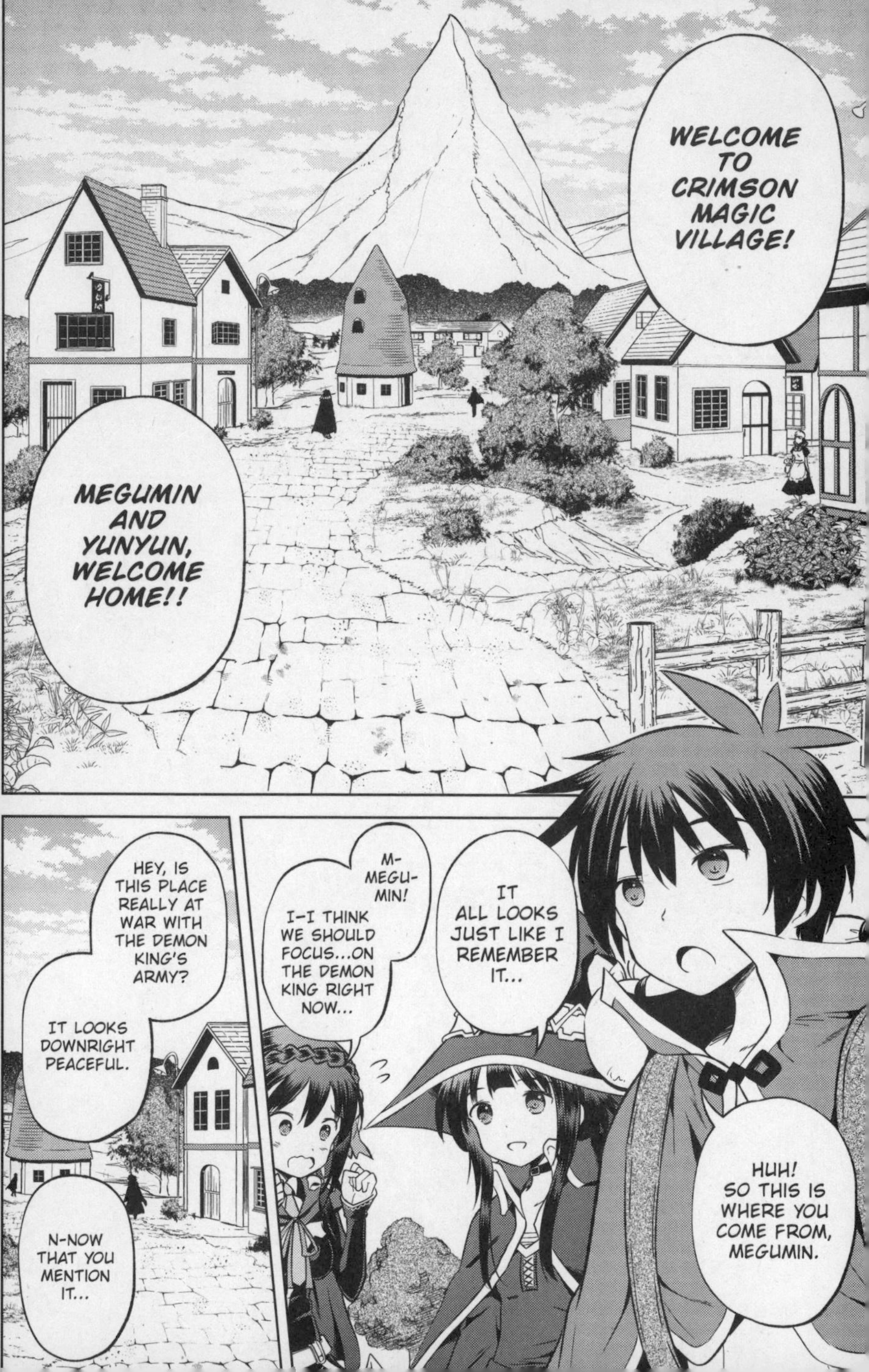
WELCOME TO CRIMSON MAGIC VILLAGE!
MEGUMIN AND YUNYUN, WELCOME HOME!!
IT ALL LOOKS JUST LIKE I REMEMBER IT...
M-MEGUMIN! I-I THINK WE SHOULD FOCUS...ON THE DEMON KING RIGHT NOW...
HUH! SO THIS IS WHERE YOU COME FROM, MEGUMIN.
HEY, IS THIS PLACE REALLY AT WAR WITH THE DEMON KING'S ARMY?
IT LOOKS DOWNRIGHT PEACEFUL.
N-NOW THAT YOU MENTION IT...

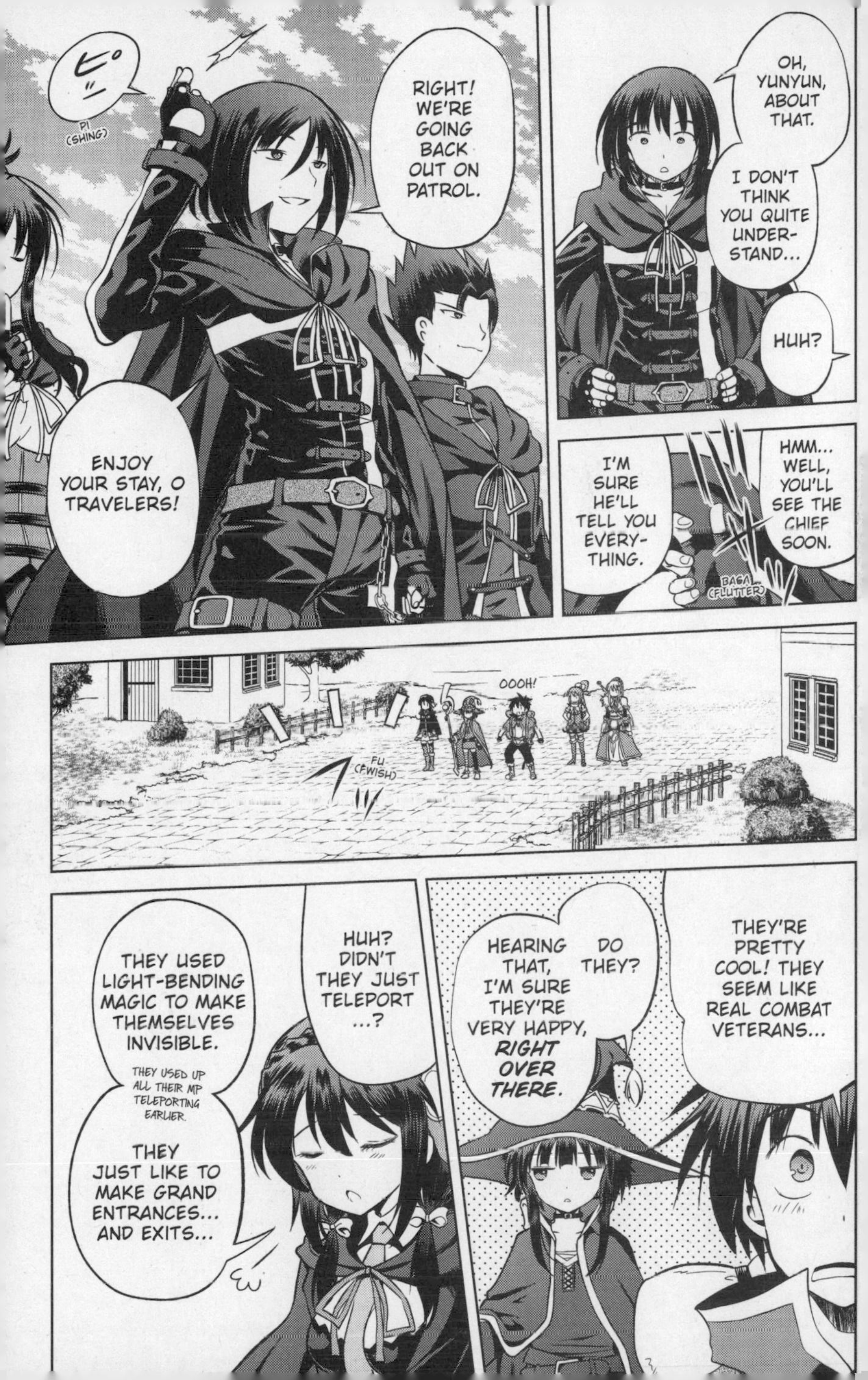
OH, YUNYUN, ABOUT THAT.
I DON'T THINK YOU QUITE UNDER-STAND...
HUH?
HMM... WELL, YOU'LL SEE THE CHIEF SOON.
I'M SURE HE'LL TELL YOU EVERY-THING.
BAGA (FLUTTER)
RIGHT! WE'RE GOING BACK OUT ON PATROL.
PI (SHING)
ENJOY YOUR STAY, O TRAVELERS!
OOOH!
FU (FWISH)
THEY'RE PRETTY COOL! THEY SEEM LIKE REAL COMBAT VETERANS...
DO THEY?
HEARING THAT, I'M SURE THEY'RE VERY HAPPY, RIGHT OVER THERE.
HUH? DIDN'T THEY JUST TELEPORT ...?
THEY USED LIGHT-BENDING MAGIC TO MAKE THEMSELVES INVISIBLE.
THEY USED UP ALL THEIR MP TELEPORTING EARLIER.
THEY JUST LIKE TO MAKE GRAND ENTRANCES... AND EXITS...

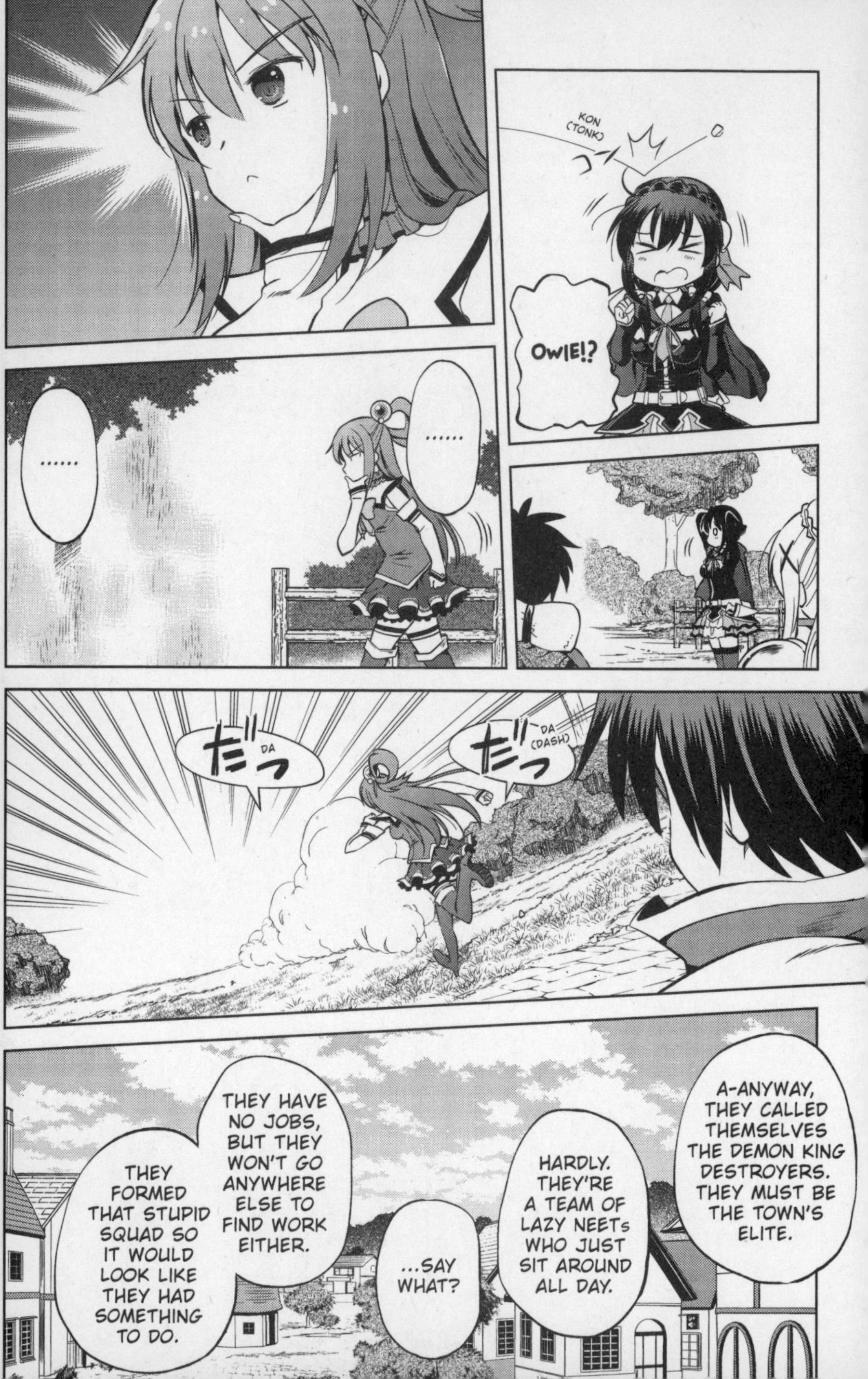
KON (TONK)
OWIE!?
......
......
だっ DA (DASH)
だっ DA
A-ANYWAY, THEY CALLED THEMSELVES THE DEMON KING DESTROYERS. THEY MUST BE THE TOWN'S ELITE.
HARDLY. THEY'RE A TEAM OF LAZY NEETs WHO JUST SIT AROUND ALL DAY.
...SAY WHAT?
THEY HAVE NO JOBS, BUT THEY WON'T GO ANYWHERE ELSE TO FIND WORK EITHER.
THEY FORMED THAT STUPID SQUAD SO IT WOULD LOOK LIKE THEY HAD SOMETHING TO DO.

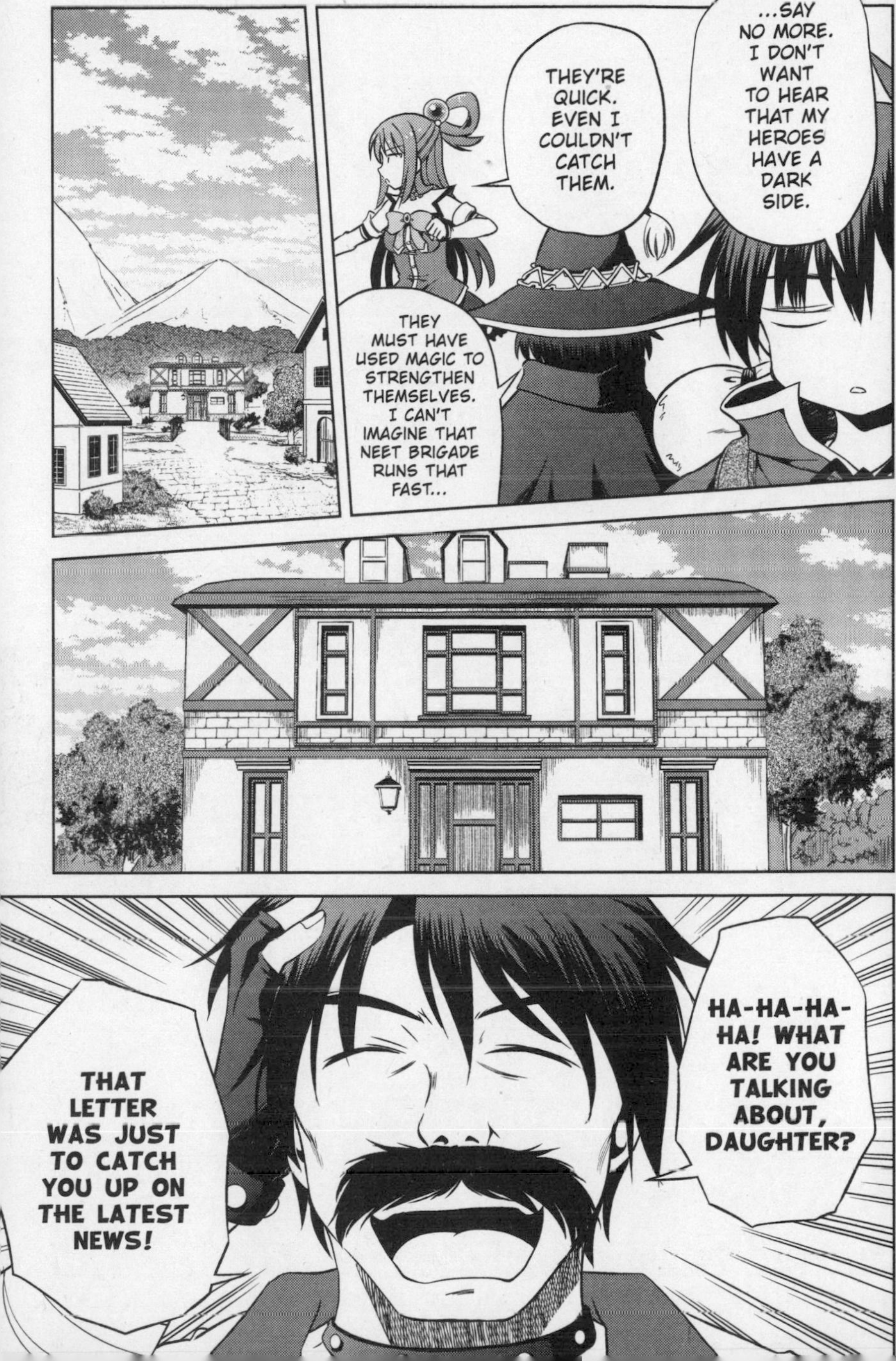
THEY'RE QUICK. EVEN I COULDN'T CATCH THEM.
THEY MUST HAVE USED MAGIC TO STRENGTHEN THEMSELVES. I CAN'T IMAGINE THAT NEET BRIGADE RUNS THAT FAST...
...SAY NO MORE. I DON'T WANT TO HEAR THAT MY HEROES HAVE A DARK SIDE.
HA-HA-HA-HA! WHAT ARE YOU TALKING ABOUT, DAUGHTER?
THAT LETTER WAS JUST TO CATCH YOU UP ON THE LATEST NEWS!

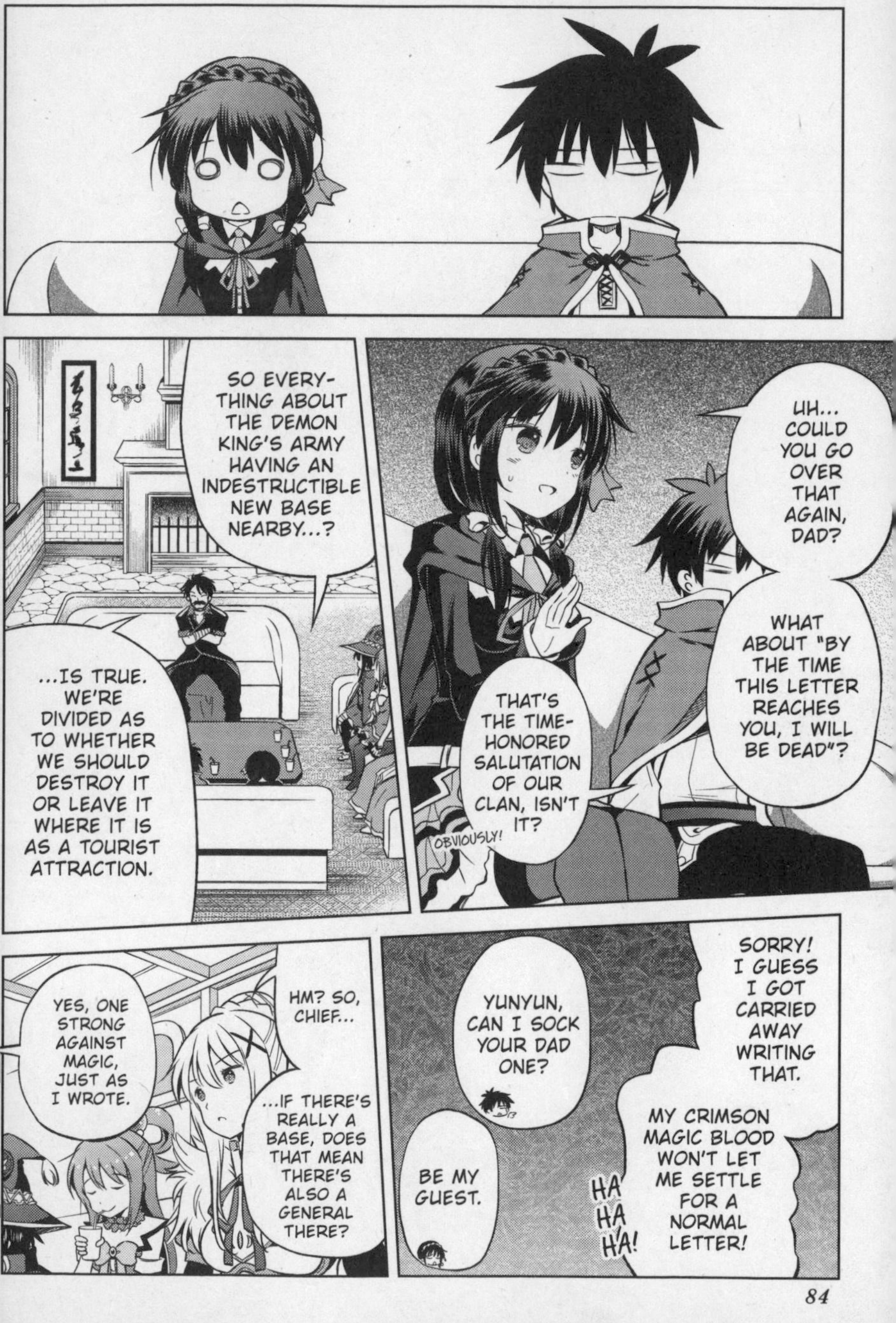
UH... COULD YOU GO OVER THAT AGAIN, DAD?
WHAT ABOUT "BY THE TIME THIS LETTER REACHES YOU, I WILL BE DEAD"?
THAT'S THE TIME-HONORED SALUTATION OF OUR CLAN, ISN'T IT?
OBVIOUSLY!
SO EVERYTHING ABOUT THE DEMON KING'S ARMY HAVING AN INDESTRUCTIBLE NEW BASE NEARBY...?
...IS TRUE. WE'RE DIVIDED AS TO WHETHER WE SHOULD DESTROY IT OR LEAVE IT WHERE IT IS AS A TOURIST ATTRACTION.
SORRY! I GUESS I GOT CARRIED AWAY WRITING THAT.
MY CRIMSON MAGIC BLOOD WON'T LET ME SETTLE FOR A NORMAL LETTER!
HA HA HA!
YUNYUN, CAN I SOCK YOUR DAD ONE?
BE MY GUEST.
HM? SO, CHIEF...
...IF THERE'S REALLY A BASE, DOES THAT MEAN THERE'S ALSO A GENERAL THERE?
YES, ONE STRONG AGAINST MAGIC, JUST AS I WROTE.

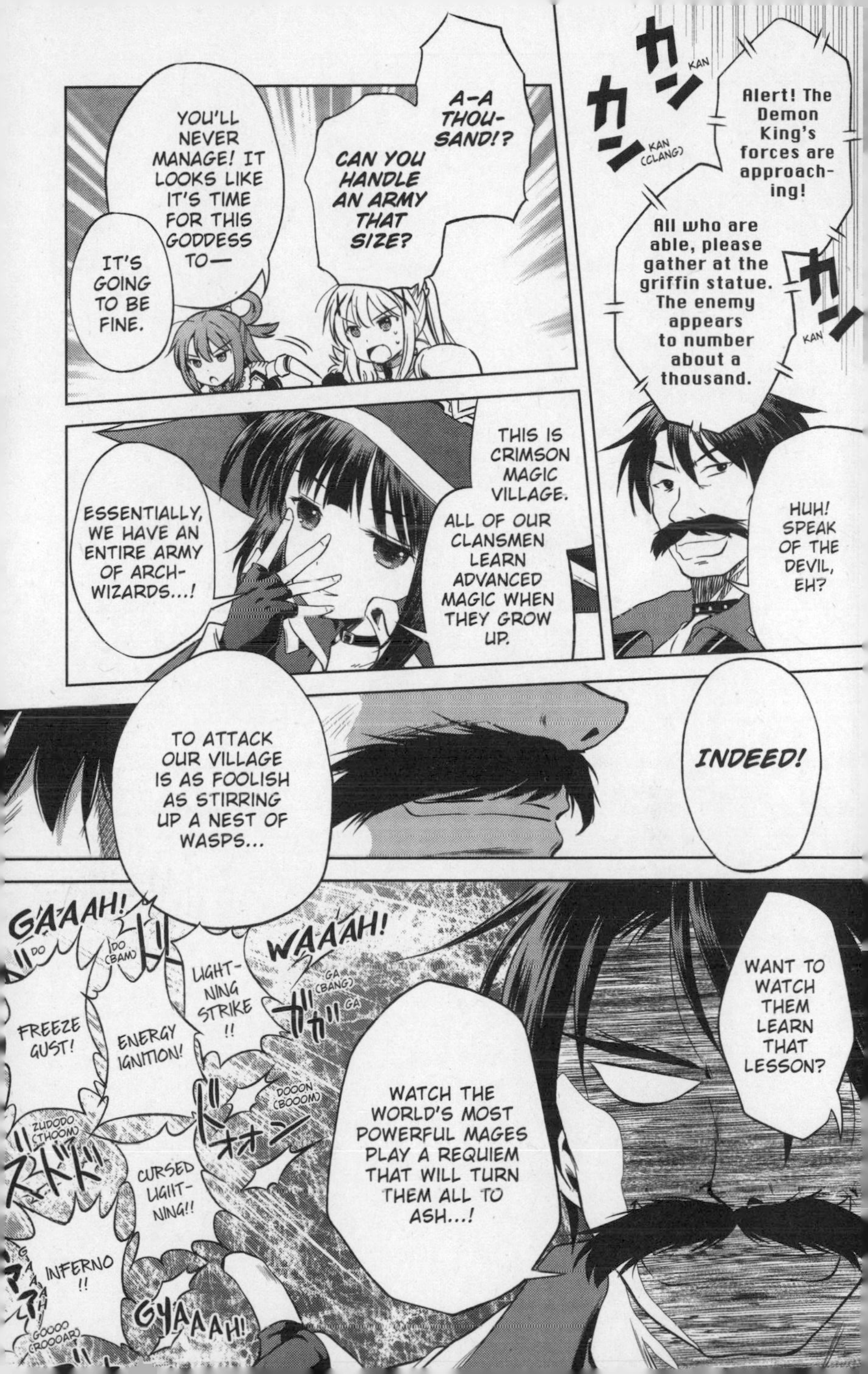
KAN
KAN (CLANG)
Alert! The Demon King's forces are approaching!
All who are able, please gather at the griffin statue. The enemy appears to number about a thousand.
KAN
A-A THOUSAND!?
CAN YOU HANDLE AN ARMY THAT SIZE?
YOU'LL NEVER MANAGE! IT LOOKS LIKE IT'S TIME FOR THIS GODDESS TO—
IT'S GOING TO BE FINE.
HUH! SPEAK OF THE DEVIL, EH?
THIS IS CRIMSON MAGIC VILLAGE.
ALL OF OUR CLANSMEN LEARN ADVANCED MAGIC WHEN THEY GROW UP.
ESSENTIALLY, WE HAVE AN ENTIRE ARMY OF ARCH-WIZARDS...!
INDEED!
TO ATTACK OUR VILLAGE IS AS FOOLISH AS STIRRING UP A NEST OF WASPS...
WANT TO WATCH THEM LEARN THAT LESSON?
WATCH THE WORLD'S MOST POWERFUL MAGES PLAY A REQUIEM THAT WILL TURN THEM ALL TO ASH...!
WAAAH!
GA (BANG) GA
LIGHTNING STRIKE!!
DO (BAM)
GAAAH!
DO
FREEZE GUST!
ENERGY IGNITION!
DOOON (BOOOM)
ZUDODO (THOOM)
CURSED LIGHTNING!!
INFERNO!!
GAAAAH
GYAAAAH!
GOOOO (ROOOAR)

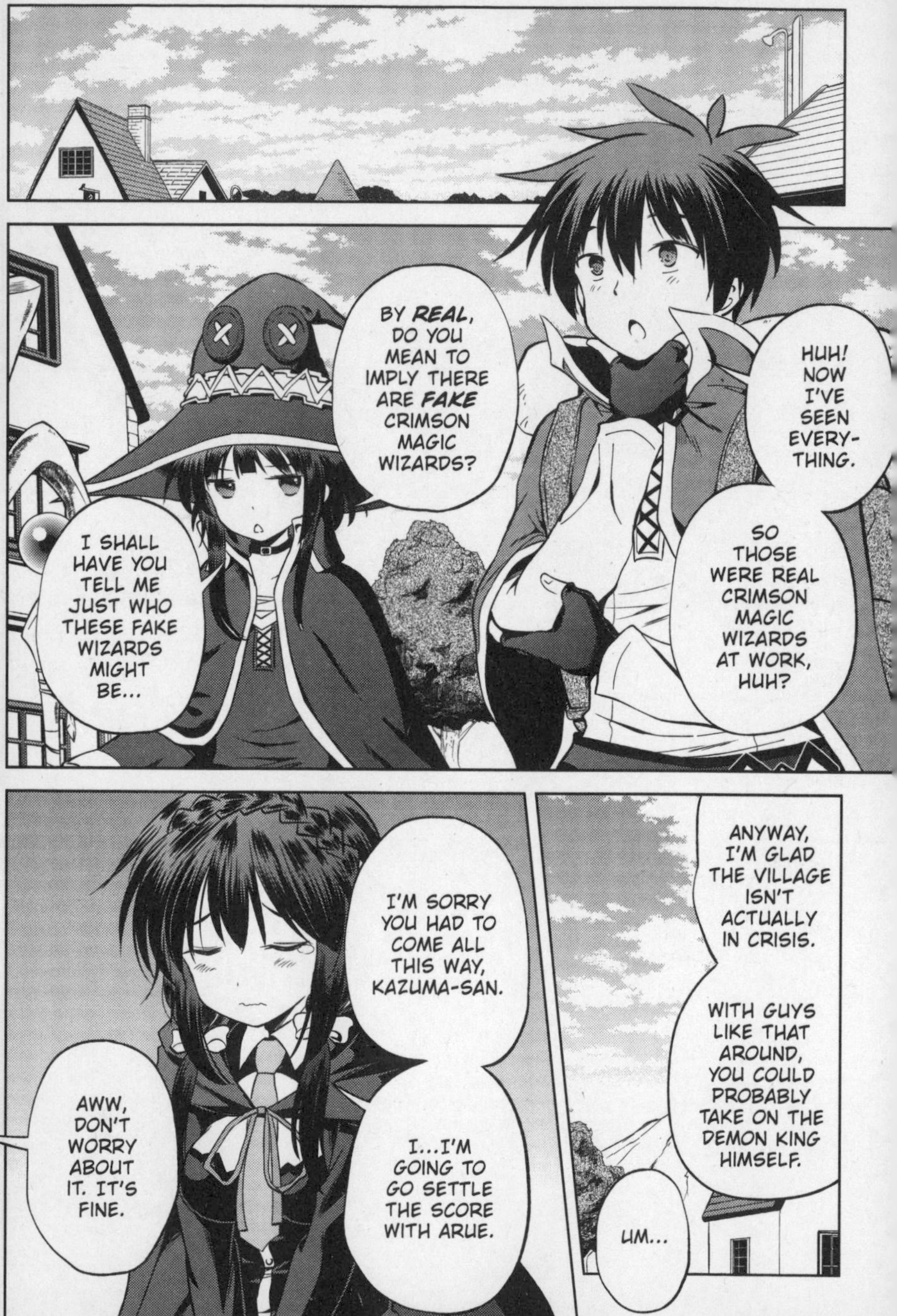
HUH! NOW I'VE SEEN EVERYTHING.
SO THOSE WERE REAL CRIMSON MAGIC WIZARDS AT WORK, HUH?
BY *REAL*, DO YOU MEAN TO IMPLY THERE ARE *FAKE* CRIMSON MAGIC WIZARDS?
I SHALL HAVE YOU TELL ME JUST WHO THESE FAKE WIZARDS MIGHT BE...
ANYWAY, I'M GLAD THE VILLAGE ISN'T ACTUALLY IN CRISIS.
WITH GUYS LIKE THAT AROUND, YOU COULD PROBABLY TAKE ON THE DEMON KING HIMSELF.
UM...
I'M SORRY YOU HAD TO COME ALL THIS WAY, KAZUMA-SAN.
I...I'M GOING TO GO SETTLE THE SCORE WITH ARUE.
AWW, DON'T WORRY ABOUT IT. IT'S FINE.

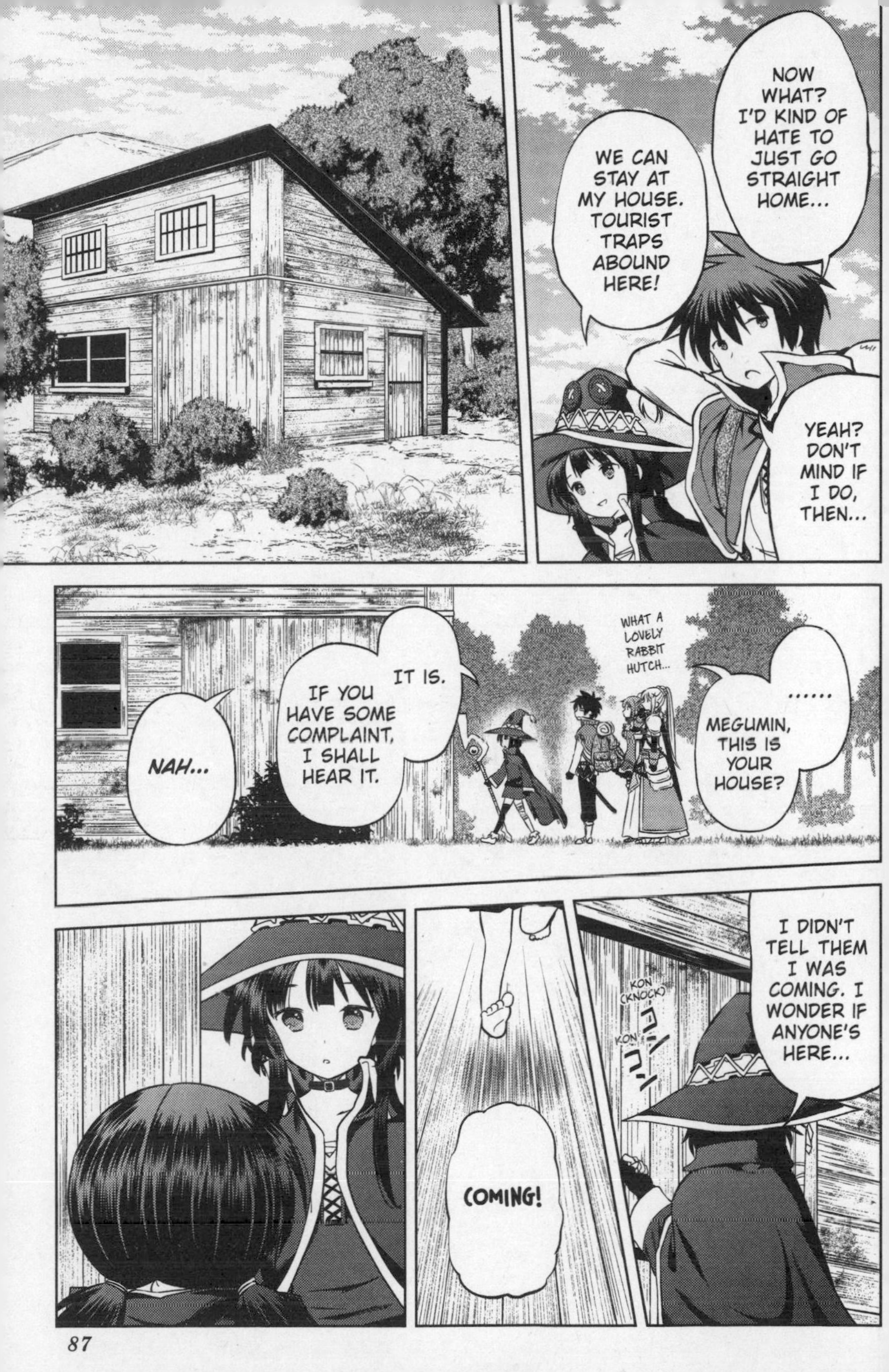
NOW WHAT? I'D KIND OF HATE TO JUST GO STRAIGHT HOME...
WE CAN STAY AT MY HOUSE. TOURIST TRAPS ABOUND HERE!
YEAH? DON'T MIND IF I DO, THEN...
......
MEGUMIN, THIS IS YOUR HOUSE?
WHAT A LOVELY RABBIT HUTCH...
IT IS.
IF YOU HAVE SOME COMPLAINT, I SHALL HEAR IT.
NAH...
I DIDN'T TELL THEM I WAS COMING. I WONDER IF ANYONE'S HERE...
KON (KNOCK)
KON
COMING!

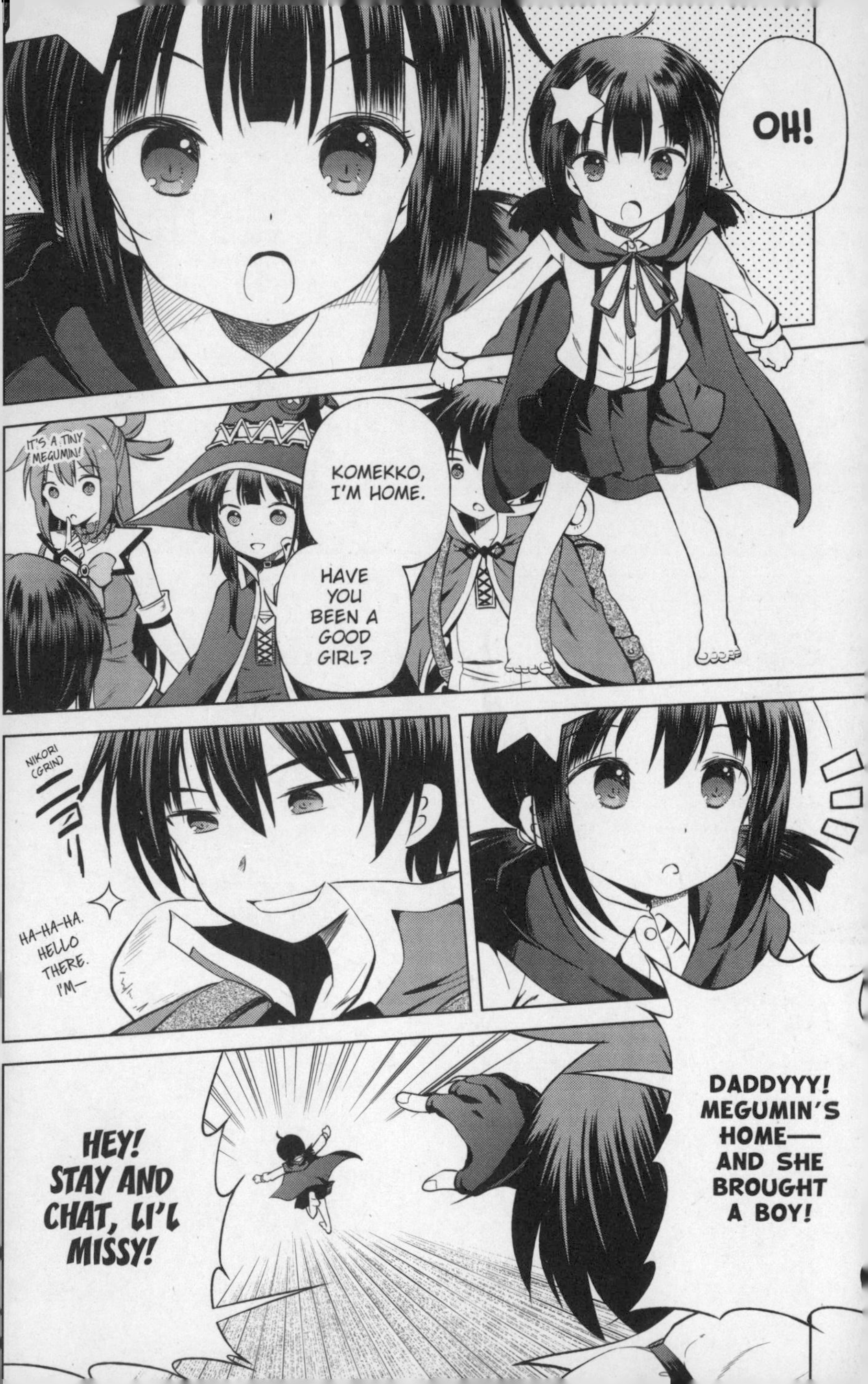
OH!
KOMEKKO, I'M HOME.
HAVE YOU BEEN A GOOD GIRL?
IT'S A TINY MEGUMIN!
NIKORI (GRIN)
HA-HA-HA. HELLO THERE. I'M—
DADDYYY! MEGUMIN'S HOME—AND SHE BROUGHT A BOY!
HEY! STAY AND CHAT, LI'L MISSY!

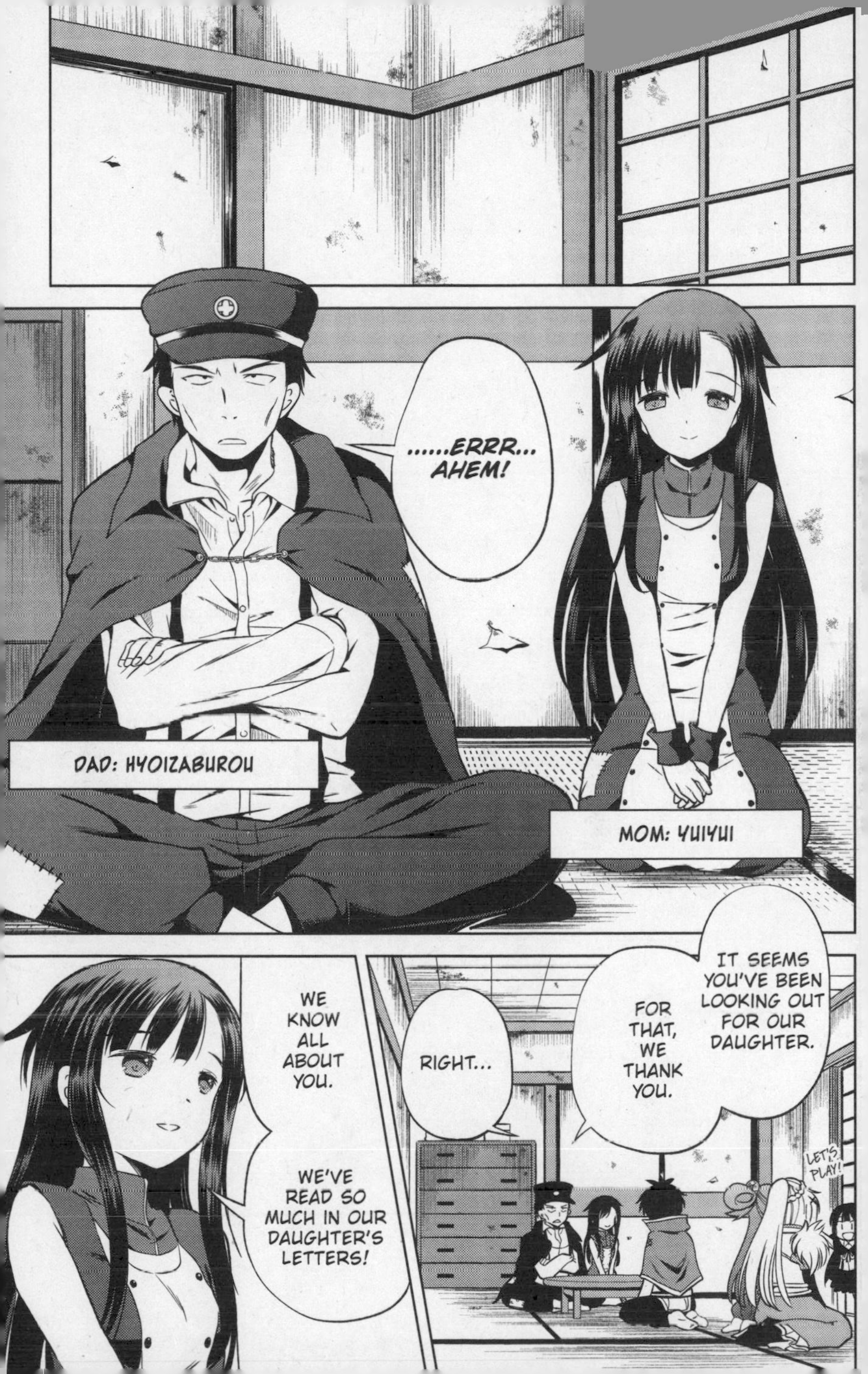
......ERRR... AHEM!
DAD: HYOIZABUROU
MOM: YUIYUI
IT SEEMS YOU'VE BEEN LOOKING OUT FOR OUR DAUGHTER.
FOR THAT, WE THANK YOU.
RIGHT...
LET'S PLAY!
WE KNOW ALL ABOUT YOU.
WE'VE READ SO MUCH IN OUR DAUGHTER'S LETTERS!

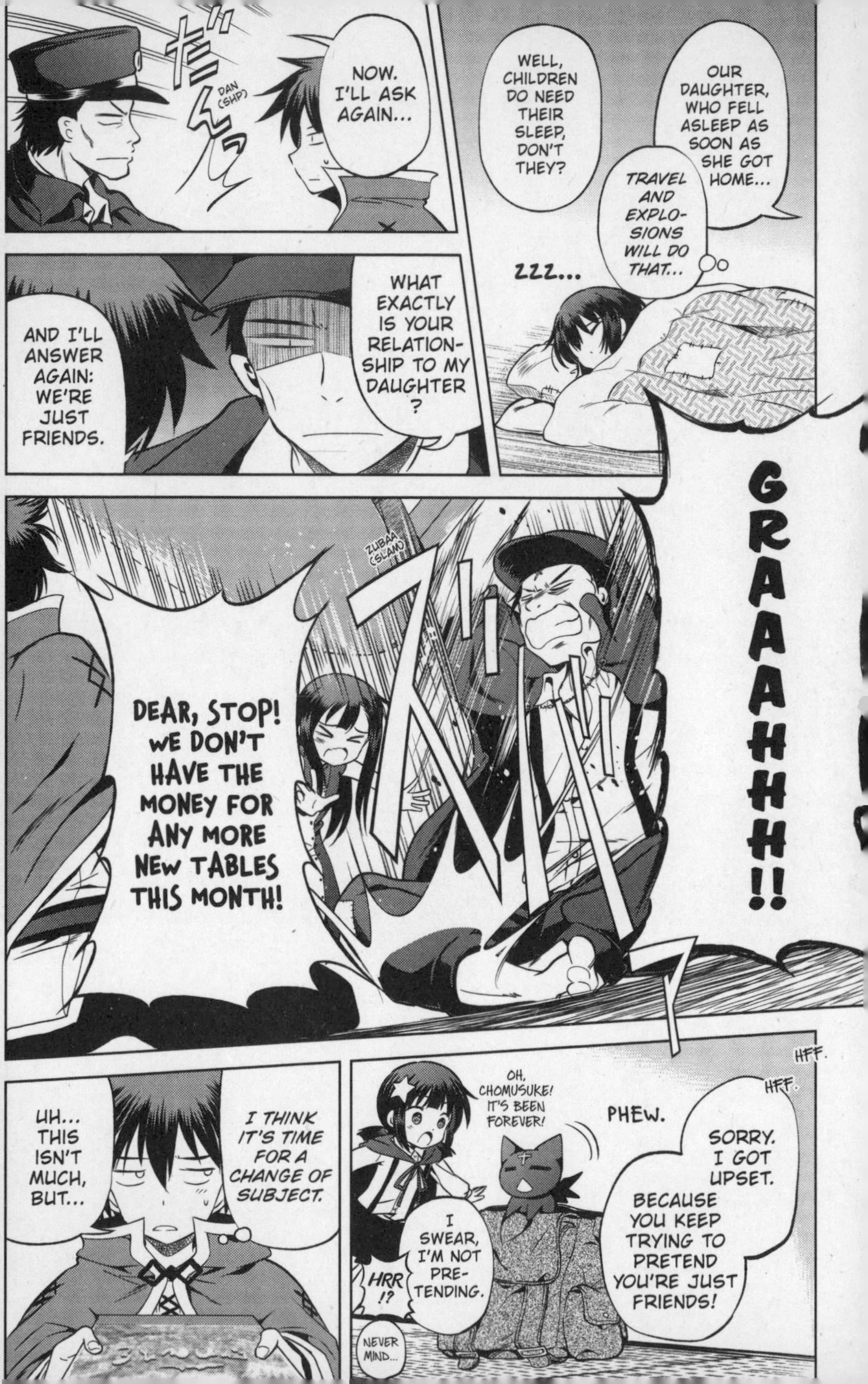
OUR DAUGHTER, WHO FELL ASLEEP AS SOON AS SHE GOT HOME...
WELL, CHILDREN DO NEED THEIR SLEEP, DON'T THEY?
TRAVEL AND EXPLOSIONS WILL DO THAT...
ZZZ...
NOW. I'LL ASK AGAIN...
DAN (SHP)
WHAT EXACTLY IS YOUR RELATIONSHIP TO MY DAUGHTER?
AND I'LL ANSWER AGAIN: WE'RE JUST FRIENDS.
GRAAAHHH!!
ZUBAA (SLAM)
DEAR, STOP! WE DON'T HAVE THE MONEY FOR ANY MORE NEW TABLES THIS MONTH!
HFF.
HFF.
SORRY. I GOT UPSET.
BECAUSE YOU KEEP TRYING TO PRETEND YOU'RE JUST FRIENDS!
PHEW.
OH, CHOMUSUKE! IT'S BEEN FOREVER!
I SWEAR, I'M NOT PRETENDING.
HRR !?
NEVER MIND...
I THINK IT'S TIME FOR A CHANGE OF SUBJECT.
UH... THIS ISN'T MUCH, BUT...

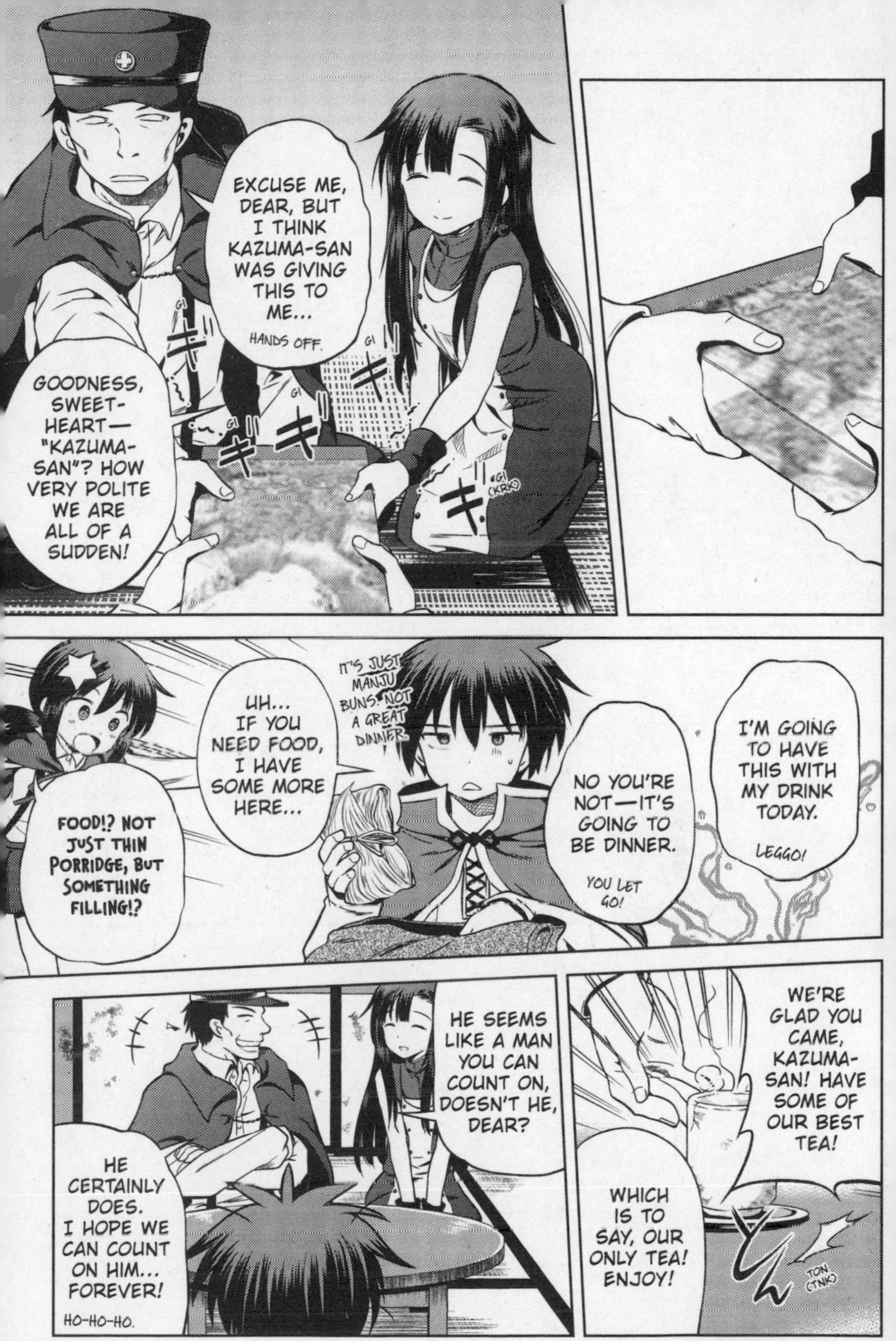
EXCUSE ME, DEAR, BUT I THINK KAZUMA-SAN WAS GIVING THIS TO ME...
HANDS OFF.
GI
GI
GI
GOODNESS, SWEETHEART—"KAZUMA-SAN"? HOW VERY POLITE WE ARE ALL OF A SUDDEN!
GI (KRK)
I'M GOING TO HAVE THIS WITH MY DRINK TODAY.
LEGGO!
NO YOU'RE NOT—IT'S GOING TO BE DINNER.
YOU LET GO!
IT'S JUST MANJU BUNS. NOT A GREAT DINNER.
UH... IF YOU NEED FOOD, I HAVE SOME MORE HERE...
FOOD!? NOT JUST THIN PORRIDGE, BUT SOMETHING FILLING!?
WE'RE GLAD YOU CAME, KAZUMA-SAN! HAVE SOME OF OUR BEST TEA!
WHICH IS TO SAY, OUR ONLY TEA! ENJOY!
TON (TNK)
HE SEEMS LIKE A MAN YOU CAN COUNT ON, DOESN'T HE, DEAR?
HE CERTAINLY DOES. I HOPE WE CAN COUNT ON HIM... FOREVER!
HO-HO-HO.

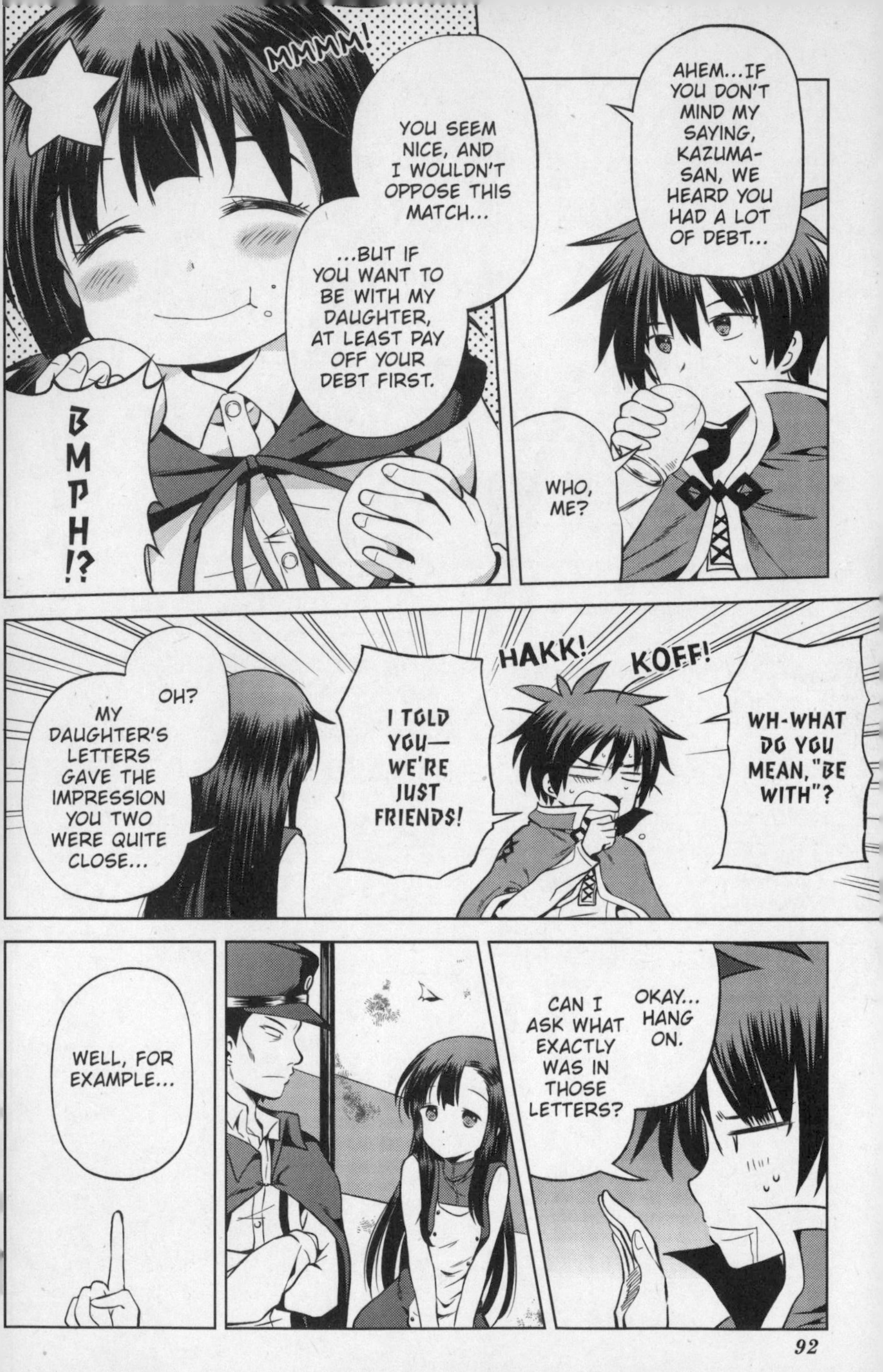
AHEM...IF YOU DON'T MIND MY SAYING, KAZUMA-SAN, WE HEARD YOU HAD A LOT OF DEBT...
WHO, ME?
MMMM!
YOU SEEM NICE, AND I WOULDN'T OPPOSE THIS MATCH...
...BUT IF YOU WANT TO BE WITH MY DAUGHTER, AT LEAST PAY OFF YOUR DEBT FIRST.
BMPH!?
WH-WHAT DO YOU MEAN, "BE WITH"?
KOFF!
HAKK!
I TOLD YOU—WE'RE JUST FRIENDS!
OH? MY DAUGHTER'S LETTERS GAVE THE IMPRESSION YOU TWO WERE QUITE CLOSE...
OKAY... HANG ON.
CAN I ASK WHAT EXACTLY WAS IN THOSE LETTERS?
WELL, FOR EXAMPLE...

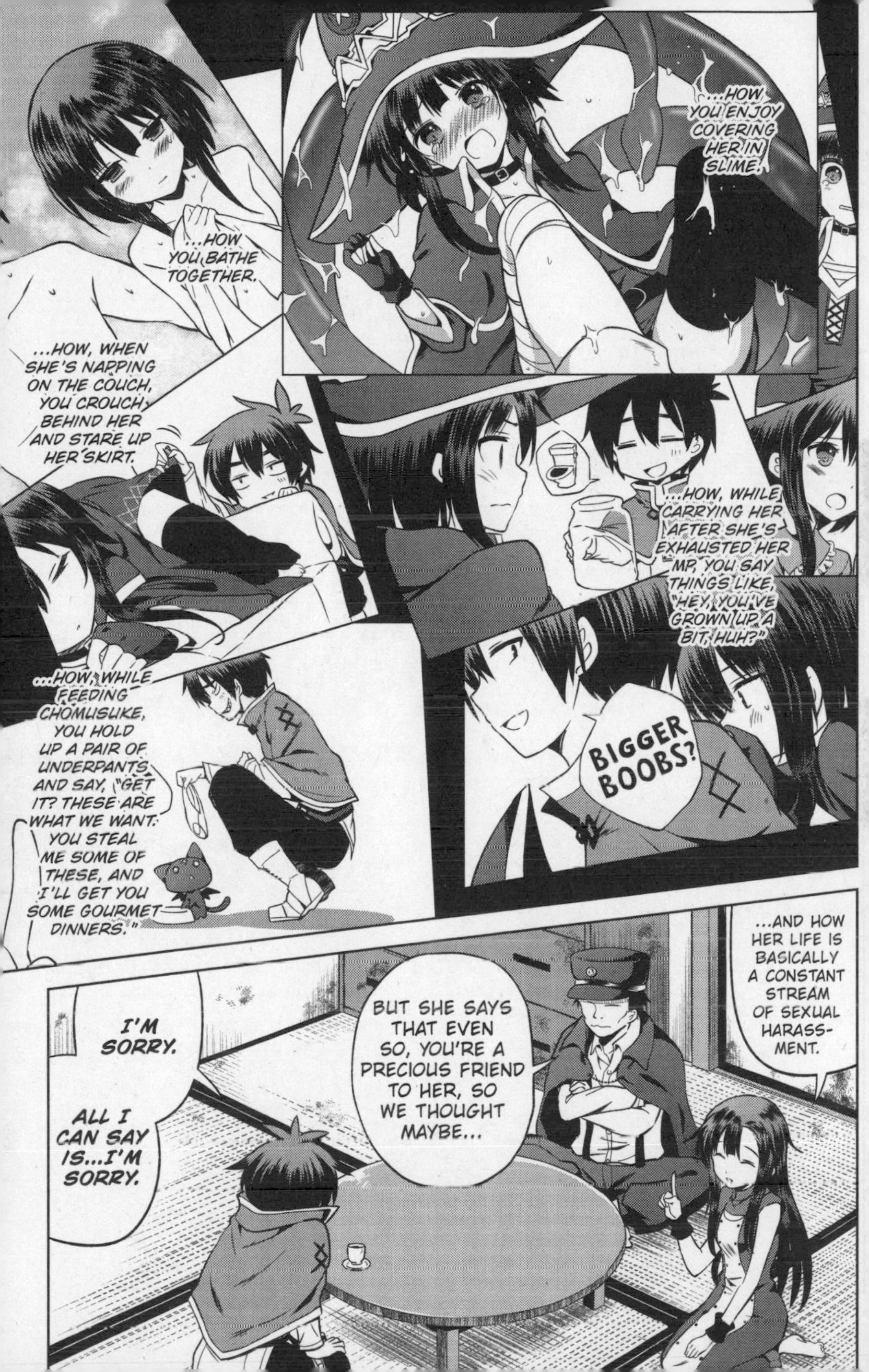
...HOW YOU ENJOY COVERING HER IN SLIME.
...HOW YOU BATHE TOGETHER.
...HOW, WHILE CARRYING HER AFTER SHE'S EXHAUSTED HER MP, YOU SAY THINGS LIKE, "HEY, YOU'VE GROWN UP A BIT, HUH?"
BIGGER BOOBS?
...HOW, WHEN SHE'S NAPPING ON THE COUCH, YOU CROUCH BEHIND HER AND STARE UP HER SKIRT.
...HOW, WHILE FEEDING CHOMUSUKE, YOU HOLD UP A PAIR OF UNDERPANTS AND SAY, "GET IT? THESE ARE WHAT WE WANT. YOU STEAL ME SOME OF THESE, AND I'LL GET YOU SOME GOURMET DINNERS."
...AND HOW HER LIFE IS BASICALLY A CONSTANT STREAM OF SEXUAL HARASS-MENT.
BUT SHE SAYS THAT EVEN SO, YOU'RE A PRECIOUS FRIEND TO HER, SO WE THOUGHT MAYBE...
I'M SORRY.
ALL I CAN SAY IS...I'M SORRY.

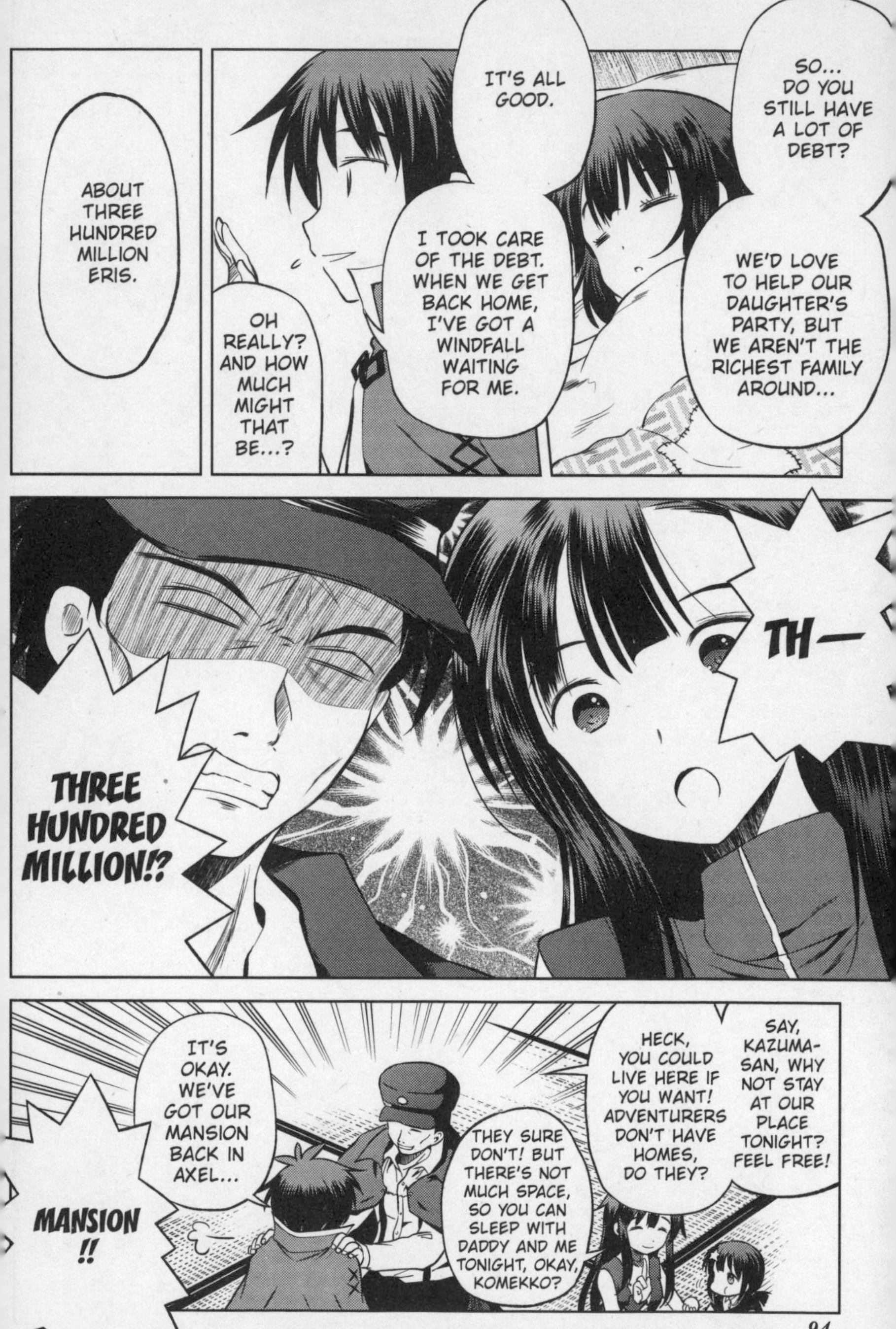
SO... DO YOU STILL HAVE A LOT OF DEBT?
WE'D LOVE TO HELP OUR DAUGHTER'S PARTY, BUT WE AREN'T THE RICHEST FAMILY AROUND...
IT'S ALL GOOD.
I TOOK CARE OF THE DEBT. WHEN WE GET BACK HOME, I'VE GOT A WINDFALL WAITING FOR ME.
OH REALLY? AND HOW MUCH MIGHT THAT BE...?
ABOUT THREE HUNDRED MILLION ERIS.
TH—
THREE HUNDRED MILLION!?
SAY, KAZUMA-SAN, WHY NOT STAY AT OUR PLACE TONIGHT? FEEL FREE!
HECK, YOU COULD LIVE HERE IF YOU WANT! ADVENTURERS DON'T HAVE HOMES, DO THEY?
THEY SURE DON'T! BUT THERE'S NOT MUCH SPACE, SO YOU CAN SLEEP WITH DADDY AND ME TONIGHT, OKAY, KOMEKKO?
IT'S OKAY. WE'VE GOT OUR MANSION BACK IN AXEL...
MANSION!!

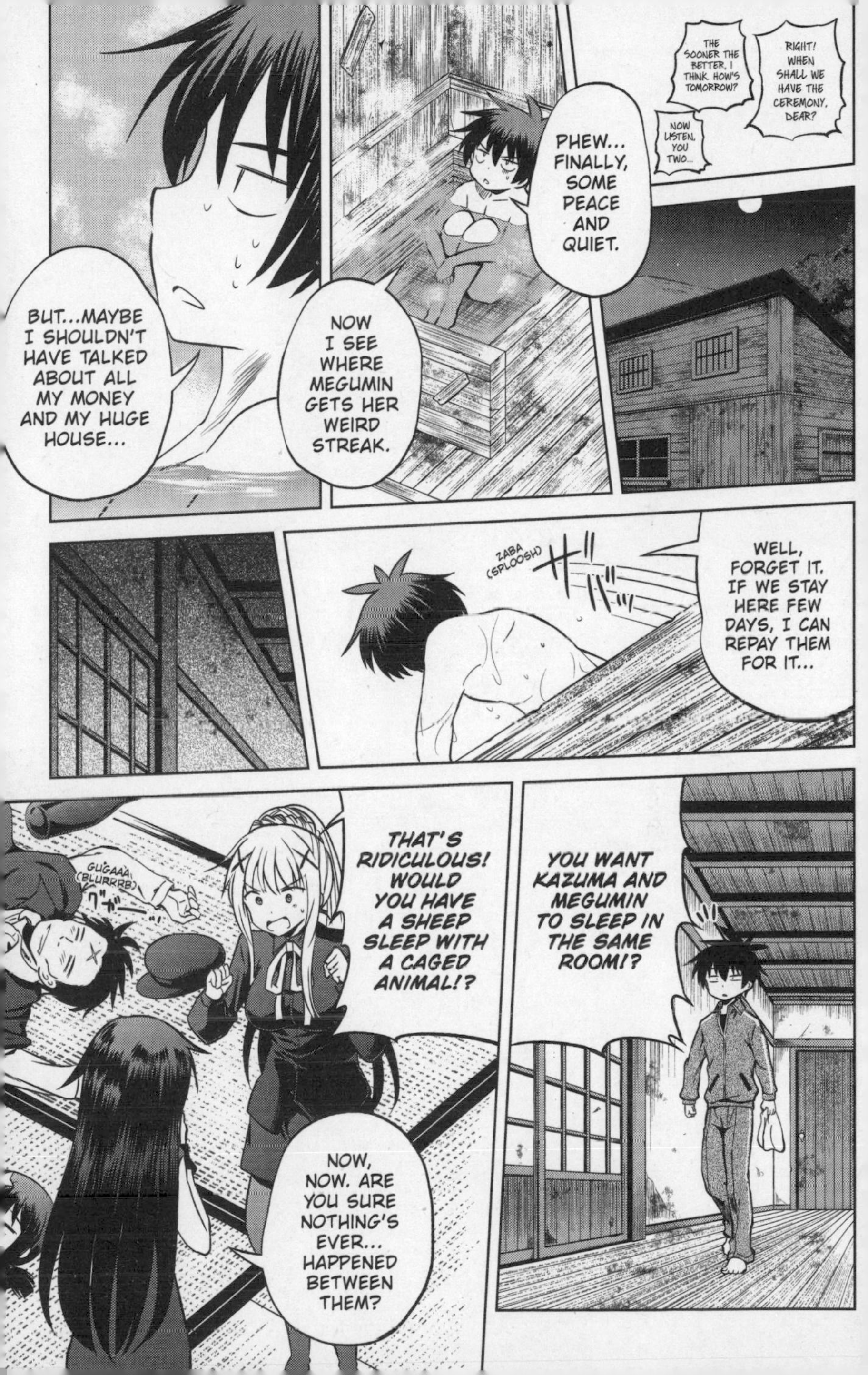
RIGHT! WHEN SHALL WE HAVE THE CEREMONY, DEAR?
THE SOONER THE BETTER, I THINK. HOW'S TOMORROW?
NOW LISTEN, YOU TWO...
PHEW... FINALLY, SOME PEACE AND QUIET.
NOW I SEE WHERE MEGUMIN GETS HER WEIRD STREAK.
BUT...MAYBE I SHOULDN'T HAVE TALKED ABOUT ALL MY MONEY AND MY HUGE HOUSE...
ZABA (SPLOOSH)
WELL, FORGET IT. IF WE STAY HERE FEW DAYS, I CAN REPAY THEM FOR IT...
YOU WANT KAZUMA AND MEGUMIN TO SLEEP IN THE SAME ROOM!?
THAT'S RIDICULOUS! WOULD YOU HAVE A SHEEP SLEEP WITH A CAGED ANIMAL!?
GUGAAA (BLURRRB)
NOW, NOW. ARE YOU SURE NOTHING'S EVER... HAPPENED BETWEEN THEM?

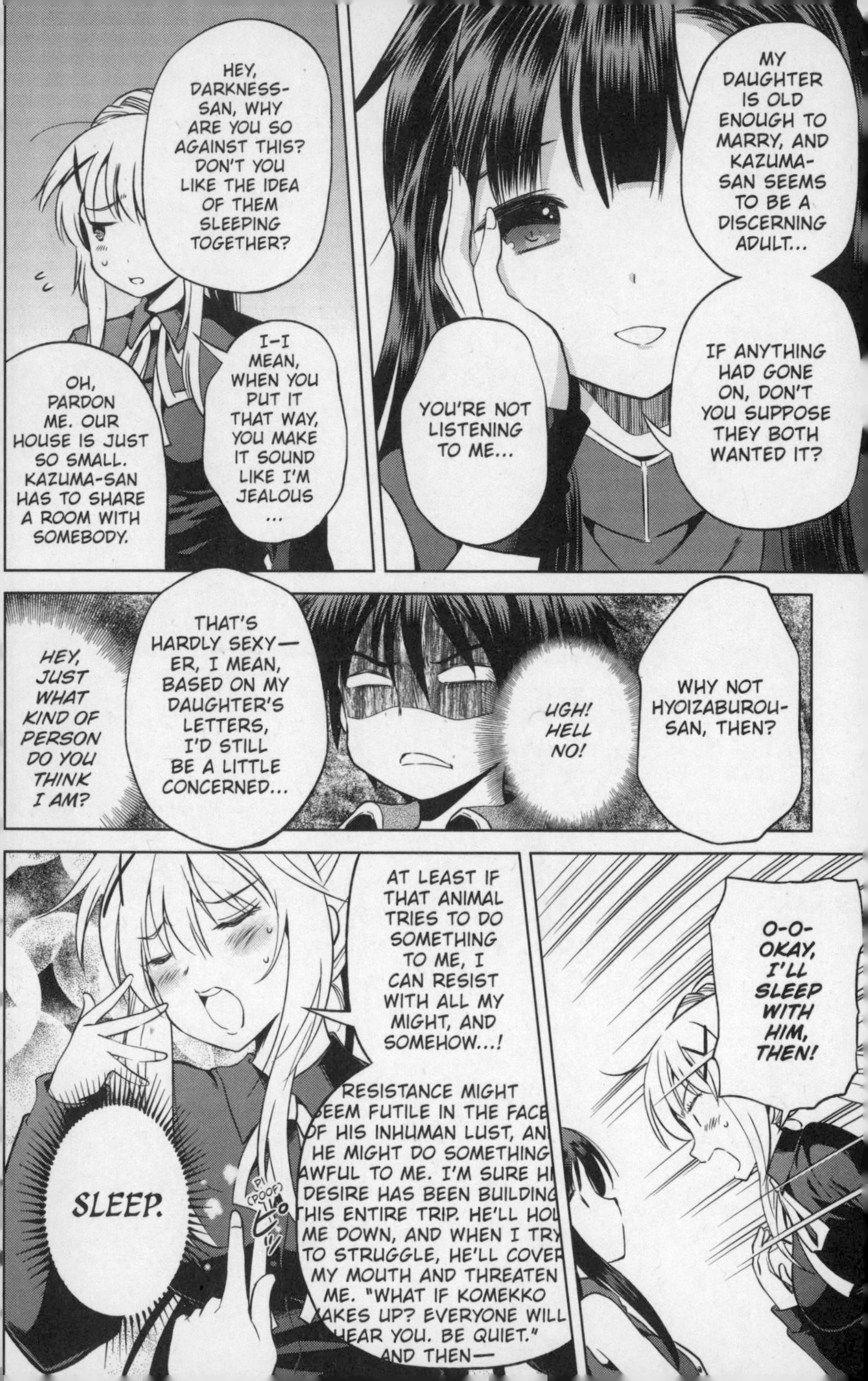
MY DAUGHTER IS OLD ENOUGH TO MARRY, AND KAZUMA-SAN SEEMS TO BE A DISCERNING ADULT...
IF ANYTHING HAD GONE ON, DON'T YOU SUPPOSE THEY BOTH WANTED IT?
YOU'RE NOT LISTENING TO ME...
HEY, DARKNESS-SAN, WHY ARE YOU SO AGAINST THIS? DON'T YOU LIKE THE IDEA OF THEM SLEEPING TOGETHER?
I-I MEAN, WHEN YOU PUT IT THAT WAY, YOU MAKE IT SOUND LIKE I'M JEALOUS...
OH, PARDON ME. OUR HOUSE IS JUST SO SMALL. KAZUMA-SAN HAS TO SHARE A ROOM WITH SOMEBODY.
WHY NOT HYOIZABUROU-SAN, THEN?
UGH! HELL NO!
THAT'S HARDLY SEXY— ER, I MEAN, BASED ON MY DAUGHTER'S LETTERS, I'D STILL BE A LITTLE CONCERNED...
HEY, JUST WHAT KIND OF PERSON DO YOU THINK I AM?
O-O-OKAY, I'LL SLEEP WITH HIM, THEN!
AT LEAST IF THAT ANIMAL TRIES TO DO SOMETHING TO ME, I CAN RESIST WITH ALL MY MIGHT, AND SOMEHOW...!
RESISTANCE MIGHT SEEM FUTILE IN THE FACE OF HIS INHUMAN LUST, AND HE MIGHT DO SOMETHING AWFUL TO ME. I'M SURE HIS DESIRE HAS BEEN BUILDING THIS ENTIRE TRIP. HE'LL HOLD ME DOWN, AND WHEN I TRY TO STRUGGLE, HE'LL COVER MY MOUTH AND THREATEN ME. "WHAT IF KOMEKKO WAKES UP? EVERYONE WILL HEAR YOU. BE QUIET." AND THEN—
PI (POOF)
SLEEP.

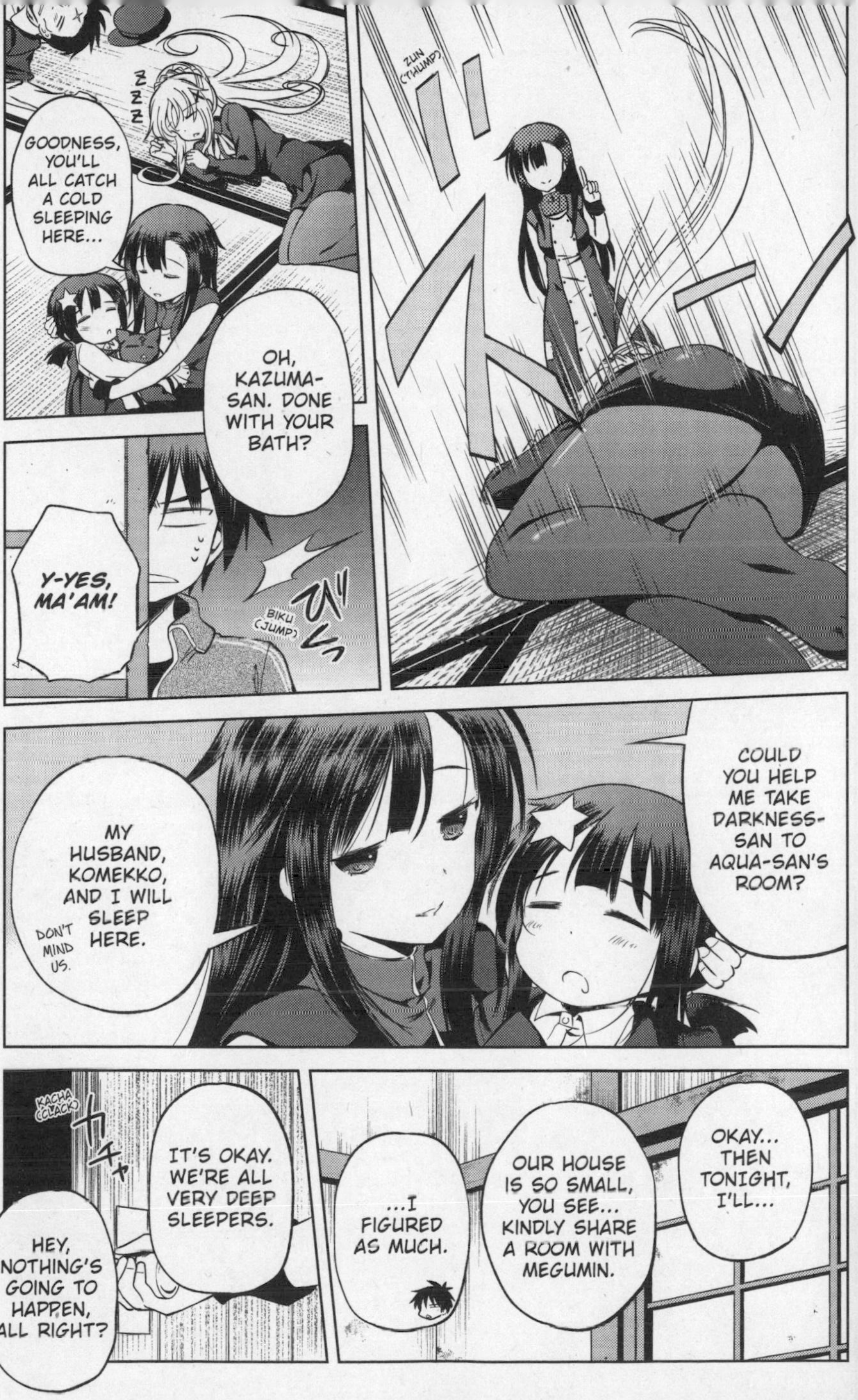
ZUN (THUMP)
ZZZ
GOODNESS, YOU'LL ALL CATCH A COLD SLEEPING HERE...
OH, KAZUMA-SAN. DONE WITH YOUR BATH?
Y-YES, MA'AM!
BIKU (JUMP)
COULD YOU HELP ME TAKE DARKNESS-SAN TO AQUA-SAN'S ROOM?
MY HUSBAND, KOMEKKO, AND I WILL SLEEP HERE.
DON'T MIND US.
OKAY... THEN TONIGHT, I'LL...
OUR HOUSE IS SO SMALL, YOU SEE... KINDLY SHARE A ROOM WITH MEGUMIN.
...I FIGURED AS MUCH.
KACHA (CLACK)
IT'S OKAY. WE'RE ALL VERY DEEP SLEEPERS.
HEY, NOTHING'S GOING TO HAPPEN, ALL RIGHT?

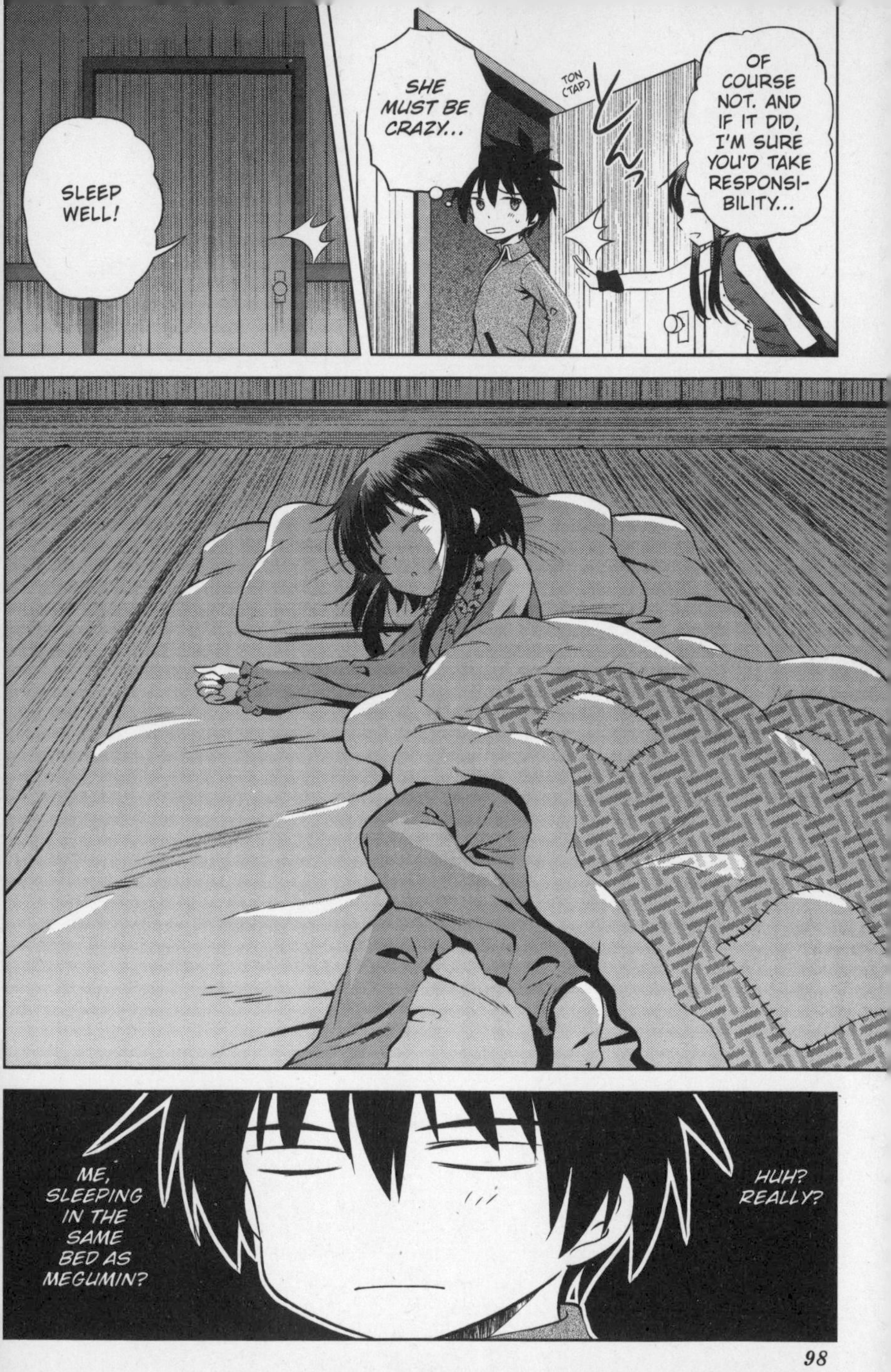
OF COURSE NOT. AND IF IT DID, I'M SURE YOU'D TAKE RESPONSI-BILITY...
TON (TAP)
SHE MUST BE CRAZY...
SLEEP WELL!
HUH? REALLY?
ME, SLEEPING IN THE SAME BED AS MEGUMIN?

GOD'S
BLESSING
ON THIS
WONDERFUL
WORLD!

8

8

GOD'S
BLESSING
ON THIS
WONDERFUL
WORLD!

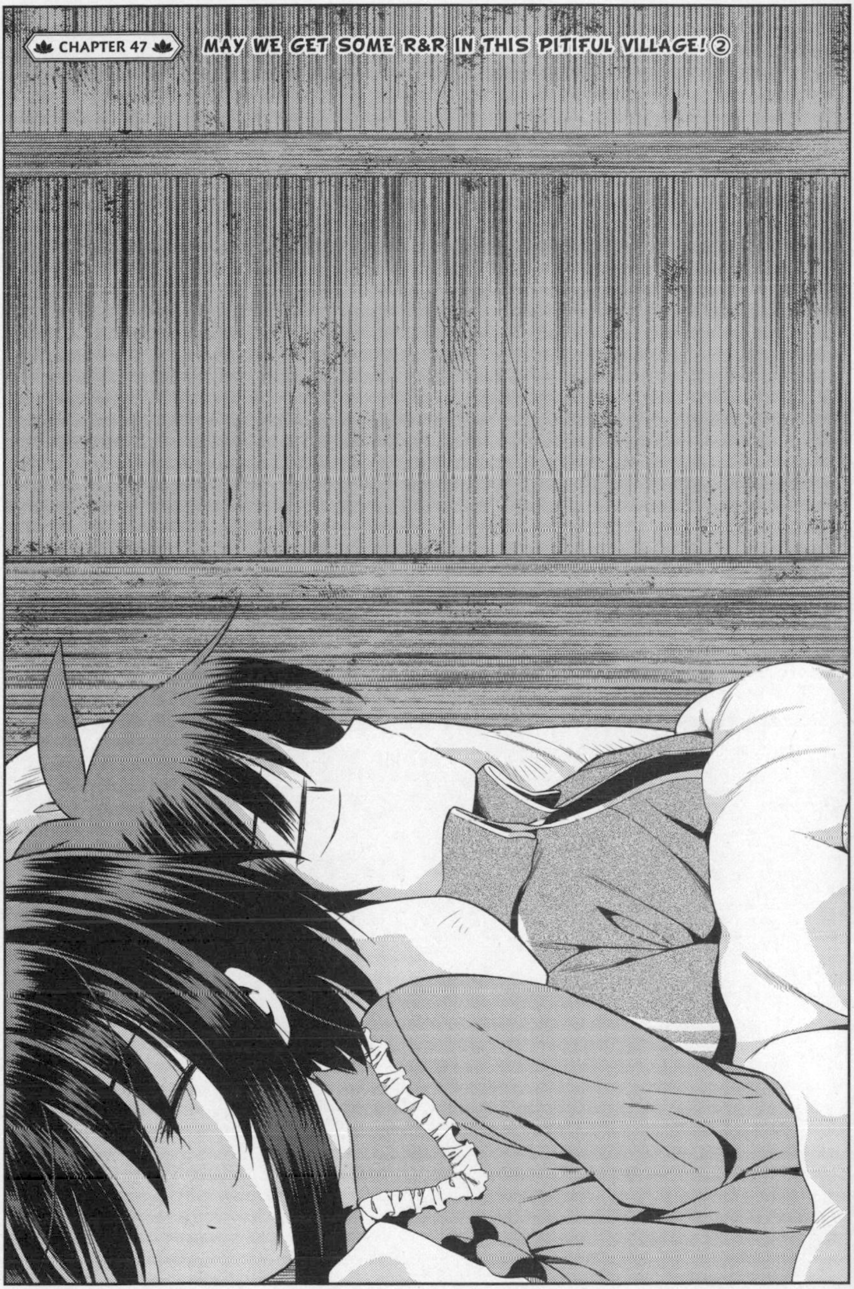
CHAPTER 47
MAY WE GET SOME R&R IN THIS PITIFUL VILLAGE! ②

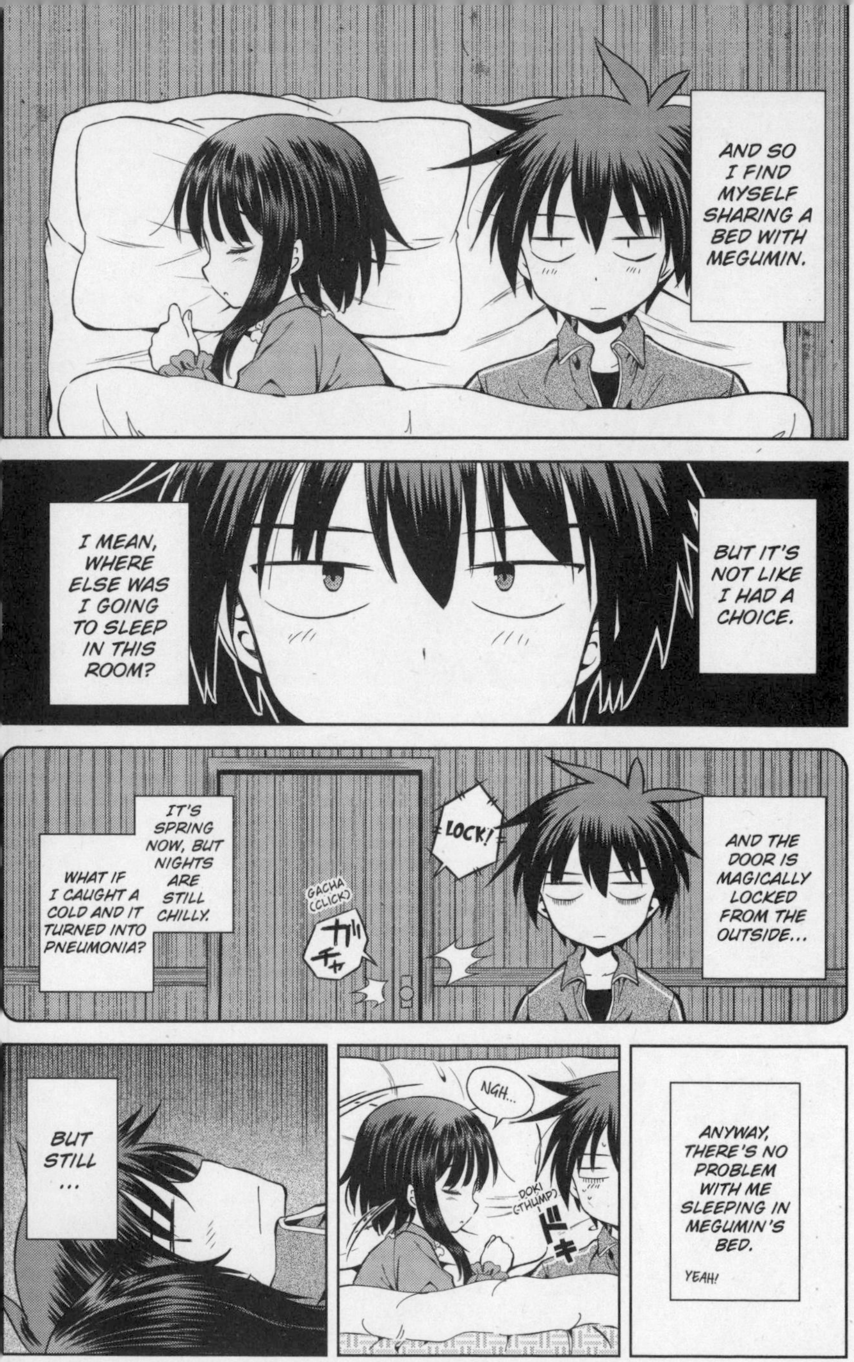
AND SO I FIND MYSELF SHARING A BED WITH MEGUMIN.
BUT IT'S NOT LIKE I HAD A CHOICE.
I MEAN, WHERE ELSE WAS I GOING TO SLEEP IN THIS ROOM?
AND THE DOOR IS MAGICALLY LOCKED FROM THE OUTSIDE...
LOCK!
GACHA (CLICK)
ガチャ
IT'S SPRING NOW, BUT NIGHTS ARE STILL CHILLY.
WHAT IF I CAUGHT A COLD AND IT TURNED INTO PNEUMONIA?
ANYWAY, THERE'S NO PROBLEM WITH ME SLEEPING IN MEGUMIN'S BED.
YEAH!
NGH...
DOKI (THUMP)
ドキ
BUT STILL ...

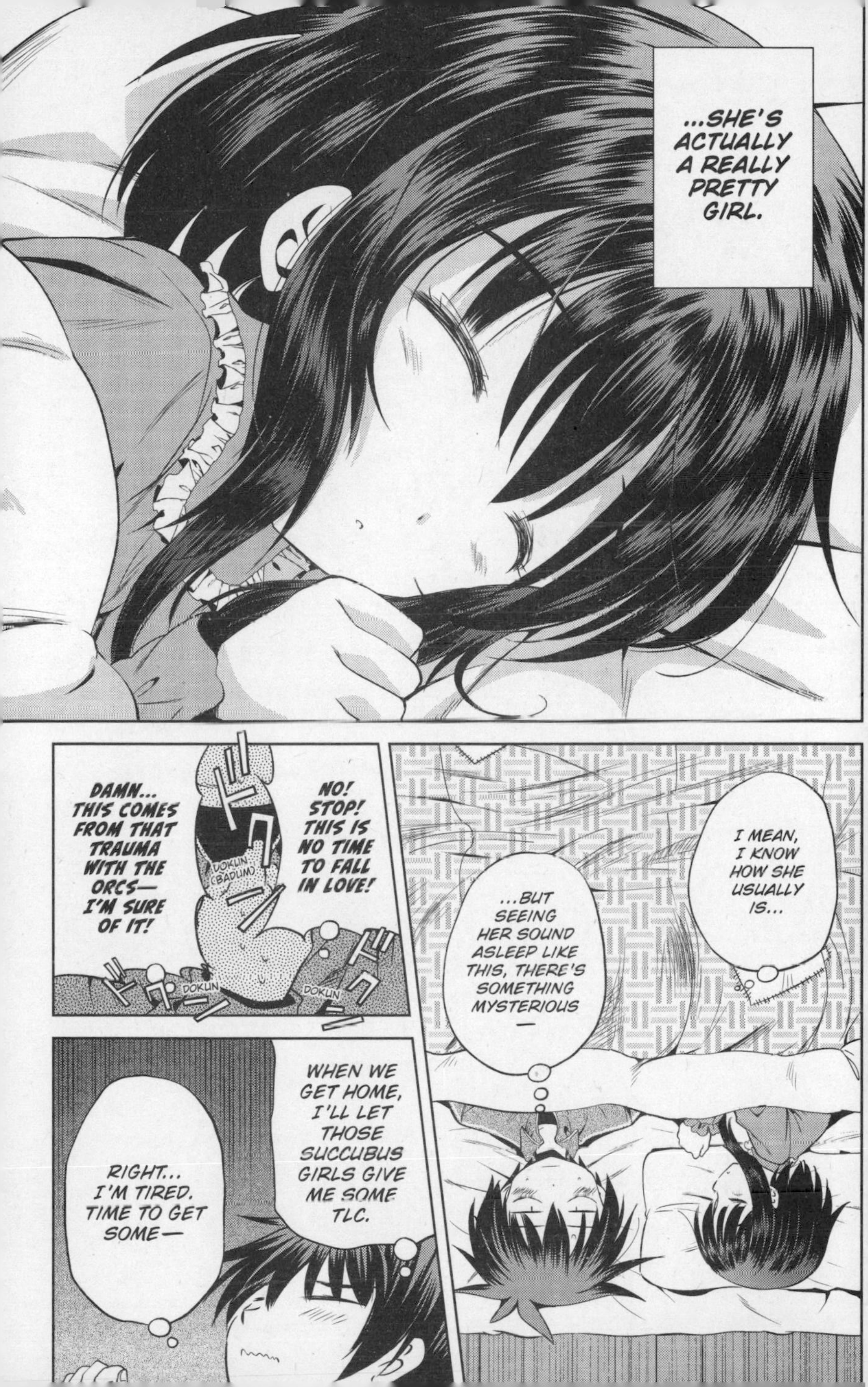

...SHE'S ACTUALLY A REALLY PRETTY GIRL.
I MEAN, I KNOW HOW SHE USUALLY IS...
...BUT SEEING HER SOUND ASLEEP LIKE THIS, THERE'S SOMETHING MYSTERIOUS—
NO! STOP! THIS IS NO TIME TO FALL IN LOVE!
DAMN... THIS COMES FROM THAT TRAUMA WITH THE ORCS— I'M SURE OF IT!
DOKUN (BADUM)
DOKUN
DOKUN
WHEN WE GET HOME, I'LL LET THOSE SUCCUBUS GIRLS GIVE ME SOME TLC.
RIGHT... I'M TIRED. TIME TO GET SOME—

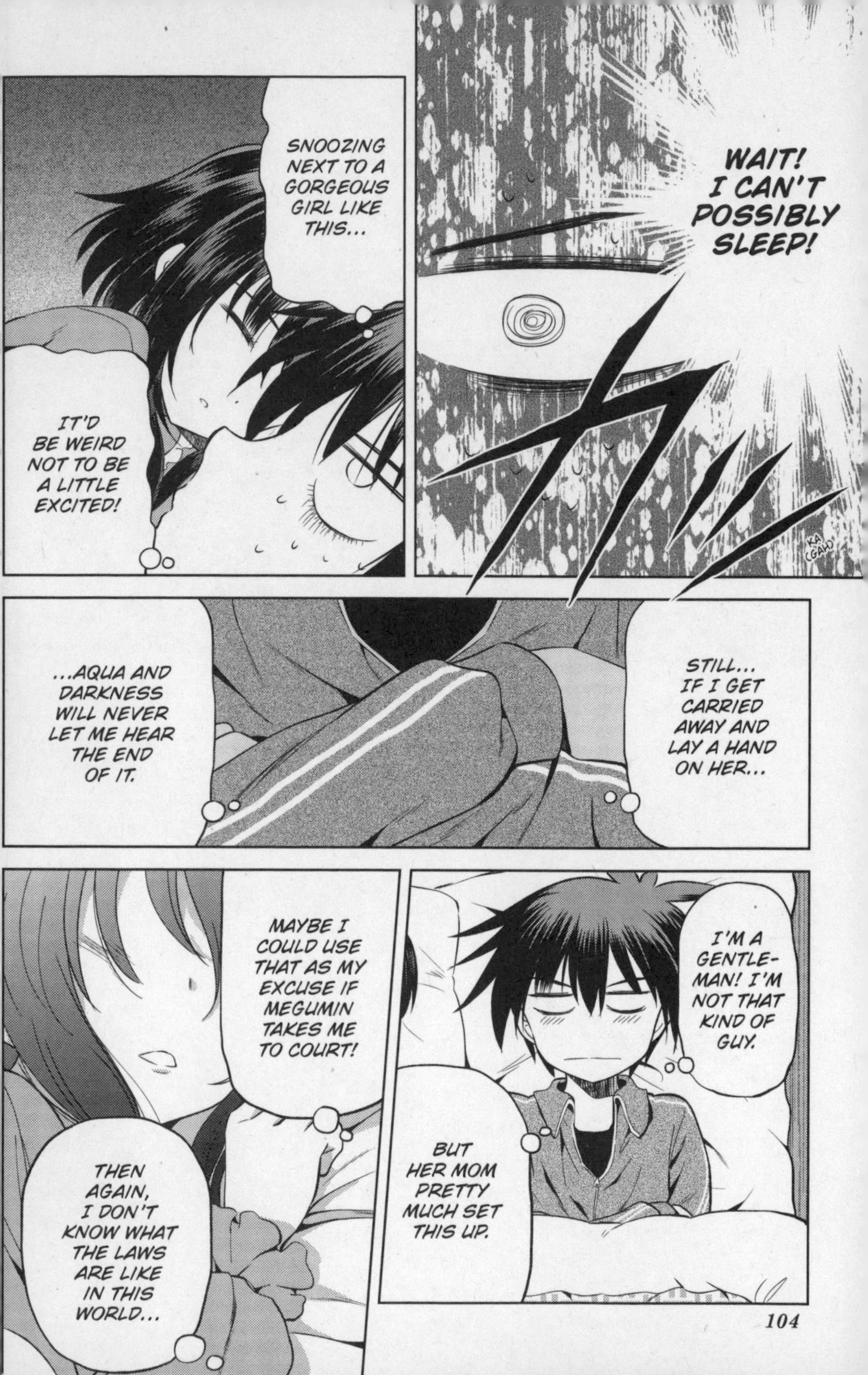

WAIT! I CAN'T POSSIBLY SLEEP!
KA (GAH)
SNOOZING NEXT TO A GORGEOUS GIRL LIKE THIS...
IT'D BE WEIRD NOT TO BE A LITTLE EXCITED!
STILL... IF I GET CARRIED AWAY AND LAY A HAND ON HER...
...AQUA AND DARKNESS WILL NEVER LET ME HEAR THE END OF IT.
I'M A GENTLE-MAN! I'M NOT THAT KIND OF GUY.
BUT HER MOM PRETTY MUCH SET THIS UP.
MAYBE I COULD USE THAT AS MY EXCUSE IF MEGUMIN TAKES ME TO COURT!
THEN AGAIN, I DON'T KNOW WHAT THE LAWS ARE LIKE IN THIS WORLD...

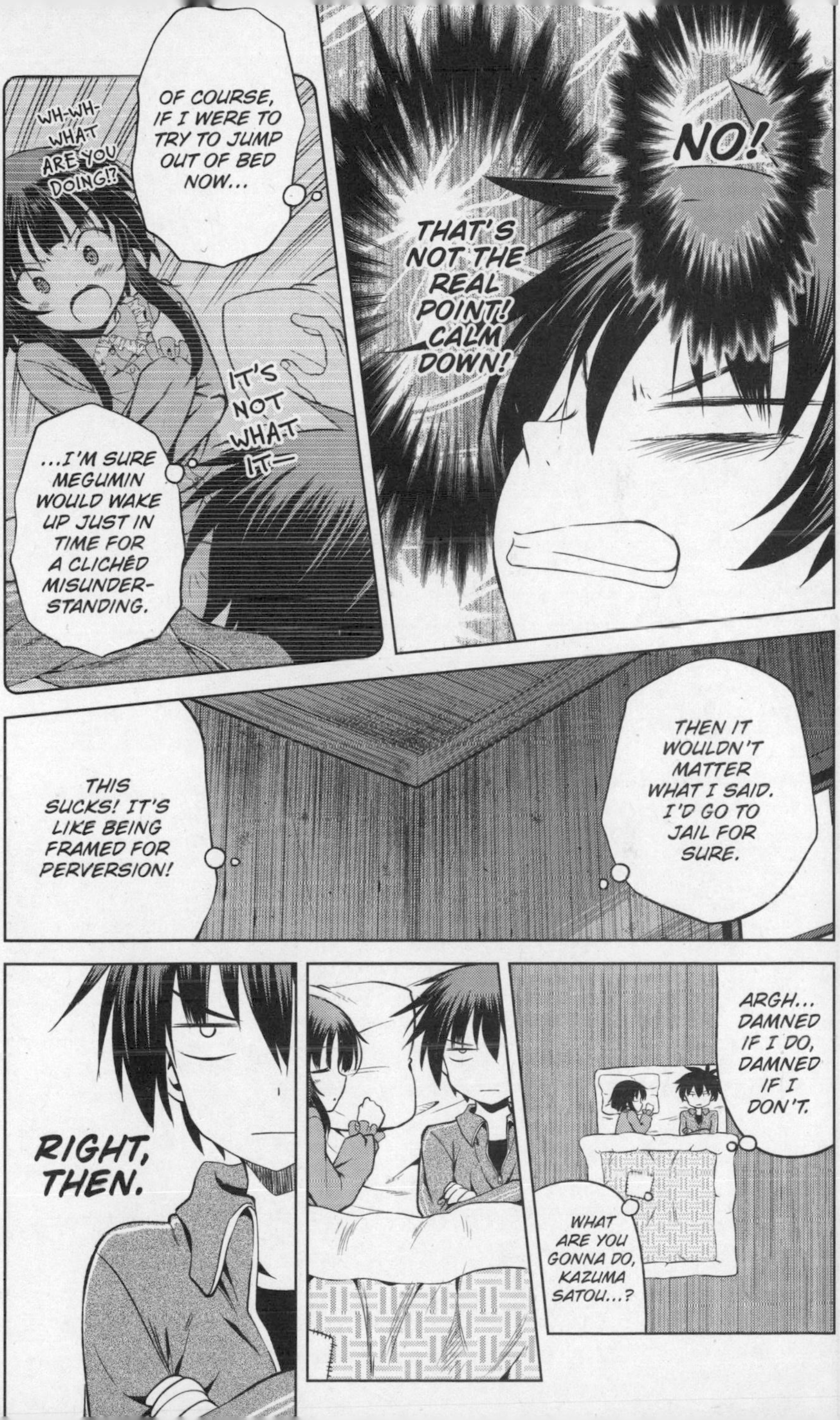
NO!
THAT'S NOT THE REAL POINT! CALM DOWN!
OF COURSE, IF I WERE TO TRY TO JUMP OUT OF BED NOW...
WH-WH-WHAT ARE YOU DOING!?
IT'S NOT WHAT IT—
...I'M SURE MEGUMIN WOULD WAKE UP JUST IN TIME FOR A CLICHÉD MISUNDER-STANDING.
THEN IT WOULDN'T MATTER WHAT I SAID. I'D GO TO JAIL FOR SURE.
THIS SUCKS! IT'S LIKE BEING FRAMED FOR PERVERSION!
ARGH... DAMNED IF I DO, DAMNED IF I DON'T.
WHAT ARE YOU GONNA DO, KAZUMA SATOU...?
RIGHT, THEN.

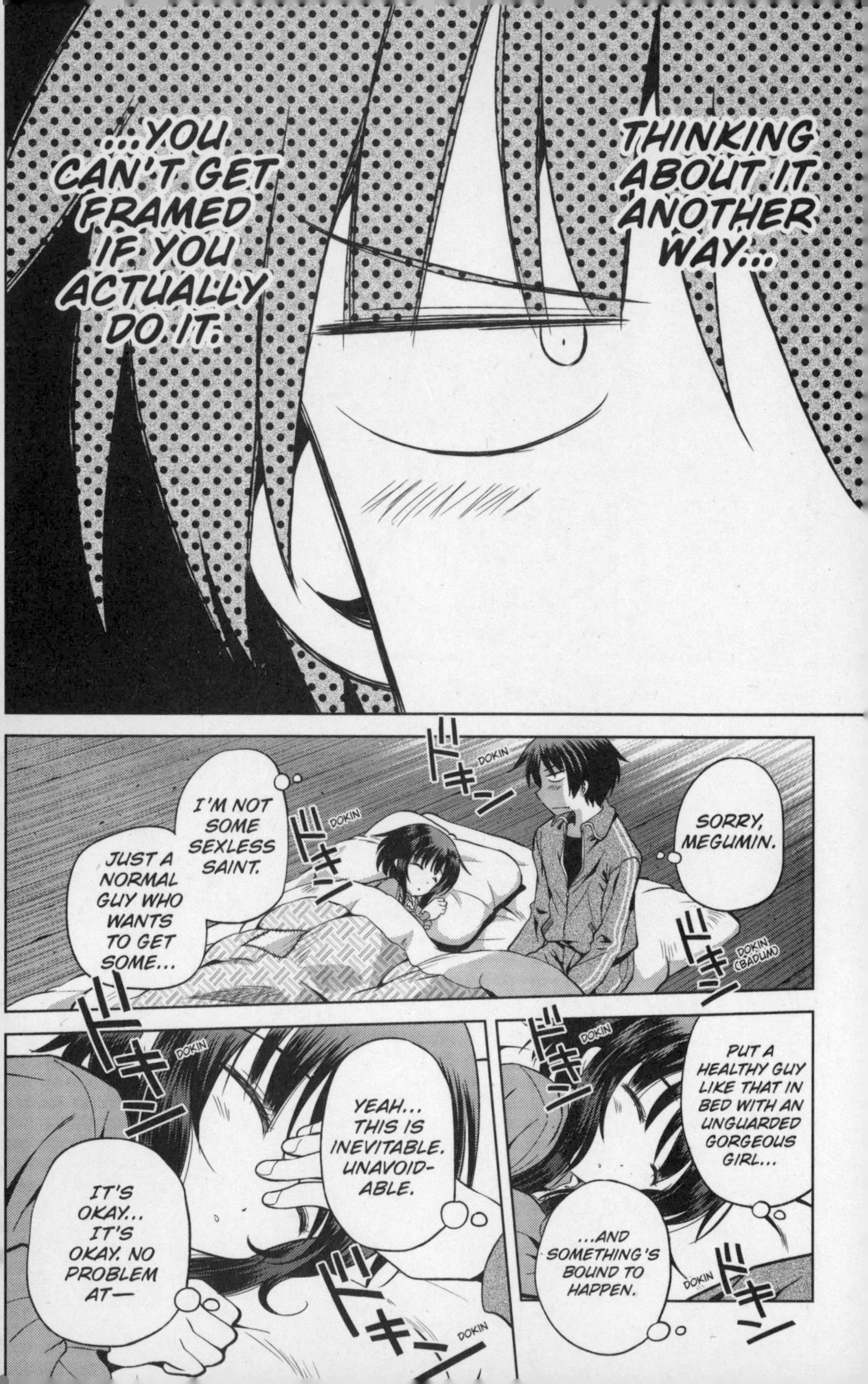
THINKING ABOUT IT ANOTHER WAY...
...YOU CAN'T GET FRAMED IF YOU ACTUALLY DO IT.
DOKIN
SORRY, MEGUMIN.
DOKIN (BADUM)
DOKIN
I'M NOT SOME SEXLESS SAINT.
JUST A NORMAL GUY WHO WANTS TO GET SOME...
DOKIN
PUT A HEALTHY GUY LIKE THAT IN BED WITH AN UNGUARDED GORGEOUS GIRL...
...AND SOMETHING'S BOUND TO HAPPEN.
DOKIN
DOKIN
YEAH... THIS IS INEVITABLE. UNAVOIDABLE.
IT'S OKAY... IT'S OKAY. NO PROBLEM AT—
DOKIN

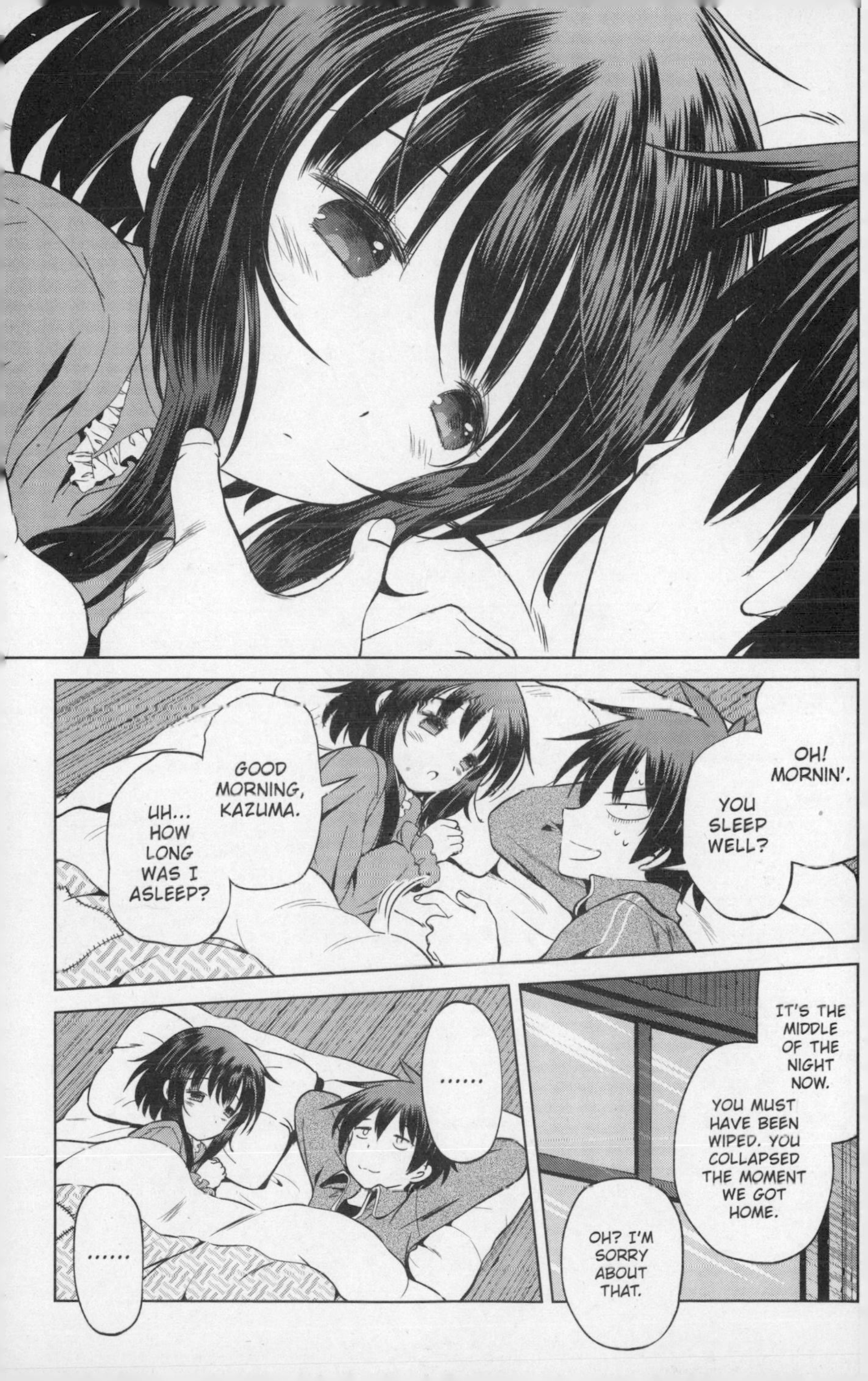
OH! MORNIN'.
YOU SLEEP WELL?
GOOD MORNING, KAZUMA.
UH... HOW LONG WAS I ASLEEP?
IT'S THE MIDDLE OF THE NIGHT NOW.
YOU MUST HAVE BEEN WIPED. YOU COLLAPSED THE MOMENT WE GOT HOME.
OH? I'M SORRY ABOUT THAT.
......
......

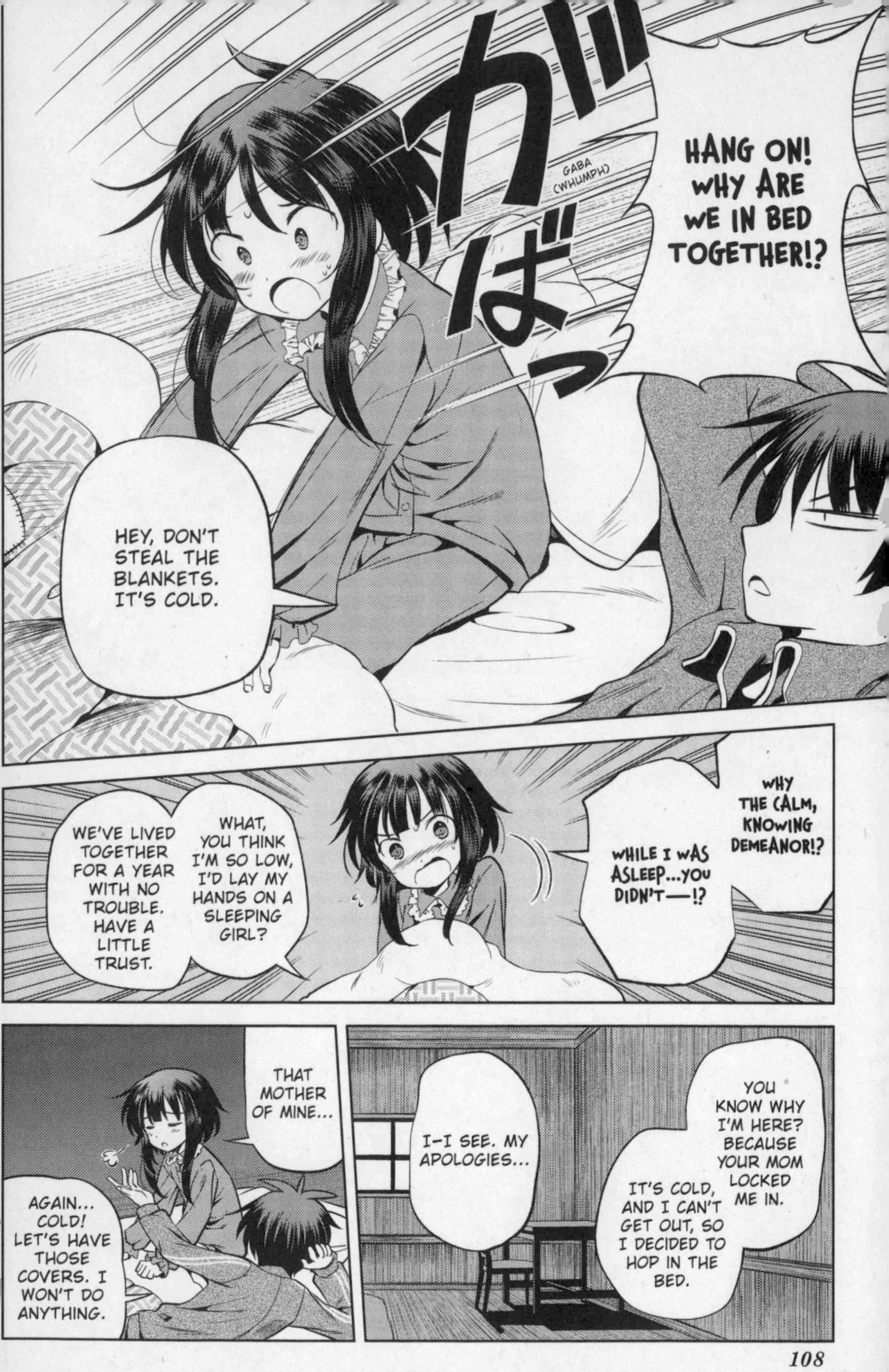
HANG ON! WHY ARE WE IN BED TOGETHER!?
GABA (WHUMPH)
HEY, DON'T STEAL THE BLANKETS. IT'S COLD.
WHY THE CALM, KNOWING DEMEANOR!?
WHILE I WAS ASLEEP...YOU DIDN'T—!?
WHAT, YOU THINK I'M SO LOW, I'D LAY MY HANDS ON A SLEEPING GIRL?
WE'VE LIVED TOGETHER FOR A YEAR WITH NO TROUBLE. HAVE A LITTLE TRUST.
YOU KNOW WHY I'M HERE? BECAUSE YOUR MOM LOCKED ME IN.
IT'S COLD, AND I CAN'T GET OUT, SO I DECIDED TO HOP IN THE BED.
I-I SEE. MY APOLOGIES...
THAT MOTHER OF MINE...
AGAIN... COLD! LET'S HAVE THOSE COVERS. I WON'T DO ANYTHING.

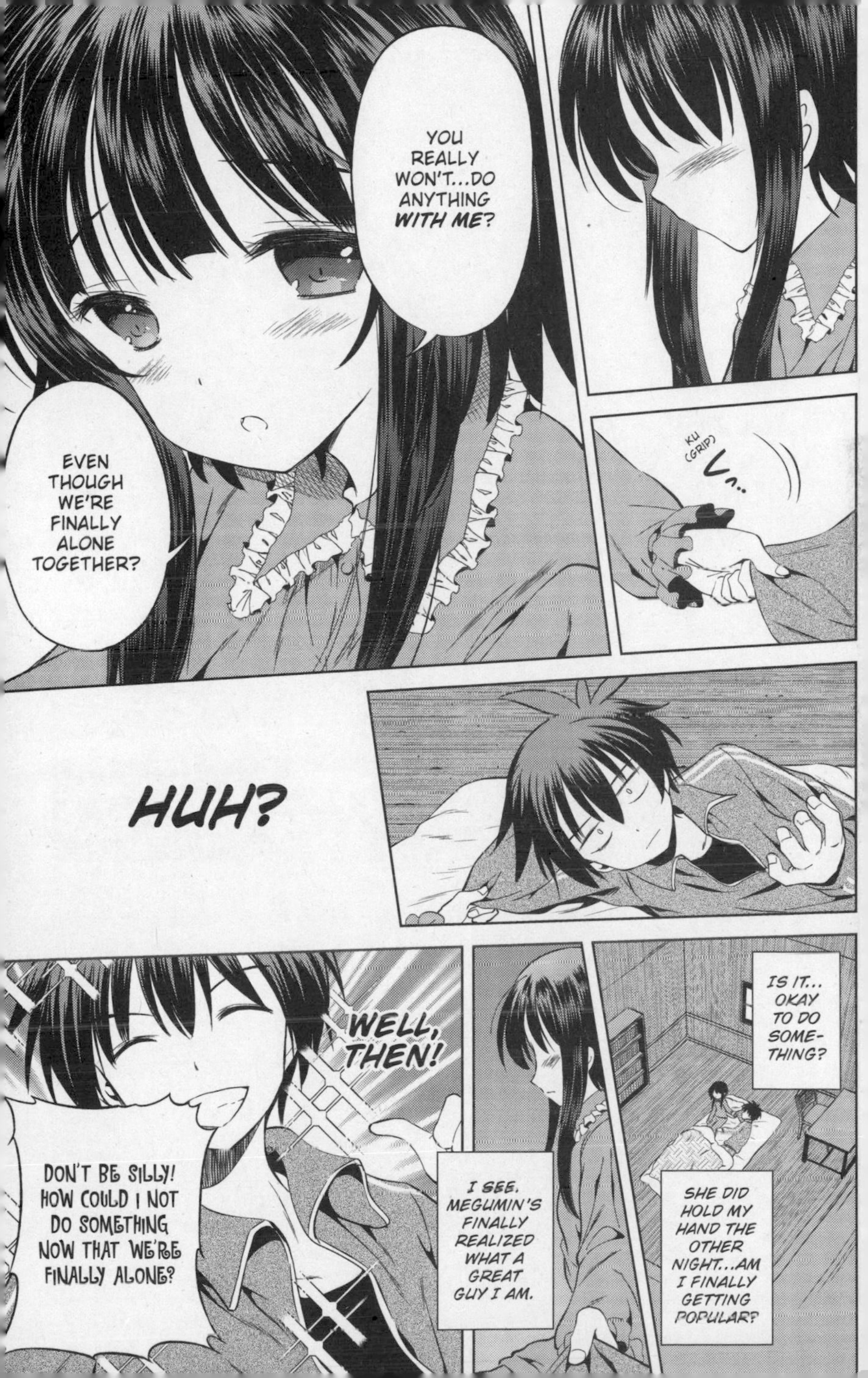
KU (GRIP)
YOU REALLY WON'T...DO ANYTHING WITH ME?
EVEN THOUGH WE'RE FINALLY ALONE TOGETHER?
HUH?
IS IT... OKAY TO DO SOME-THING?
SHE DID HOLD MY HAND THE OTHER NIGHT...AM I FINALLY GETTING POPULAR?
I SEE. MEGUMIN'S FINALLY REALIZED WHAT A GREAT GUY I AM.
WELL, THEN!
DON'T BE SILLY! HOW COULD I NOT DO SOMETHING NOW THAT WE'RE FINALLY ALONE?

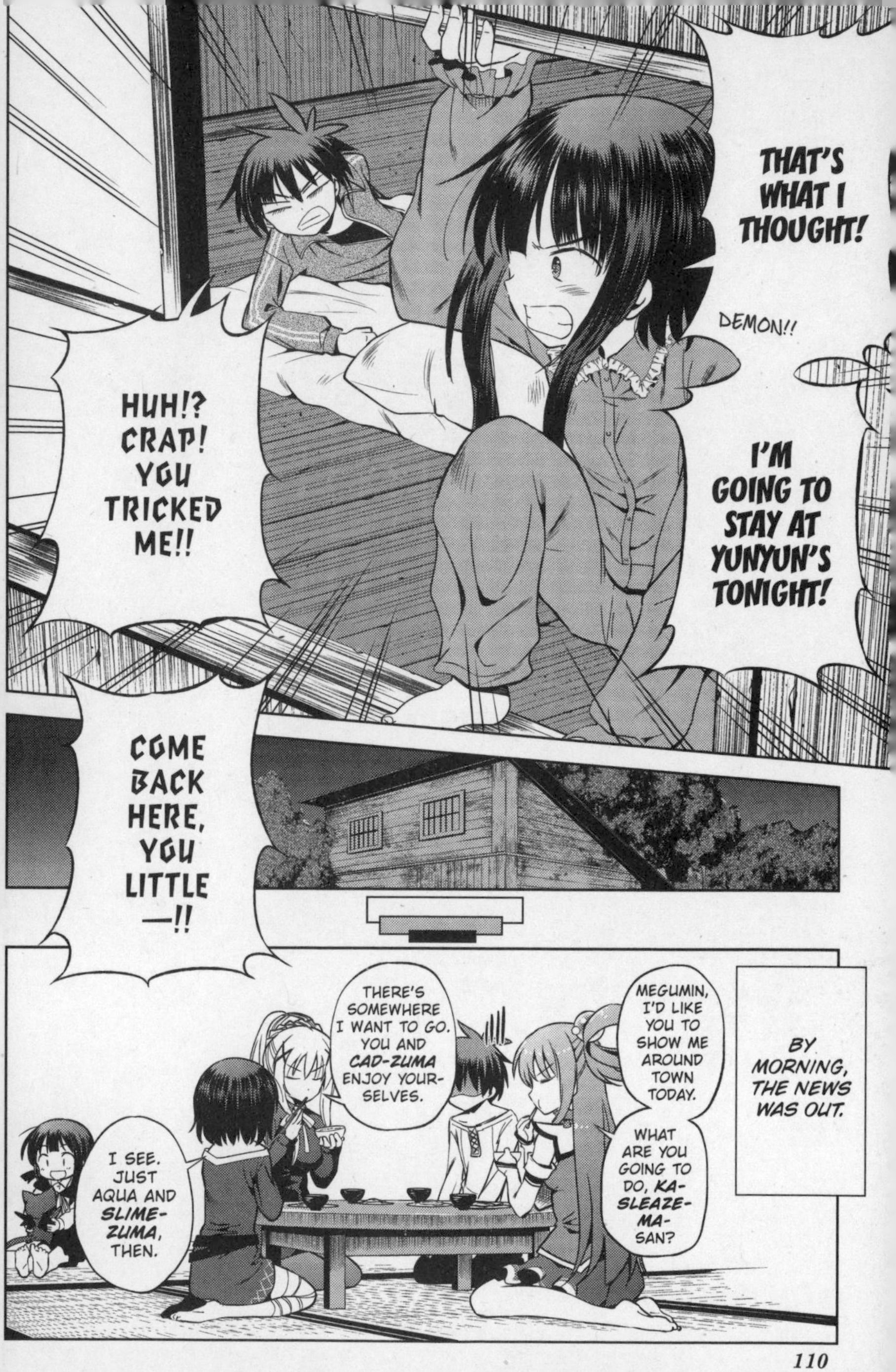
THAT'S WHAT I THOUGHT!
DEMON!!
I'M GOING TO STAY AT YUNYUN'S TONIGHT!
HUH!? CRAP! YOU TRICKED ME!!
COME BACK HERE, YOU LITTLE—!!
BY MORNING, THE NEWS WAS OUT.
MEGUMIN, I'D LIKE YOU TO SHOW ME AROUND TOWN TODAY.
WHAT ARE YOU GOING TO DO, *KASLEAZEMA*-SAN?
THERE'S SOMEWHERE I WANT TO GO. YOU AND *CAD-ZUMA* ENJOY YOURSELVES.
I SEE. JUST AQUA AND *SLIME-ZUMA*, THEN.

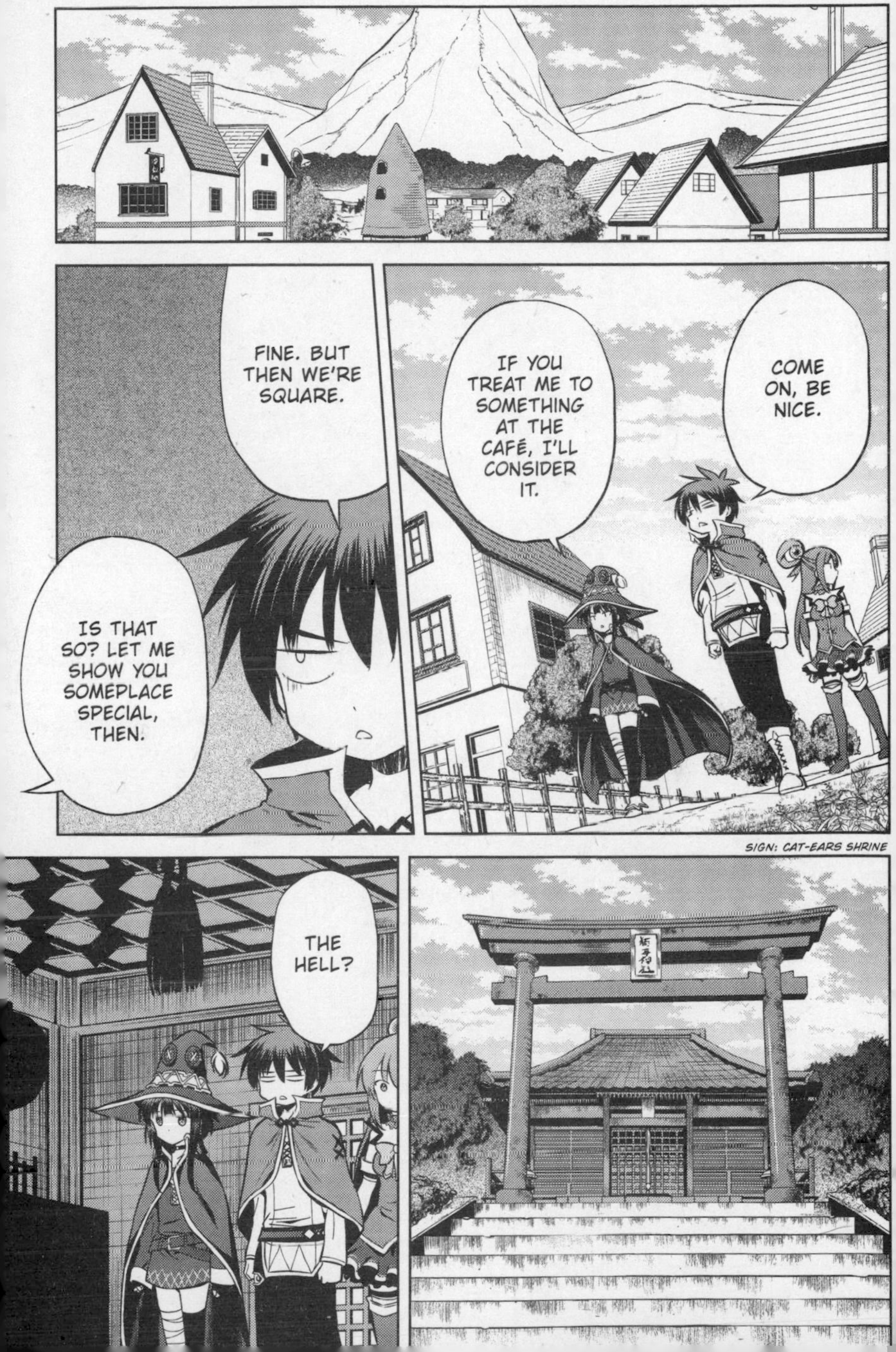
COME ON, BE NICE.
IF YOU TREAT ME TO SOMETHING AT THE CAFÉ, I'LL CONSIDER IT.
FINE. BUT THEN WE'RE SQUARE.
IS THAT SO? LET ME SHOW YOU SOMEPLACE SPECIAL, THEN.
SIGN: CAT-EARS SHRINE
THE HELL?

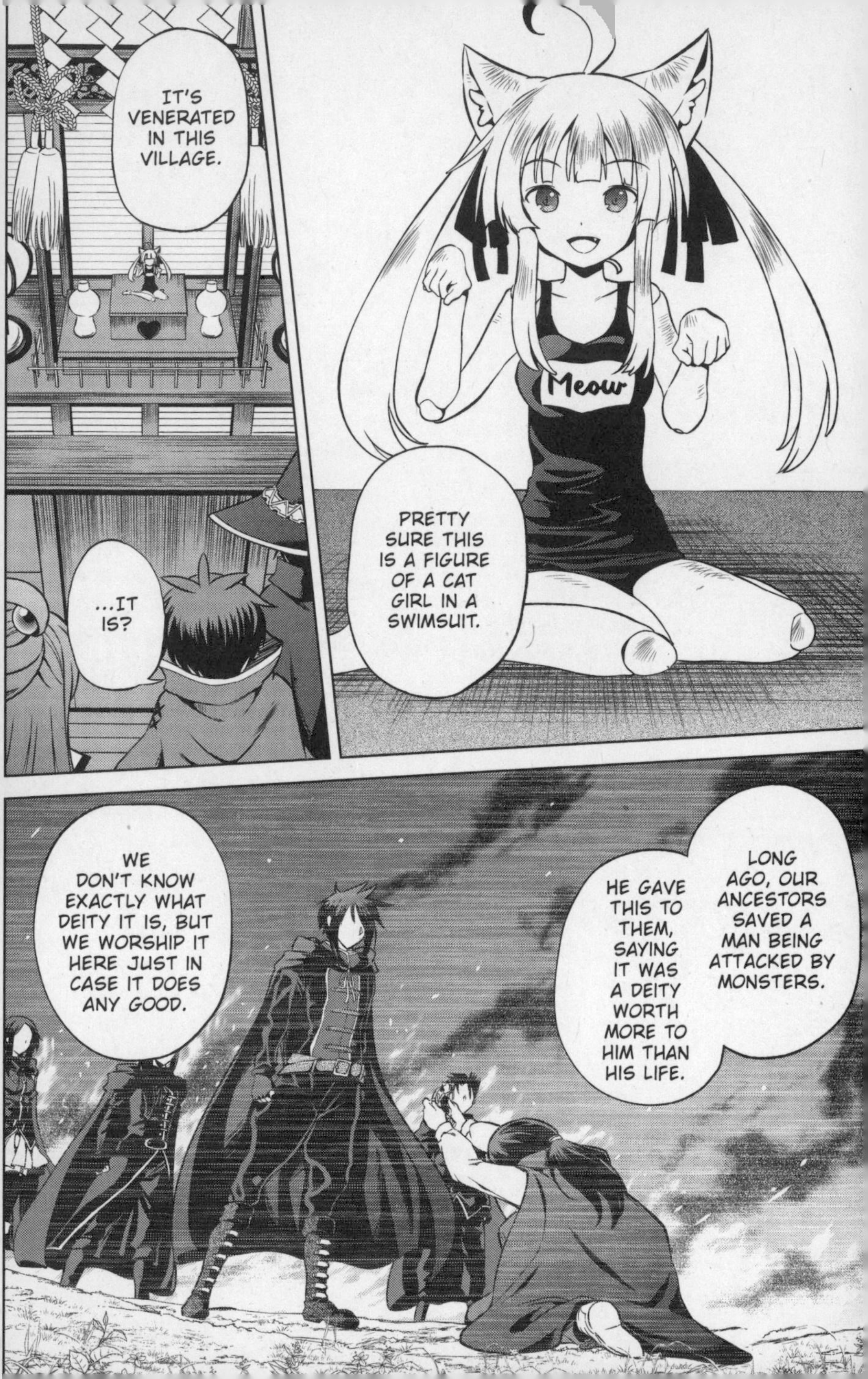
Meow
PRETTY SURE THIS IS A FIGURE OF A CAT GIRL IN A SWIMSUIT.
IT'S VENERATED IN THIS VILLAGE.
...IT IS?
LONG AGO, OUR ANCESTORS SAVED A MAN BEING ATTACKED BY MONSTERS.
HE GAVE THIS TO THEM, SAYING IT WAS A DEITY WORTH MORE TO HIM THAN HIS LIFE.
WE DON'T KNOW EXACTLY WHAT DEITY IT IS, BUT WE WORSHIP IT HERE JUST IN CASE IT DOES ANY GOOD.

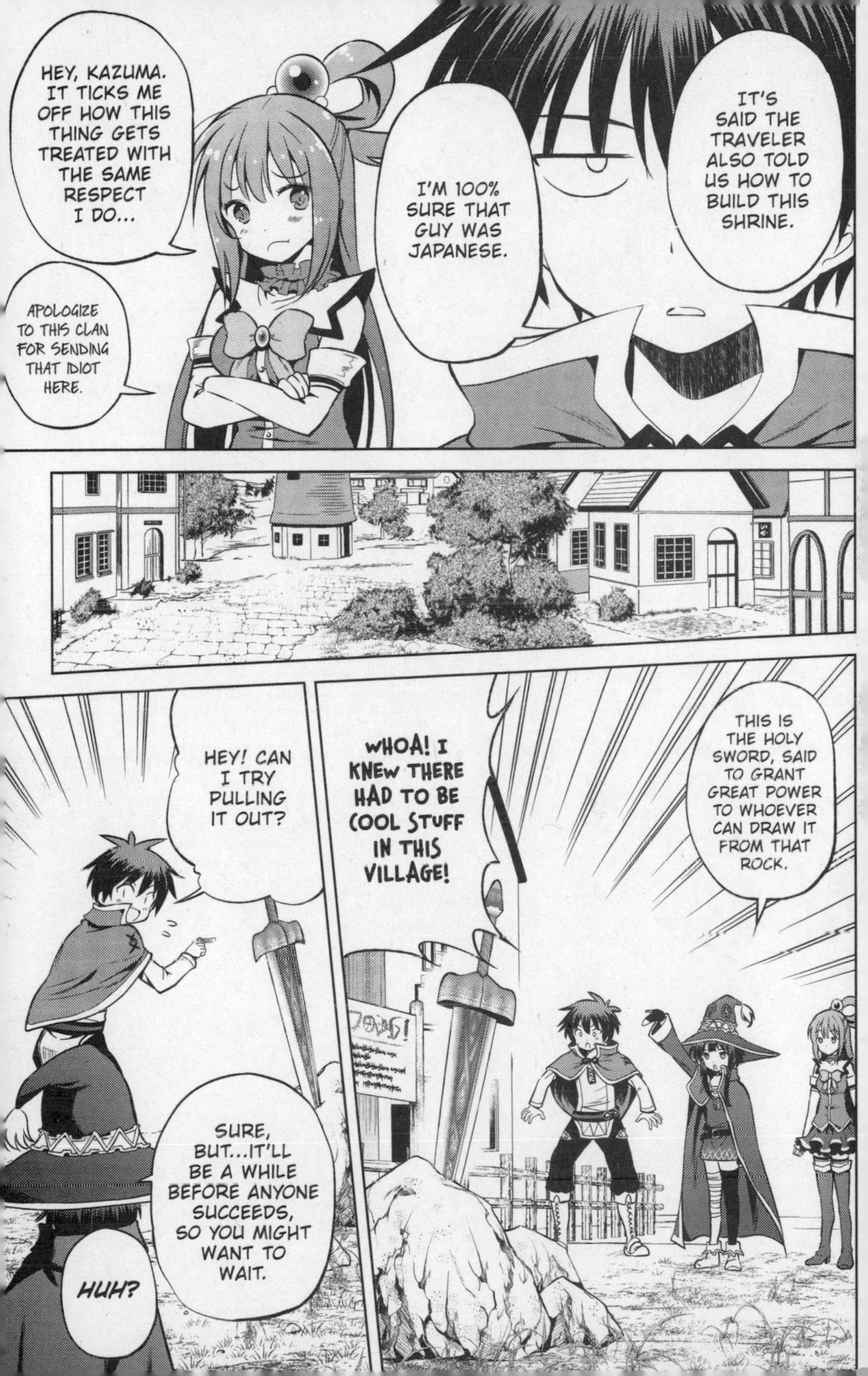
IT'S SAID THE TRAVELER ALSO TOLD US HOW TO BUILD THIS SHRINE.
I'M 100% SURE THAT GUY WAS JAPANESE.
HEY, KAZUMA. IT TICKS ME OFF HOW THIS THING GETS TREATED WITH THE SAME RESPECT I DO...
APOLOGIZE TO THIS CLAN FOR SENDING THAT IDIOT HERE.
THIS IS THE HOLY SWORD, SAID TO GRANT GREAT POWER TO WHOEVER CAN DRAW IT FROM THAT ROCK.
WHOA! I KNEW THERE HAD TO BE COOL STUFF IN THIS VILLAGE!
HEY! CAN I TRY PULLING IT OUT?
SURE, BUT...IT'LL BE A WHILE BEFORE ANYONE SUCCEEDS, SO YOU MIGHT WANT TO WAIT.
HUH?

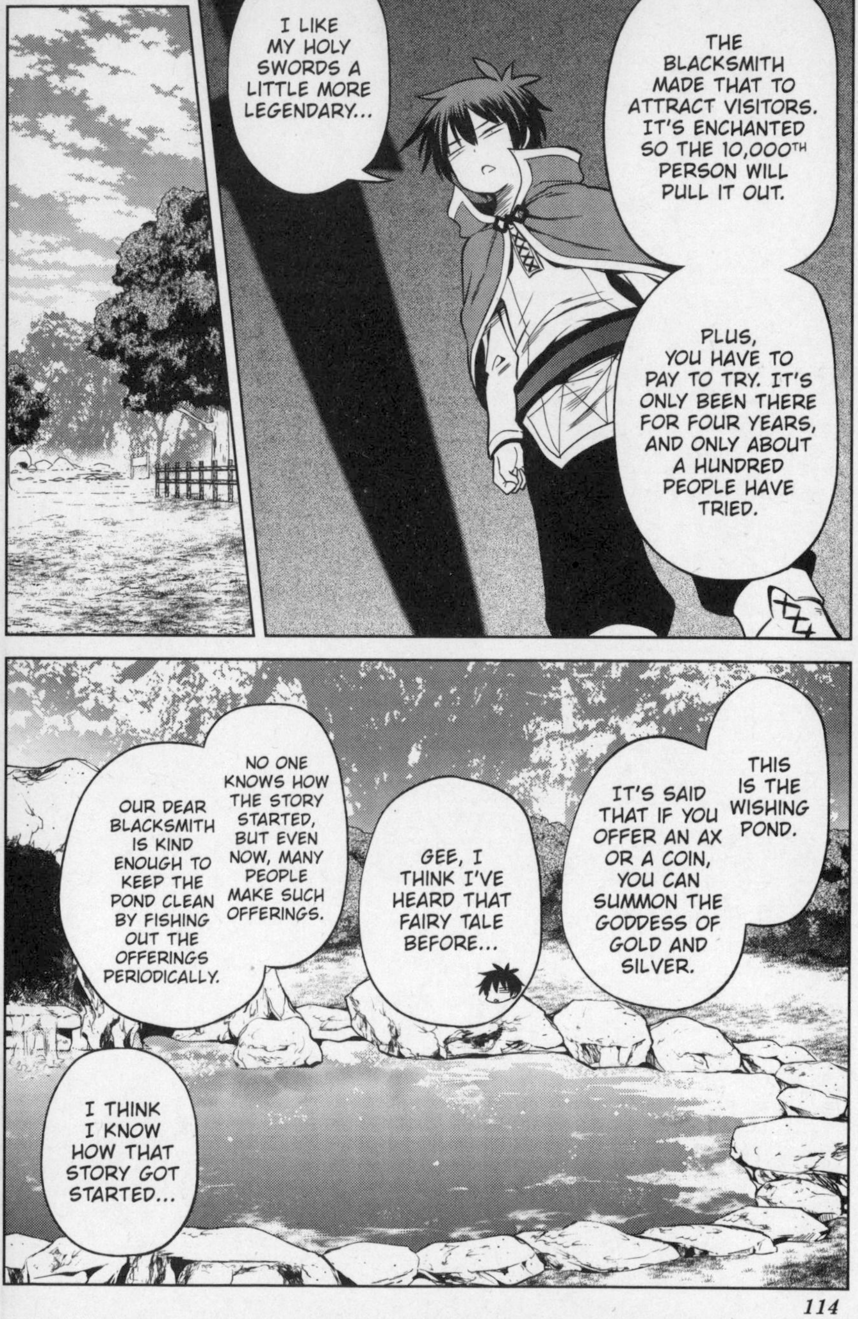
THE BLACKSMITH MADE THAT TO ATTRACT VISITORS. IT'S ENCHANTED SO THE 10,000TH PERSON WILL PULL IT OUT.
PLUS, YOU HAVE TO PAY TO TRY. IT'S ONLY BEEN THERE FOR FOUR YEARS, AND ONLY ABOUT A HUNDRED PEOPLE HAVE TRIED.
I LIKE MY HOLY SWORDS A LITTLE MORE LEGENDARY...
THIS IS THE WISHING POND.
IT'S SAID THAT IF YOU OFFER AN AX OR A COIN, YOU CAN SUMMON THE GODDESS OF GOLD AND SILVER.
GEE, I THINK I'VE HEARD THAT FAIRY TALE BEFORE...
NO ONE KNOWS HOW THE STORY STARTED, BUT EVEN NOW, MANY PEOPLE MAKE SUCH OFFERINGS.
OUR DEAR BLACKSMITH IS KIND ENOUGH TO KEEP THE POND CLEAN BY FISHING OUT THE OFFERINGS PERIODICALLY.
I THINK I KNOW HOW THAT STORY GOT STARTED...

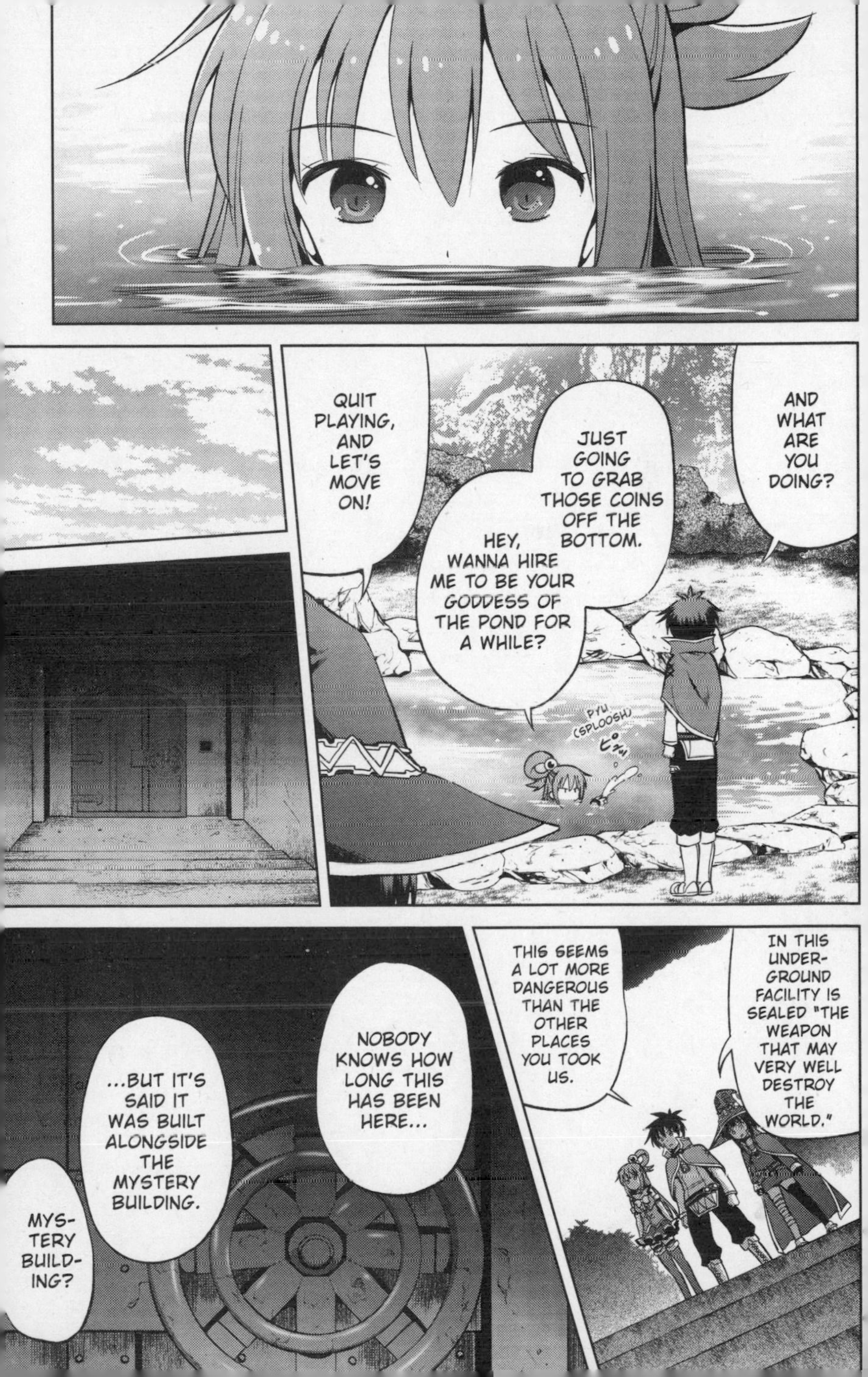
AND WHAT ARE YOU DOING?
JUST GOING TO GRAB THOSE COINS OFF THE BOTTOM. HEY, WANNA HIRE ME TO BE YOUR GODDESS OF THE POND FOR A WHILE?
QUIT PLAYING, AND LET'S MOVE ON!
PYU (SPLOOSH)
IN THIS UNDERGROUND FACILITY IS SEALED "THE WEAPON THAT MAY VERY WELL DESTROY THE WORLD."
THIS SEEMS A LOT MORE DANGEROUS THAN THE OTHER PLACES YOU TOOK US.
NOBODY KNOWS HOW LONG THIS HAS BEEN HERE...
...BUT IT'S SAID IT WAS BUILT ALONGSIDE THE MYSTERY BUILDING.
MYSTERY BUILDING?

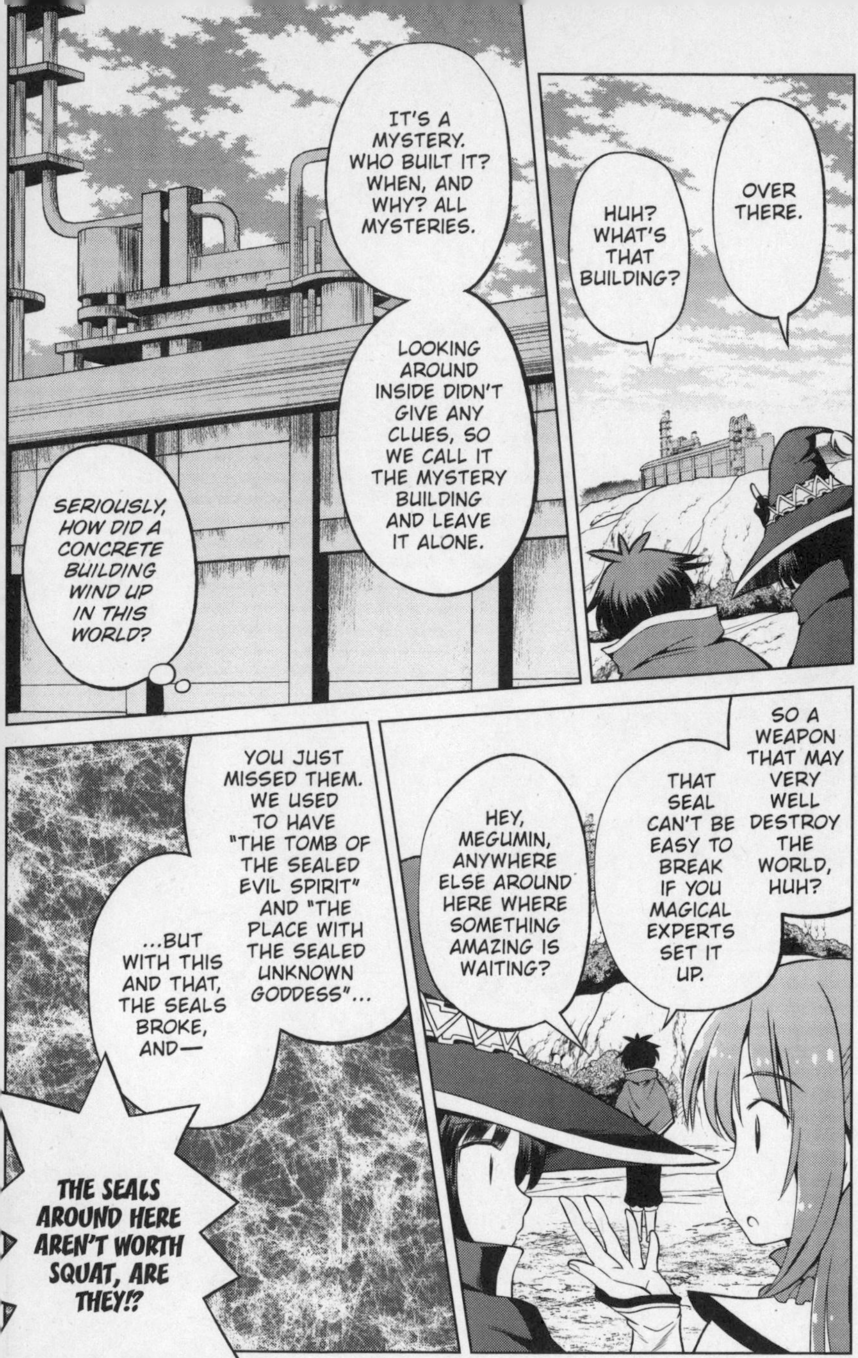
OVER THERE.
HUH? WHAT'S THAT BUILDING?
IT'S A MYSTERY. WHO BUILT IT? WHEN, AND WHY? ALL MYSTERIES.
LOOKING AROUND INSIDE DIDN'T GIVE ANY CLUES, SO WE CALL IT THE MYSTERY BUILDING AND LEAVE IT ALONE.
SERIOUSLY, HOW DID A CONCRETE BUILDING WIND UP IN THIS WORLD?
SO A WEAPON THAT MAY VERY WELL DESTROY THE WORLD, HUH?
THAT SEAL CAN'T BE EASY TO BREAK IF YOU MAGICAL EXPERTS SET IT UP.
HEY, MEGUMIN, ANYWHERE ELSE AROUND HERE WHERE SOMETHING AMAZING IS WAITING?
YOU JUST MISSED THEM. WE USED TO HAVE "THE TOMB OF THE SEALED EVIL SPIRIT" AND "THE PLACE WITH THE SEALED UNKNOWN GODDESS"...
...BUT WITH THIS AND THAT, THE SEALS BROKE, AND—
THE SEALS AROUND HERE AREN'T WORTH SQUAT, ARE THEY!?

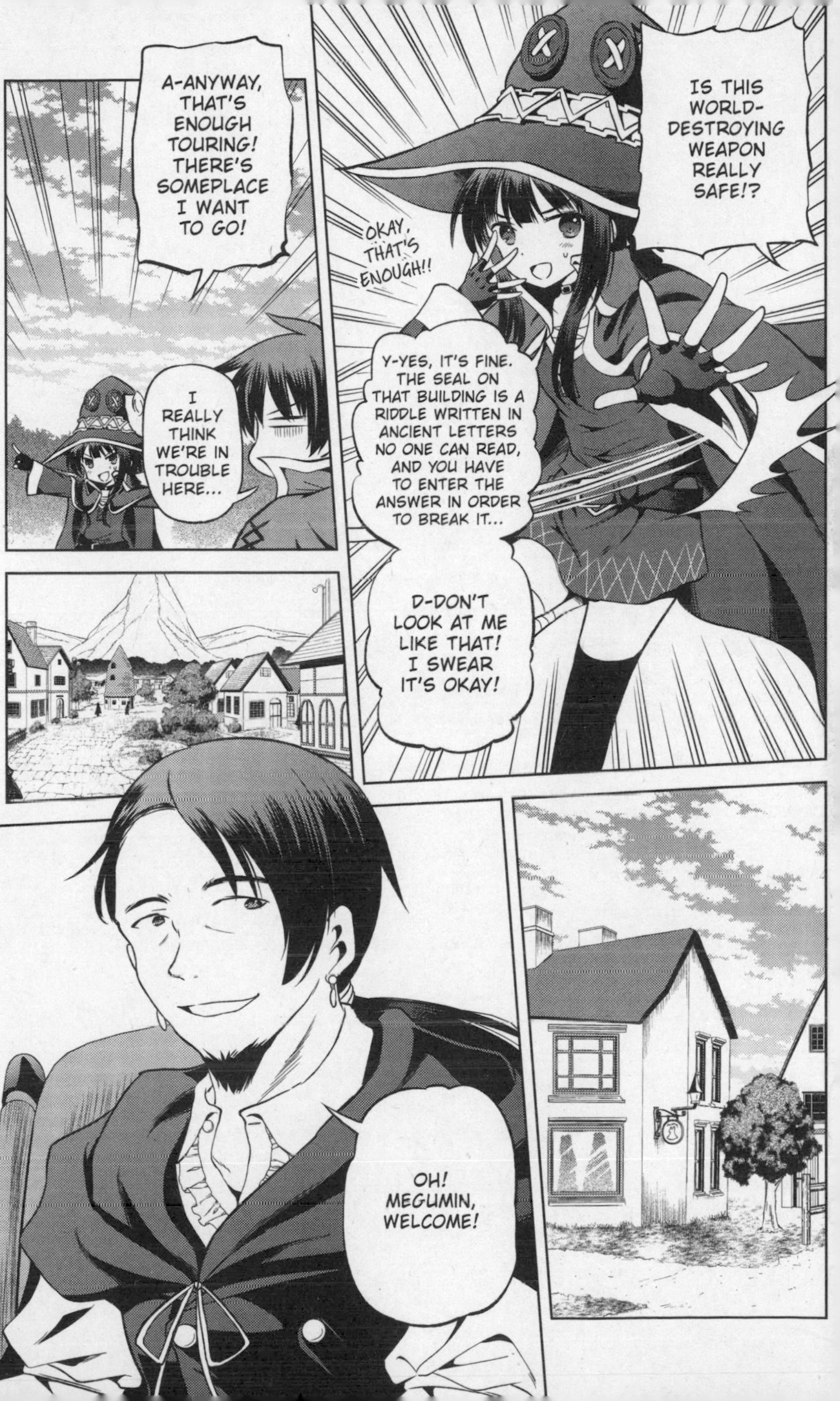
IS THIS WORLD-DESTROYING WEAPON REALLY SAFE!?
OKAY, THAT'S ENOUGH!!
Y-YES, IT'S FINE. THE SEAL ON THAT BUILDING IS A RIDDLE WRITTEN IN ANCIENT LETTERS NO ONE CAN READ, AND YOU HAVE TO ENTER THE ANSWER IN ORDER TO BREAK IT...
D-DON'T LOOK AT ME LIKE THAT! I SWEAR IT'S OKAY!
A-ANYWAY, THAT'S ENOUGH TOURING! THERE'S SOMEPLACE I WANT TO GO!
I REALLY THINK WE'RE IN TROUBLE HERE...
OH! MEGUMIN, WELCOME!

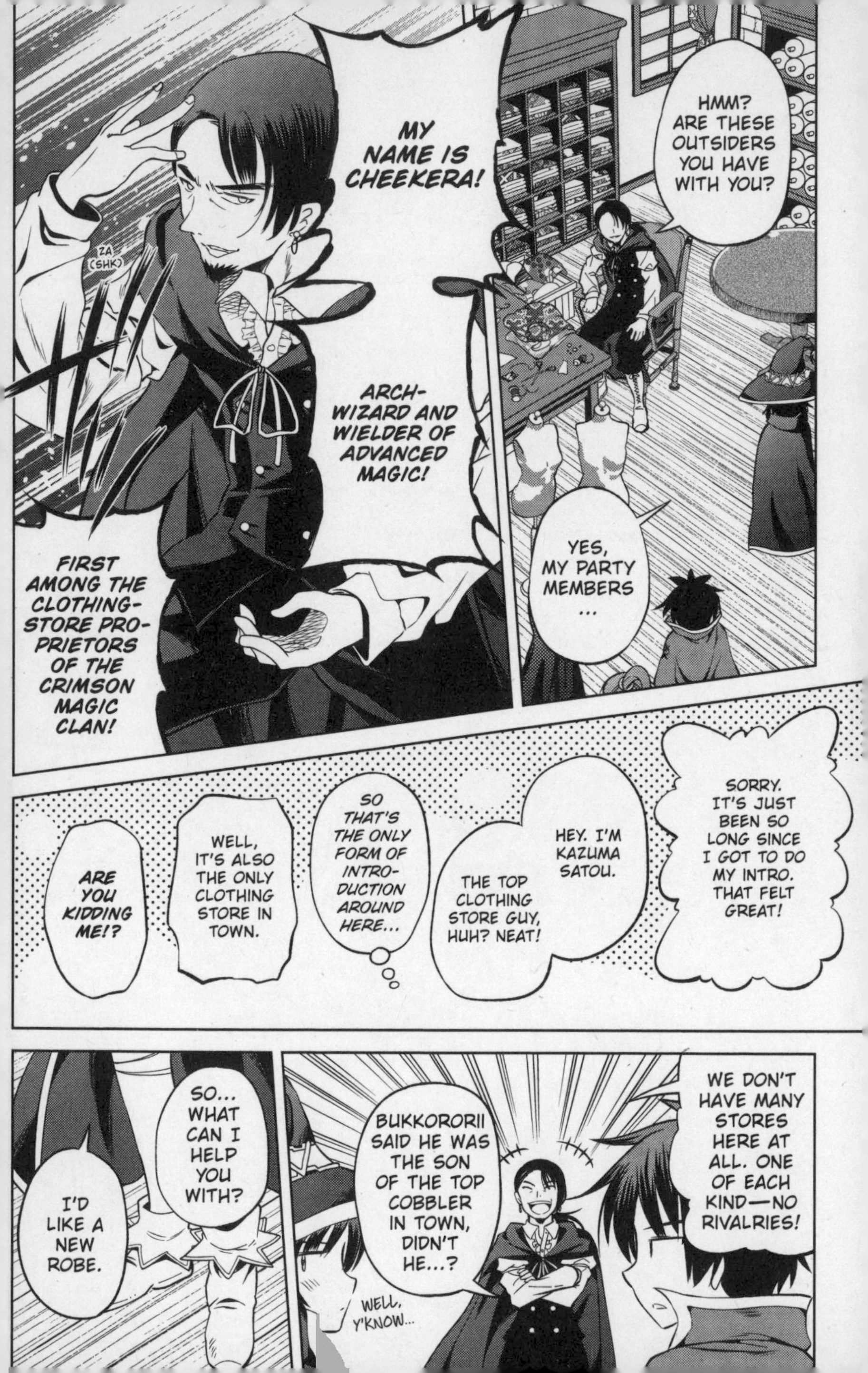
HMM? ARE THESE OUTSIDERS YOU HAVE WITH YOU?
YES, MY PARTY MEMBERS...
MY NAME IS CHEEKERA!
ARCH-WIZARD AND WIELDER OF ADVANCED MAGIC!
FIRST AMONG THE CLOTHING-STORE PROPRIETORS OF THE CRIMSON MAGIC CLAN!
ZA (SHK)
SORRY. IT'S JUST BEEN SO LONG SINCE I GOT TO DO MY INTRO. THAT FELT GREAT!
HEY. I'M KAZUMA SATOU.
THE TOP CLOTHING STORE GUY, HUH? NEAT!
SO THAT'S THE ONLY FORM OF INTRO-DUCTION AROUND HERE...
WELL, IT'S ALSO THE ONLY CLOTHING STORE IN TOWN.
ARE YOU KIDDING ME!?
WE DON'T HAVE MANY STORES HERE AT ALL. ONE OF EACH KIND—NO RIVALRIES!
BUKKORORII SAID HE WAS THE SON OF THE TOP COBBLER IN TOWN, DIDN'T HE...?
WELL, Y'KNOW...
SO... WHAT CAN I HELP YOU WITH?
I'D LIKE A NEW ROBE.

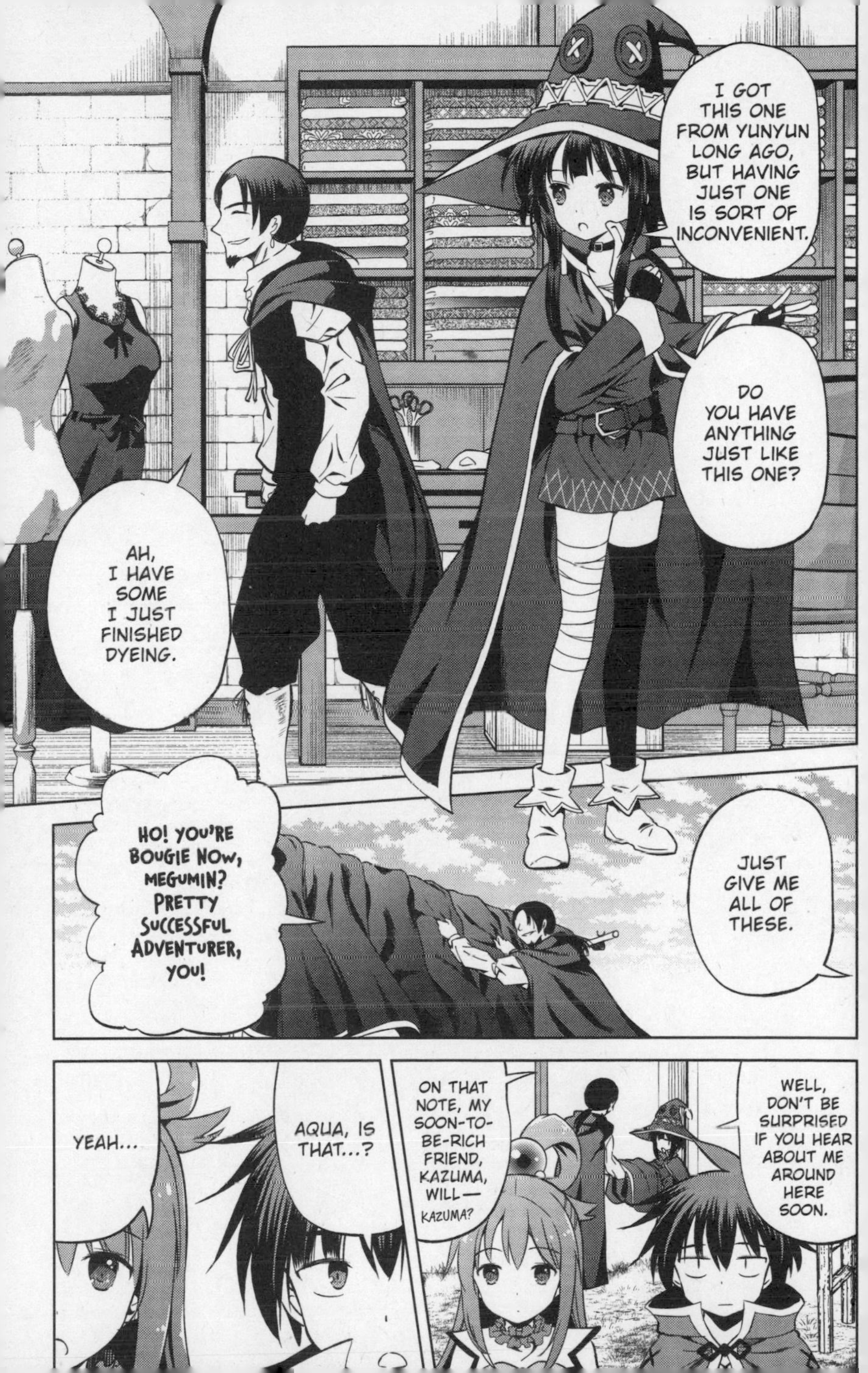
I GOT THIS ONE FROM YUNYUN LONG AGO, BUT HAVING JUST ONE IS SORT OF INCONVENIENT.
DO YOU HAVE ANYTHING JUST LIKE THIS ONE?
AH, I HAVE SOME I JUST FINISHED DYEING.
JUST GIVE ME ALL OF THESE.
HO! YOU'RE BOUGIE NOW, MEGUMIN? PRETTY SUCCESSFUL ADVENTURER, YOU!
WELL, DON'T BE SURPRISED IF YOU HEAR ABOUT ME AROUND HERE SOON.
ON THAT NOTE, MY SOON-TO-BE-RICH FRIEND, KAZUMA, WILL—
KAZUMA?
AQUA, IS THAT...?
YEAH...

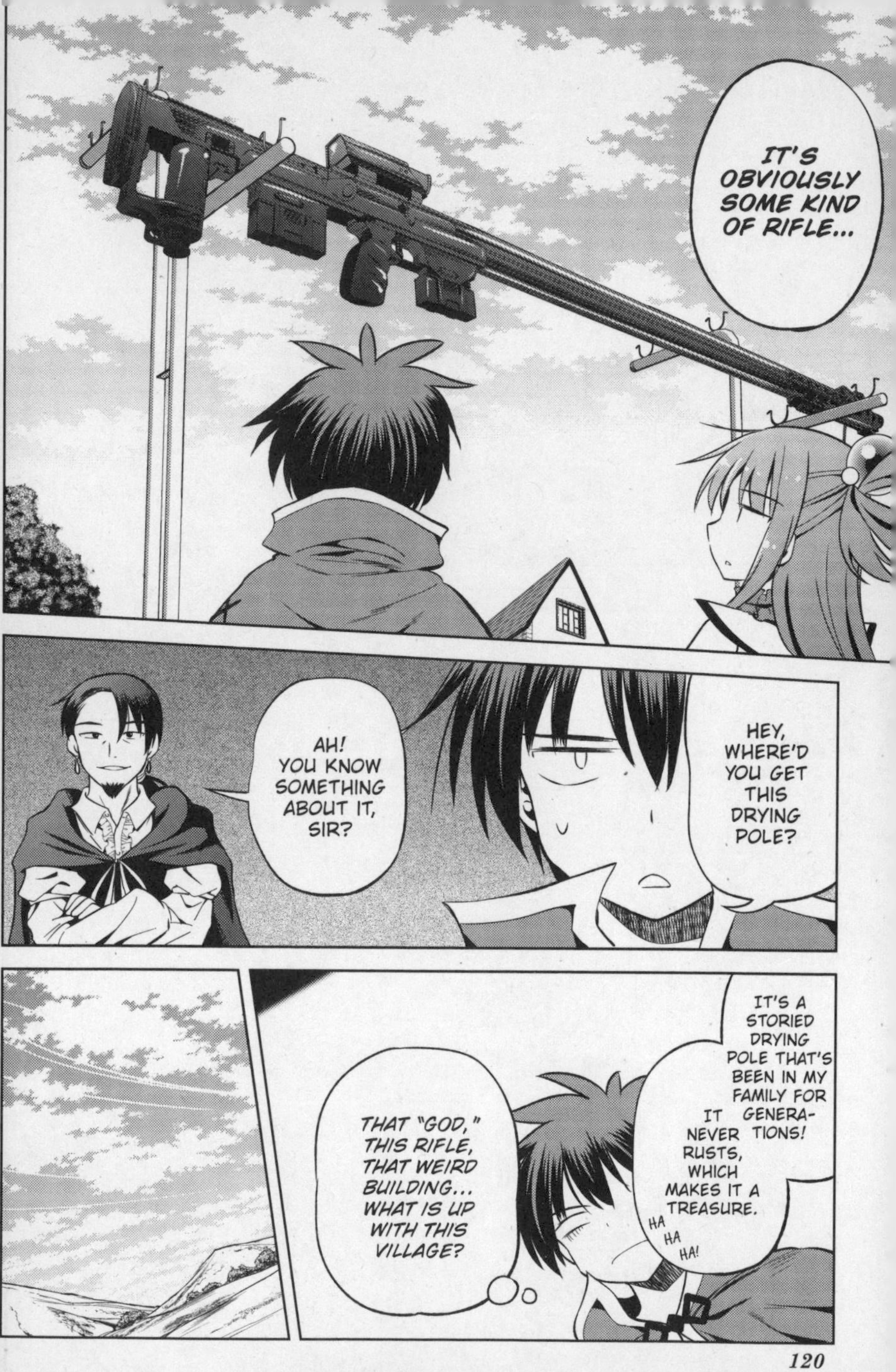
IT'S OBVIOUSLY SOME KIND OF RIFLE...
HEY, WHERE'D YOU GET THIS DRYING POLE?
AH! YOU KNOW SOMETHING ABOUT IT, SIR?
IT'S A STORIED DRYING POLE THAT'S BEEN IN MY FAMILY FOR GENERATIONS!
IT NEVER RUSTS, WHICH MAKES IT A TREASURE.
HA HA HA!
THAT "GOD," THIS RIFLE, THAT WEIRD BUILDING... WHAT IS UP WITH THIS VILLAGE?

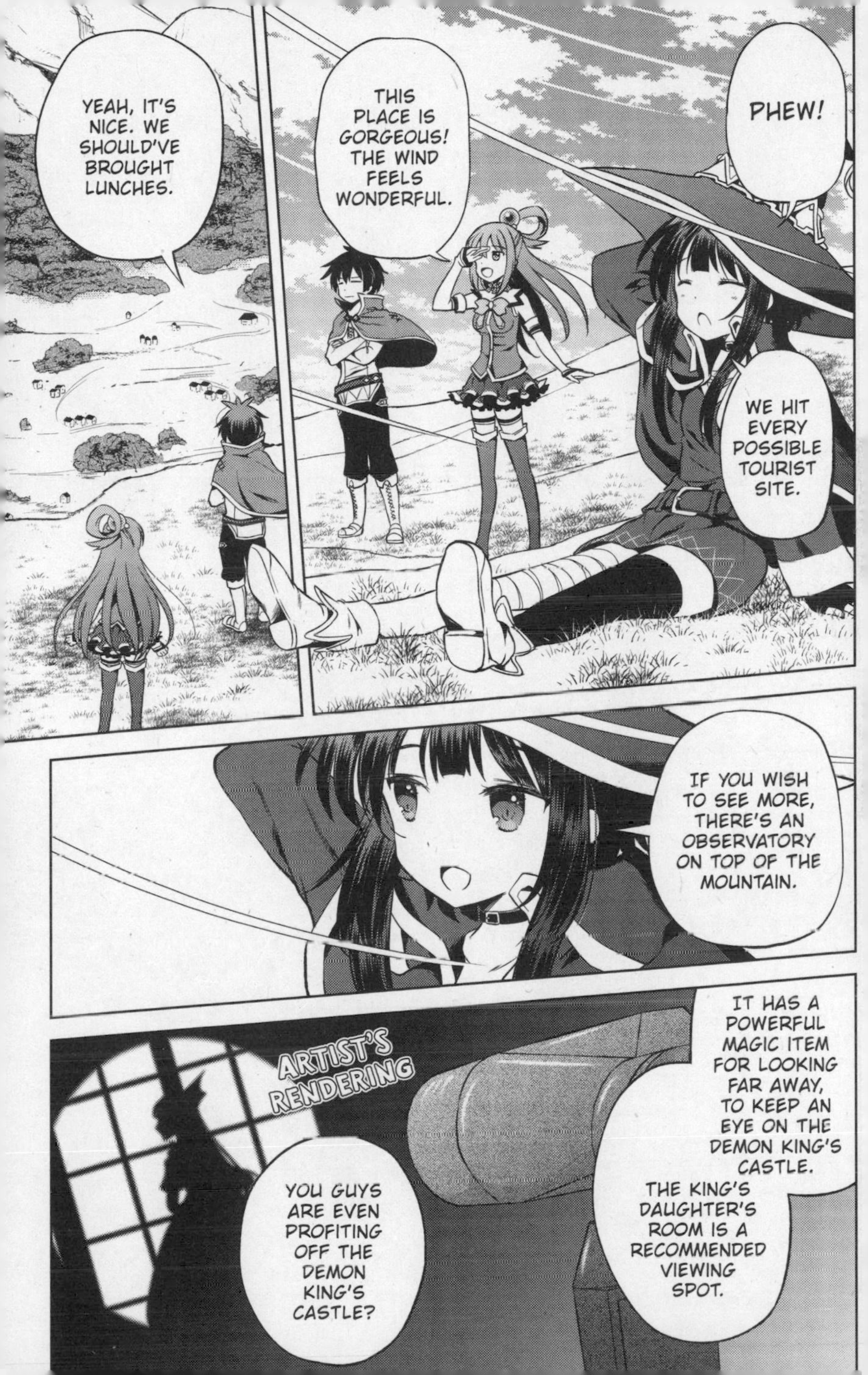
PHEW!
WE HIT EVERY POSSIBLE TOURIST SITE.
THIS PLACE IS GORGEOUS! THE WIND FEELS WONDERFUL.
YEAH, IT'S NICE. WE SHOULD'VE BROUGHT LUNCHES.
IF YOU WISH TO SEE MORE, THERE'S AN OBSERVATORY ON TOP OF THE MOUNTAIN.
IT HAS A POWERFUL MAGIC ITEM FOR LOOKING FAR AWAY, TO KEEP AN EYE ON THE DEMON KING'S CASTLE.
THE KING'S DAUGHTER'S ROOM IS A RECOMMENDED VIEWING SPOT.
ARTIST'S RENDERING
YOU GUYS ARE EVEN PROFITING OFF THE DEMON KING'S CASTLE?

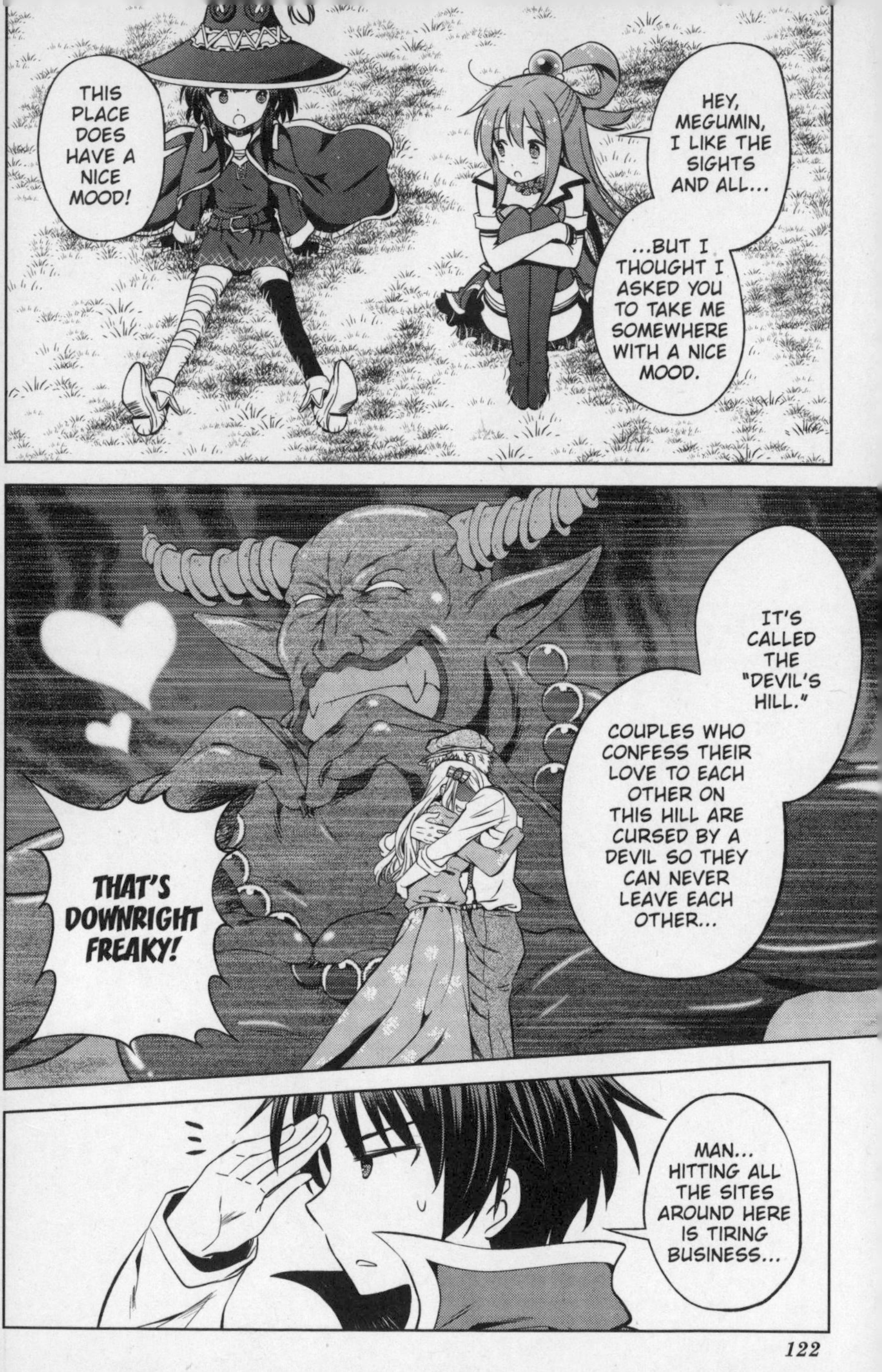
HEY, MEGUMIN, I LIKE THE SIGHTS AND ALL...
...BUT I THOUGHT I ASKED YOU TO TAKE ME SOMEWHERE WITH A NICE MOOD.
THIS PLACE DOES HAVE A NICE MOOD!
IT'S CALLED THE "DEVIL'S HILL."
COUPLES WHO CONFESS THEIR LOVE TO EACH OTHER ON THIS HILL ARE CURSED BY A DEVIL SO THEY CAN NEVER LEAVE EACH OTHER...
THAT'S DOWNRIGHT FREAKY!
MAN... HITTING ALL THE SITES AROUND HERE IS TIRING BUSINESS...

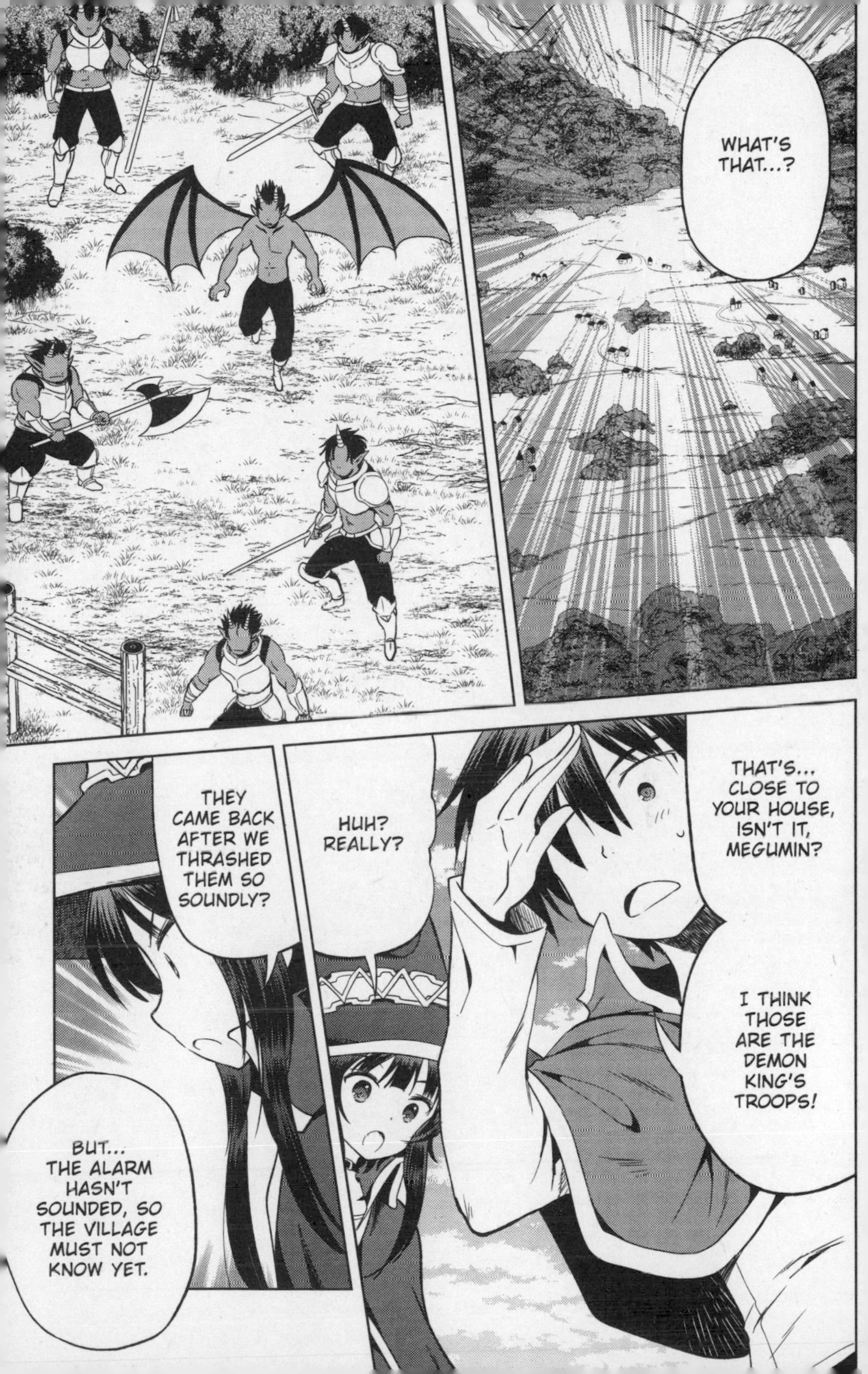
WHAT'S THAT...?
THAT'S... CLOSE TO YOUR HOUSE, ISN'T IT, MEGUMIN?
I THINK THOSE ARE THE DEMON KING'S TROOPS!
HUH? REALLY?
THEY CAME BACK AFTER WE THRASHED THEM SO SOUNDLY?
BUT... THE ALARM HASN'T SOUNDED, SO THE VILLAGE MUST NOT KNOW YET.

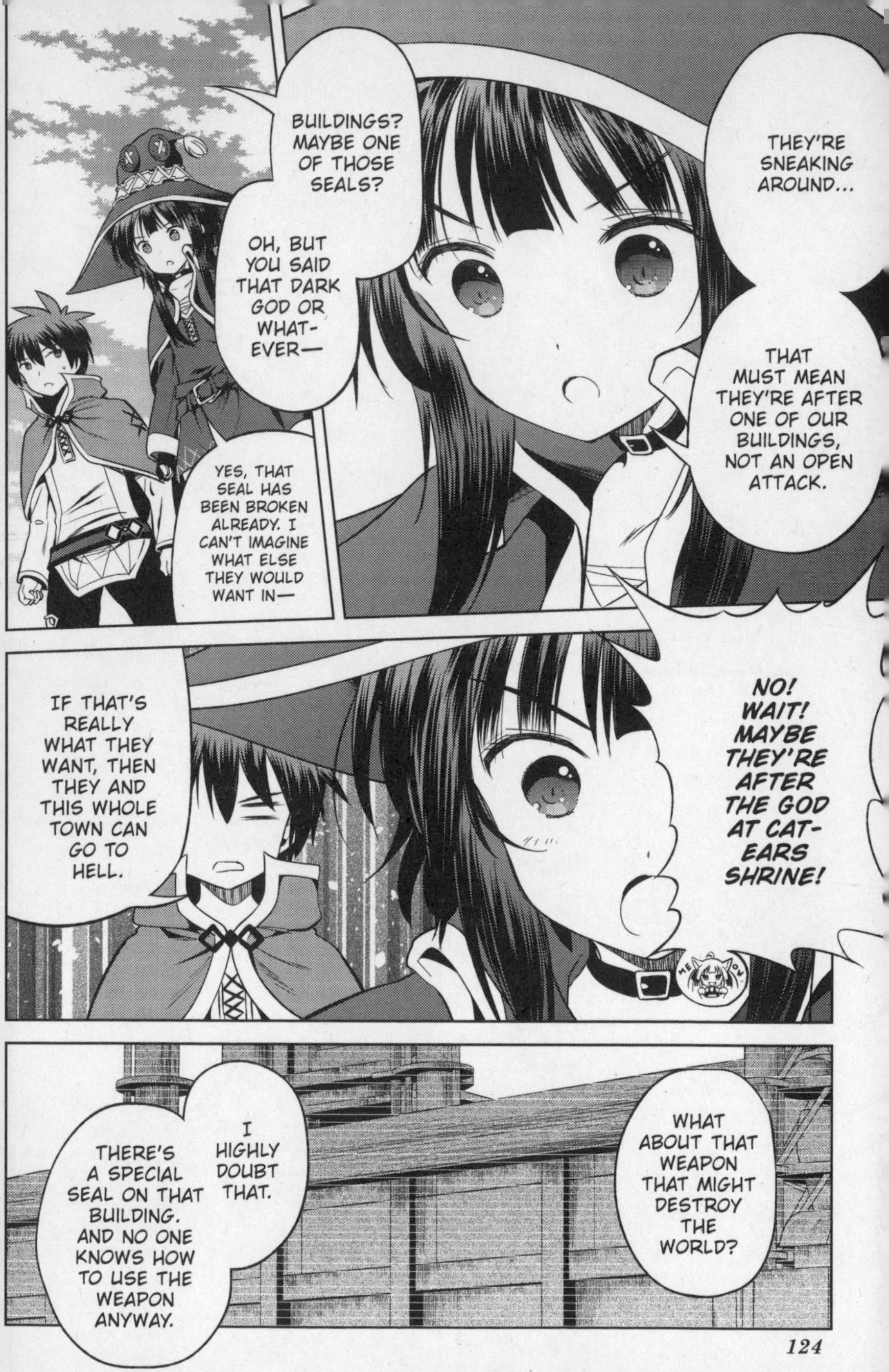
THEY'RE SNEAKING AROUND...
THAT MUST MEAN THEY'RE AFTER ONE OF OUR BUILDINGS, NOT AN OPEN ATTACK.
BUILDINGS? MAYBE ONE OF THOSE SEALS?
OH, BUT YOU SAID THAT DARK GOD OR WHAT-EVER—
YES, THAT SEAL HAS BEEN BROKEN ALREADY. I CAN'T IMAGINE WHAT ELSE THEY WOULD WANT IN—
NO! WAIT! MAYBE THEY'RE AFTER THE GOD AT CAT-EARS SHRINE!
MEOW
IF THAT'S REALLY WHAT THEY WANT, THEN THEY AND THIS WHOLE TOWN CAN GO TO HELL.
WHAT ABOUT THAT WEAPON THAT MIGHT DESTROY THE WORLD?
I HIGHLY DOUBT THAT.
THERE'S A SPECIAL SEAL ON THAT BUILDING. AND NO ONE KNOWS HOW TO USE THE WEAPON ANYWAY.

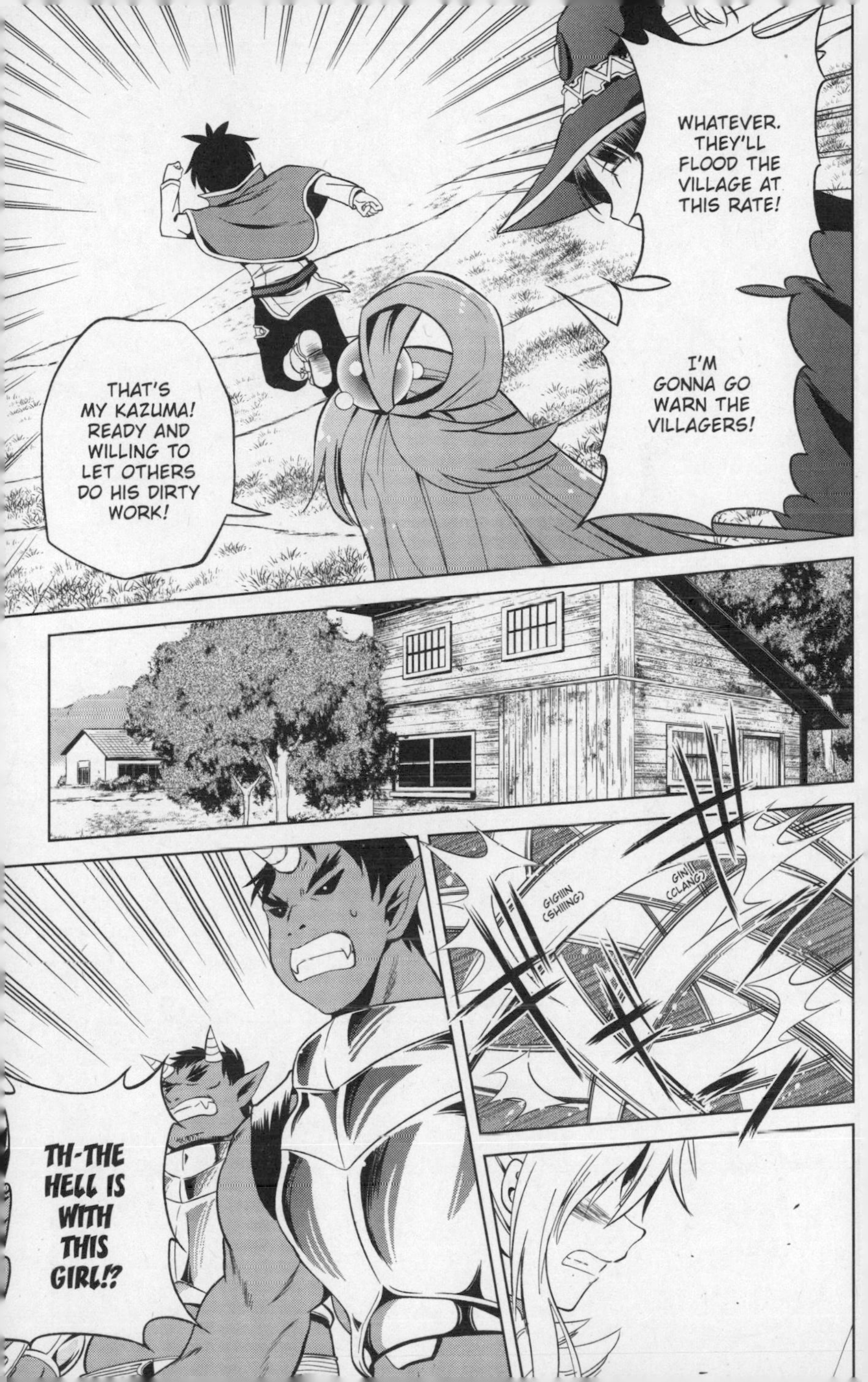
WHATEVER. THEY'LL FLOOD THE VILLAGE AT THIS RATE!
I'M GONNA GO WARN THE VILLAGERS!
THAT'S MY KAZUMA! READY AND WILLING TO LET OTHERS DO HIS DIRTY WORK!
GIN (CLANG)
GIGIIIN (SHIIING)
TH-THE HELL IS WITH THIS GIRL!?

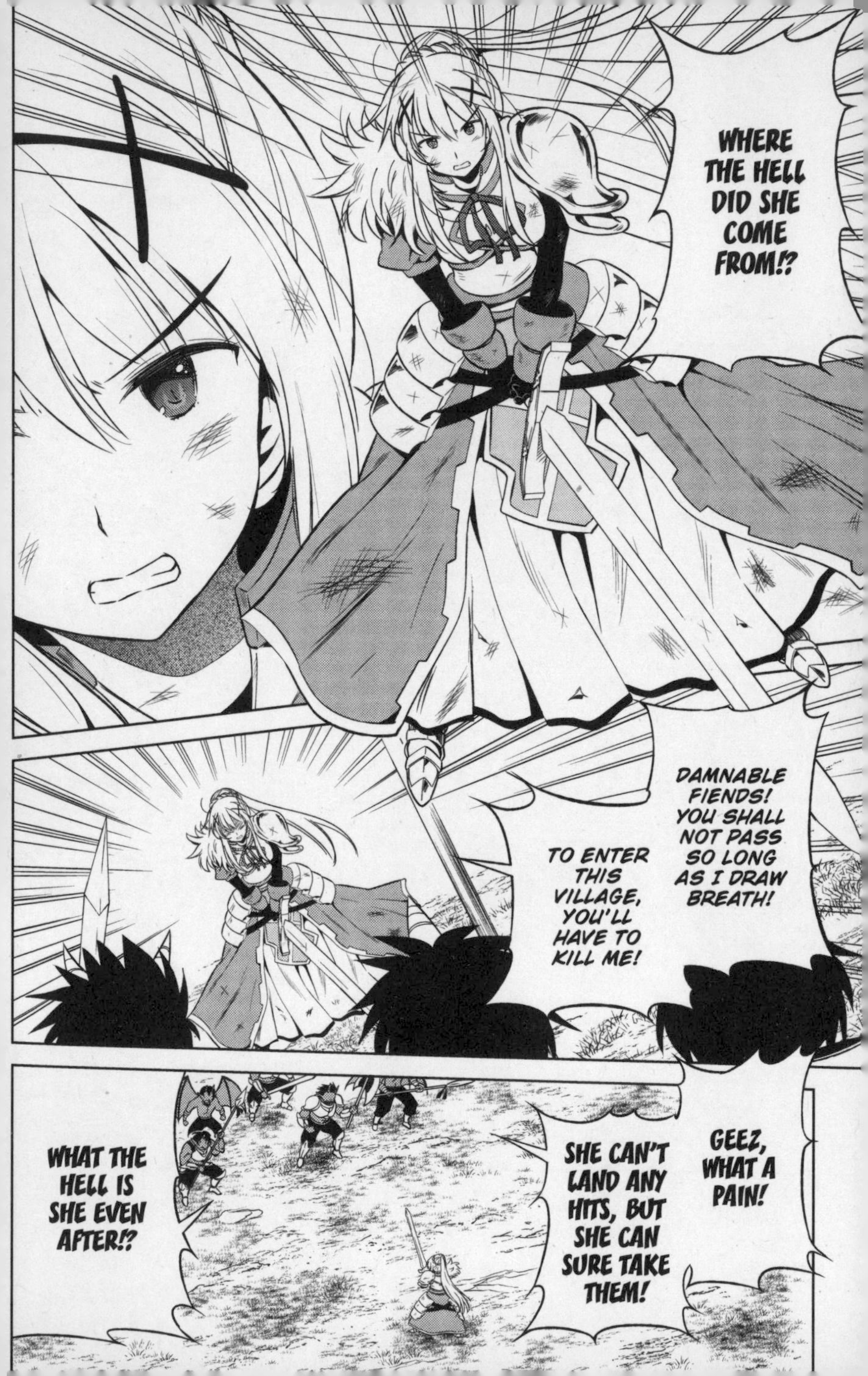
WHERE THE HELL DID SHE COME FROM!?
DAMNABLE FIENDS! YOU SHALL NOT PASS SO LONG AS I DRAW BREATH!
TO ENTER THIS VILLAGE, YOU'LL HAVE TO KILL ME!
GEEZ, WHAT A PAIN!
SHE CAN'T LAND ANY HITS, BUT SHE CAN SURE TAKE THEM!
WHAT THE HELL IS SHE EVEN AFTER!?

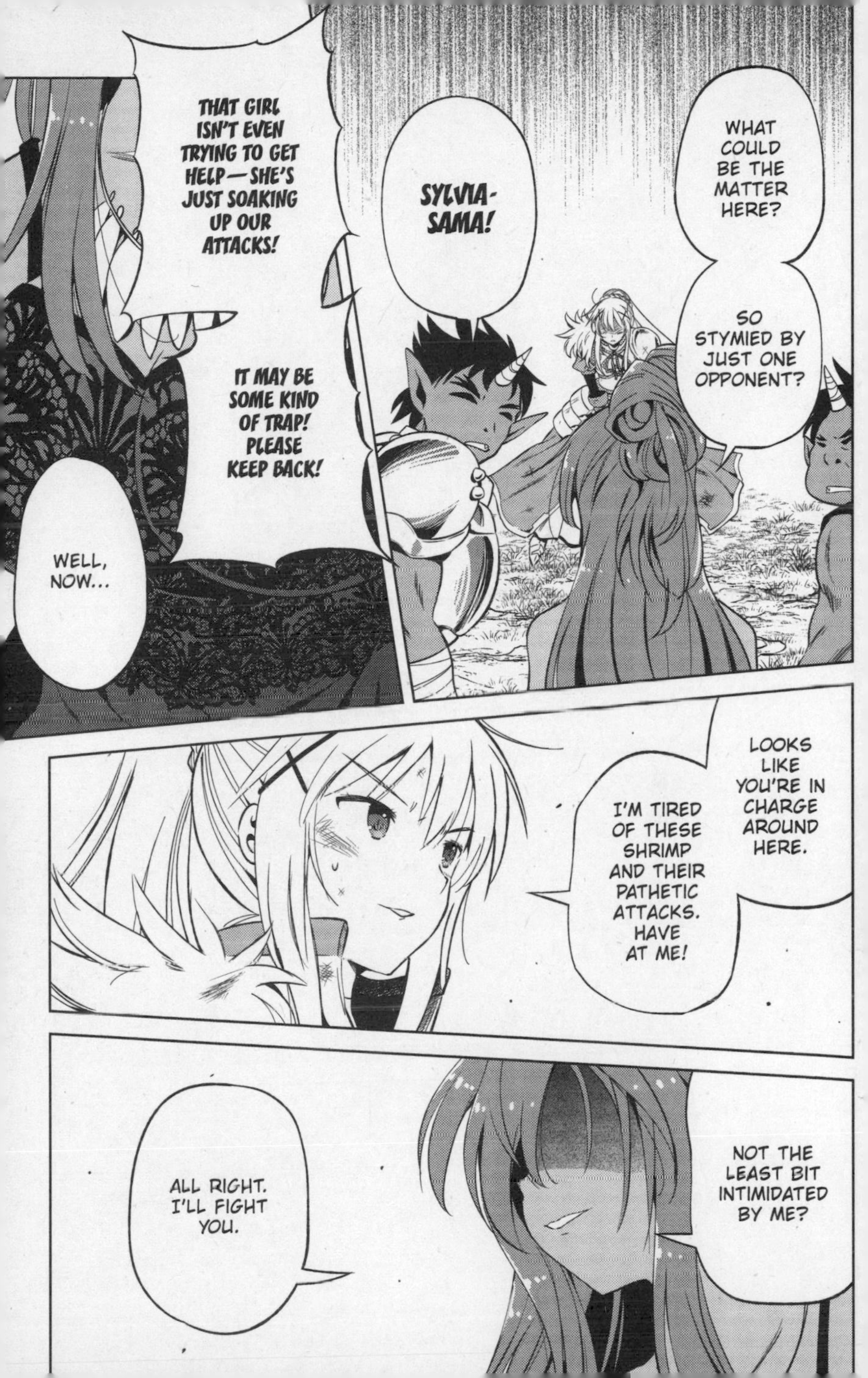
WHAT COULD BE THE MATTER HERE?
SO STYMIED BY JUST ONE OPPONENT?
SYLVIA-SAMA!
THAT GIRL ISN'T EVEN TRYING TO GET HELP—SHE'S JUST SOAKING UP OUR ATTACKS!
IT MAY BE SOME KIND OF TRAP! PLEASE KEEP BACK!
WELL, NOW...
LOOKS LIKE YOU'RE IN CHARGE AROUND HERE.
I'M TIRED OF THESE SHRIMP AND THEIR PATHETIC ATTACKS. HAVE AT ME!
NOT THE LEAST BIT INTIMIDATED BY ME?
ALL RIGHT. I'LL FIGHT YOU.

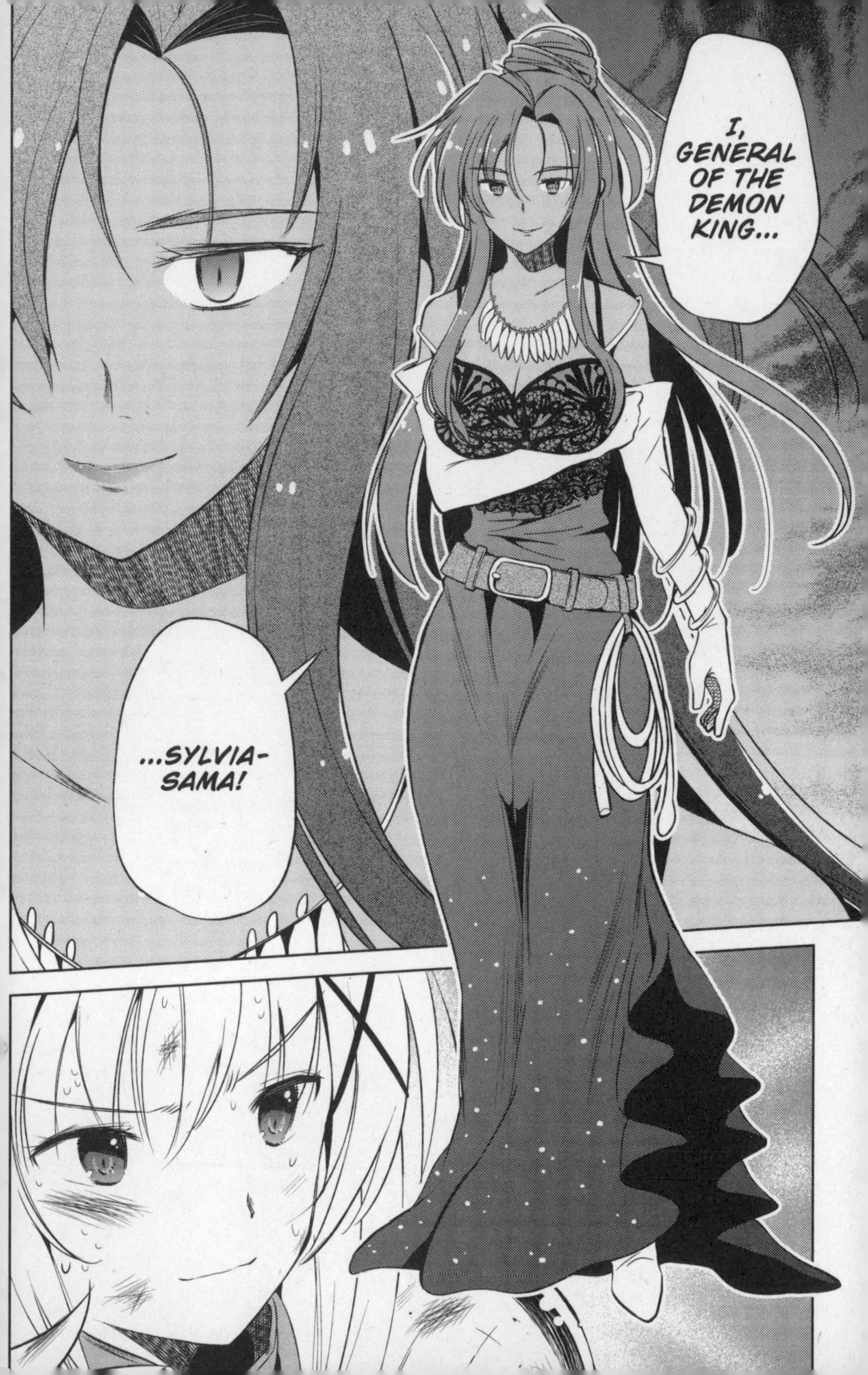
I, GENERAL OF THE DEMON KING...
...SYLVIA-SAMA!

GOD'S
BLESSING
ON THIS
WONDERFUL
WORLD!

8

8

GOD'S
BLESSING
ON THIS
WONDERFUL
WORLD!

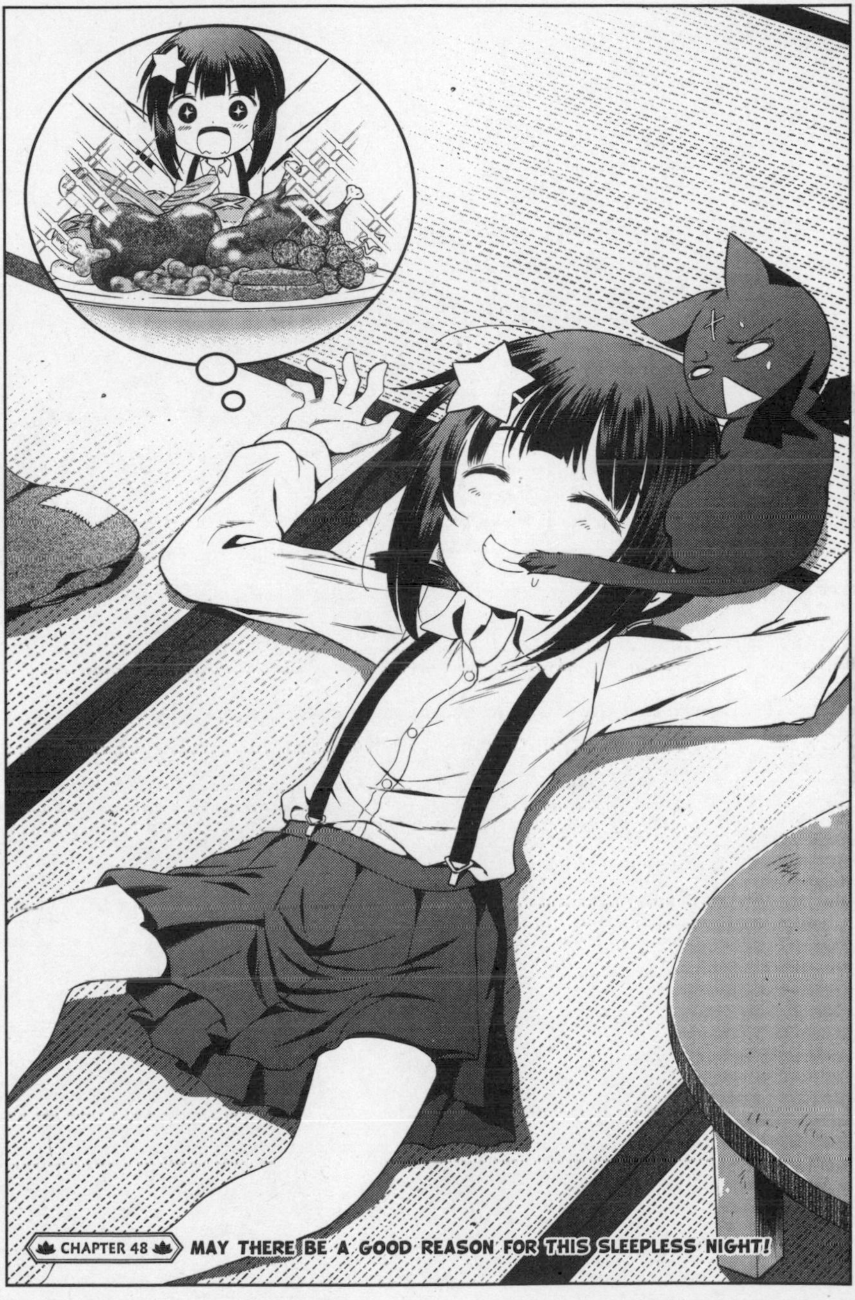
CHAPTER 48
MAY THERE BE A GOOD REASON FOR THIS SLEEPLESS NIGHT!

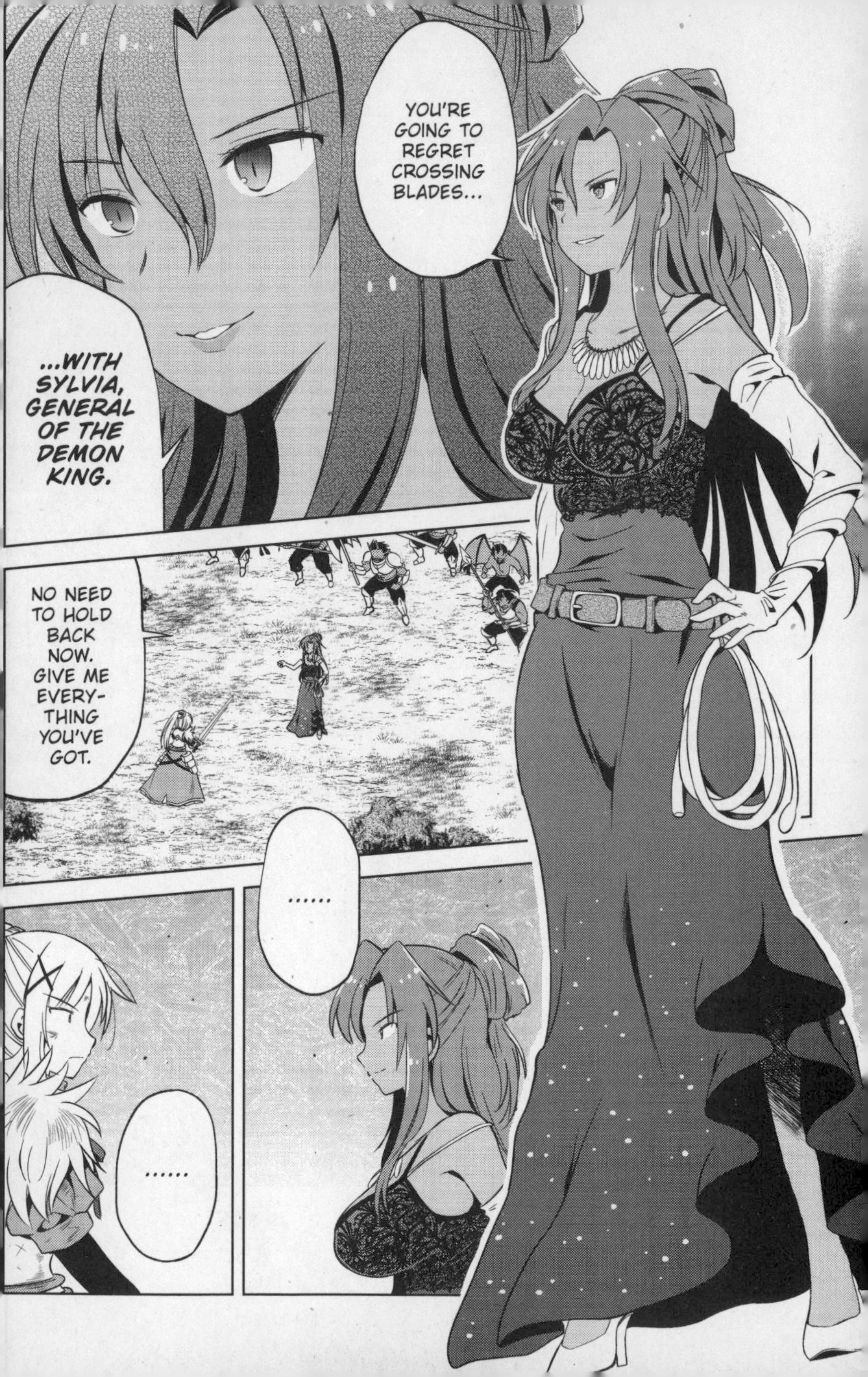
YOU'RE GOING TO REGRET CROSSING BLADES...
...WITH SYLVIA, GENERAL OF THE DEMON KING.
NO NEED TO HOLD BACK NOW. GIVE ME EVERY-THING YOU'VE GOT.
......
......

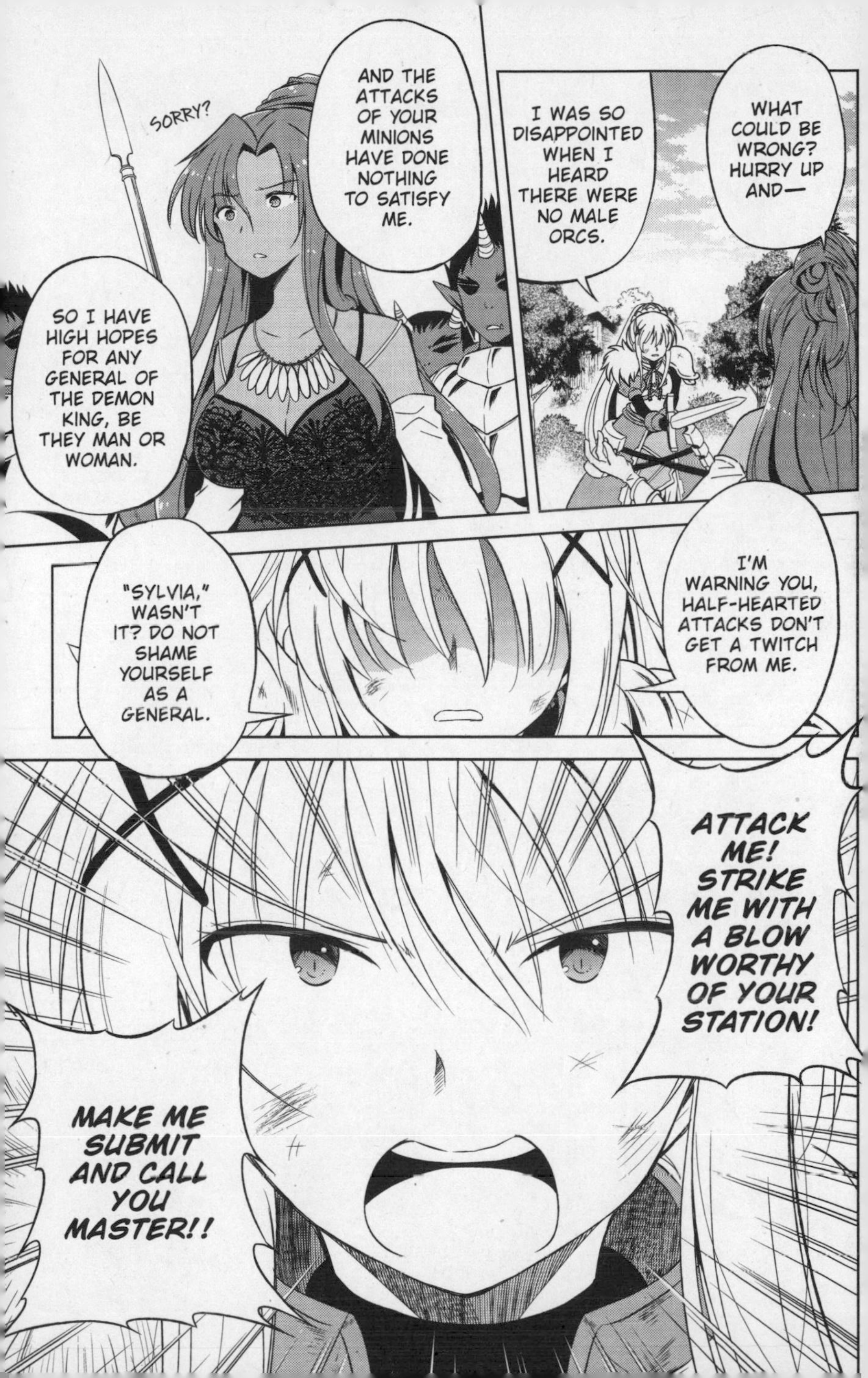
WHAT COULD BE WRONG? HURRY UP AND—
I WAS SO DISAPPOINTED WHEN I HEARD THERE WERE NO MALE ORCS.
AND THE ATTACKS OF YOUR MINIONS HAVE DONE NOTHING TO SATISFY ME.
SORRY?
SO I HAVE HIGH HOPES FOR ANY GENERAL OF THE DEMON KING, BE THEY MAN OR WOMAN.
I'M WARNING YOU, HALF-HEARTED ATTACKS DON'T GET A TWITCH FROM ME.
"SYLVIA," WASN'T IT? DO NOT SHAME YOURSELF AS A GENERAL.
ATTACK ME! STRIKE ME WITH A BLOW WORTHY OF YOUR STATION!
MAKE ME SUBMIT AND CALL YOU MASTER!!

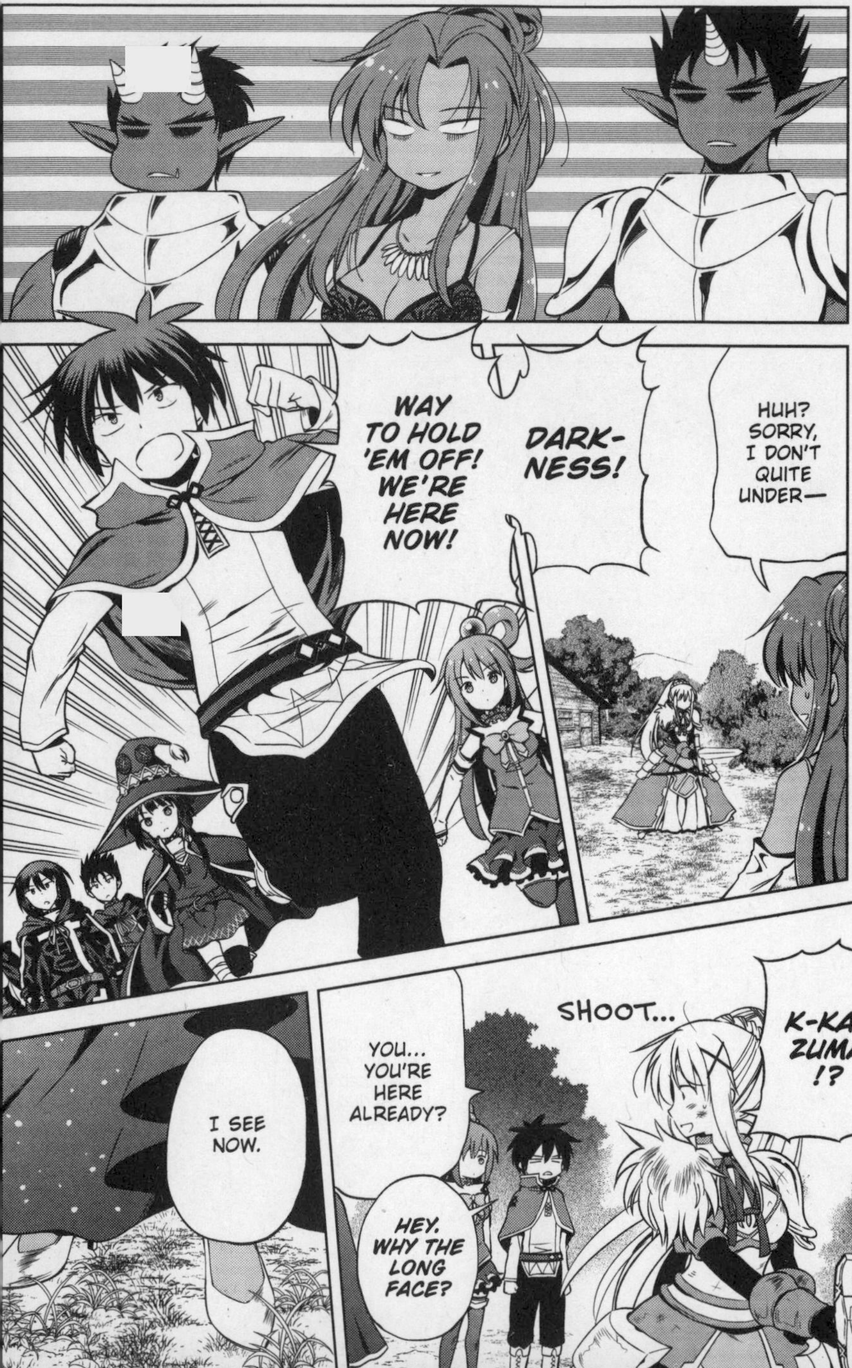
HUH? SORRY, I DON'T QUITE UNDER—
DARK-NESS!
WAY TO HOLD 'EM OFF! WE'RE HERE NOW!
K-KA-ZUMA !?
SHOOT...
YOU... YOU'RE HERE ALREADY?
HEY. WHY THE LONG FACE?
I SEE NOW.

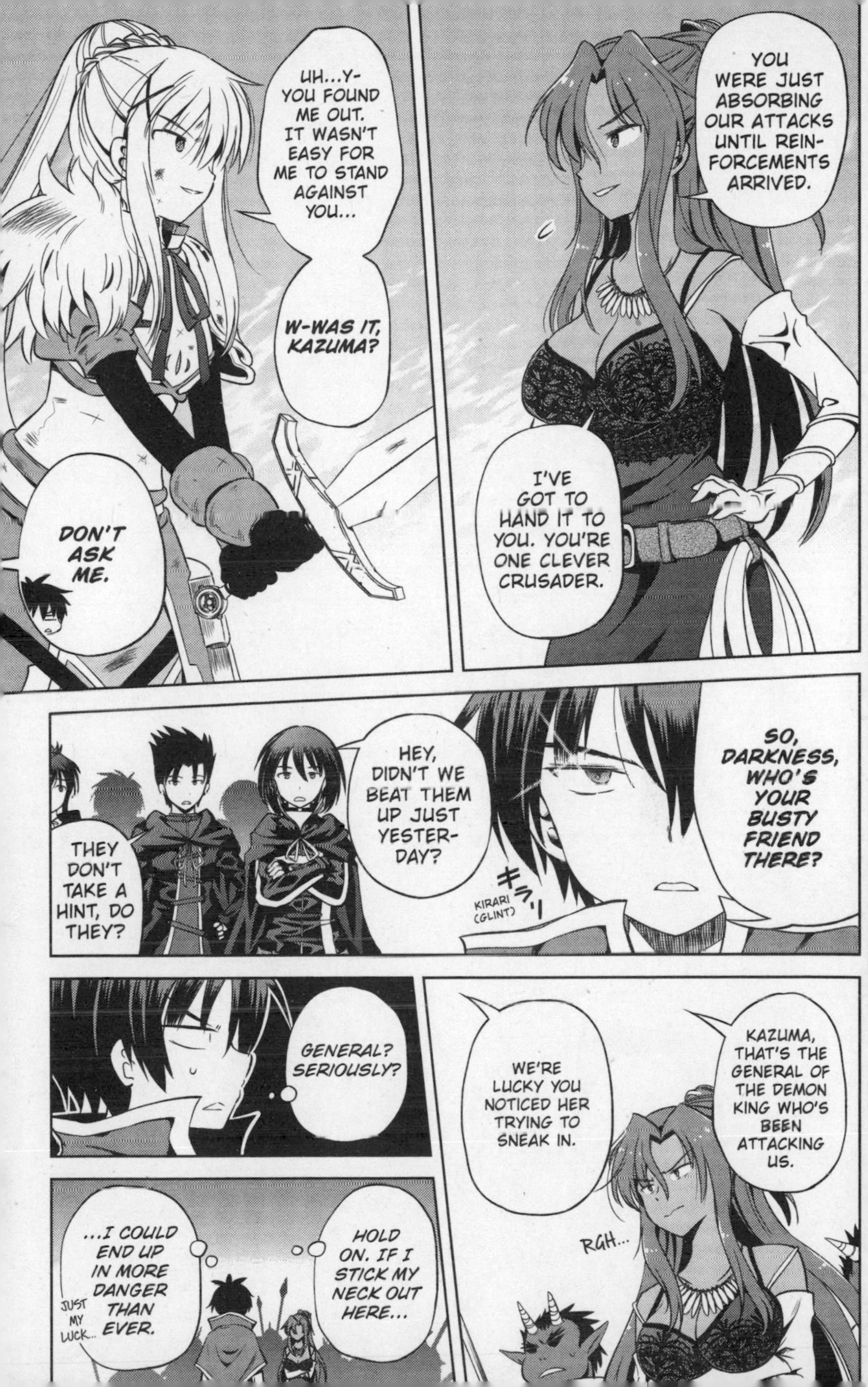
YOU WERE JUST ABSORBING OUR ATTACKS UNTIL REIN-FORCEMENTS ARRIVED.
I'VE GOT TO HAND IT TO YOU. YOU'RE ONE CLEVER CRUSADER.
UH...Y-YOU FOUND ME OUT. IT WASN'T EASY FOR ME TO STAND AGAINST YOU...
W-WAS IT, KAZUMA?
DON'T ASK ME.
SO, DARKNESS, WHO'S YOUR BUSTY FRIEND THERE?
KIRARI (GLINT)
HEY, DIDN'T WE BEAT THEM UP JUST YESTER-DAY?
THEY DON'T TAKE A HINT, DO THEY?
KAZUMA, THAT'S THE GENERAL OF THE DEMON KING WHO'S BEEN ATTACKING US.
WE'RE LUCKY YOU NOTICED HER TRYING TO SNEAK IN.
RGH...
GENERAL? SERIOUSLY?
HOLD ON. IF I STICK MY NECK OUT HERE...
...I COULD END UP IN MORE DANGER THAN EVER.
JUST MY LUCK...

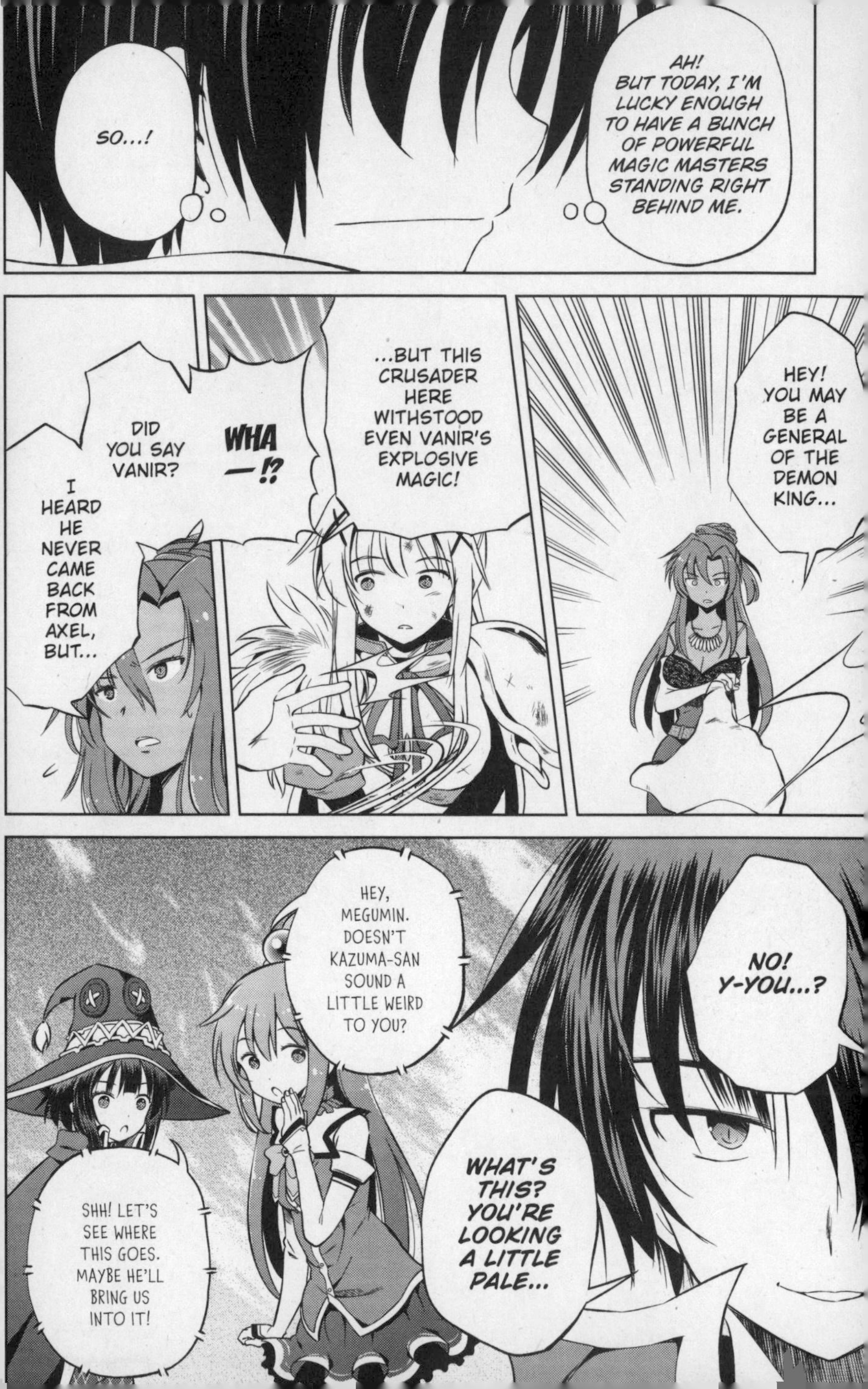
AH! BUT TODAY, I'M LUCKY ENOUGH TO HAVE A BUNCH OF POWERFUL MAGIC MASTERS STANDING RIGHT BEHIND ME.
SO...!
HEY! YOU MAY BE A GENERAL OF THE DEMON KING...
...BUT THIS CRUSADER HERE WITHSTOOD EVEN VANIR'S EXPLOSIVE MAGIC!
WHA—!?
DID YOU SAY VANIR?
I HEARD HE NEVER CAME BACK FROM AXEL, BUT...
NO! Y-YOU...?
HEY, MEGUMIN. DOESN'T KAZUMA-SAN SOUND A LITTLE WEIRD TO YOU?
WHAT'S THIS? YOU'RE LOOKING A LITTLE PALE...
SHH! LET'S SEE WHERE THIS GOES. MAYBE HE'LL BRING US INTO IT!

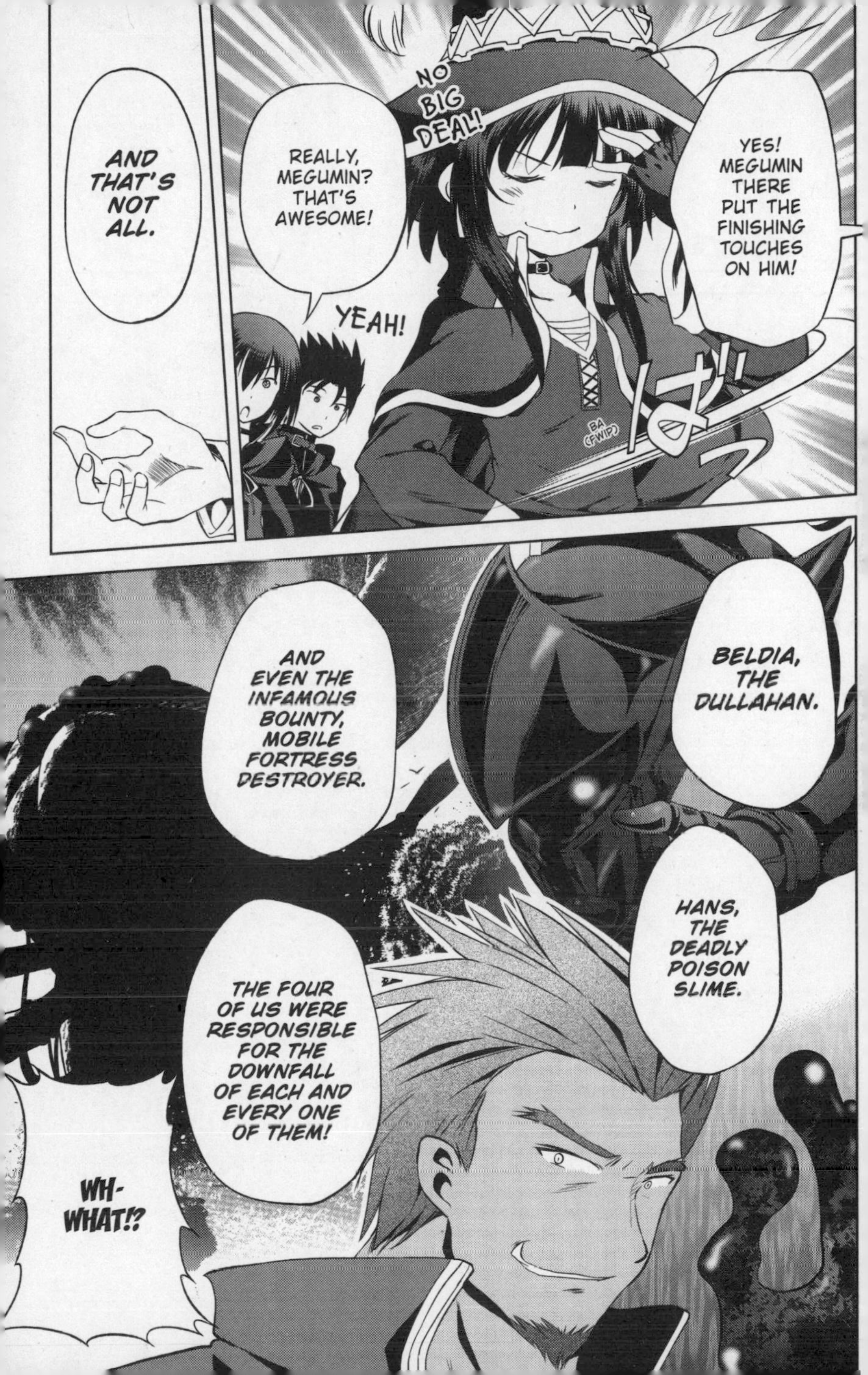
YES! MEGUMIN THERE PUT THE FINISHING TOUCHES ON HIM!
NO BIG DEAL!
ばっ
BA (FWIP)
REALLY, MEGUMIN? THAT'S AWESOME!
YEAH!
AND THAT'S NOT ALL.
BELDIA, THE DULLAHAN.
AND EVEN THE INFAMOUS BOUNTY, MOBILE FORTRESS DESTROYER.
HANS, THE DEADLY POISON SLIME.
THE FOUR OF US WERE RESPONSIBLE FOR THE DOWNFALL OF EACH AND EVERY ONE OF THEM!
WH-WHAT!?

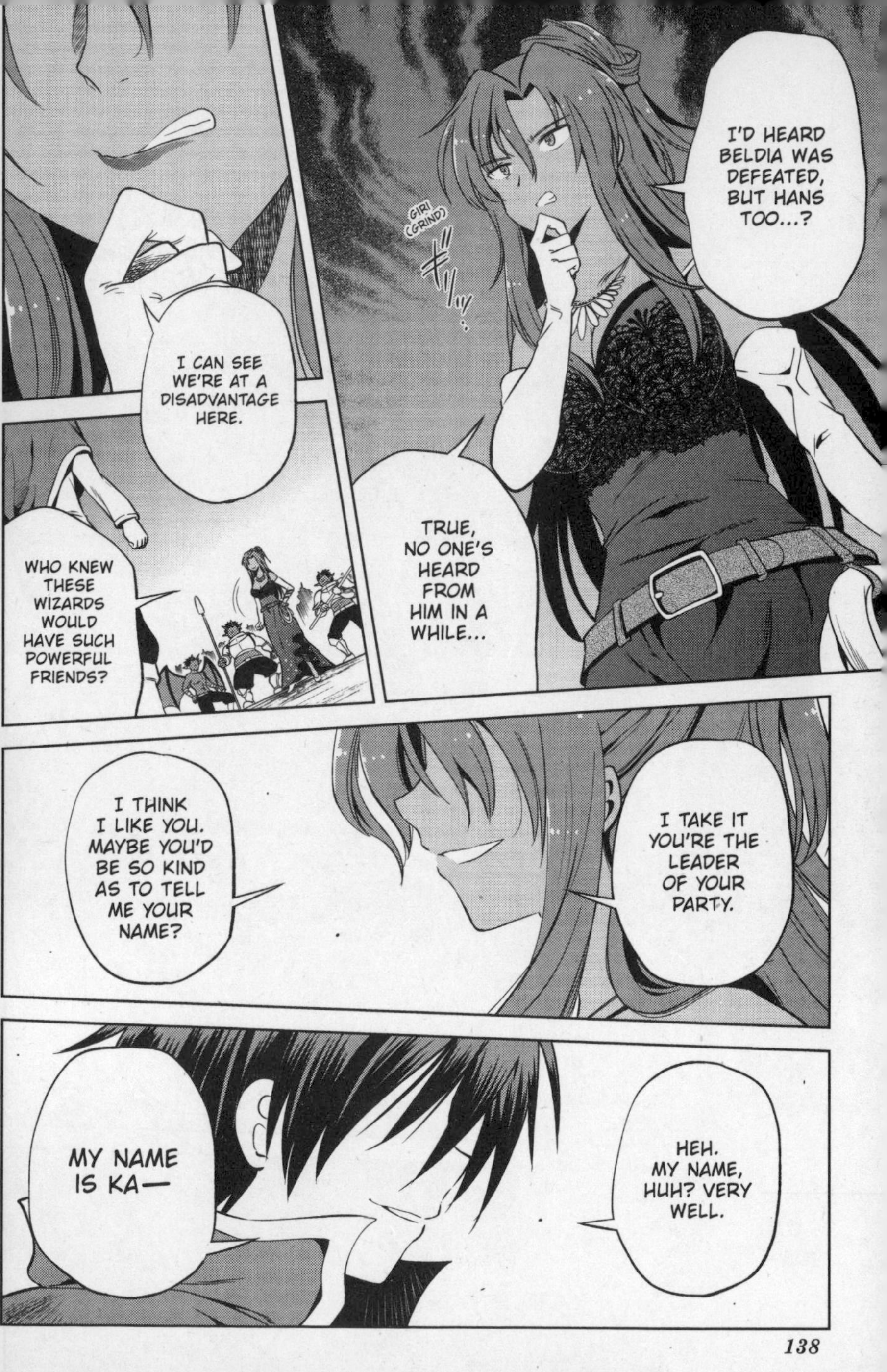
I'D HEARD BELDIA WAS DEFEATED, BUT HANS TOO...?
GIRI (GRIND)
ギリッ
TRUE, NO ONE'S HEARD FROM HIM IN A WHILE...
I CAN SEE WE'RE AT A DISADVANTAGE HERE.
WHO KNEW THESE WIZARDS WOULD HAVE SUCH POWERFUL FRIENDS?
I TAKE IT YOU'RE THE LEADER OF YOUR PARTY.
I THINK I LIKE YOU. MAYBE YOU'D BE SO KIND AS TO TELL ME YOUR NAME?
HEH. MY NAME, HUH? VERY WELL.
MY NAME IS KA—

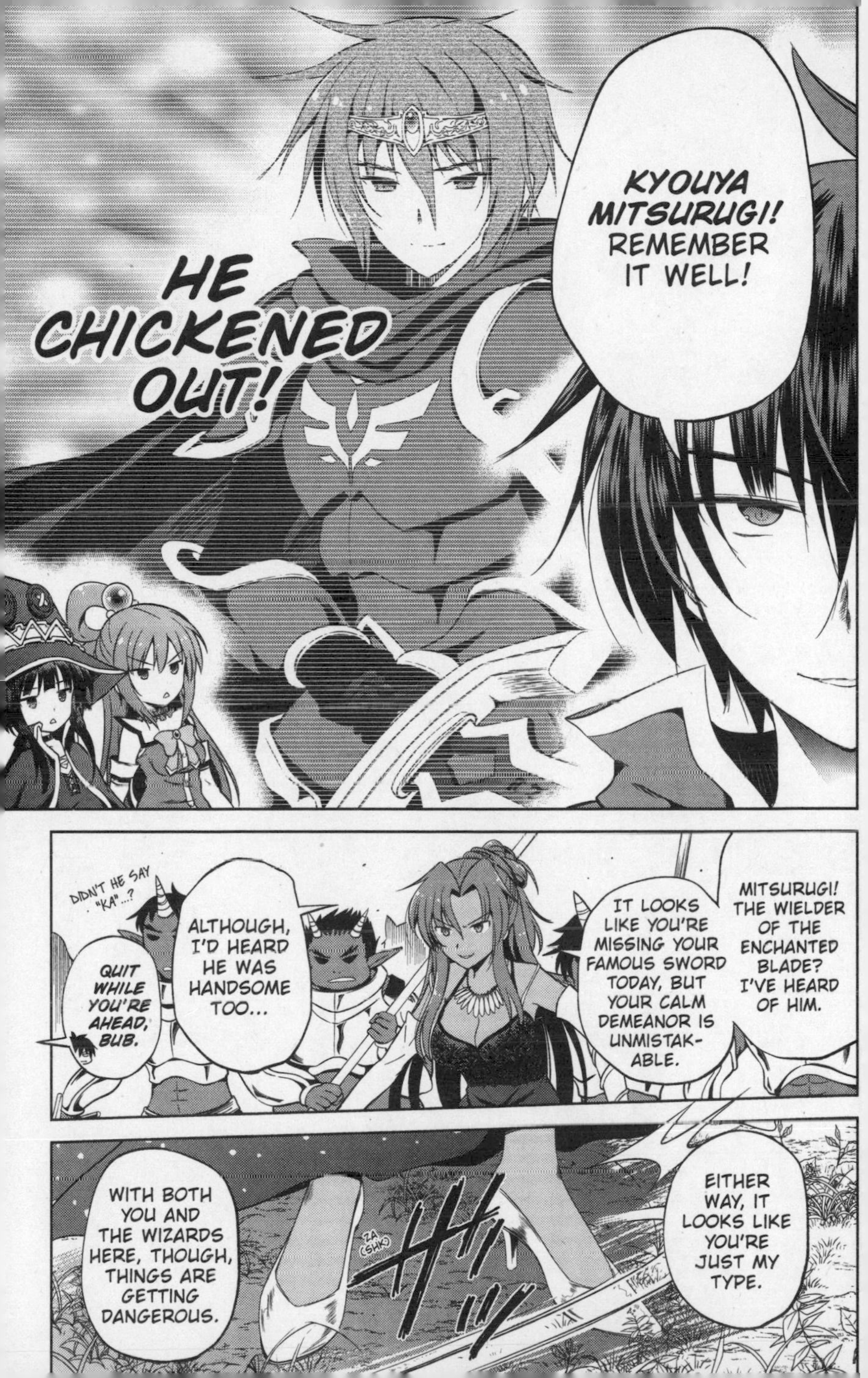
KYOUYA MITSURUGI! REMEMBER IT WELL!
HE CHICKENED OUT!
MITSURUGI! THE WIELDER OF THE ENCHANTED BLADE? I'VE HEARD OF HIM.
IT LOOKS LIKE YOU'RE MISSING YOUR FAMOUS SWORD TODAY, BUT YOUR CALM DEMEANOR IS UNMISTAK-ABLE.
ALTHOUGH, I'D HEARD HE WAS HANDSOME TOO...
DIDN'T HE SAY "KA"...?
QUIT WHILE YOU'RE AHEAD, BUB.
EITHER WAY, IT LOOKS LIKE YOU'RE JUST MY TYPE.
ZA (SHK)
WITH BOTH YOU AND THE WIZARDS HERE, THOUGH, THINGS ARE GETTING DANGEROUS.

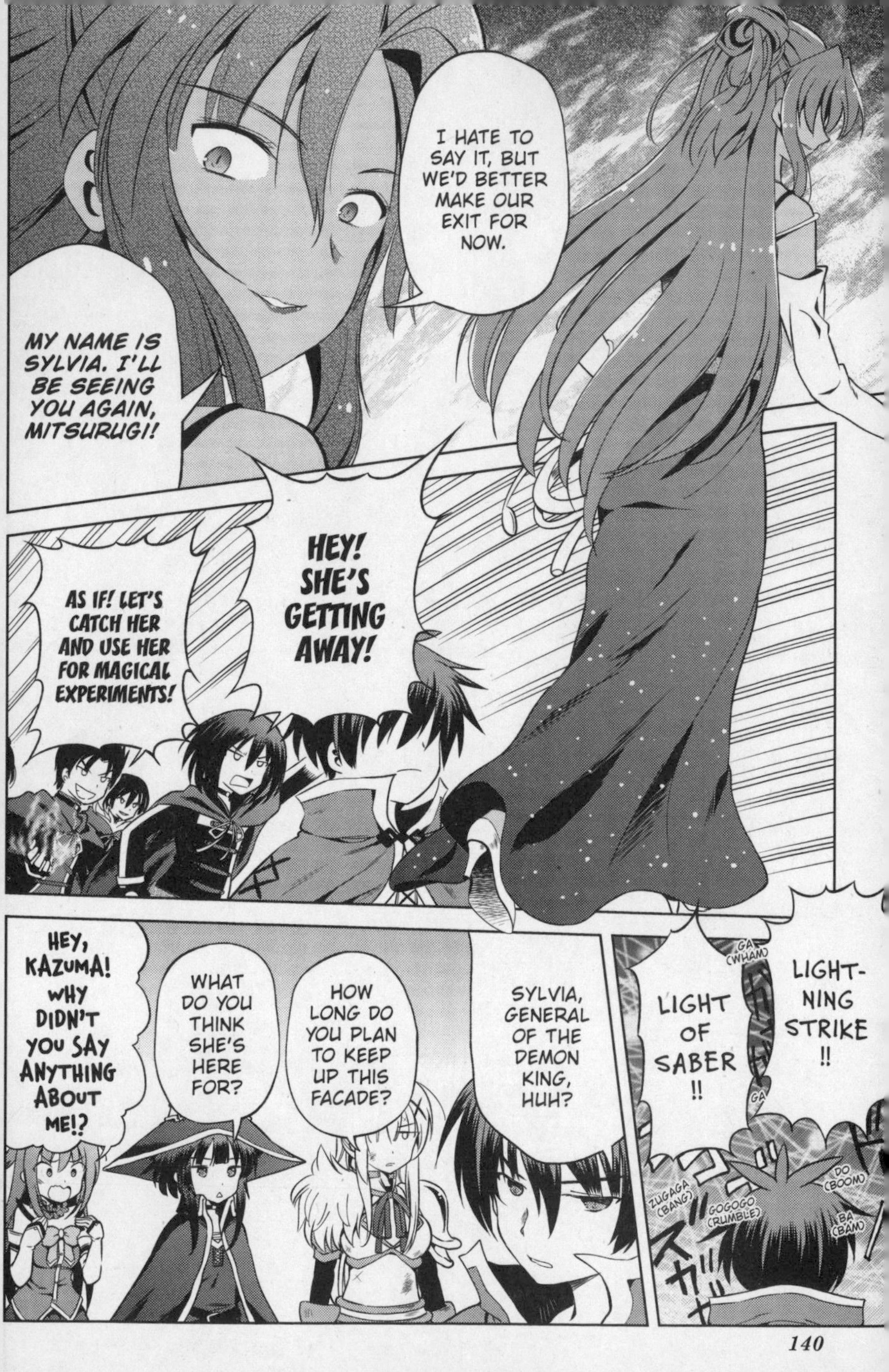
I HATE TO SAY IT, BUT WE'D BETTER MAKE OUR EXIT FOR NOW.
MY NAME IS SYLVIA. I'LL BE SEEING YOU AGAIN, MITSURUGI!
HEY! SHE'S GETTING AWAY!
AS IF! LET'S CATCH HER AND USE HER FOR MAGICAL EXPERIMENTS!
GA (WHAM)
LIGHTNING STRIKE!!
LIGHT OF SABER!!
GA
DO (BOOM)
ZUGAGA (BANG)
GOGOGO (RUMBLE)
BA (BAM)
SYLVIA, GENERAL OF THE DEMON KING, HUH?
HOW LONG DO YOU PLAN TO KEEP UP THIS FACADE?
WHAT DO YOU THINK SHE'S HERE FOR?
HEY, KAZUMA! WHY DIDN'T YOU SAY ANYTHING ABOUT ME!?

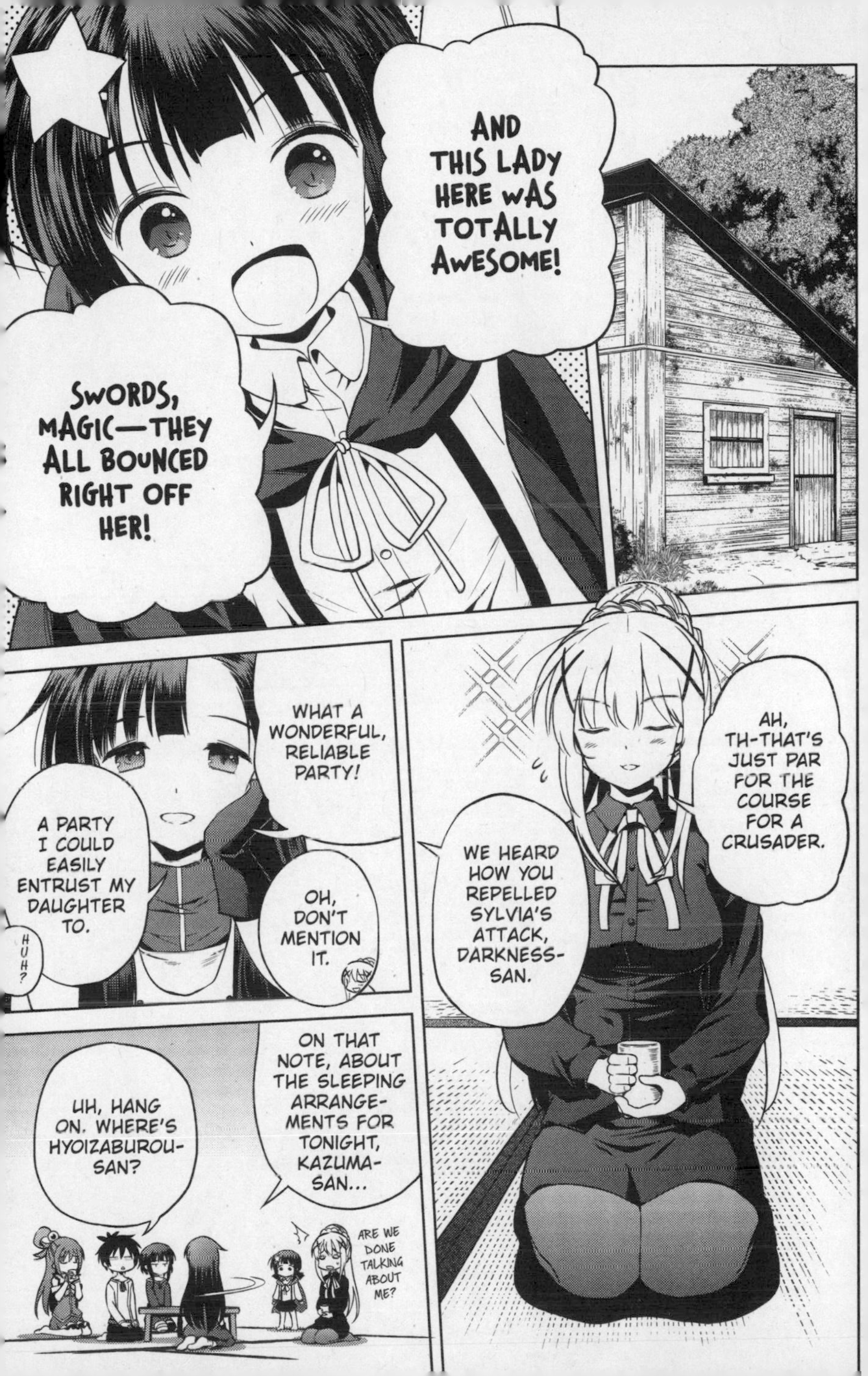
AND THIS LADY HERE WAS TOTALLY AWESOME!
SWORDS, MAGIC—THEY ALL BOUNCED RIGHT OFF HER!
WE HEARD HOW YOU REPELLED SYLVIA'S ATTACK, DARKNESS-SAN.
AH, TH-THAT'S JUST PAR FOR THE COURSE FOR A CRUSADER.
WHAT A WONDERFUL, RELIABLE PARTY!
A PARTY I COULD EASILY ENTRUST MY DAUGHTER TO.
OH, DON'T MENTION IT.
HUH?
ON THAT NOTE, ABOUT THE SLEEPING ARRANGE-MENTS FOR TONIGHT, KAZUMA-SAN...
UH, HANG ON. WHERE'S HYOIZABUROU-SAN?
ARE WE DONE TALKING ABOUT ME?

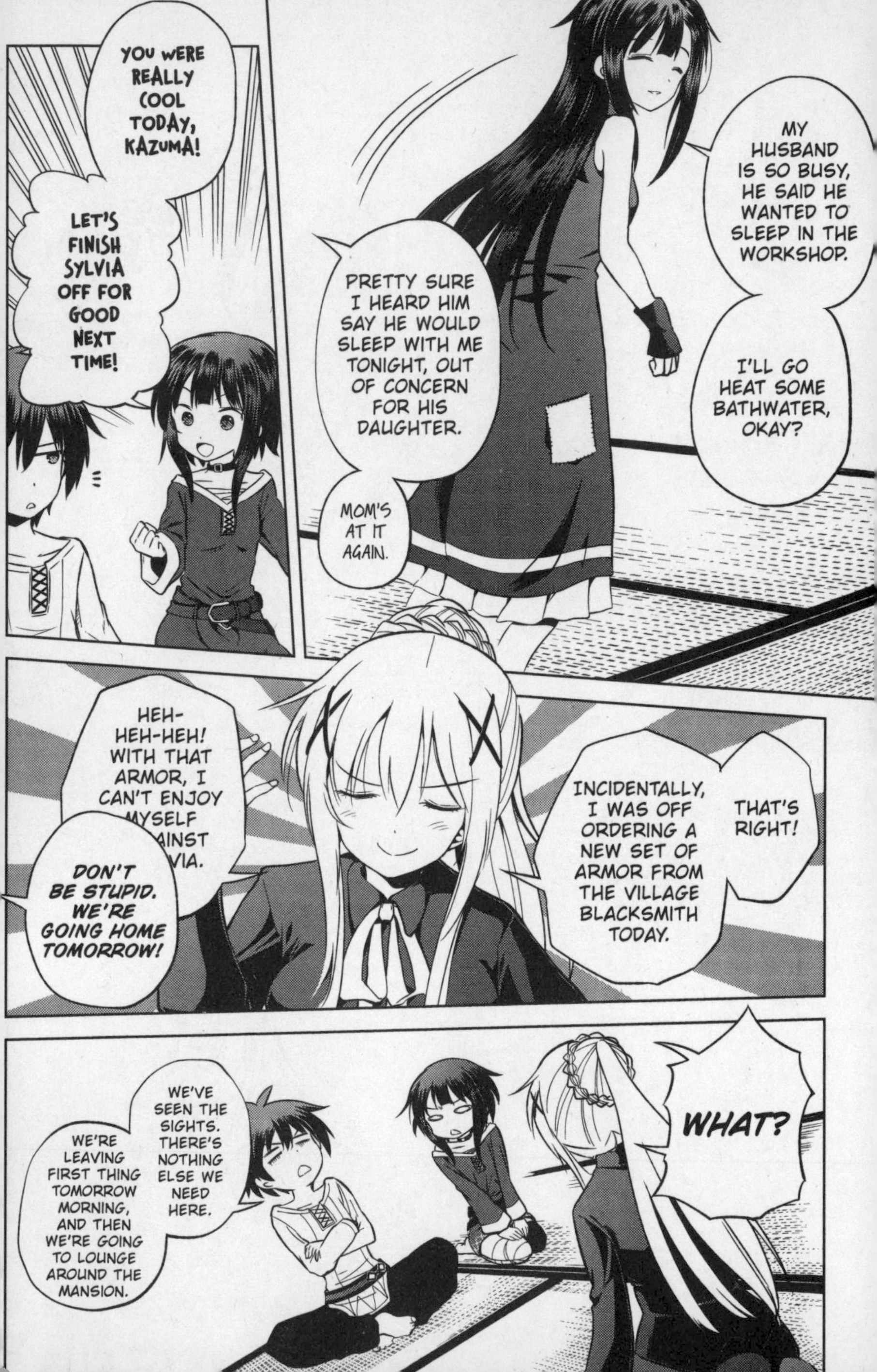
MY HUSBAND IS SO BUSY, HE SAID HE WANTED TO SLEEP IN THE WORKSHOP.
I'LL GO HEAT SOME BATHWATER, OKAY?
PRETTY SURE I HEARD HIM SAY HE WOULD SLEEP WITH ME TONIGHT, OUT OF CONCERN FOR HIS DAUGHTER.
MOM'S AT IT AGAIN.
YOU WERE REALLY COOL TODAY, KAZUMA!
LET'S FINISH SYLVIA OFF FOR GOOD NEXT TIME!
THAT'S RIGHT!
INCIDENTALLY, I WAS OFF ORDERING A NEW SET OF ARMOR FROM THE VILLAGE BLACKSMITH TODAY.
HEH-HEH-HEH! WITH THAT ARMOR, I CAN'T ENJOY MYSELF
DON'T BE STUPID. WE'RE GOING HOME TOMORROW!
WHAT?
WE'VE SEEN THE SIGHTS. THERE'S NOTHING ELSE WE NEED HERE.
WE'RE LEAVING FIRST THING TOMORROW MORNING, AND THEN WE'RE GOING TO LOUNGE AROUND THE MANSION.

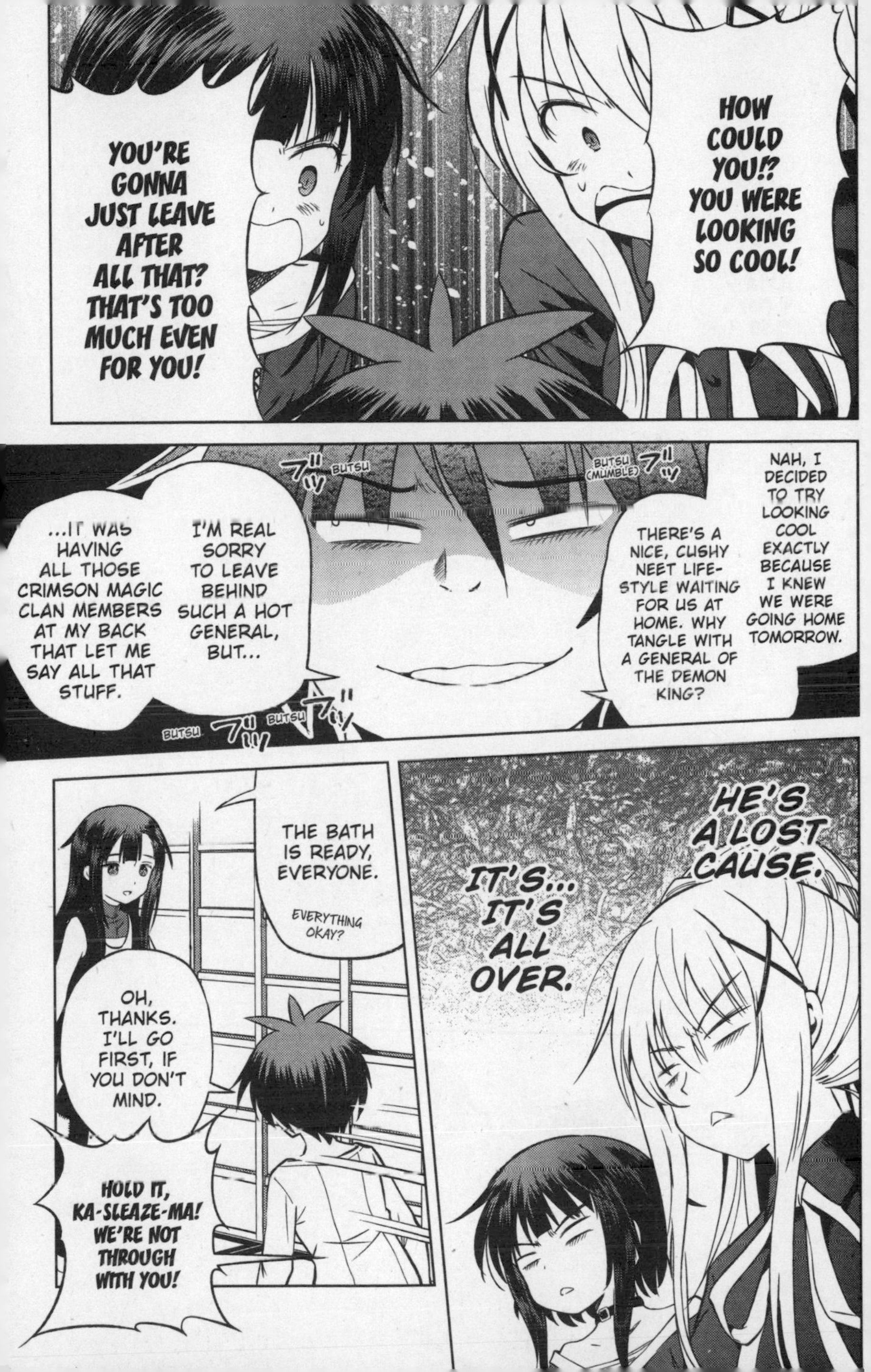
HOW COULD YOU!? YOU WERE LOOKING SO COOL!
YOU'RE GONNA JUST LEAVE AFTER ALL THAT? THAT'S TOO MUCH EVEN FOR YOU!
NAH, I DECIDED TO TRY LOOKING COOL EXACTLY BECAUSE I KNEW WE WERE GOING HOME TOMORROW.
BUTSU (MUMBLE)
THERE'S A NICE, CUSHY NEET LIFE-STYLE WAITING FOR US AT HOME. WHY TANGLE WITH A GENERAL OF THE DEMON KING?
BUTSU
I'M REAL SORRY TO LEAVE BEHIND SUCH A HOT GENERAL, BUT...
...IT WAS HAVING ALL THOSE CRIMSON MAGIC CLAN MEMBERS AT MY BACK THAT LET ME SAY ALL THAT STUFF.
BUTSU
BUTSU
HE'S A LOST CAUSE.
IT'S... IT'S ALL OVER.
THE BATH IS READY, EVERYONE.
EVERYTHING OKAY?
OH, THANKS. I'LL GO FIRST, IF YOU DON'T MIND.
HOLD IT, KA-SLEAZE-MA! WE'RE NOT THROUGH WITH YOU!

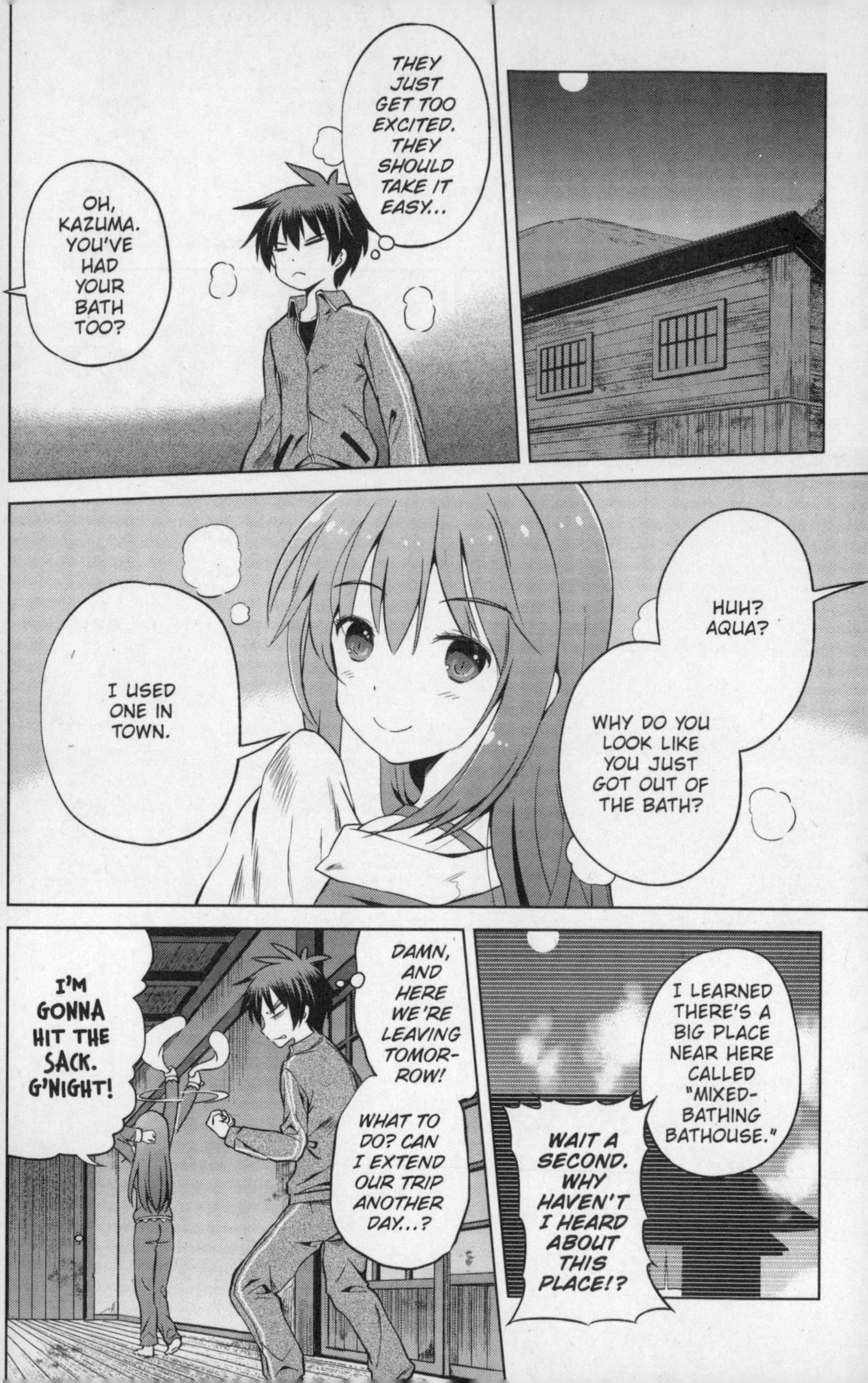
THEY JUST GET TOO EXCITED. THEY SHOULD TAKE IT EASY...
OH, KAZUMA. YOU'VE HAD YOUR BATH TOO?
HUH? AQUA?
WHY DO YOU LOOK LIKE YOU JUST GOT OUT OF THE BATH?
I USED ONE IN TOWN.
I LEARNED THERE'S A BIG PLACE NEAR HERE CALLED "MIXED-BATHING BATHOUSE."
WAIT A SECOND. WHY HAVEN'T I HEARD ABOUT THIS PLACE!?
DAMN, AND HERE WE'RE LEAVING TOMOR-ROW!
I'M GONNA HIT THE SACK. G'NIGHT!
WHAT TO DO? CAN I EXTEND OUR TRIP ANOTHER DAY...?

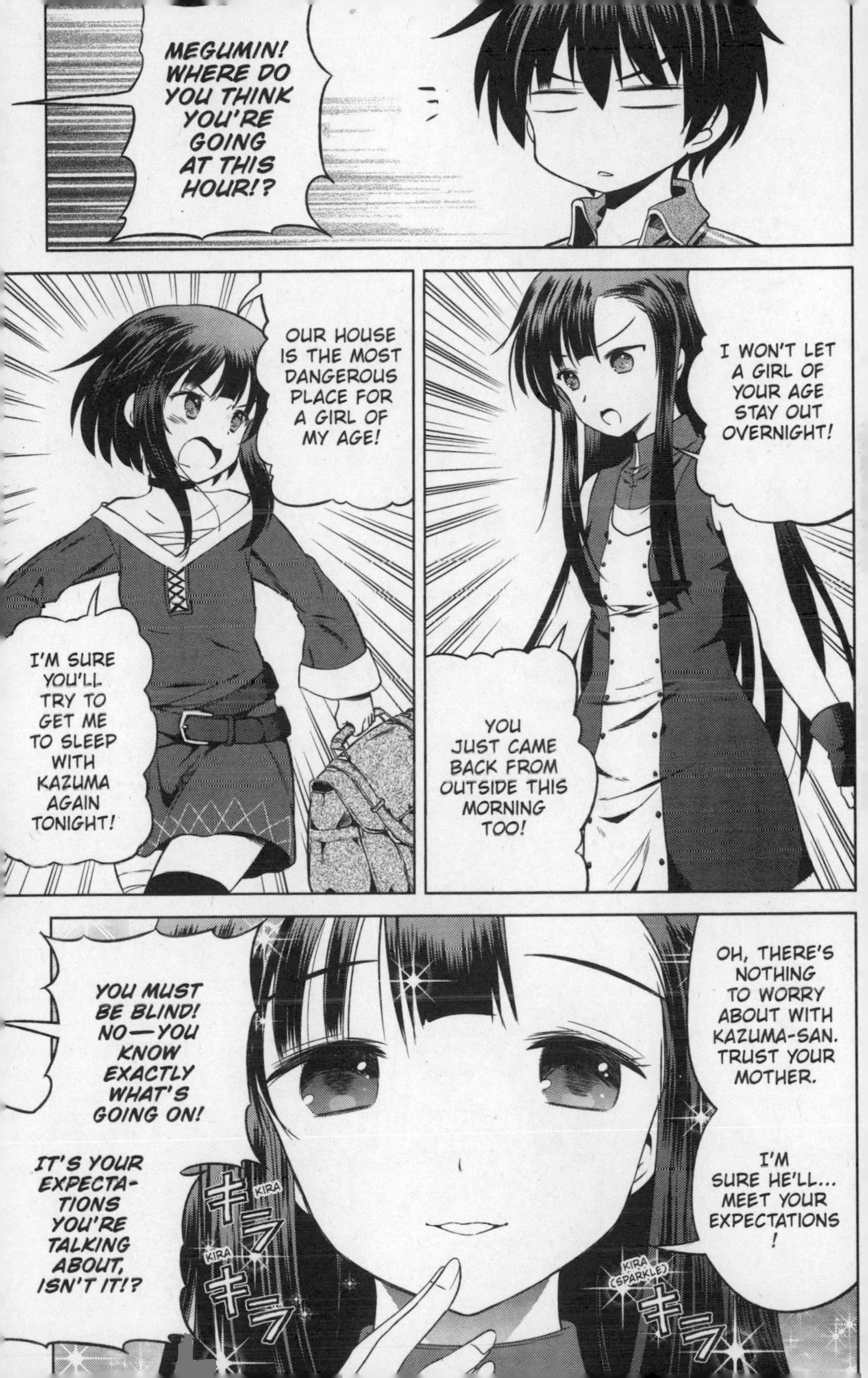
MEGUMIN! WHERE DO YOU THINK YOU'RE GOING AT THIS HOUR!?
I WON'T LET A GIRL OF YOUR AGE STAY OUT OVERNIGHT!
YOU JUST CAME BACK FROM OUTSIDE THIS MORNING TOO!
OUR HOUSE IS THE MOST DANGEROUS PLACE FOR A GIRL OF MY AGE!
I'M SURE YOU'LL TRY TO GET ME TO SLEEP WITH KAZUMA AGAIN TONIGHT!
OH, THERE'S NOTHING TO WORRY ABOUT WITH KAZUMA-SAN. TRUST YOUR MOTHER.
I'M SURE HE'LL... MEET YOUR EXPECTATIONS!
キラ KIRA (SPARKLE)
キラ KIRA
キラ KIRA
YOU MUST BE BLIND! NO—YOU KNOW EXACTLY WHAT'S GOING ON!
IT'S YOUR EXPECTATIONS YOU'RE TALKING ABOUT, ISN'T IT!?

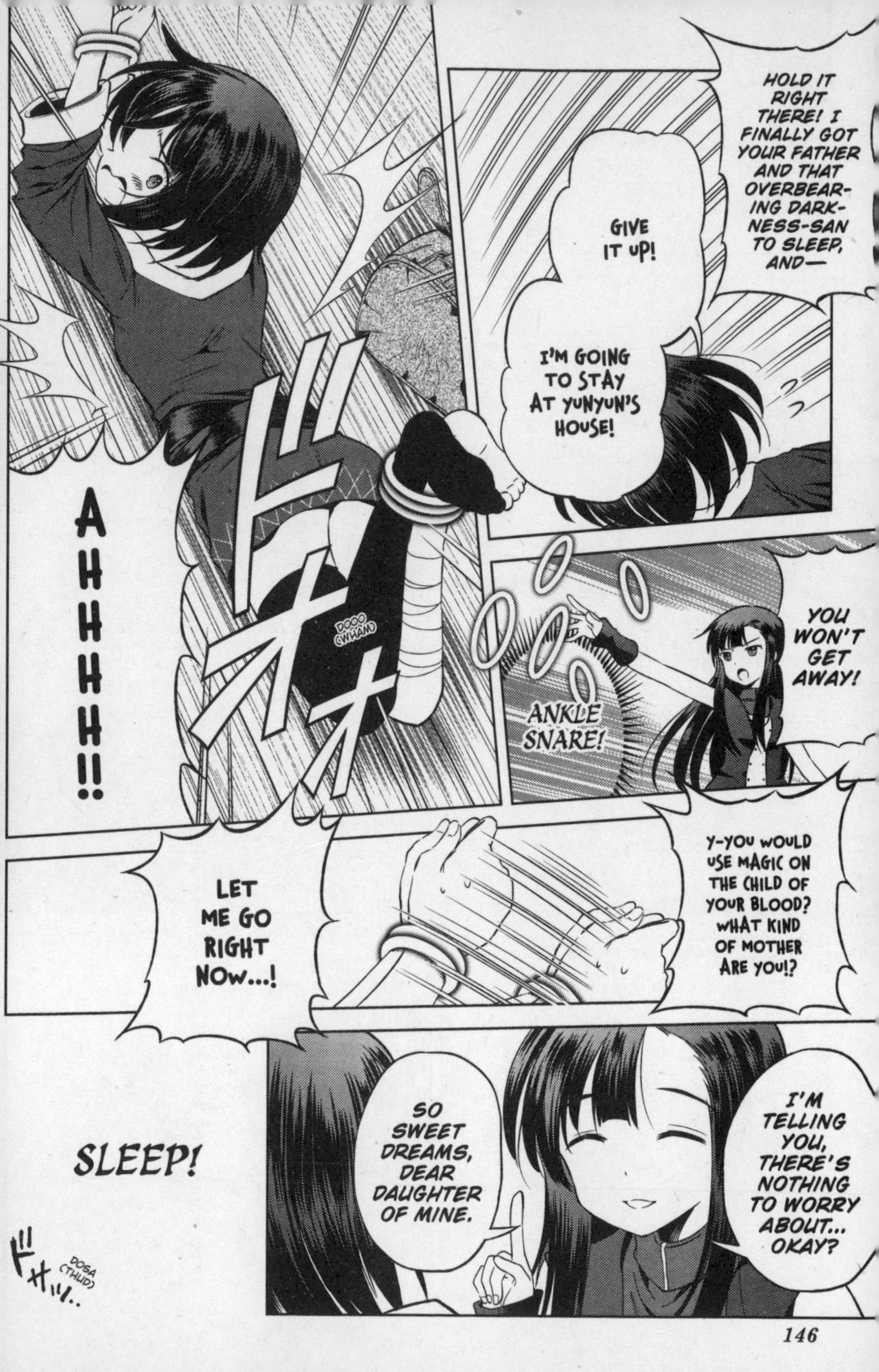
HOLD IT RIGHT THERE! I FINALLY GOT YOUR FATHER AND THAT OVERBEARING DARKNESS-SAN TO SLEEP, AND—
GIVE IT UP!
I'M GOING TO STAY AT YUNYUN'S HOUSE!
YOU WON'T GET AWAY!
ANKLE SNARE!
DOOO (WHAM)
AHHHH!!
Y-YOU WOULD USE MAGIC ON THE CHILD OF YOUR BLOOD? WHAT KIND OF MOTHER ARE YOU!?
LET ME GO RIGHT NOW...!
I'M TELLING YOU, THERE'S NOTHING TO WORRY ABOUT... OKAY?
SO SWEET DREAMS, DEAR DAUGHTER OF MINE.
SLEEP!
DOSA (THUD)

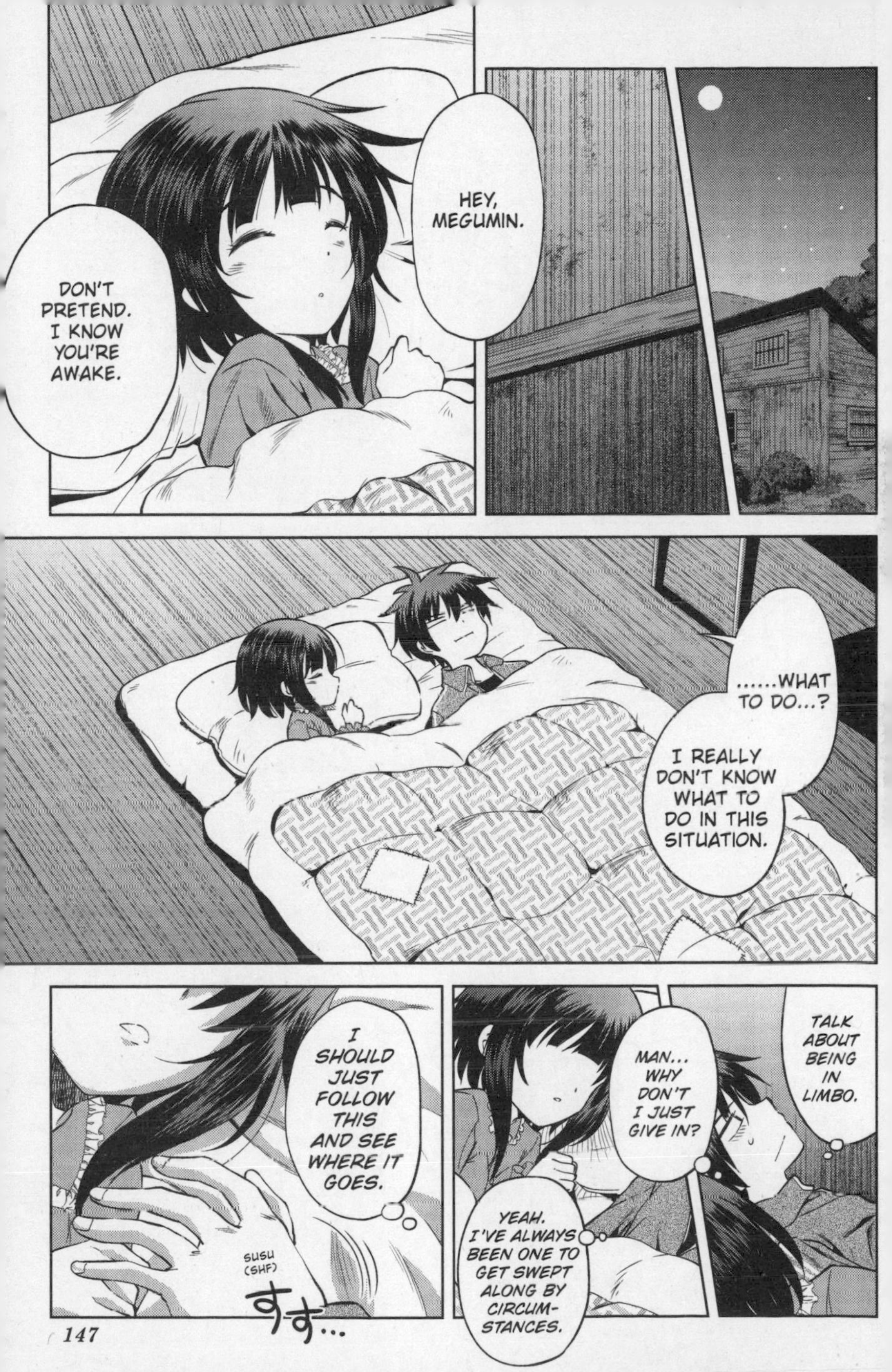
HEY, MEGUMIN.
DON'T PRETEND. I KNOW YOU'RE AWAKE.
......WHAT TO DO...?
I REALLY DON'T KNOW WHAT TO DO IN THIS SITUATION.
TALK ABOUT BEING IN LIMBO.
MAN... WHY DON'T I JUST GIVE IN?
YEAH. I'VE ALWAYS BEEN ONE TO GET SWEPT ALONG BY CIRCUM-STANCES.
I SHOULD JUST FOLLOW THIS AND SEE WHERE IT GOES.
SUSU (SHF)
すす…

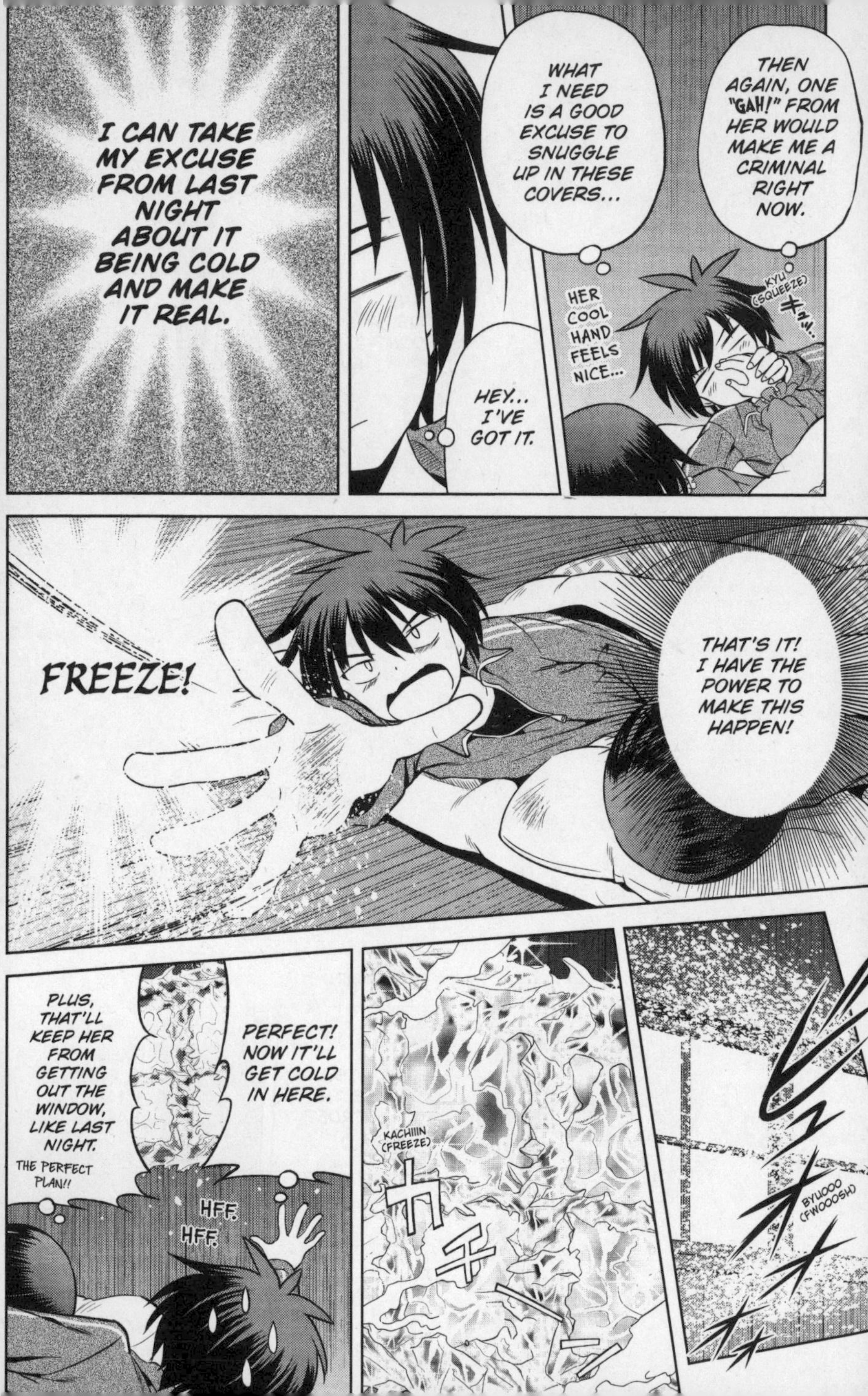
THEN AGAIN, ONE "GAH!" FROM HER WOULD MAKE ME A CRIMINAL RIGHT NOW.
KYU (SQUEEZE)
HER COOL HAND FEELS NICE...
WHAT I NEED IS A GOOD EXCUSE TO SNUGGLE UP IN THESE COVERS...
HEY... I'VE GOT IT.
I CAN TAKE MY EXCUSE FROM LAST NIGHT ABOUT IT BEING COLD AND MAKE IT REAL.
THAT'S IT! I HAVE THE POWER TO MAKE THIS HAPPEN!
FREEZE!
BYUOOO (FWOOOSH)
KACHIIN (FREEZE)
PERFECT! NOW IT'LL GET COLD IN HERE.
PLUS, THAT'LL KEEP HER FROM GETTING OUT THE WINDOW, LIKE LAST NIGHT.
THE PERFECT PLAN!!
HFF. HFF.

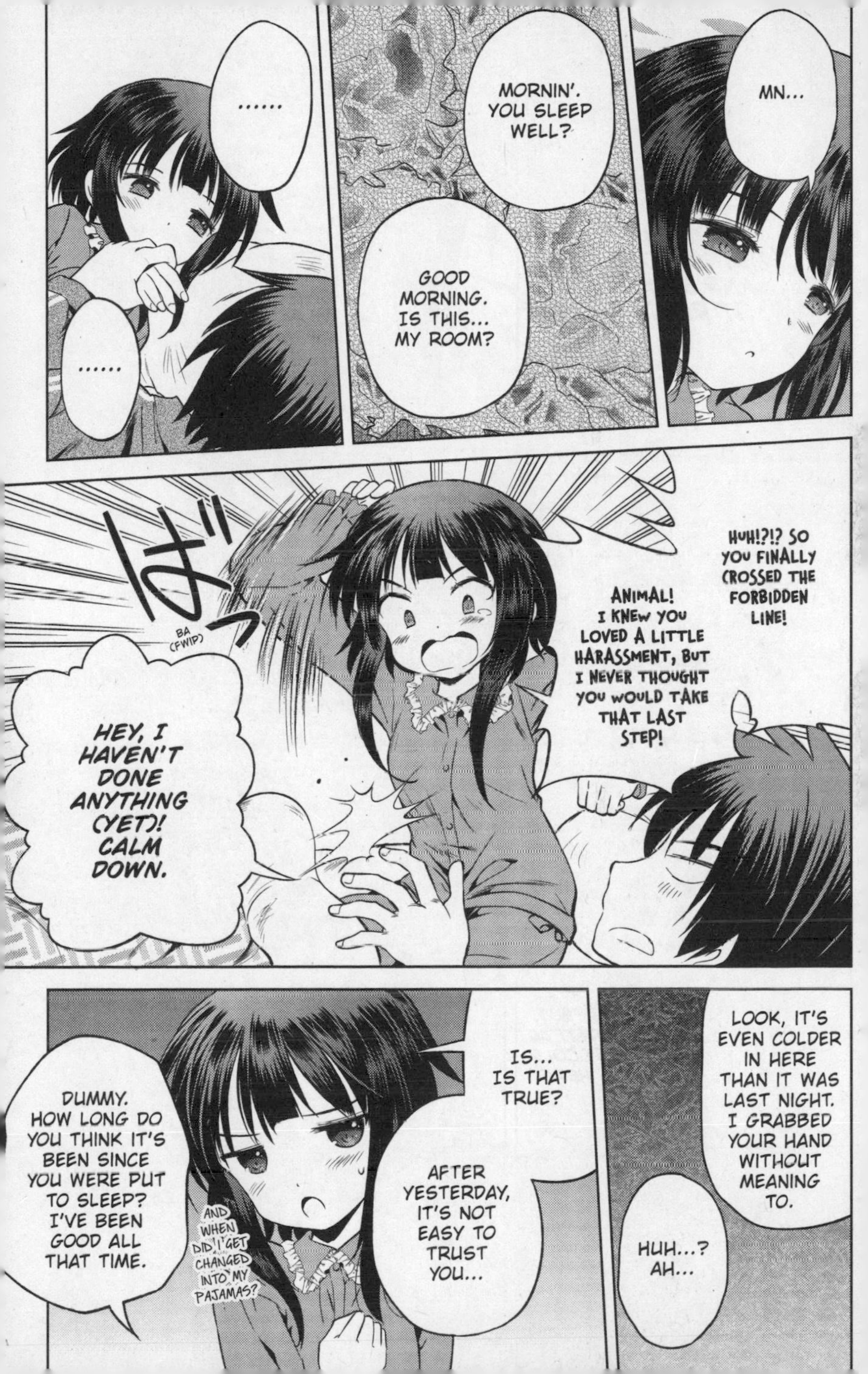
MN...
MORNIN'. YOU SLEEP WELL?
GOOD MORNING. IS THIS... MY ROOM?
......
......
HUH!?!? SO YOU FINALLY CROSSED THE FORBIDDEN LINE!
ANIMAL! I KNEW YOU LOVED A LITTLE HARASSMENT, BUT I NEVER THOUGHT YOU WOULD TAKE THAT LAST STEP!
ばっ
BA (FWIP)
HEY, I HAVEN'T DONE ANYTHING (YET)! CALM DOWN.
LOOK, IT'S EVEN COLDER IN HERE THAN IT WAS LAST NIGHT. I GRABBED YOUR HAND WITHOUT MEANING TO.
HUH...? AH...
IS... IS THAT TRUE?
AFTER YESTERDAY, IT'S NOT EASY TO TRUST YOU...
AND WHEN DID I GET CHANGED INTO MY PAJAMAS?
DUMMY. HOW LONG DO YOU THINK IT'S BEEN SINCE YOU WERE PUT TO SLEEP? I'VE BEEN GOOD ALL THAT TIME.

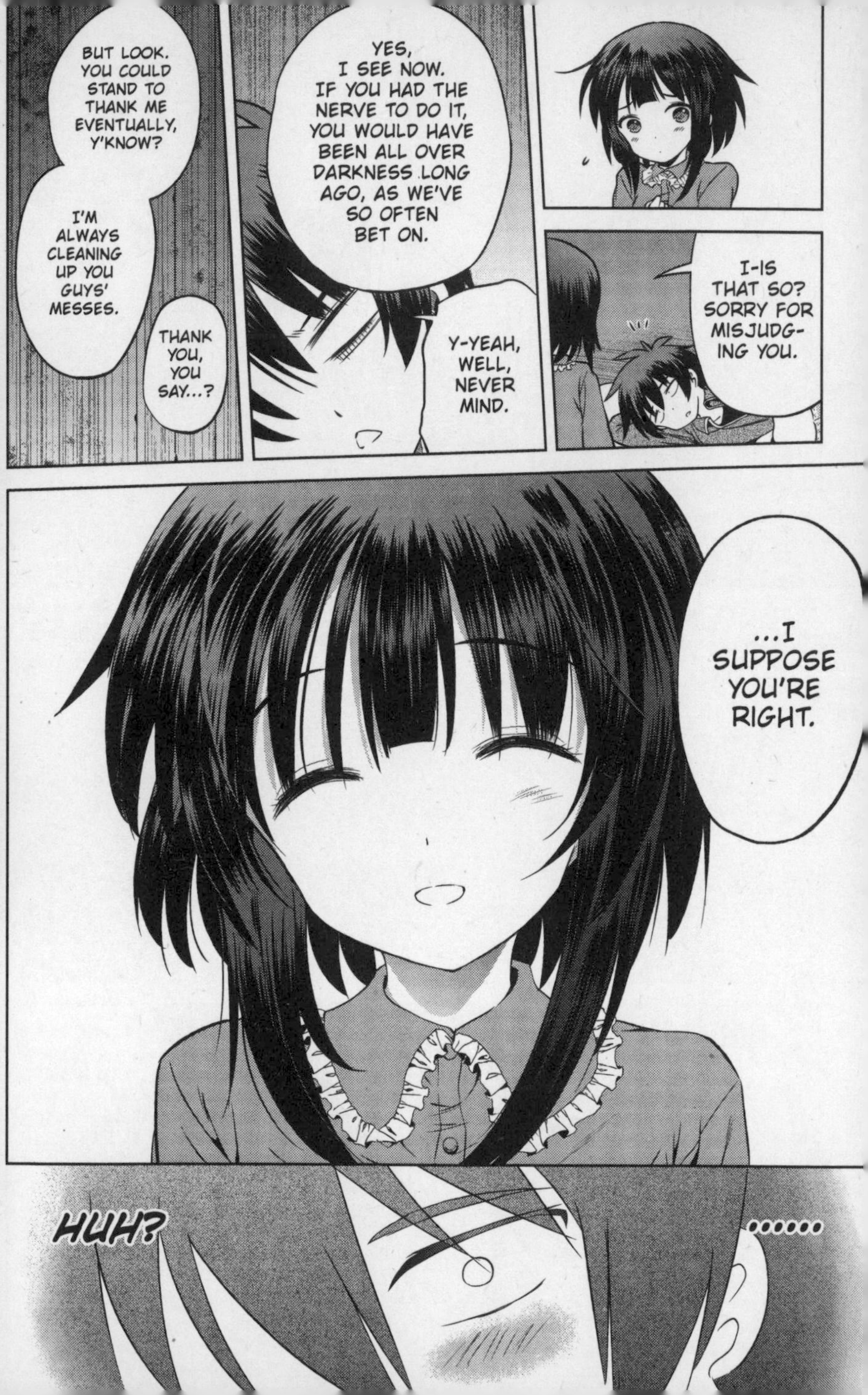
I-IS THAT SO? SORRY FOR MISJUDG-ING YOU.
YES, I SEE NOW. IF YOU HAD THE NERVE TO DO IT, YOU WOULD HAVE BEEN ALL OVER DARKNESS LONG AGO, AS WE'VE SO OFTEN BET ON.
Y-YEAH, WELL, NEVER MIND.
BUT LOOK. YOU COULD STAND TO THANK ME EVENTUALLY, Y'KNOW?
I'M ALWAYS CLEANING UP YOU GUYS' MESSES.
THANK YOU, YOU SAY...?
...I SUPPOSE YOU'RE RIGHT.
......
HUH?

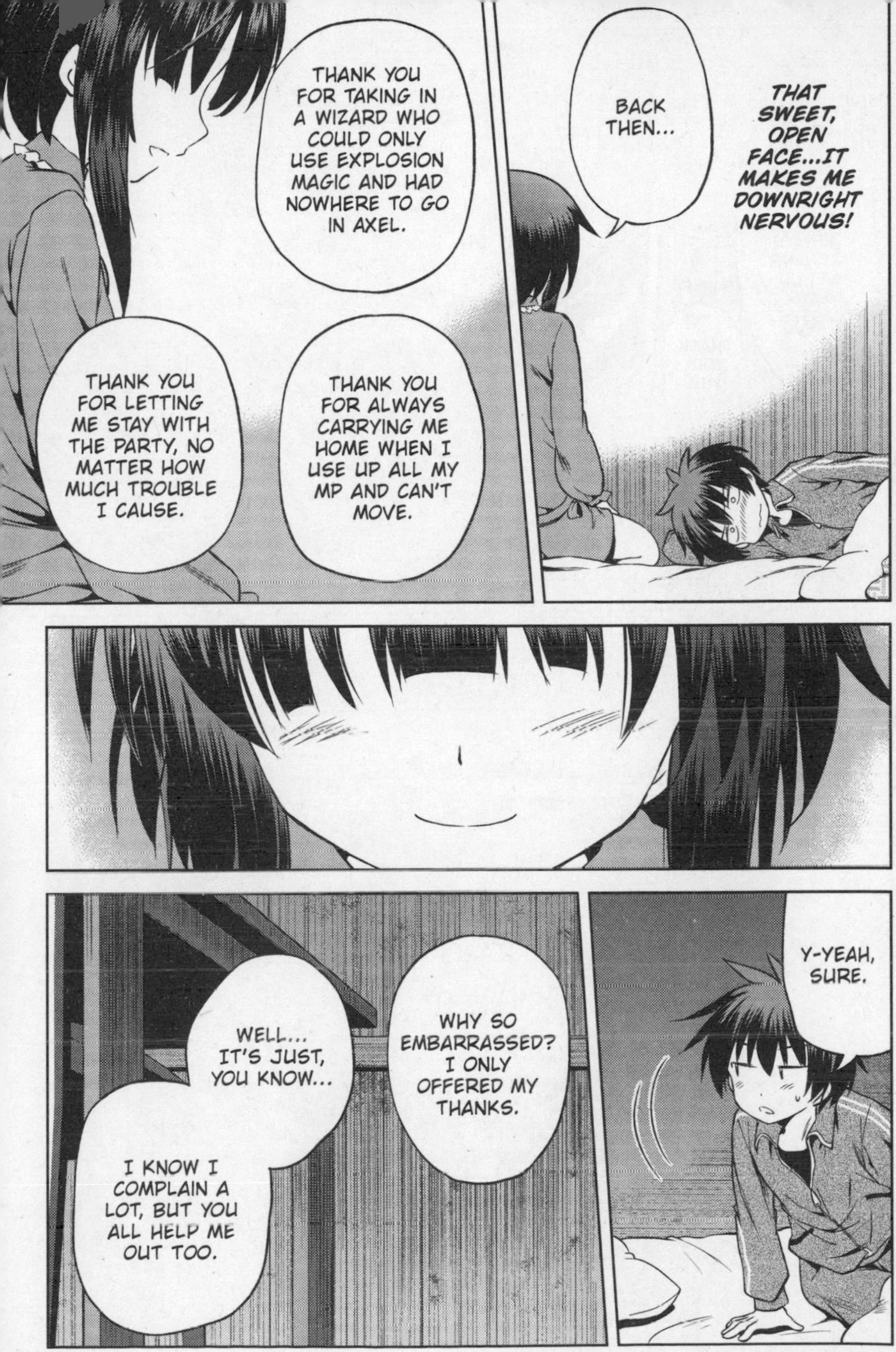
BACK THEN...
THAT SWEET, OPEN FACE...IT MAKES ME DOWNRIGHT NERVOUS!
THANK YOU FOR TAKING IN A WIZARD WHO COULD ONLY USE EXPLOSION MAGIC AND HAD NOWHERE TO GO IN AXEL.
THANK YOU FOR ALWAYS CARRYING ME HOME WHEN I USE UP ALL MY MP AND CAN'T MOVE.
THANK YOU FOR LETTING ME STAY WITH THE PARTY, NO MATTER HOW MUCH TROUBLE I CAUSE.
Y-YEAH, SURE.
WHY SO EMBARRASSED? I ONLY OFFERED MY THANKS.
WELL... IT'S JUST, YOU KNOW...
I KNOW I COMPLAIN A LOT, BUT YOU ALL HELP ME OUT TOO.

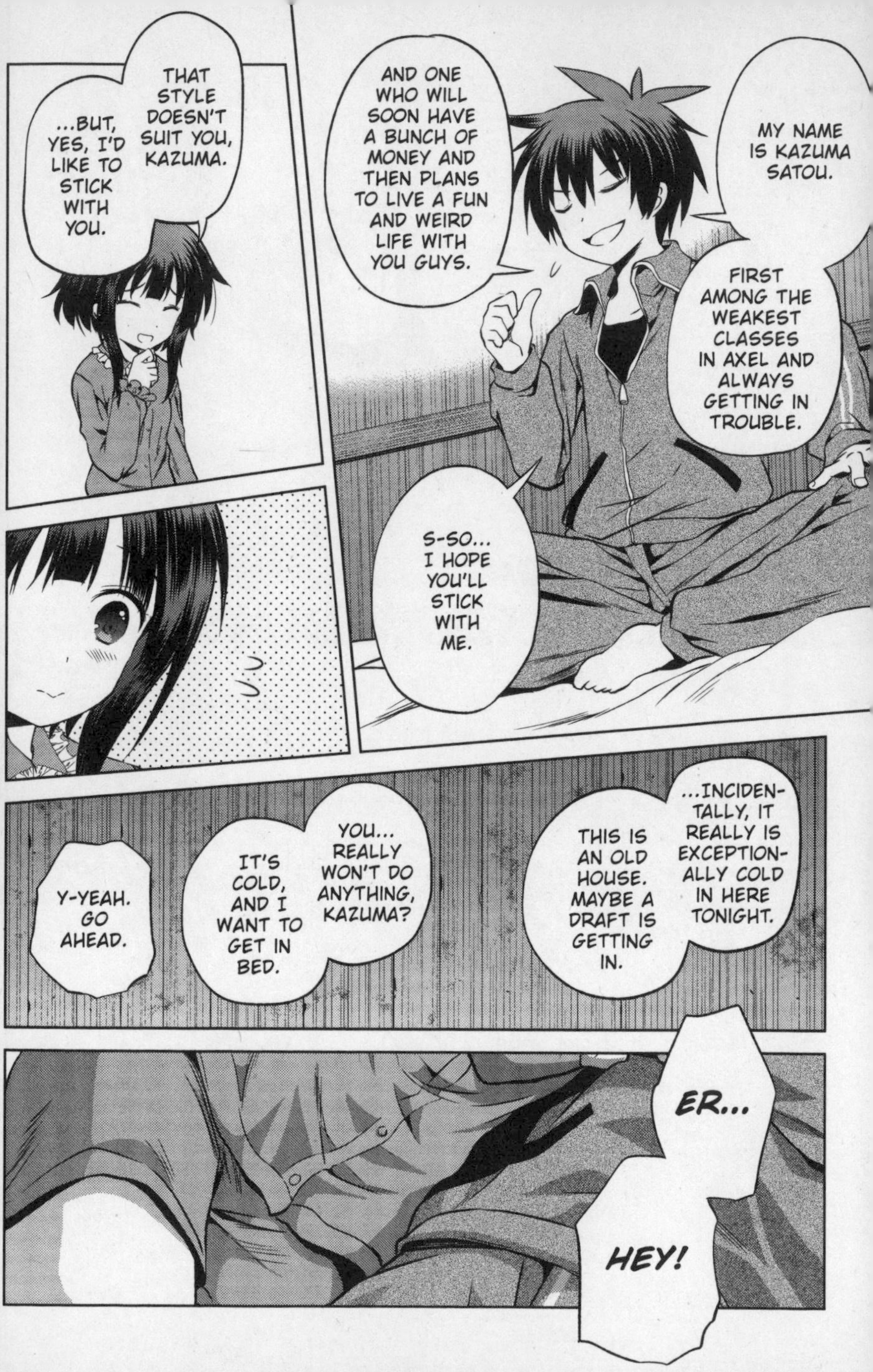
MY NAME IS KAZUMA SATOU.
FIRST AMONG THE WEAKEST CLASSES IN AXEL AND ALWAYS GETTING IN TROUBLE.
AND ONE WHO WILL SOON HAVE A BUNCH OF MONEY AND THEN PLANS TO LIVE A FUN AND WEIRD LIFE WITH YOU GUYS.
S-SO... I HOPE YOU'LL STICK WITH ME.
THAT STYLE DOESN'T SUIT YOU, KAZUMA.
...BUT, YES, I'D LIKE TO STICK WITH YOU.
...INCIDEN-TALLY, IT REALLY IS EXCEPTION-ALLY COLD IN HERE TONIGHT.
THIS IS AN OLD HOUSE. MAYBE A DRAFT IS GETTING IN.
YOU... REALLY WON'T DO ANYTHING, KAZUMA?
IT'S COLD, AND I WANT TO GET IN BED.
Y-YEAH. GO AHEAD.
ER...
HEY!

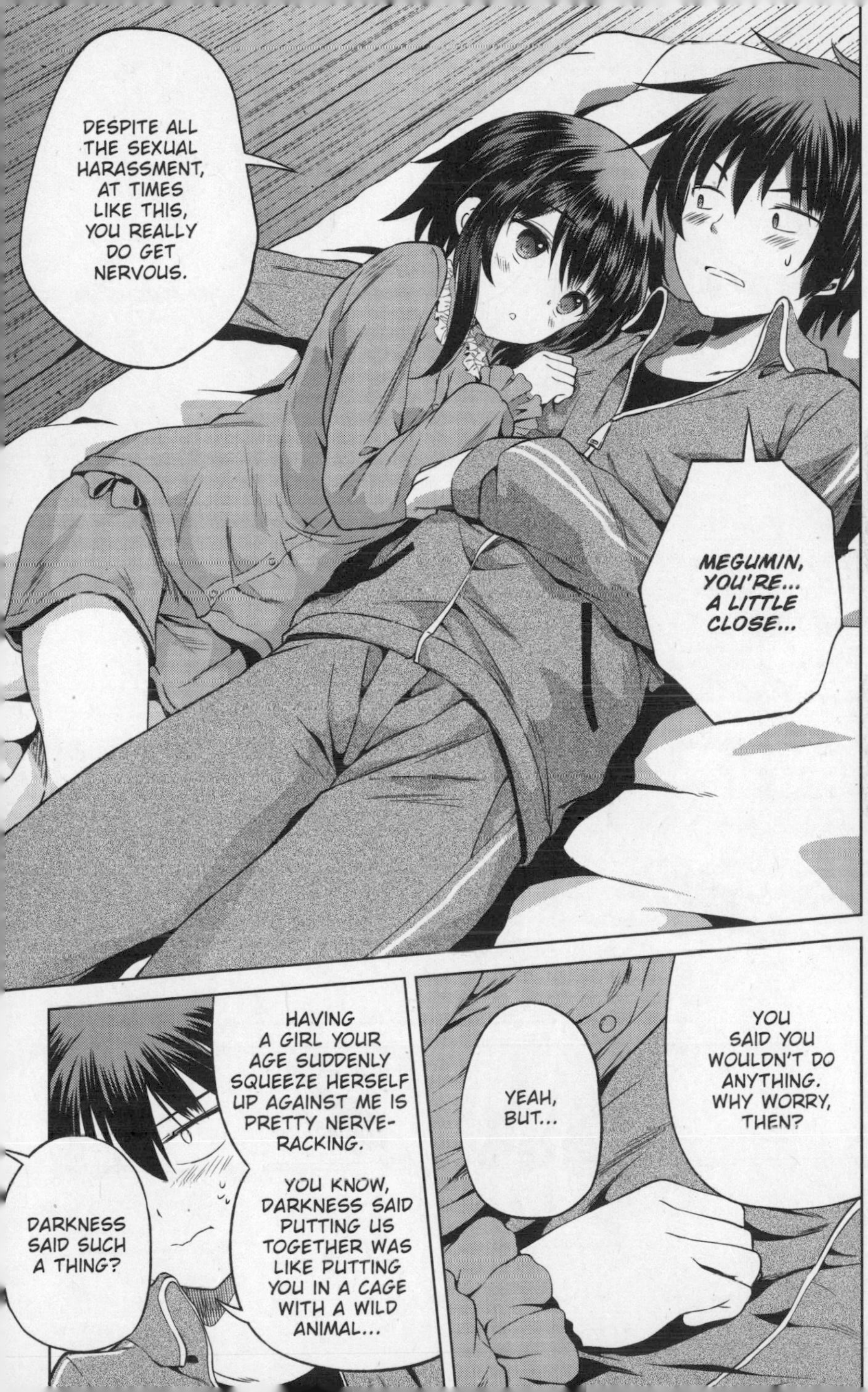
MEGUMIN, YOU'RE... A LITTLE CLOSE...
DESPITE ALL THE SEXUAL HARASSMENT, AT TIMES LIKE THIS, YOU REALLY DO GET NERVOUS.
YOU SAID YOU WOULDN'T DO ANYTHING. WHY WORRY, THEN?
YEAH, BUT...
HAVING A GIRL YOUR AGE SUDDENLY SQUEEZE HERSELF UP AGAINST ME IS PRETTY NERVE-RACKING.
YOU KNOW, DARKNESS SAID PUTTING US TOGETHER WAS LIKE PUTTING YOU IN A CAGE WITH A WILD ANIMAL...
DARKNESS SAID SUCH A THING?

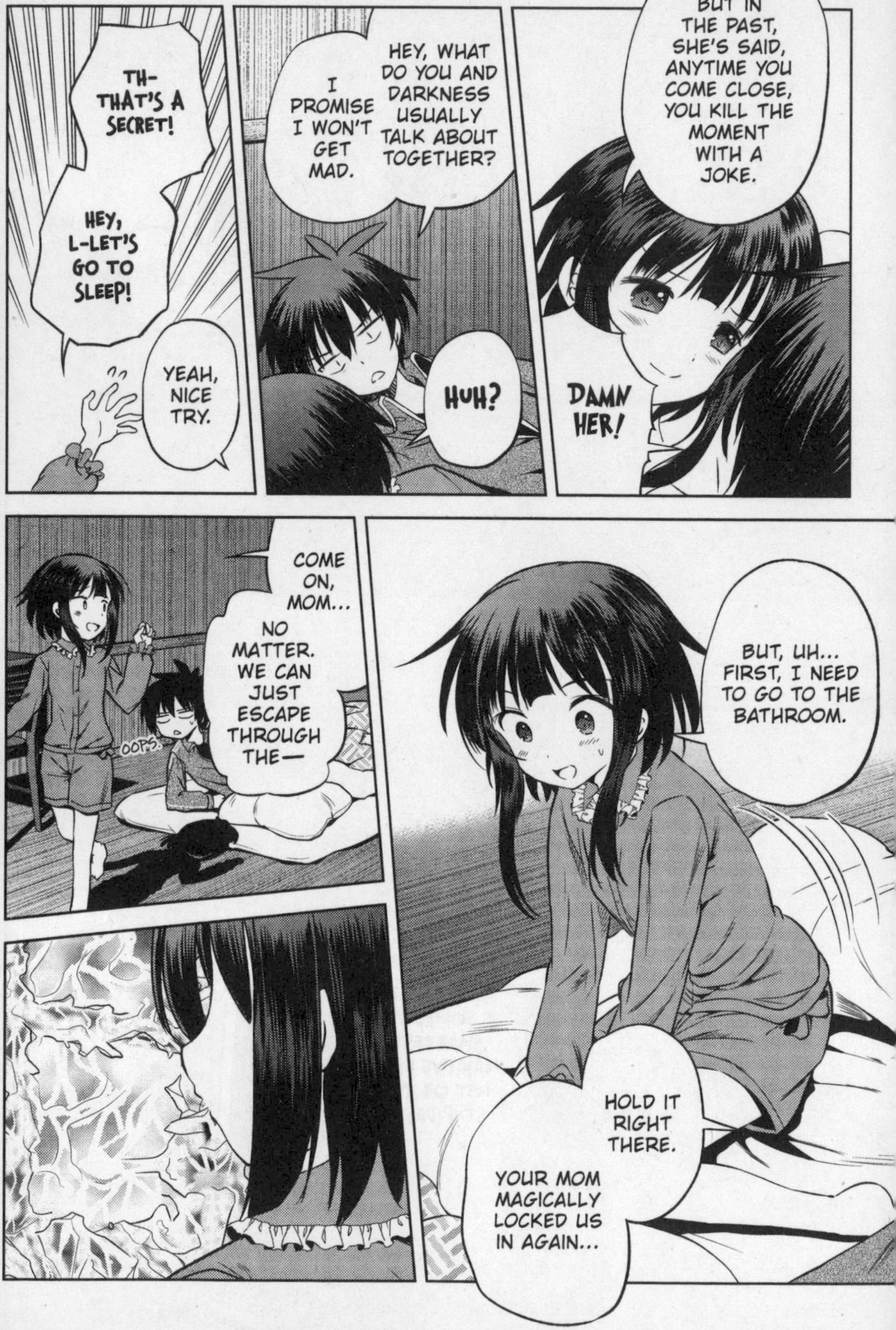
BUT IN THE PAST, SHE'S SAID, ANYTIME YOU COME CLOSE, YOU KILL THE MOMENT WITH A JOKE.
DAMN HER!
HEY, WHAT DO YOU AND DARKNESS USUALLY TALK ABOUT TOGETHER?
I PROMISE I WON'T GET MAD.
HUH?
TH-THAT'S A SECRET!
HEY, L-LET'S GO TO SLEEP!
YEAH, NICE TRY.
BUT, UH... FIRST, I NEED TO GO TO THE BATHROOM.
COME ON, MOM...
NO MATTER. WE CAN JUST ESCAPE THROUGH THE—
OOPS.
HOLD IT RIGHT THERE.
YOUR MOM MAGICALLY LOCKED US IN AGAIN...

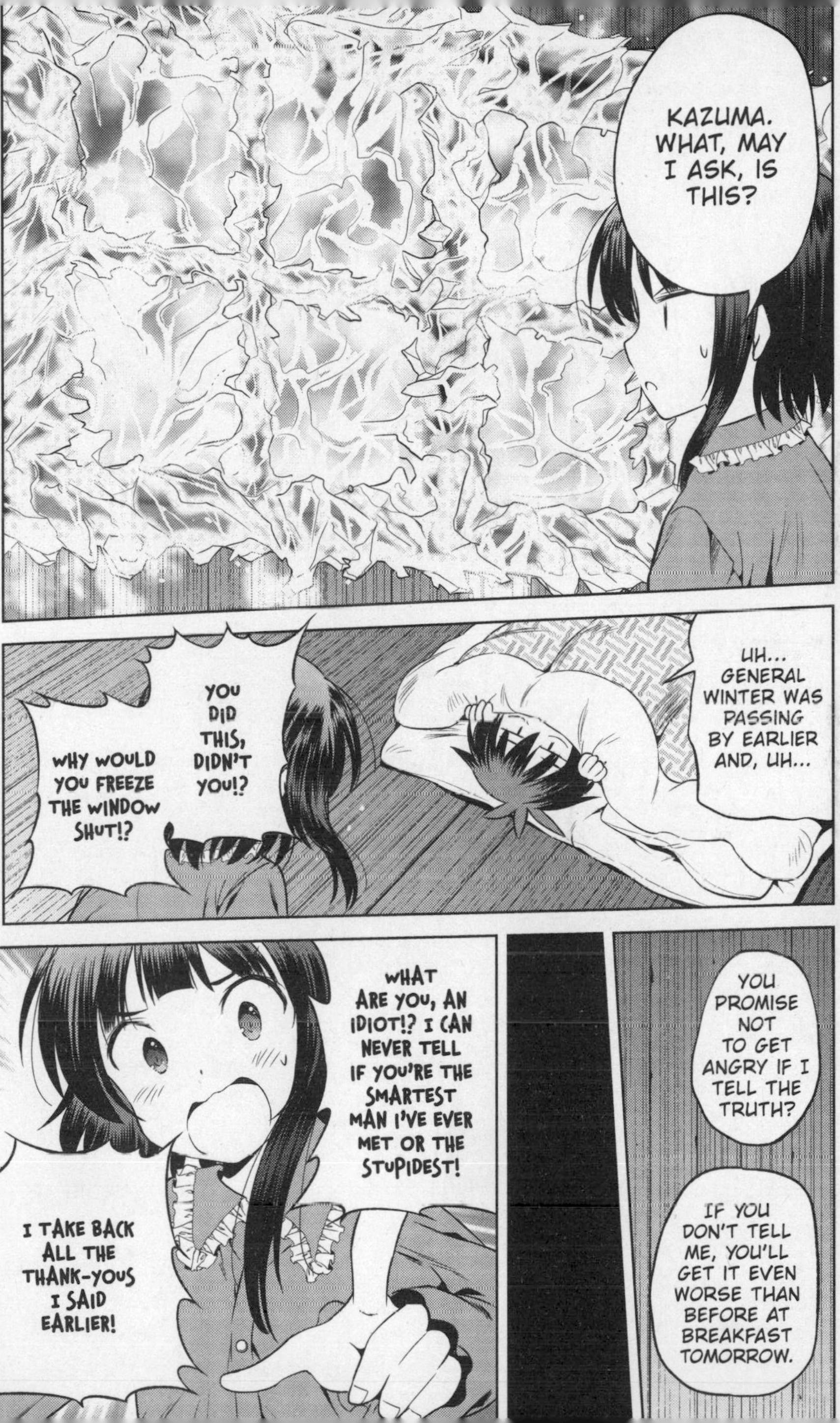
KAZUMA. WHAT, MAY I ASK, IS THIS?
UH... GENERAL WINTER WAS PASSING BY EARLIER AND, UH...
YOU DID THIS, DIDN'T YOU!?
WHY WOULD YOU FREEZE THE WINDOW SHUT!?
YOU PROMISE NOT TO GET ANGRY IF I TELL THE TRUTH?
IF YOU DON'T TELL ME, YOU'LL GET IT EVEN WORSE THAN BEFORE AT BREAKFAST TOMORROW.
WHAT ARE YOU, AN IDIOT!? I CAN NEVER TELL IF YOU'RE THE SMARTEST MAN I'VE EVER MET OR THE STUPIDEST!
I TAKE BACK ALL THE THANK-YOUS I SAID EARLIER!

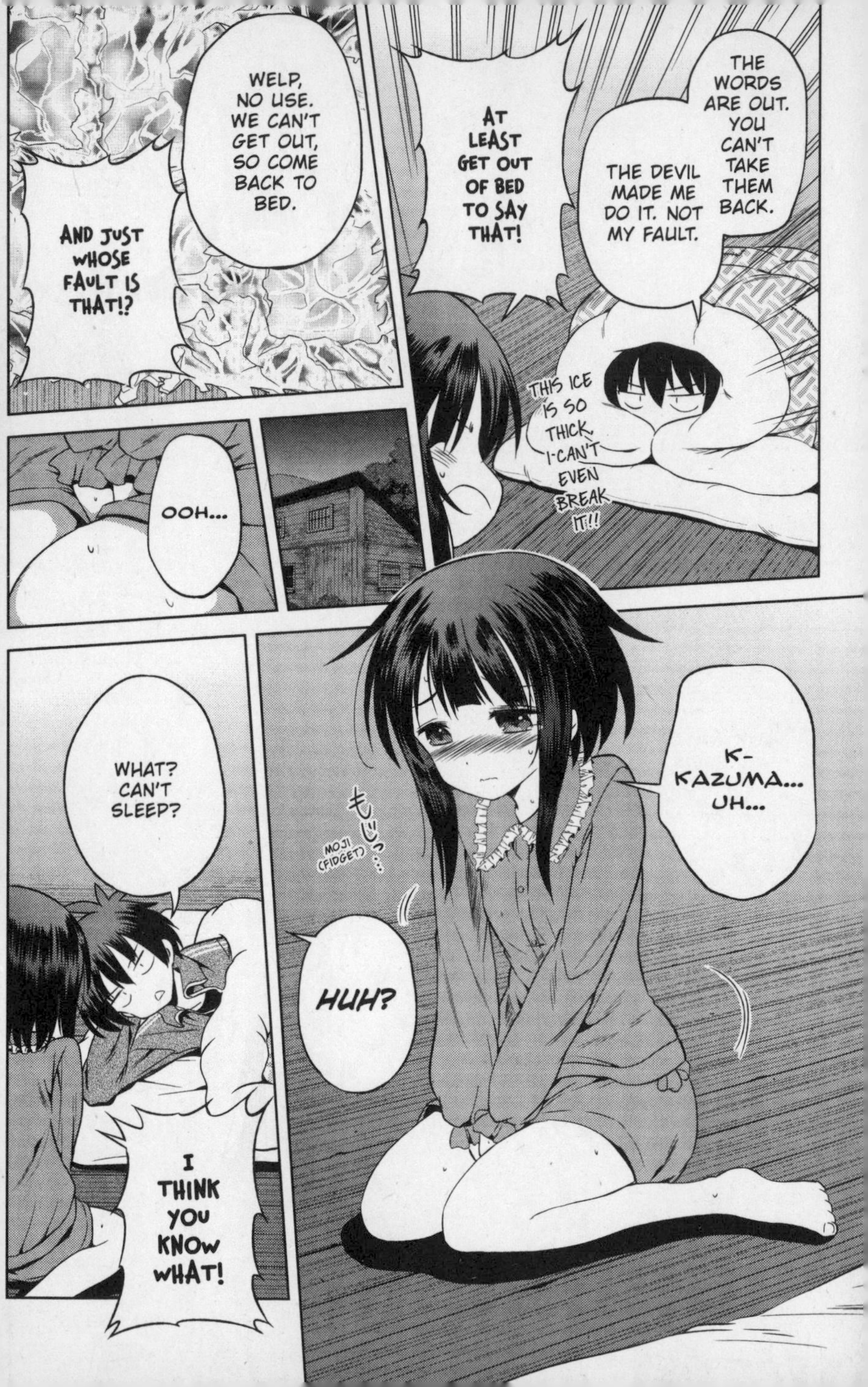
THE WORDS ARE OUT. YOU CAN'T TAKE THEM BACK.
THE DEVIL MADE ME DO IT. NOT MY FAULT.
AT LEAST GET OUT OF BED TO SAY THAT!
THIS ICE IS SO THICK, I-CAN'T EVEN BREAK IT!!
WELP, NO USE. WE CAN'T GET OUT, SO COME BACK TO BED.
AND JUST WHOSE FAULT IS THAT!?
OOH...
K-KAZUMA... UH...
もじっ...
MOJI (FIDGET)
HUH?
WHAT? CAN'T SLEEP?
I THINK YOU KNOW WHAT!

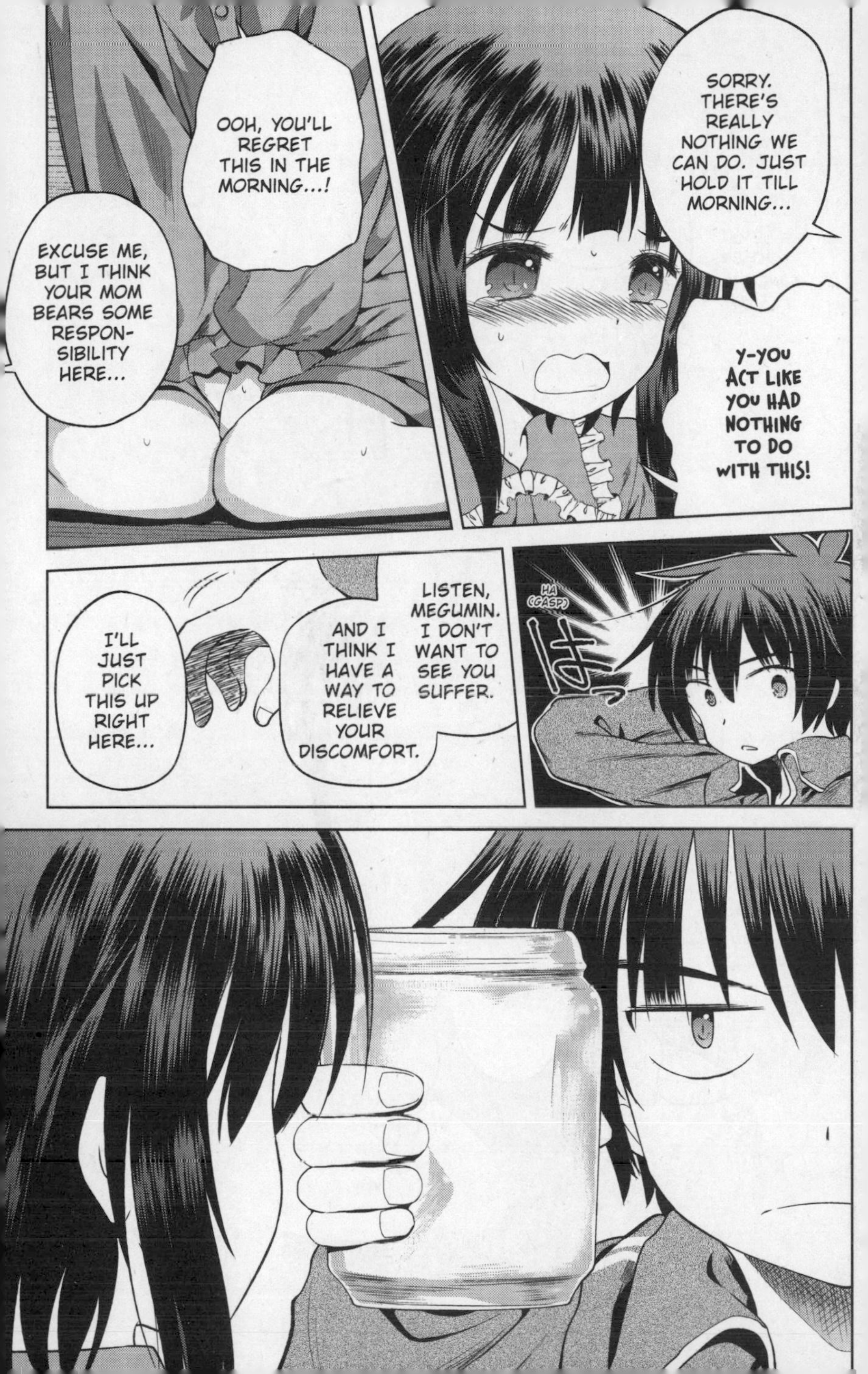
SORRY. THERE'S REALLY NOTHING WE CAN DO. JUST HOLD IT TILL MORNING...
Y-YOU ACT LIKE YOU HAD NOTHING TO DO WITH THIS!
OOH, YOU'LL REGRET THIS IN THE MORNING...!
EXCUSE ME, BUT I THINK YOUR MOM BEARS SOME RESPON-SIBILITY HERE...
HA (GASP)
はっ
LISTEN, MEGUMIN. I DON'T WANT TO SEE YOU SUFFER.
AND I THINK I HAVE A WAY TO RELIEVE YOUR DISCOMFORT.
I'LL JUST PICK THIS UP RIGHT HERE...

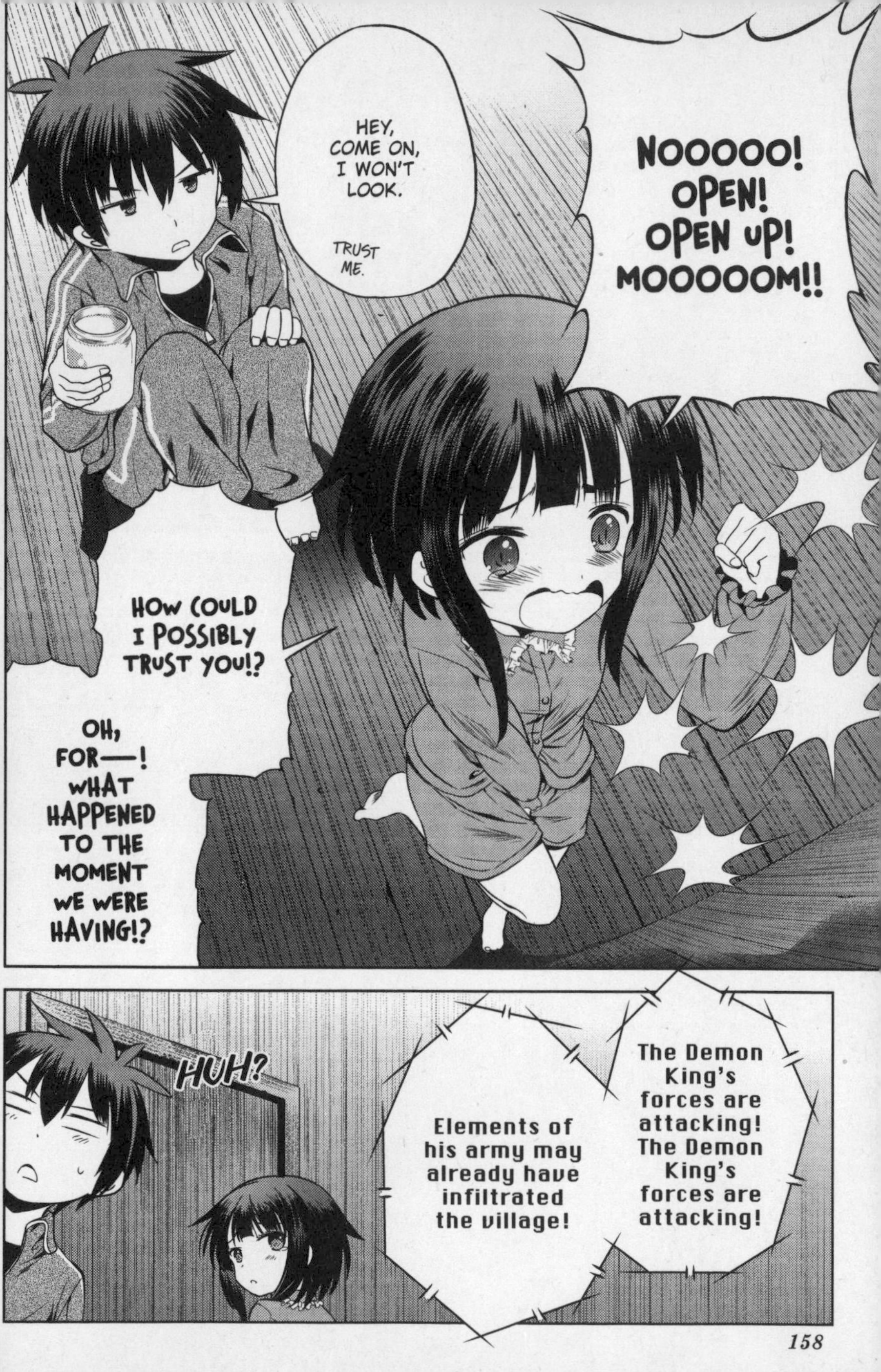
NOOOOO! OPEN! OPEN UP! MOOOOOM!!
HEY, COME ON, I WON'T LOOK.
TRUST ME.
HOW COULD I POSSIBLY TRUST YOU!?
OH, FOR—! WHAT HAPPENED TO THE MOMENT WE WERE HAVING!?
The Demon King's forces are attacking! The Demon King's forces are attacking!
Elements of his army may already have infiltrated the village!
HUH?

GOD'S
BLESSING
ON THIS
WONDERFUL
WORLD!

8

8

GOD'S
BLESSING
ON THIS
WONDERFUL
WORLD!

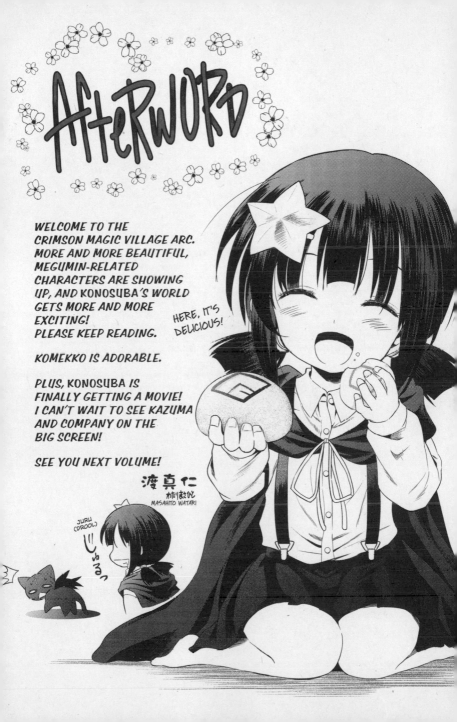

AFTERWORD

WELCOME TO THE CRIMSON MAGIC VILLAGE ARC. MORE AND MORE BEAUTIFUL, MEGUMIN-RELATED CHARACTERS ARE SHOWING UP, AND KONOSUBA'S WORLD GETS MORE AND MORE EXCITING! PLEASE KEEP READING.

KOMEKKO IS ADORABLE.

PLUS, KONOSUBA IS FINALLY GETTING A MOVIE! I CAN'T WAIT TO SEE KAZUMA AND COMPANY ON THE BIG SCREEN!

SEE YOU NEXT VOLUME!

渡真仁
わたりまさひと
MASAHITO WATARI

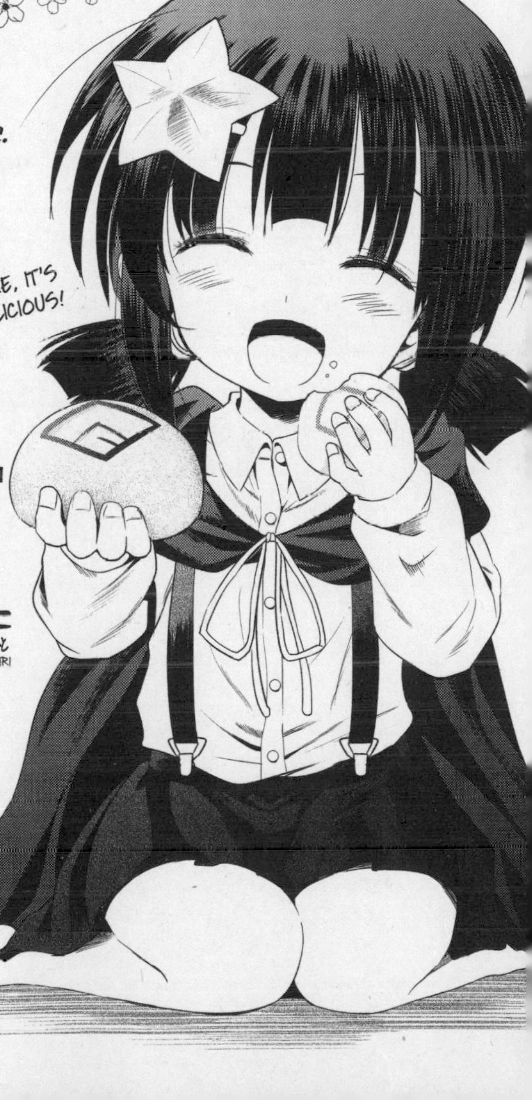
HERE, IT'S DELICIOUS!

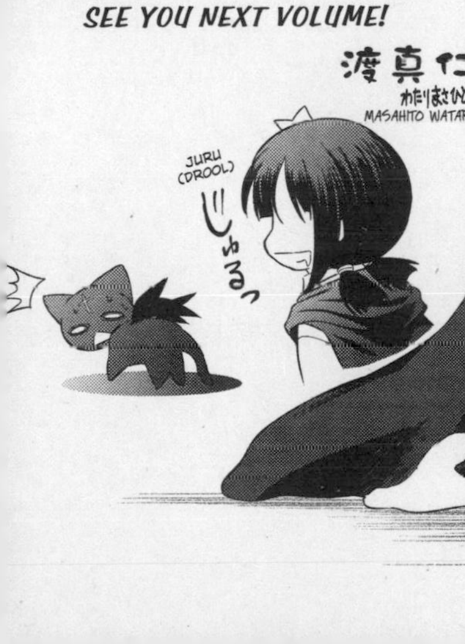
JURU (DROOL)
じゅるっ

KONOSUBA: GOD'S BLESSING ON THIS WONDERFUL WORLD! 8

Natsume Akatsuki

TRANSLATION: Kevin Steinbach ● **LETTERING**: Rochelle Gancio

KONO SUBARASHII SEKAI NI SYUKUFUKU WO! Volume 8
©MASAHITO WATARI 2018
©NATSUME AKATSUKI, KURONE MISHIMA 2018
First published in Japan in 2018 by Kadokawa Corporation, Tokyo. English translation rights arranged with KADOKAWA Corporation, Tokyo through Tuttle-Mori Agency, Inc., Tokyo.

Yen Press
1290 Avenue of the Americas
New York, NY 10104

Visit us at yenpress.com
facebook.com/yenpress
twitter.com/yenpress
yenpress.tumblr.com
instagram.com/yenpress

First Yen Press Edition: April 2019

Yen Press is an imprint of Yen Press, LLC.
The Yen Press name and logo are trademarks of Yen Press, LLC.

Library of Congress Control Number: 2016946112

ISBNs: 978-1-9753-0416-4 (paperback)
       978-1-9753-5796-2 (ebook)

10 9 8 7 6 5 4 3 2 1

WOR

Printed in the United States of America